Project Europe

Today it often appears as though the European Union has entered existential crisis after decades of success, condemned by its adversaries as a bureaucratic monster eroding national sovereignty: at best wasteful, at worst dangerous. How did we reach this point and how has European integration impacted on ordinary people's lives – not just in the member states, but also beyond? Did the predecessors of today's EU really create peace after the Second World War, as is often argued? How about its contribution to creating prosperity? What was the role of citizens in this process, and can the EU justifiably claim to be a 'community of values'? Kiran Klaus Patel's bracing look back at the myths and realities of integration challenges conventional wisdoms of Europhiles and Euro-sceptics alike and shows that the future of Project Europe will depend on the lessons that Europeans derive from its past.

Kiran Klaus Patel is Professor of European History at Ludwig Maximilian University of Munich (LMU). His previous publications include *The New Deal: A Global History* (2016), which was co-winner of the 2017 World History Association Bentley Book Prize.

KIRAN KLAUS PATEL

PROJECT EUROPE

A HISTORY

CAMBRIDGE
UNIVERSITY PRESS

CAMBRIDGE
UNIVERSITY PRESS

University Printing House, Cambridge CB2 8BS, United Kingdom

One Liberty Plaza, 20th Floor, New York, NY 10006, USA

477 Williamstown Road, Port Melbourne, VIC 3207, Australia

314–321, 3rd Floor, Plot 3, Splendor Forum, Jasola District Centre, New Delhi – 110025, India

79 Anson Road, #06–04/06, Singapore 079906

Cambridge University Press is part of the University of Cambridge.

It furthers the University's mission by disseminating knowledge in the pursuit of education, learning, and research at the highest international levels of excellence.

www.cambridge.org
Information on this title: www.cambridge.org/9781108494960
DOI: 10.1017/9781108848893

Originally published in 2018 by C. H. Beck as *Projekt Europa: Eine kritische Geschichte*, written in German by Kiran Klaus Patel (ISBN 9783406727689)

First published in English by Cambridge University Press in 2020, written by Kiran Klaus Patel, translated by Meredith Dale

Printed in the United Kingdom by TJ International Ltd, Padstow Cornwall

A catalogue record for this publication is available from the British Library.

Library of Congress Cataloging-in-Publication Data
NAMES: Patel, Kiran Klaus, author. | Dale, Meredith, translator.
TITLE: Project Europe : myths and realities of European integration / Kiran Klaus Patel ; translated by Meredith Dale.
OTHER TITLES: Projekt Europa. English
DESCRIPTION: Cambridge ; New York, NY : Cambridge University Press, 2020. | "Originally published in 2018 by C.H.Beck as Projekt Europa: Eine Kritische Geschichte, written in German by Kiran Klaus Patel (ISBN 9783406727689)." | Includes bibliographical references and index.
IDENTIFIERS: LCCN 2019042235 (print) | LCCN 2019042236 (ebook) | ISBN 9781108494960 (hardback) | ISBN 9781108848893 (ebook)
SUBJECTS: LCSH: European Union – History. | Europe – Economic integration – History. | Europe – Politics and government – 1945–
CLASSIFICATION: LCC JN30 .P389513 2020 (print) | LCC JN30 (ebook) | DDC 341.242/2–dc23
LC record available at https://lccn.loc.gov/2019042235
LC ebook record available at https://lccn.loc.gov/2019042236

ISBN 978-1-108-49496-0 Hardback

CONTENTS

FIGURES, MAPS AND TABLES

Figures

Maps

Tables

ABBREVIATIONS

ACP	*African, Caribbean and Pacific Group of States*
CAP	*Common Agricultural Policy*
CEN	*Comité européen de normalisation*
CENELEC	*Comité européen de normalisation en électronique et en électrotechnique*
CEPT	*Conférence européenne des administrations des postes et des télécommunications*
CMO	*Common Market Organisation*
Comecon	*Council for Mutual Economic Assistance*
COREPER	*Comité des représentants permanents*
CSCE	*Conference on Security and Cooperation in Europe*
DG	*Directorate-General*
EC	*European Community*
ECJ	*European Court of Justice*
ECMT	*European Conference of Ministers of Transport*
ECSC	*European Coal and Steel Community*
ECU	*European Currency Unit*
EDC	*European Defence Community*
EEC	*European Economic Community*
EFTA	*European Free Trade Association*
EMS	*European Monetary System*
EMU	*Economic and Monetary Union*
EP	*European Parliament*
EPC	*European Political Community*
EPU	*European Payments Union*
ERM	*European Exchange Rate Mechanism*

EU	*European Union*
Euratom	*European Atomic Energy Community*
FLN	*Front de Libération Nationale*
FPÖ	*Freiheitliche Partei Österreichs*
GATT	*General Agreement on Tariffs and Trade*
GDP	*Gross Domestic Product*
ILO	*International Labour Organization*
NATO	*North Atlantic Treaty Organization*
OECD	*Organisation for Economic Co-operation and Development*
OEEC	*Organisation for European Economic Co-operation*
ÖVP	*Österreichische Volkspartei*
SGCI	*Secrétariat général du Comité interministériel pour les questions de coopération économique européenne*
SPD	*Sozialdemokratische Partei Deutschlands*
SPÖ	*Sozialdemokratische Partei Österreichs*
UEF	*Union of European Federalists*
UEM	*United Europe Movement*
UN	*United Nations*
UNECE	*United Nations Economic Commission for Europe*
WEU	*Western European Union*

Frontispiece: Banksy's mural in Dover, of a man on a ladder chiselling one of the stars out of the EU flag. Courtesy of Pest Control Office, Banksy, Dover, 2017

PROLOGUE

In 2017, the British street artist Banksy painted a mural of a man on a ladder chiselling one of the stars out of the EU flag. The painting is on a building in Dover, which has been one of Britain's most important connections to mainland Europe since ancient times. Today its port handles almost 20 per cent of Britain's trade. While we may not know who 'Banksy' really is, there can be no doubt that his work is a commentary on the British decision to leave the European Union, or Brexit.

Today it often appears as though the European Union's best days are behind it, that it has entered existential crisis after decades of success. Before Brexit there was Grexit and trouble in the Eurozone. Now we see squabbling over refugees. The question of failure or collapse of the integration project is on everyone's lips. The walls are crumbling, the demolition crew is on its way and the EU is operating in crisis mode.

Against the troubles of the present, the early history of the European project since the 1950s shines all the brighter, at least according to some. In 2012 the European Union received the Nobel Peace Prize on the grounds that it and its forerunners 'have for over six decades contributed to the advancement of peace and reconciliation, democracy and human rights in Europe'.[1] Those achievements are felt to be in danger today, more than one star threatens to fall from the deep-blue sky. So Banksy's monumental artwork, which fills the end wall of a three-storey building, represents a fitting commentary on one of the most burning issues for Europe today.

Figure 1: Banksy's mural in Dover. Glyn Kirk/AFP/Getty Images

At second glance we discover there is more to the image. Closer examination reveals that there were already cracks in the wall before Banksy's demolition man started swinging his hammer. He is destroying the star, but leaving little mark on the wall. And the ladder is very long and looks rather wobbly. How much will he demolish? And is the man perhaps in more danger than the flag?

Other aspects remain unsaid. The number of stars has always been twelve, since the 1950s. That did not change with enlargement, and will not change with Brexit. In fact for its first thirty years the flag was not even the symbol of the EU or its predecessors, but of the much less prominent Council of Europe. If Banksy had painted his mural in 1973, when the United Kingdom joined the European Community, nobody would have understood it. Back then, the symbol was obscure. Today media in places as far-flung as the United States, Uruguay, Thailand and Russia report the story; everyone understands what the symbol means and why it is important. But the questions do not end with the depicted flag; the same applies to the choice of location. Banksy chose a building already slated for demolition – so will the loss of one star change the broader course of events at all? And how to read that the mural was painted over in 2019?

And with that, I have outlined the questions addressed in this volume. The EU's crisis today appears uniquely deep. But is the situation really so unusual? The EU's self-image could not be more positive. It stands for peace, prosperity, values and integration. Its adversaries condemn it as a bureaucratic monster munching up national sovereignty: at best wasteful, at worst dangerous.

Whatever one thinks of the outcome, in retrospect it appears as though the precursors of today's European Union created the whole show all on their own and practically inevitably. As I will demonstrate in this book, the EU's exaggerated self-image exacerbates the contemporary perception of crisis, because phenomena we have actually already seen before are interpreted as new and threatening. And at the same time the core of today's problem is overlooked. The volume scrutinises many of the myths that have grown up around the history of European integration, along with the criticisms the EU so frequently finds itself confronted with. This is a critical history that asks how and why the EU really emerged and what it achieved, digging beyond the political rhetoric and cheap polemics. What we find is that it has fundamentally changed over the course of its history, and how improbable its undeniable importance today would have appeared just a few decades ago. Many of the aspects we today project back onto the early years in fact only took shape much more recently.

In order to gain a proper understanding we must free ourselves from a number of methodological corsets. The first of these is an excessive concentration on motives and driving forces. While that is the approach adopted by most authors to date, most people are more interested in the concrete effects and results of European integration. And about these we know astonishingly little, echoing the way the EU in general has remained very abstract and intangible for most ordinary people. They are not alone in this. In fact many historians describing the history of Europe in the twentieth century devote little space to European integration and plainly believe it to be a rather marginal factor.[2] In this volume I show how the European Community already had important effects in certain spheres at an early stage, and in others above all from the 1970s and 1980s. But these were not always the areas to which the EU itself attributes important effects in retrospect. This becomes very clear if we look beyond the internal dynamics between the member states and consider what European integration meant for global problems like the Cuban Missile Crisis, world trade policy and the end of the Cold War – and for Algerian vintners, Argentine generals and Japanese carmakers. Altogether the foundations for the defining position the EU occupies today were laid before the Maastricht Treaty of 1992.

Secondly, I am not interested in chronicling every step towards integration as the coming together of equal sovereign states that have agreed on shared rules and institutions and recapitulating the history of the organisation. Given the amount that happened, we would just get lost in the technical details or, even more likely, bored with an endless succession of negotiating rounds. At the same time, this approach easily creates a teleological narrative where deepening and expansion are the only modes of history, interrupted by occasional phases of standstill overcome by heroic efforts.[3] This is frequently written as a succession of conflicts between great men (and a few women) where the roles are clear: Jean Monnet, Konrad Adenauer, Alcide de Gasperi and Paul-Henri Spaak, Jacques Delors and Helmut Kohl are the goodies, the pro-European visionaries; Charles de Gaulle, Andreas Papandreou and Margaret Thatcher the biggest villains. In the euro-sceptic version the roles are simply reversed. In fact we have long known that Monnet, Adenauer and Spaak also pursued national interests and had no truck with idealistic notions of abolishing the nation state,[4] while de Gaulle and Thatcher made a lot of noise but got along astonishingly well with the EC in certain questions. At the same time, a focus on political leaders overlooks the frequently much more interesting actors in the second row. Follow-on decisions and bureaucratic routine in concrete policy areas often turn out to be more important than the personalities of the heads of state and government. A chronological approach also easily loses sight of the fact that the European option never represented the only alternative to the nation state. Finally, this approach also suppresses the absolutely decisive question of how the effects of the negotiations played out, away from the political spotlight.

Instead, each of the following eight chapters examines a central issue in connection with the history of the EU. What was its contribution to peace and security? Did it really create economic growth and prosperity as so often asserted? I also explore the central tensions in the integration process, for example between participation and technocracy. Each chapter stands on its own. Apart from the first, they can be read in any order – although a proper overview will only emerge when all the parts are reflected together.

The problem-orientated approach chosen here should not be confused with organisation by policy area. For example, refugee and asylum policy plays no role in this book because it only came to prominence after the period discussed here. Nevertheless the various chapters do generate an understanding of the basic structures of more recent debates. A systematising approach reveals the asynchronicities – and the surprising coincidences – between the dynamics in areas as different as peace and security, prosperity and growth, and values and norms.

Thirdly it is a challenge to maintain analytical distance to the arguments of supporters and opponents of the integration process since the 1940s. The most obvious example is the assumption that European integration in today's European Union differs fundamentally from other forms of international cooperation and should therefore be examined in isolation. For one side this is reason to praise the process; for the other to condemn it even more strongly as artificial. It is true that the EU today occupies a special status unavailable to organisations like the Council of Europe or the OECD. But that was not always the case, as I show in Chapter 1. There I also discuss how the EC was ultimately able to achieve precedence over other international organisations in Western Europe – and went on to rise out of that sphere altogether. But later developments should not be projected back onto the early years. For example the EC actually played a fairly marginal role in securing peace in the first two post-war decades – but later became more significant in this respect. In order to arrive at a balanced analysis we need to measure the precursors of today's EU against other forms of international cooperation in Europe. This is why it is so important to compare a multitude of sources and perspectives. It would also be false to merely concentrate on one national outlook. Instead it is imperative to contrast this with other perspectives. Understanding the history of European integration means listening to the others.

Words are never easy, and the term 'Europe' is especially tricky. 'Whoever speaks of Europe is wrong', wrote Reich Chancellor Otto von Bismarck in the margins of a letter in 1876. His scribbled note in French referred to a Russian call to respond jointly to a crisis in the name of Europe.[5] To Bismarck Europe did not represent a genuinely political concept; solidarity in the name of the continent was an impossibility.

History since 1945 has proved him wrong. Nevertheless his biting comment indicates an important point. We have become accustomed to saying 'Europe' when we mean the European Union, and vice versa. Yet the EU has never included the whole of Europe, and the institutional and legal EU is much more concrete than the rather vague idea of Europe. One can criticise the confusion of Europe with the EU and its precursors as a presumptive and ahistorical distortion. Or one can investigate the history of the twentieth century in order to understand why a rather narrow organisation that initially comprised just six Western European states is today so frequently equated with Europe as a whole. That is what this book is about.

When discussing the history of cooperation and integration in Europe one must also distinguish carefully between planning, implementation and impact, regardless of whether they occurred in the scope of the EC or another organisational context. For there was often a rather complex relationship between the intended and the realised; intentions should not be confused with effects. Nor did planning always precede realisation as clearly as most of the existing descriptions of the history of European integration would have it, when they start from the ideas and seek to describe their successive realisation. Of course much had been written about peace through European federation since the end of the Middle Ages and one could present an impressive ancestral gallery: Dante Alighieri, Immanuel Kant and Victor Hugo to start with. But for most of the time these and similar ideas remained extremely marginal. The kind of international economic and technical cooperation that began in the nineteenth century – in areas such as cross-border infrastructures (for example navigation on the Rhine), reducing trade protectionism or later developing electricity grids – was at least as important for the history of European integration since 1945.[6] While the Great War was quickly followed by the Second and permanent peace remained elusive, a parade of almost unknown organisations notched up impressive achievements in the sphere of second-order problems. Nevertheless in 1945 political integration in Europe was still only one possible future among many – and a rather unlikely one at that.

And still. In the beginning was the Second World War. Without it – without the destruction, the delegitimisation of hypertrophic nationalism, the decline of European global dominance and the fear of further German aggression – European integration would never have shifted from the realm of the thinkable to the realm of the politically plausible.

At the same time another war was needed as the indispensable context for turning possibility into reality: the Cold War. The shared fear of communism and the emerging Soviet-led Eastern Bloc functioned as an external brace holding the states together – and explains why 'European' integration increasingly applied only to Western Europe. This does not mean that the integration process was completely determined by the Cold War, though; otherwise the process would have ended in 1989.[7]

This eastward-looking anti-hegemonic anti-communism was accompanied by an ambivalent relationship towards the West. Many early proponents of European integration also sought to position Western Europe as a 'third force' vis-à-vis the United States, and as such to escape the superpower polarity. This idea found support in the late 1940s and 1950s especially in Western European social democratic parties, for example in France, the Netherlands and West Germany, as well as the left wing of the British Labour Party. De Gaulle also pursued a similar course on Europe.

The United States nevertheless massively supported the integration process. The US security guarantee – which made it Western Europe's hegemonic power – thus became one of the defining framework conditions for all moves towards European cooperation and integration from the late 1940s.

The terminology itself demonstrates just how hard it is to define European integration. The entities that were to become the European Union of today often changed their form, responsibilities and even name. The EU originated in the European Coal and Steel Community (ECSC) founded in 1951, and two other organisations established in 1957 by the so-called Treaties of Rome, the European Economic Community (EEC) and Euratom. That sounds rather technical and indeed it was. Only over time did these three largely independent organisations join more closely together, and for the period until the Maastricht Treaty one should actually speak of the 'European Communities' in the plural. From the 1970s the European Political Cooperation and the summits of heads of state and government gradually institutionalised, initially outside the three core Communities. Maastricht rearranged the organisational structure. The institutional framework appears confusing, but is not really difficult to explain. It indicates that the history of European integration is full of far-reaching hopes, unintended consequences, initially invisible new starts and slow reorientations. These contexts shaped not only the history of the EC's precursors, but also other initiatives for European cooperation (of which more below).

In the following I refer to the pre-Maastricht European Communities in the singular, and not only for reasons of legibility. Interestingly in certain European languages – including German and French – the entity was increasingly discussed in the singular from the 1970s and the European Community was increasingly equated with Europe.[8] In English the term 'Common Market', with its very different allusions, tended to be preferred.

In another respect too, the EC is difficult to grasp. There was not one big blueprint for its development. Rather than a unified will we frequently encounter a complex web of different and contradictory motives. National affiliation was by no means always the determining factor when representatives of different states met. Often enough political/ideological affiliations meant more: federalists, technocrats, Christian conservatives, social democrats and so on hobnobbed with their own circles, and the same applies to the different generations with their respective experiences and expectations. So the EC became a stage on which intergovernmental negotiations and international political dramas played out. Non-state actors, such as representatives of major companies and various economic sectors, journalists and trade unionists, also left their marks. In many questions the EC became significantly more than just the platform or instrument of national interests, gradually assuming the semblance of a proactive subject capable of planning and implementing. In these cases it frequently succeeded – precisely on the grounds of its vagueness – in representing more than the sum of its member states and pursuing an independent course. Altogether the EC therefore sometimes recalls a puppet played by the large member states; sometimes Superman, and sometimes Robert Musil's *Man Without Qualities*: an actor with great potential and a sense of possibility searching for a meaningful existence.

Understanding the history of European integration not as the implementation of a grand plan, but taking seriously the diversity and vicissitudes of the associated projects, changes the perspective. The heart of the matter is not the 'ever closer union' invoked in slightly varying forms in all major treaties since 1957:[9] the impression that European integration followed this model at least until the Maastricht

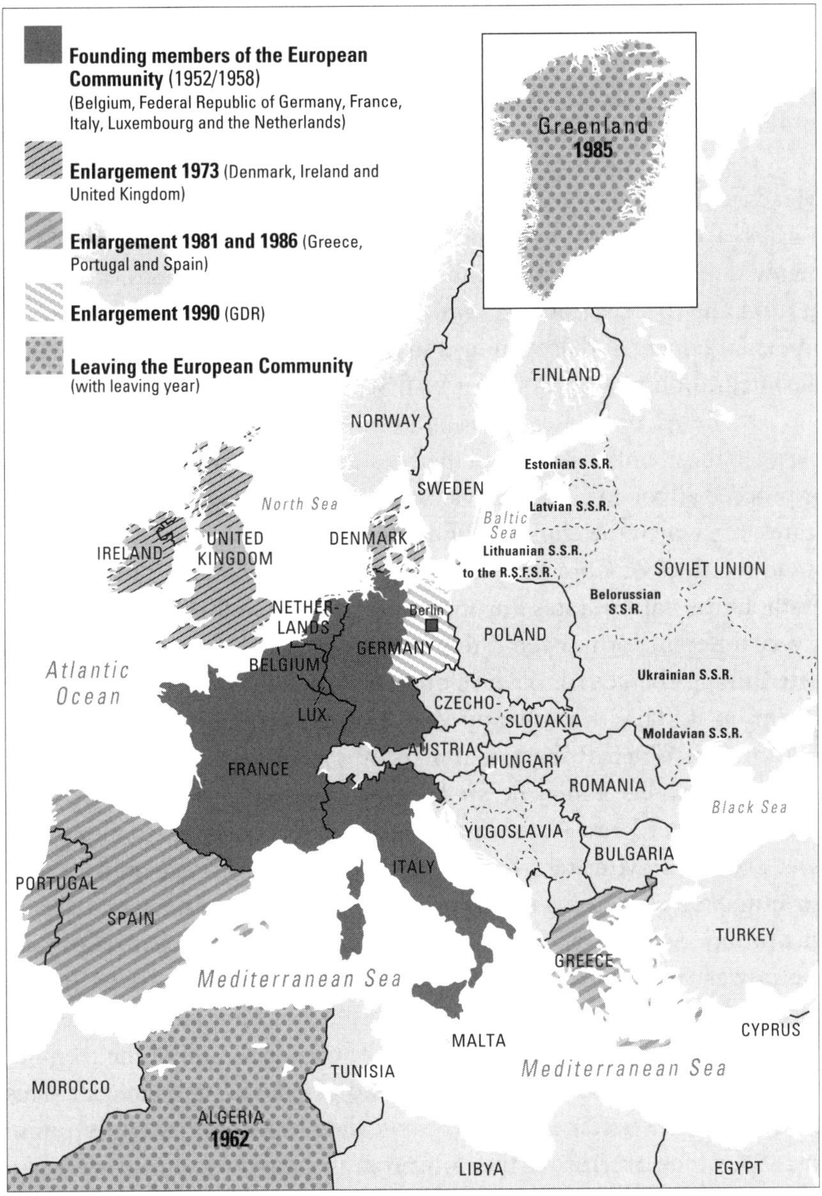

Map 1: Changes in EC membership until 1992. © Peter Palm, Berlin/Germany

Treaty is superficial. Academic and public discussion to date has always been obsessed with successive enlargement rounds. The six founding states were joined in 1973 by the United Kingdom, Ireland and Denmark. Greece followed in 1981; Spain and Portugal in 1986; and even before Maastricht the EC crossed the (now defunct) Iron Curtain in 1990 when the territory of East Germany joined on German reunification. Under this widespread perspective the EC was always expanding, and Brexit presented the first fundamental shock.

In fact Algeria and Greenland both left the EC long before Maastricht. In very general terms enlargement and deepening were always accompanied by important countervailing tendencies. Even below the level of formal membership there were processes of disintegration and dysfunctionality, which relativise both the story of successive enlargement and deepening and the currently fashionable view that the integration process is set for its first ever reversal.

Many of these tensions resulted from diverging interests between the member states and their resistance to permitting integration to proceed all too far. The EC was first and foremost a creature of nation states, for which the choice for Europe was an effective means to withstand the tides of Cold War tension, decolonisation and globalisation. Without the nation states European integration would have unfolded in a very different form. Even if they did not always succeed in absolutely determining the course of developments, they did place their decisive stamp on it. That was already visible in the establishment of the EC institutions. When Robert Schuman in 1950 presented the plan that came to bear his name, he spoke only of a supranational executive organ, the later High Authority. This organ was quickly supplemented by a Council of Ministers, because there was no way the member states' governments were going to relinquish their powers completely to a new institution. A parliamentary Common Assembly somewhat relativised the power of the governments and an independent Court of Justice provided legal oversight. Altogether this created a complex system of checks and balances in which the roles of the Community, the member states and other actors were continuously being rebalanced. This occurred most spectacularly in the so-called Luxembourg compromise in 1966, which overturned the slow progression from more intergovernmental to more supranational set out in the original treaties. There were also further changes in the interplay of the institutions, with the representations of the member states today playing a larger role in certain questions than they did in the 1970s and 1980s.

Indeed, as we will see below, the 1970s represented a phase of deep transformation where the EC acquired a truly significant role for the first time. Whether we consider its contribution to peace, to growth and prosperity, to safeguarding values or – even more fundamentally – its precedence over other forums of international cooperation in Western Europe, in each case the 1970s represented a phase of immense growth in significance. The Hague Summit in December 1969 represented a significant milestone, without of course attributing all those developments to that one meeting. That is surprising given that the 1970s were long regarded as a phase of crisis and have even been described as the 'dark ages' of European integration.[10]

Many of the new departures of the 1970s grew and intensified in the following decade. In certain respects the Maastricht Treaty could be better characterised as the conclusion of the process because the basis for onward development was already created two decades earlier. Of course subsequent changes should not be underestimated either: while most people in the 1990s still believed they could ignore the role of the EU, that has changed fundamentally since the late 2000s. But the reasons why the effects of European integration are so far-reaching are to be found in the 1970s and 1980s.

Hence, my discussion concentrates on the decades of the Cold War, ending with the Maastricht Treaty. This restriction is also necessary because that is the period for which it is possible to base research on archival sources and the latest historical literature. My source-rich multi-perspectival approach is quite simply not yet possible for the more recent period since the early 1990s.

Ultimately, this volume thus paints quite a different picture of the history of European integration than the one with which we are familiar. It seeks to chisel through the wall of leaden boredom that many people associate with the subject. The EC's typical strategies of de-dramatising decisions through legal means, through shared processes and hard-fought compromises need to be understood as a procedural mode that posits itself explicitly as an alternative to national egotism, symbolic enactment and the urge for global power. As we will see, the European Community was initially more fragile and less important than was long thought, before gaining real significance in the 1970s precisely when many contemporaries saw it mired in existential crisis. The precursors of today's EU turned out to be a great deal more resilient than was hitherto believed.

Only in that knowledge do we understand why the present crisis is so much more fundamental in nature than its predecessors. Until the 1970s the questions the EC was responsible for tended to be of secondary importance, and it shared tasks with a whole string of other international organisations. Today we are in a very different situation. With the EU now the absolutely decisive forum for so many policy areas it has become much more vulnerable to fundamental crisis. Where problems are now handled within one and the same organisation they can more easily flashover from one area to another. That could not have happened in the EC of the 1960s, which basically represented a large Common Market with a complicated agricultural policy, while other questions remained the responsibility of the Council of Europe, OECD and other forums.

But the history has more than one lesson. Paradoxically one can understand the 1970s and early 1980s not only as the EC's severest test of the Cold War era, but also one of its most productive and character-building periods. As today, there was no pre-existing plan for tackling the problems – which is precisely why the Community was able to adapt to new challenges and grasp new opportunities.

History is always open-ended. The present is always a door to the unknown. I would not dream of claiming to know the EU's future. But awareness of the history of the European integration process is central to understanding the times we live in and shaping the way forward.

1 EUROPE AND EUROPEAN INTEGRATION

After months of wrangling agreement had finally been reached. Article 1 of its Statute stated the purpose of the new organisation: 'to achieve a greater unity between its members for the purpose of safeguarding and realising the ideals and principles which are their common heritage and facilitating their economic and social progress.' According to the preamble, its focus was to be broader than the merely economic or social. The new organisation was to 'bring European States into closer association' and serve first and foremost 'the pursuit of peace'. And they plainly meant it seriously: the text speaks of 'closer unity', 'closer association' and 'greater unity'.[1]

Yet this was not the European Union or one of its precursors. The document cited above was the 1949 Statute of the Council of Europe – which still exists today, but is nowhere near as important or well known as the EU.

These days 'Europe' is automatically assumed to mean the European Union and Brussels. Most European states are members of the EU, and it is the EU that guarantees open internal borders, supports structurally weak regions and occasionally steps in to pluck a member out of crisis. The fate of its member states is – for both better and worse – intimately bound up with that of the Union as a whole. These days, the European Union is frequently identified more with Europe's problems than with their solutions. And if a state decides to leave, the repercussions are felt throughout the organisation and across the globe. It is so easy to equate Europe with the European Union, or at least with international cooperation in Europe.

That temptation has only grown over the past quarter-century. It even affects historians, who often seem to regard the EU as the only international organisation in Western Europe during the Cold War, or at least far and away the most important. One might easily conclude that European integration began in an international void; that nations basically had to choose between national sovereignty and integration on the EC model. This underestimates two aspects: firstly, the EC was a fragile latecomer in an already densely populated field of international organisations; seventy years ago (and more recently too) it in fact appeared rather unlikely that this particular organisation would one day come to be identified with Europe as a whole, or even just with Western Europe. And secondly, the integration process was not only shaped by the histories of the participating states and the general historical context, but also was influenced by a veritable web of relationships with other Western European organisations and transnational forums. This forms an important and to date largely neglected dimension of the integration process, especially in relation to the Cold War. Europe was never just the EU, and the EU (and its precursors) was never all of Europe. So we need to understand how that equivalence became so strong and how the EC was able to morph from humble origins into Europe's pre-eminent international entity.

One of Many

The fifteen years following the end of the Second World War saw the emergence of a warren of sometimes overlapping, sometimes competing international organisations in Europe, especially Western Europe. Their creation was driven by the lessons of the economic and social crises of the past, and the recent experience of global war, genocide and mass displacement. Never again should radical nationalism and ideologies of autarchy be permitted to plunge the world into chaos and devastation. Cooperation and connection were held to be the best form of prevention. Yet it was not a completely fresh start, given the number of individuals and ideas that had already been around during the inter-war years.[2] The continuities remained in the shadows, however, as the protagonists of integration worked to present their project as a completely new beginning.

By the 1950s internationalisation and globalisation had reached a point where the states of Western Europe no longer formed self-contained entities – if they ever had. The question was simply which of several available European or international solutions they wished to choose. During the brief phase from 1945 to 1948 about 100 international organisations were founded worldwide.[3] By 1949 one Norwegian expert felt moved to complain that the 'number of international organizations has grown tremendously, and it continues to grow. At present, a world-wide public is under the impression that international effort is suffering from undue multiplicity, lack of coordination, wastefulness, and paper worship.'[4] Yet the trend was about to intensify: between 1951 and 1960 the total number of international organisations worldwide swelled from 832 to a grand total of 1,255. The pressures of the Cold War placed the geographical focus on the North Atlantic, and especially Western Europe.[5]

At this juncture the EC was thus merely one among many. Its remit revolved principally around economic matters, but even there it was by no means alone. More than twenty other international organisations dealing with such questions sprouted in Western Europe during the first fifteen years after the Second World War. Some are still comparatively well known, such as the Council of Europe and the OECD, alongside many others such as the United Nations Economic Commission for Europe (UNECE), EFTA and the European Payments Union.[6] A few, such as the Geneva-based International Labour Organization (ILO), pre-dated the war. The ILO had originally been part of the League of Nations, and now became a specialised agency of the United Nations. At this point the EC clearly possessed no monopoly in the broad field of European economic cooperation.

There was another factor too: in comparison to many other initiatives at the international level, the EC was strikingly small, a dwarf rather than a giant. The UNECE, founded in 1947 under the auspices of the United Nations, represented the first significant post-war effort to promote European cooperation. Originally it brought together eighteen states: France and the United Kingdom in Western Europe for example, but also Eastern European states like Czechoslovakia and Poland, as well as the two superpowers, the United States and the Soviet Union. The UNECE understood itself as an all-European institution whose role was to coordinate the reconstruction of Europe and keep the spirit of the wartime alliance alive. The latter became obsolete just months after it was set up, as the escalating Cold War quickly led to the formation of three camps: East, West and neutral. From there on its work became a last-ditch scrabble to build bridges between the blocs, with limited success. In 1948, just one year after UNECE, sixteen Western European states (largely also members of UNECE) formed the Organization for European Economic Co-operation (OEEC). The OEEC coordinated cooperation between Western European states in the framework of the US-led Marshall Plan. The Council of Europe entered the scene in 1949 with just ten members, followed in 1951 by the six-member ECSC as the first direct precursor of today's European Union. But that was no reason to dissolve any of the organisations already established. Instead, UNECE, OEEC, the Council of Europe and ECSC were like Russian matryoshka dolls, of which the ECSC was the smallest and youngest.[7]

Nor could the ECSC be said to have been addressing the most urgent problem of the age. Even if economic questions consumed a great deal of energy after 1945, the public's greatest concern after two devastating world wars was peace. In West Germany, for example, a survey in 1950 showed 57 per cent of citizens expecting a third world war within ten years. According to another survey, two-thirds felt that times were too uncertain to plan for the longer term.[8] While the life-threatening shortages of the immediate post-war years were overcome comparatively quickly, fears that the next global conflict would potentially destroy all of humanity persisted, making peace the greatest concern of many Europeans. Of course the ECSC made a contribution to preserving peace by promoting Franco-German reconciliation and establishing reciprocal controls in the crucial coal and steel industries. But its contribution to preventing war was rather indirect, whereas other organisations placed the issue front and centre. For example, France, the United Kingdom and the Benelux states established a military pact in 1948, which became the Western European Union (WEU) in 1954 after West Germany and Italy were admitted. In matters of war and peace, the WEU was more important than the EC. In another central policy area, human rights, the Council of Europe – rather than the EC – played a leading role from the outset.[9]

There was a broader context, too. As well as being an integral part of a group of Western European organisations, the 'little Western Europe' of the emerging EC was also tied into a broader Western political setting. It was part of a North Atlantic region that was increasingly defined in ideological terms. Reflecting the lessons of the Great Depression, the New Deal and the Second World War, the United States pursued a decidedly internationalist and multilateral approach after 1945, especially as Cold War tensions grew from 1947 onwards.[10] In the second half of the 1940s Washington played a central role in creating international institutions, such as NATO as the security alliance welding Western Europe to the West's superpower. In the economic realm, the international trade organisation GATT and the Bretton Woods institutions underpinned the capitalist international monetary order, with the World Bank and the International Monetary Fund as the central pillars. Together these bodies created the security foundations and specific economic framework in which the EC came to be embedded. In addition, there were literally dozens of bilateral alliances and treaties, within Europe and across the world. One contemporary critic accused US Secretary of State John Foster Dulles of veritable 'pactomania'.[11]

Another factor also shaped the EC's place on the international stage: explicit competition from other Western European organisations. This applies most clearly to EFTA, the British-led initiative established in 1960 as an open alternative to the EC, after the United Kingdom initially chose not to join the ECSC and remained outside the process of establishing the EC. Instead, the British government put forward proposals in 1952 and 1957/58 that would have curtailed the role of the ECSC and the emerging EC in Western Europe. After these attempts failed, the United Kingdom joined with six other Western European states to create a direct rival to the EC, placing greater priority on free trade and pursuing looser forms of cooperation.[12] So alternatives to EC-style integration certainly existed, and there was even an immediate rival within Western Europe. By 1955 the continent was more divided economically and politically than it had been a decade earlier.

Post-war cooperation in Europe becomes a maze of partly overlapping, partly competing organisations: ECSC, UNECE, OEEC, WEU, EC. How on earth could one keep track? And to complete the confusion, they often had different acronyms in different languages. The ECSC was the EGKS in German and CECA in French and Italian. Sometimes an organisation changed its name over time, like the Brussels Pact that became WEU, or the OEEC, which turned into the OECD in 1961 (OCDE in French, OCSE in Italian and OESO in Dutch). Not to forget the many dozens at subsidiary technical levels, such as the European Conference of Postal and Telecommunications Administrations (CEPT)

Map 2: The member states of the UNECE, OEEC, Council of Europe and EC, 1958. © Peter Palm, Berlin/Germany

FINLAND
SWEDEN
Estonian S.S.R.
SOVIET UNION
Latvian S.S.R.
Lithuanian S.S.R.
Baltic Sea
Belorussian S.S.R.
POLAND
EAST GERMANY
Ukrainian S.S.R.
CZECHOSLOVAKIA
Moldavian S.S.R.
AUSTRIA
HUNGARY
ROMANIA
Black Sea
YUGOSLAVIA
BULGARIA
TURKEY
ITALY
ALBANIA
GREECE
Mediterranean Sea

and the European Conference of Ministers of Transport (ECMT). Europe, a great tureen of alphabet soup!

Ultimately the EC emerged at the intersection of three processes. Firstly, it was part and parcel of the West, with a fundamentally capitalist orientation and the United States as its benign guardian. Some of the organisations mentioned above originated in the final phase of the war or even earlier; others were only created after 1945. The period when the EC was founded coincided exactly with the ascendancy of the idea of a specific 'Atlantic community'. This referenced not only the centrality of US influence in Western Europe, but also the importance of mutual interests and values – buttressed by a whole range of shared institutions from NATO to Bretton Woods. In 1964 one expert noted that no issue in international relations was 'so conducive to the outpouring of words, often very tenuously related to recognizable political fact, as that of Atlantic community'.[13] And it was more than just words, as the lists of organisations above demonstrate.[14]

Secondly, and closely connected to the first point, the creation of the EC stood at the end of a process where the Cold War increasingly shaped and narrowed the options for European cooperation. Nothing illustrates this as clearly as the trajectory from the UNECE through the OEEC and the Council of Europe to the EC. Although launched as an all-European initiative, the Marshall Plan was only ostensibly open to the Soviet Union and ultimately provoked the establishment in 1949 of a rival east of the Iron Curtain: the Council for Mutual Economic Assistance (Comecon). The next development was the Council of Europe in 1950, which still included neutral states among its founders. That was no longer the case when the ECSC was established in 1951; its members were unequivocally committed to the Western camp – even if there were still hopes that it would lead to a European third way. UNECE now played a less prominent role, its all-European configuration increasingly at odds with the logic of the Cold War.

Two things about the ECSC stand out: firstly, West Germany was one of the founding members, according it a status it had hitherto been denied (obviously, in the case of UNECE and OEEC, which had been established before West Germany came into existence in 1949). In other words, just half a decade after 1945, fear of Germany – despite two world wars and other conflicts – was already overshadowed by anti-communism and the logic of the Cold War. In the course of the 1950s the young West German state successively gained admission to international bodies, including specialised agencies of the United Nations like the International Labour Organization.[15] So the ECSC was not the only organisation to champion peace with West Germany – but it was the first European body to focus on Franco-German reconciliation. That should not be underestimated.

The second notable point about the ECSC was that the United Kingdom and the Scandinavian countries remained outside; by this time it had become quite clear that they were not interested in such close cooperation, at least for the time being. The post-war hopes of rebuilding Europe as a neutral third force between the superpower blocs transpired to be increasingly unrealistic. From the 1940s international organisations instead became the forums from which the Eastern and Western blocs emerged, policing cohesion and discipline within their respective camps.[16] The EC thus stood not for unity, but for Europe's division into east and west. None of these decisions were uncontroversial; in the early 1960s, for example, de Gaulle sought to overcome the East–West division – even at the price of friction within the West – but his efforts were doomed to failure.[17]

And so the Cold War is deeply ingrained into the integration process. Really Joseph Stalin deserved the first Charlemagne Prize for services to European integration, quipped the Franco-German scholar Alfred Grosser: 'Without that shared fear there would never have been a Community.'[18] Just as the founding of the OEEC spurred the creation of Comecon, moves in the East were soon accelerating political developments in Western Europe. In 1951, for example, former French prime minister Paul Reynaud published *Unite or Perish*, arguing for a Western European confederation: 'Compare the Cominform with the Council of Europe. What speed and efficiency on one side! What slowness and inefficiency on the other!'[19] Even in later phases the sense of external pressure remained strong. For instance, when Norway withdrew its application to join the EC at the last minute in September 1972, some argued that the country should now be left to fend for itself. A few days after the decision, the British embassy in Oslo observed that this was wrong-minded: the implications for the Cold War had to be remembered.[20] This applied all the more in view of Soviet gloating over this 'serious blow to "NATO and EEC circles"'.[21]

The third characteristic of the EC, besides its Western pedigree and its Cold War dimensions, has to do with its relationship to other organisations within Western Europe. Several of them partly overlapped with the EC, sometimes maintained a labour-sharing relationship and sometimes stood in direct competition (as in the case of the Council of Europe and even more so EFTA). In comparison to these organisations the EC certainly did not initially stand out in terms of the number of member states or the breadth of its responsibilities (or only in the sense that it was smaller and more narrowly configured than, for example, the Council of Europe). All of these organisations – including the EC – were pursuing regional integration within Europe, rather than European integration. In comparison to UNECE, the OEEC or the Council of Europe the EC was conspicuously small – although there were naturally also smaller cooperation formats, for example at the bilateral level, in the Benelux context, and in Scandinavia. In the course of the first post-war decade Western Europe had learned that 'effective action becomes inordinately more difficult' where – as in the case of the Council of Europe – the 'circle of membership is drawn very broadly'.[22] It was by no means obvious that the EC's principle of 'small but excellent' would win the day. At the beginning of the 1960s it was certainly not a foregone conclusion that the EC would one day leave the OEEC/OECD far behind.

None of these organisations encompassed all of Europe, yet almost all aspired to represent the continent, as illustrated above in the Statute of the Council of Europe. Pathos-laden preambles and the moniker 'European' were de rigueur. Yet in the case of the EEC, the very word that would in the longer run define the EC/EU project was rather an afterthought. While the ECSC staked a clearly European claim from the Schuman Declaration onwards, negotiations over the EEC initially proceeded under the technical designation 'Common Market'. The symbolic 'European Economic Community' only came later, shortly before conclusion of the treaty. While that was apparently a mere detail, one OEEC official noted in 1958 that the change lent the organisation more 'sex-appeal'. Working towards a Common Market was one thing, aspiring to a European Community a great deal more noble. By adopting an explicitly 'European' identity, the EC projected itself beyond the economic sphere and the legalese of the treaties.[23]

Sui Generis

It is often asserted that the EC stood out from normal international organisations in one specific respect: it alone was supranational.[24]

In other words, it alone was able to take legally binding majority decisions with immediate effect within the member states, without these first having to be implemented in national law. Supranationality is frequently also understood as meaning the ability of an organisation to take on particular tasks, for example in the area of administration, thus substituting policy conducted at the level of the nation state. In this understanding all other organisations are intergovernmental, with each member state possessing a veto and their sovereignty thus remaining unaffected.[25]

Closer examination of this assertion is revealing, however. Firstly, neither the ECSC nor the later EC was fully supranational (nor is the EU today). The High Authority of the ECSC fulfilled the criteria better than the later EC, but was still answerable to an intergovernmental Special Council of Ministers, largely at the insistence of Belgium and the Netherlands. The Dutch negotiator, Dirk Spierenburg, stressed that the mandate of the High Authority was 'more technical in character', while the Council of Ministers possessed 'a more political character'.[26] A supranational arrangement would have looked rather different. The transfer of powers always remained partial and was certainly not set in stone in the treaties. The immediate effect of EC law in the member states, for example, was established piecemeal by the European Court of Justice through a series of rulings beginning in the early 1960s. Under the treaties, the possibility of making legally binding majority decisions was also subject to significant constraints for a defined transitional period. And in 1966, before it expired, the parties agreed to depart from the original plan and switch to a more strongly intergovernmental course (the Luxembourg compromise).[27] All in all, the EC only approximated the ideal of supranational governance. While it certainly possessed unique features, the supranational aspects were by no means ascendent. As such, the EC was not at this stage fundamentally different from other international organisations and regional forums. To the question of the long-term significance of the unique features, we will return later.

Secondly, the latest research challenges the conventional assertion that the ECSC was the first institution to possess supranational elements. In fact, a little-known treaty of 1804 between France and the Holy Roman Empire – regulating tolls and navigation on the Rhine – already possessed all the central attributes of supranationality. Admittedly, the treaty was short-lived, soon to be replaced by the somewhat better-known Central Commission for Navigation on the Rhine of 1816.[28] Nevertheless, it certainly demonstrates that supranationality is older than generally assumed. The emergence of modern sovereign nation-statehood went hand in hand with elements relativising it.

Possible precursors and limits to supranationality played no role in the debates of the 1950s and 1960s, however. Instead, the protagonists of the newly established EC institutions emphasised the absolute novelty of the situation. The Joint Declaration of the Ministers Signatory to the Treaty Establishing the European Coal and Steel Community in 1951, for example, declared that with the new 'organization, involving a hundred and sixty million Europeans, the Contracting Parties have given proof of their determination to set up the first supranational institution and thus to lay the real foundations of an organized Europe'.[29] And Walter Hallstein, the powerful first president of the EEC Commission, described his organisation as a creation *sui generis*, which he sharply differentiated from all other forms of cooperation in Europe.[30] No other term expresses the asserted uniqueness and visionary claim of the EC better than these two words of scholarly Latin. Politicians and experts across fields and disciplines were soon expanding the myth, gradually consolidating an image that remains definitional to this day.[31]

At least in the early stages it was by no means certain how important this slight difference at the institutional level was ultimately to become. This applies all the more so if we take another institution into consideration: the Parliament. The term 'parliament' suggests an assembly of representatives of the people, possessing legislative powers. Yet the Parliament of the EC was relatively toothless at first. And, equally importantly, NATO, the WEU and the Council of Europe also created parliamentary assemblies within their institutional structures in the early 1950s, as did other organisations such as the Nordic Council. In no respect did the EC's organ stand out from this crowd. If any of them could assert that claim, it was the Consultative Assembly of the Council of Europe, which became the context and model for other organisations. For example the WEU's Parliamentary Assembly, established in 1954, was composed of the Council of Europe representatives from the WEU states. And when the Consultative Assembly of the Council of Europe met for the first time in 1949, it was attended by the heads of state and government of all the participating countries. In its early years, the EC's proponents could only dream of such symbolic capital.[32]

In fact, the EC owed its reputation as a special and supranational entity not least to its most influential critic. Charles de Gaulle, French president in the formative years from 1959 to 1969, made no secret of his opposition to a model with the potential to create a United States of Europe. When he was elected many supporters of the integration process feared that he might kill off the young EC on account of its supranational elements.[33] That option was certainly on the table – confirming how shaky the EC's status in the field of international cooperation was at that time. In fact de Gaulle recognised that the system as it stood did not actually disadvantage France, but instead opened up a wealth of opportunities. Through his sometimes brusque and harsh power politics, and even more his passionate interventions at crucial junctures, he ensured that the EC's supranational elements remained limited and unable to override central national interests. His tirades against Brussels were notorious; but because the EC was not in fact galloping towards a United States of Europe, even Gaullist France was able to find a profitable accommodation and succeeded in deriving great benefit from the integration process.[34] At the same time de Gaulle was not alone: great lip-service notwithstanding, fundamental scepticism towards supranationality was widespread in other states too.[35]

The EC may have wanted to be completely unlike the others, but initially this remained more an aspiration, an assertion. In the early years it was one rather small club among many, with only slight differences to other international organisations in Western Europe. On account of the primacy of Franco-German reconciliation, its supranational elements and other factors to which we will come below, the EC did in fact possess great potential – even if this was not necessarily obvious at the time. All this underlines how improbable it actually was that the EU would rise to become the primary and increasingly also the dominant forum of cooperation and integration in Europe.

Three into One

Although I have thus far mainly used the term 'European Community' in the singular, the name itself resulted from a historical process whose outcome was initially by no means certain. The EC not only had to relate to other Western European organisations; it took a whole decade before its several Communities merged into just one. And even then it was frequently referred to in the plural. Belgium, France, Italy, Luxembourg, the Netherlands and West Germany established the ECSC in 1951; six years later, in March 1957, the same six states signed another two treaties creating two new organisations: the European Economic Community and Euratom. The new Communities were neither part of the ECSC nor completely separate new entities. Instead this was an arrangement that could be compared to conjoined triplets (although the first was born five years before the other two). Each of the three organisations had its own Commission (the ECSC's, just to complicate matters, being named the High Authority) and separate Councils of Ministers, comprising the relevant ministers from the six states. But they also shared a number of institutions, principally the Parliamentary Assembly and the Court of Justice.

The policy areas handled by this institutional patchwork were also rather haphazard. The ECSC stood for a sectoral intervention creating shared rules for the coal and steel sectors in the six member states. Euratom followed a similar sectoral approach for nuclear power. The EEC, on the other hand, possessed a broader mandate, given that it was set up to establish a Common Market with free movement of goods, services, people and capital, and common external trade rules. The EEC Treaty also contained vague ideas about establishing other common policies, such as a Common Agricultural Policy and a Common Transport Policy. Unlike the ECSC Treaty, in which the rules were spelled out in detail (*traité loi*), the EEC Treaty tended more towards broadly couched powers (*traité cadre*). This approach had consequences: within ten years the Agricultural Policy had become the EEC's most visible and controversial policy area, while the Transport Policy did not get off the ground until the 1990s – *traité cadre* opened up broad possibilities, but also increased the risk of failure.[36] There was no overarching concept laying out which areas the EC should concentrate on and which legal instruments it should use. Much more decisive was what the governments were able to agree in the treaty negotiations, and sometimes in the process of implementing what they had decided.

This point is illustrated very well by two projects that were ultimately never realised. The two Communities established in 1957 were dwarfed by the grand plans aired during the brief half-decade between the founding of the ECSC and the Treaties of Rome. During this interval the six ECSC states discussed the creation of a European Defence Community (EDC), which would have established a European army. But that venture was torpedoed in 1954 by the French National Assembly (particularly its communist and Gaullist members), along with the attempt to create a kind of constitution for the six member states in the guise of the European Political Community (EPC). Even before de Gaulle's return to power, these radical plans went too far for a majority of the deputies assembled in Paris. The EDC and EPC would have impinged upon core aspects of state sovereignty and greatly deepened the integration process. Measured against these plans and expectations, the Communities that eventually appeared in 1952 and in 1957 remained tiny and quickly concentrated on the production of and trade in coal, steel, agricultural goods and nuclear materials, as well as creating a Common Market. What they lacked was the overarching roof that the EPC had sought to provide. So the two Communities established in 1957 represented successes for the project but stood on the ruins of much grander plans.

The EEC and Euratom also presented challenges and risks for the ECSC. The early days saw important figures leaving the ECSC for the two new organisations (and elsewhere). Pierre Uri, one of Monnet's closest advisors in the High Authority, had already spent a great deal of time in Brussels during the negotiations for the Treaties of Rome, and resigned in July 1959. Several central positions, such as Director of the ECSC's Financial Division, remained vacant for years. And there were frequent disputes over matters such as the precise functioning of the shared and separate organs. When EEC Commission president Hallstein announced his intention to give the opening speech to the new shared Parliamentary Assembly, for example, he was met with a storm of protest from the ECSC's High Authority: they were the older body and therefore entitled to precedence. So especially in the early years there was much friction, driven by personal vanities and institutional rivalries.[37]

It quickly became apparent that the relationship between the three Communities would be neither harmonious nor equal. The ECSC's expectation that it would continue to lead the pack was quickly dashed.[38] But even between the other two organisations it was initially unclear which would come out on top. Jean Monnet, for example, believed it would be Euratom. Given that the ECSC was already dealing with coal, the power sector seemed the obvious lead. And this was also a field where energy and security converged, as it was no secret that the power of the atom also had military uses.[39] It is hard to imagine now, but this was an era of absolutely utopian expectations for nuclear power. Some experts even believed that there would soon be nuclear-powered aircraft, and that civilian nuclear power was the key to solving all the great social and energy challenges of the future. The philosopher Ernst Bloch, for example, gushed at the end of the 1950s about the atom's contribution to peace, how it 'creates fertile land out of the desert, and spring out of ice'. Nuclear power, he said, grants humankind 'the energy, which would otherwise have to be obtained in millions of hours of labour, ready for use in slim containers and in highly concentrated form'.[40] The treaty negotiations themselves were coloured by the 'perspective of a new industrial revolution far exceeding that of the preceding hundred years', as the Italian Foreign Ministry noted.[41] Those high-flying hopes were soon brought crashing back to earth. There were also other reasons why Euratom was soon reduced to a marginal role, whereas the EEC now called the tune – even though many member states, including France and West Germany, had started off with grave doubts about the Common Market project on a variety of economic grounds.[42] It is instructive that the authoritative account of the history of the High Authority sees the founding of the two new Communities as one of the main reasons for its demise.[43] All these aspects relativise the conventional narrative asserting that the integration process steadily deepened and widened in the course of the Cold War.

The fragmented character of the early Communities was starkly revealed by an official visit to the United States in June 1959. Rather than conducting concrete negotiations, the trip was intended to symbolise Washington's support for the European integration process.[44] But who would the EC send? Although the trip was so symbolically laden, they chose to send no fewer than all three presidents of the Communities: the Belgian Paul Finet for the ECSC, the Frenchman Étienne Hirsch for Euratom and the German Walter Hallstein for the EEC. A trinity of European unity. The Americans wanted to generate good publicity, and wondered what symbol to use for their European guests. In the end they opted for the flags of the six member states, as the Communities did not yet have a symbol of their own.[45] Three into one turned out to be a tricky operation.

Gothic and Other Structures

Many other aspects remained thoroughly provisional too. While the members of the Council of Europe agreed in 1949 to make Strasbourg the seat of its institutions, the governments of the EC states remained unable to agree a clear and permanent solution until the 1990s. National prestige and local interests permitted only provisional arrangements for locating the institutions of the Communities.[46] Until the mid-1960s there was not even a legal basis for the complicated arrangement that had crystallised by that point, under which Strasbourg, Luxembourg and Brussels served as the seats of the EC's most important organs.[47] The provisional character of the Communities was particularly obvious in the case of their Parliament, which met in Strasbourg (while its secretariat remained in Luxembourg and its committees convened in Brussels): for decades it lacked its own premises and was forced to borrow the Council of Europe's assembly room. In fact, at that time 'Brussels' was largely in Luxembourg: while it

Figure 2: Assembly room of the Council of Europe (1950), later also used by the European Parliament. Stringer/AFP/Getty Images

is the Belgian capital that has today become synonymous with the EU, the High Authority, as the executive organ of the ECSC, was originally based in Luxembourg. Europe is often praised or cursed as a 'utopia'. The word originates from ancient Greek and literally means 'no-place'. Astonishingly fitting.

The Merger Treaty of 1965 brought the conjoined siblings closer together, although without yet melding entirely. French foreign minister Maurice Couve de Murville had already underlined the distinction in 1962: the point was to merge the executives of the three organisations rather than applying EEC rules to coal and steel.[48] Nevertheless, that process now created the 'European Communities', which were increasingly frequently referred to in the singular, even though each of the organisations remained legally separate. While the High Authority went into the negotiations still believing that it would be able to preserve its position of greater autonomy than the executives of Euratom and the EEC, the member states ultimately agreed on a model that was less supranational and more strongly orientated on the Treaties of Rome. The Communities were now called the EC, although it was increasingly seen as principally the EEC. The ECSC was relegated from son-and-heir to stepchild, and one of the younger siblings took over the reins.[49]

This brought a little more clarity to the formation, although the situation remains extremely complex to this day: the Treaty of Lisbon subsumed the EC into the EU, while Euratom remained separate (although its structures are now completely integrated within the EU). New headquarters have sprung up – Frankfurt am Main for the European Central Bank, Warsaw for Frontex – even as Brussels is today more strongly identified with the EU than ever before. Since the 1967 fusion there has also been just one Commission president, but matters have not necessarily become any simpler. For example, when the EU received the Nobel Peace Prize in 2012 three gentlemen again made the trip: in Oslo the prize was received jointly by the presidents of the European Council, the European Commission and the European Parliament – Herman van Rompuy, José Manuel Barroso and Martin Schulz. During the post-war era the Commission worked to represent the entire Community externally as if it were a state. This earned it harsh criticism, especially from Charles de Gaulle, who regarded this as an unbearable impertinence. In other words, the threesome of 2012 was a very different story to the one of 1959. Today there is just one Union – but it is not more supranational than its precursors. At the Nobel Peace

Prize award ceremony, van Rompuy represented the member states to draw a line against possible federalist tendencies.

All this will seem very confusing to most people today. Those interested in history may find the complex and rather fragmented structure of the EC reminiscent of the legal complexity of the early modern era, which certain contemporaries already regarded as 'erratic' and 'monstrous', stemming from a mixture of 'indulgence', 'ambition' and 'agitation'.[50] The structure of the EC, too, reflected more the sum of power interests and compromises between participating states and shared organs than any grand overarching idea. That is not to say that that is necessarily negative. The early modern structures themselves not only attracted criticism; one contemporary saw them as a 'durable Gothic structure, in which one may live very well even if its construction does not obey all the rules of architecture'.[51] Both interpretations can easily be applied to the EU too, and to the ensemble of European organisations as a whole.

There were also positive sides to the parallelism of international organisations, with their overlaps, rivalries and inefficiencies. Conflicts between member states were often restricted to just one of the forums, and as such contained. When President de Gaulle paralysed the EC for six months in 1965 with the Empty Chair Crisis, France still continued to fulfil its obligations in the Council of Europe, OECD, WEU and elsewhere.[52] The EC found a solution by January 1966. Just a few months later de Gaulle sparked the next crisis by withdrawing France from NATO's integrated military command structure. But this was again just a finely calculated pinprick, not a wholesale abandonment of cooperation within the Western (or Western European) camp. France remained a member of NATO itself and business as usual reigned in the EC.[53] Ultimately all the member states shared an interest in keeping the show on the road. Crises and criticism – sometimes presented with great drama, especially by the French – always concentrated on a specific international organisation. Because there were so many, it all functioned like a system of firewalls that isolated crises and limited the harm they could do. At the same time this permitted actors to play in different registers. In one international crisis of the late 1960s, for example, the British Foreign Office noted with cynical pragmatism that 'our policies in Council of Europe should be decided in the light of the moral and other issues involved, while questions of military co-operation should be treated in the NATO context'.[54] The thought expressed so openly here was also often applied similarly to the EC. And in calmer periods the various forums served to discuss the roles and responsibilities of the different organisations. For instance, in the 1960s the relationship between EC and EFTA in the upcoming GATT negotiations was explored in the WEU forum. And when it came to transatlantic economic negotiations, Western Europe's political and economic elites sought to consult and coordinate above and beyond the various organisations.[55] Occasionally the diversity of forums also permitted a differential accentuation of interests. The beauty of the architecture could perhaps be questioned, but when it mattered, the walls proved astonishingly stable.

The Most Crucial of All

In view of the numerous rivals for the title of prima donna in the field of Western European organisations, and the difficulties encountered along the road to 'the' European Community, how did the EC manage to become the decisive forum in Western Europe (and soon beyond) within the space of just three decades from the late 1950s to the end of the Cold War?

Several factors came together here. In the early phase it was important for the EC to establish a degree of task-sharing in the field of international cooperation. Left to its own devices, it would have been overwhelmed by the enormous challenges of the era. It included some of the most important states of Western Europe, which on the one hand sought to avoid duplication and overlap between the different organisations – and on the other hand found advantage in being able to play across an entire range of institutions. If NATO was responsible for defending security, the Council of Europe for protecting human rights, and the Bretton Woods organisations for guarding the economic framework, the EC had time to consolidate and develop gradually. It lived cocooned within a web of other institutions, the distribution of responsibilities subject to a never-ending process of fine-tuning. This was especially true where hardly any of these organisations were explicitly dedicated to a clearly defined policy area, and many of them sought to expand and deepen their sphere of activity for reasons of institutional self-preservation. For example, the WEU, as a military alliance, originally also had a cultural remit, which it formally transferred to the Council of Europe in 1960.[56] When environmental policy was 'invented' at the international level around 1970, the OECD, the Council of Europe and even NATO played a role.[57] Tasks were continuously being rebalanced and redistributed, and the EC certainly did not bear sole or principal responsibility for ensuring international cooperation. That made its job easier and left it space for development. So being less prominent in the early phase turned into an advantage in the medium term.

Especially in its early days the EC was able to profit from the fact that international cooperation was established practice. The routines of cooperation – travel, meeting, talking with and about one another in a multilingual environment – were familiar and had spread beyond the tight circles of classical diplomacy. The EC was able to draw on knowledge accumulated by the UNECE, OEEC and others. Without statistics and other internationally gathered information it was more or less impossible to formulate a political initiative at the European level. That might sound rather abstract. What it meant in practice was if the ECSC wanted to construct housing for coal and steel workers it had to know where the need was greatest. In fact, many of the crucial meetings on the road to the Treaties of Rome were held within the framework of the WEU or the OEEC, and thus outwith the institutional vessel of the six-member ECSC.[58]

In terms of personnel, too, the young EC drew on a pool of veterans of other organisations. The Belgian Paul-Henri Spaak had already served as president of the first United Nations General Assembly and as president of the Consultative Assembly of the Council of Europe before he became president of the Parliamentary Assembly of the ECSC in 1952.[59] Tony Rollman from Luxembourg led policy on steel in the High Authority after previously fulfilling similar roles in UNECE and OEEC.[60] Now one might object here that in such small countries a select circle is often responsible for a wide spectrum of responsibilities. But the Frenchman Jean Monnet, father of the Schuman Plan and first president of the High Authority, had previously gathered formative experience in the world of international organisations, with the First World War Allied Maritime Transport Council and the inter-war League of Nations as significant staging points.[61] His compatriot Robert Marjolin, a generation younger than Monnet, was appointed OEEC secretary-general in 1948 and resigned from that post shortly before the negotiations over the Treaties of Rome got going properly. From 1958 he served as one of France's two EEC commissioners.[62] The much lauded 'founding fathers' of the EC made sure they kept their options open.

But there was also a place for experts and senior officials who had earned their spurs in very different forms of internationalism. The Director-General of the Statistical Office of the European Communities, Rolf Wagenführ, served until 1945 in Albert Speer's Ministry of Armament and War Production, building a career preparing statistics and plans for Hitler's war economy.[63] Many representatives of the steel sector, who worked together from 1952 in the ECSC, already knew one another from contexts of collaboration and resistance under Nazi rule.[64] So the experiences of different generations and systems flowed into the EC's repertoire. Many roads led to Brussels.

At the same time the nascent EC succeeded in warding off hostile takeover attempts. A string of such challenges came already in the second half of the 1950s, the most significant when the United Kingdom initially proposed its free trade area model as a broader framework for the European Community. The initiative that ended with EFTA as an alternative to the EC was hatched between 1956 and 1959 as a kiss of death. The talks for this British initiative, incidentally, were held under the auspices of the OEEC, which in turn points to the close connections between the different international organisations. Paris led the charge in rejecting a move that could have killed off the fledgling EC.[65] Another example: at about the same time the presidents of the parliaments of the Council of Europe and the WEU proposed merging the Parliament proposed for the three Communities with those of their own organisations. Instead of speaking only for the ECSC, Euratom and EEC, this super-parliament would also have included the Council of Europe and WEU. At first glance one might think responsibility for more member states and policy fields would have strengthened the organ. However, given the different institutional arrangements of the respective organisations, this would in fact have paralysed the Parliament and made it into an illusionary giant.[66] A third example takes us to the early 1960s, and demonstrates that London certainly held no monopoly on such suffocating initiatives. This time the French government under de Gaulle proposed a new venture for European integration. The so-called Fouchet Plans would have deepened integration at the political, cultural and military levels – but without supranational components. And because this would also have endangered the existing Communities, the initiative found little favour among the member states.[67]

Additionally, many of the hopes initially projected on other international organisations remained unfulfilled. The disappointment and disillusionment were greatest in relation to the Council of Europe. Supporters of a supranational model had hoped to turn that organisation into the starting point for their United States of Europe. Although its 1949 Statute quoted at the beginning of the chapter still breathed that spirit, British and Scandinavian resistance had by that point already ensured that the remit was restricted and the structure intergovernmental. With a Committee of Ministers functioning on the unanimity principle, it was foreseeable that the Council of Europe would not be making any great leaps. When its Consultative Assembly under Spaak nevertheless quickly set about working towards greater powers, the governments of the United Kingdom and the Scandinavian countries soon put their foot down.[68] The Council of Europe was less technocratic than the later EC, and in contrast to the EC's economic model it stood for the idea of cultural and ethical (re)unification; a set of ideas that have recently been fittingly described as a 'romantic project'.[69] That is precisely the reason why it attracted so much pushback. Many federalists found this deeply frustrating, first and foremost Spaak, who threw in the towel in December 1951, resigning in disappointment as president of the Consultative Assembly.[70] The Council of Europe, and also, for example, UNECE, were thus forced to dial back originally far-reaching political ambitions. Instead of grand plans they now concentrated on technical aspects of cooperation and led – as a memorandum of the West German representation in Strasbourg noted in relation to the Council of Europe – 'an unobtrusive existence'.[71] This is what cleared the space on the international stage that the EC was soon to claim as its own. The Schuman Declaration of 1950 chose its words wisely when it spoke of 'solidarity of the deed': words aplenty had been spoken, and by now there were already more than enough institutions too.[72]

The way federalist hopes in particular jumped like sparks from one institution to the next before lighting a weak flame that was to burn permanently in the EC can be illustrated especially clearly in relation to the concept of 'integration'. Until the end of the 1940s those discussing European unification had generally spoken of 'federalism', 'federation' or 'union' to describe their objectives. The triumph of the term 'integration' only began in the context of the Marshall Plan and American analyses and hopes relating to Western Europe. In the guise of Paul G. Hoffman, director of the Economic Cooperation Administration (responsible for the Marshall Plan), an American in fact played a central role in popularising the term. In the end the Marshall Plan failed to fulfil such hopes and the term slowly 'migrated' onwards, ultimately finding itself increasingly applied to the EC.[73]

Yet at the beginning of the 1960s it was by no means clear that the 'little European' project of the Six would not suffer the fate of so many other Western European organisations: launched to great fanfare, but quickly reduced to a largely technical existence with little – and still less systemic – influence on international cooperation. The press reporting on the signing of the Treaties of Rome in 1957 is fascinating in this respect. Many media outlets reported approvingly, and some with great enthusiasm and sweeping praise. But reports frequently contained a healthy dose of scepticism. The *Frankfurter Allgemeine Zeitung*, for example: 'This is a grand decision. And if it turns out to be successful, it will be a grand achievement.'[74] This was journalism in the optative: wishes for the future were uppermost, less so the current state of affairs and achievements to date. Overall the EC did not stand out compared to other international organisations in the Western European press reporting of the 1950s and 1960s; in other words, journalists were not yet according it special status as the leading forum.[75]

The great openness of future perspectives was in turn revealed by the stance of the United States. Washington supported the European integration process like no other outside entity,[76] not least because of the trust they placed in Jean Monnet, Paul-Henri Spaak, Konrad Adenauer and a few other favoured interlocutors who mostly associated themselves with the EC. Post-war cooperation hinged on elite networks and the level of trust established between some of the key players. Having said that, Washington initially avoided committing itself solely to the EC. This is seen especially at the symbolic level. A good eighteen months after the visit of the three EC presidents, OEEC secretary-general Thorkil Kristensen travelled to Washington. He was received with similar pomp as the EC representatives, even though the European Community claimed to be very different and fundamentally more important than the organisation Kristensen represented.[77]

Through into the early 1960s the OEEC/OECD remained the principal challenger for the title of the Most Important Western European Organisation. It had more members than the EC, was also dedicated to economic questions, and was more closely connected to the United States as Western hegemon – which was sometimes an advantage, sometimes a drawback. The European Payments Union was founded in 1950 under its auspices, and the European Productivity Agency – which was also bound up with the OEEC – played an important role in establishing and coordinating Western European economic policies in the 1950s.[78] To that extent the OEEC – emerging from the Marshall Plan – unfolded an impressive dynamism. Against this background one high-ranking US expert reported in 1956 that 'among national representatives and Secretariat officials ... it has often been boasted that the Organization for European Economic Cooperation (OEEC) is the most successful of the many many postwar experiments in international organization'.[79] The OEEC was not destined for greatness, however. It was ultimately too closely associated with the United States to become the leading forum in Europe. While European integration unfolded under American dominance, there was always a significant camp that saw unification as a counterweight to American hegemony.

Having said this, it was remarkable that the OEEC survived the 1950s at all. The end of the Marshall Plan marked the fulfilment of its original task, and for several months its end appeared nigh. What happened next was something witnessed frequently with international organisations in post-war Western Europe: an existing institution sought a new mission. After complex negotiations its member states agreed to make it responsible for economic affairs in Western Europe (the ECSC not being an option as it dealt only with coal and steel). The reorientation was an important success for the OEEC, but led it straight into another crisis at the end of the 1950s, when it became the forum for the conflict between the EEC and London over British plans for a free trade area. When Western Europe split into EEC and EFTA, the OEEC again found itself under scrutiny. Once again it was not disbanded, but completely transformed into an international organisation propagating the capitalist model in the West and operating as a development agency in the former colonies of the Global South.[80]

All these aspects underline how unlikely it appeared that the EC would turn into the pre-eminent international forum in Western Europe. There was no master plan laying out how the EC would become the leader of the pack – profiting from both the experience of others and a kind of international division of labour, and eventually doing away with its rivals. Instead the story was one of multitudinous negotiations and hard-fought distribution fights out of which the EC astonishingly often – although not always – emerged the winner. Only with hindsight does the process take shape. While in the mid-1960s the French elites wanted to strengthen the EC's security role at the expense of NATO, the West Germans certainly did not. In the Cold War era the German stance won the day.[81] Nor did biographies point clearly towards the EC. The Belgian diplomat Jean-Charles Snoy et d'Oppuers, for example, was still clearly an OEEC man during the negotiations for the Treaties of Rome, and no great friend of the EC project. Even if he was among the actual signatories of the treaties, he noted decades later in his memoirs: 'and I still believe today that the OEEC system played a larger role in the first steps towards European integration than the ECSC'.[82]

Three Driving Forces

So how was the EC able to bounce back as the decisive forum time and again? Three factors stand out – not as driving forces for any sort of European cooperation, but explaining why the EC incrementally became a different creature in comparison to all other international organisations in Western Europe.[83] Firstly, the Community's focus on a Customs Union and a Common Market (originating in the EEC) turned out to be crucial in the long run. That economic logic produced many functional connections to other areas. This was already recognised in the 1950s, in the sense of spillover effects from one policy area to another:[84] the creation of the Common Market had repercussions in other areas such as hygiene standards, consumer protection, vocational training and social policy. Research has long demonstrated that such spillovers did not come about automatically: the integration dynamic did not always spring from one policy area to another, and where it did this certainly did not occur without external prompting. What mattered more is that there were groups and institutions insisting on supposed or actual inherent necessities and fighting to expand the powers of the EC – be they the Commission, the Parliament, transnational interest groups, or individual member states. For example in agriculture: once, Common Market Organisations existed for cereals, meat, dairy products and vegetables; it was only a matter of time before the vintners, the olive growers and even the flax and hemp farmers demanded similar arrangements. In environmental policy the European Commission in particular sought to protect consumers. Or another example: from the 1970s the EC developed the rudiments of its own cultural policy. There were phases where the European Court of Justice played a significant role in clarifying the extent to which cultural goods were subject to the general rules of the Common Market. In each case the logic of the market raised questions that rubbed off on other policy areas – that then had to be accordingly promoted or constrained.[85] The Council of Europe, for example, was responsible for the vital matter of human rights. But in discharging this overtly political responsibility it found itself facing much greater resistance than the EC with its more technocratic and seemingly apolitical attire. In view of the overwhelming predominance of the nation state as the model for political order, the 'romantic' programme of European cultural and ethical unification associated with the Council of Europe offered much less spillover into other areas, or at least fewer actors successfully advocating such a course.

At the same time the 'spillovers' created by the economic logic of the EC did not result from abstract functional compulsions or anonymous mechanisms. They were the work of people. The officials of the European Commission played an important part: especially in the early years, many of them presented their great expertise with enormous confidence and self-assurance. The Council of Ministers also played a significant role in this connection, although the states were naturally free to articulate their interests in other international organisations too. More important was the EC's strong focus on economic questions, which mobilised representatives of commerce and industry. Whether these were advocates for the European wine sector or the steel cartels of the Saar-Lor-Lux region, they had a history of working together and increasingly regarded the EC as the vehicle for their interests. For a long time employers were more influential than trade unions, although over time the EC became increasingly important for the latter, as it did for environmental groups and consumer rights advocates. It was much longer before human rights, as the Council of Europe's number one priority, mobilised civil society groups in any comparable manner. The transnational milieu that played such a role in the economics-driven EC always remained smaller in the Council of Europe.

Secondly there was European law. The piecemeal emergence of a legal culture of its own with a strong binding character, from legislation to implementation, gave the Community a great advantage over other Western European organisations. The latter were generally reliant on voluntary cooperation by their member states to implement broadly couched agreements into national law. Under certain conditions citizens of the Community were also able to appeal directly to the European Court of Justice, which was not the case with organisations like the OECD or the Council of Europe. This also lent a specific dynamic to the ECJ and the development of law in the Community.[86] Otherwise 'European law', as taught at universities across the world, would not – as it does – mean the law created by the EC and today the EU. At a very general level, the role of the ECJ was frequently decisive in expanding the powers of the EC, not least by a very broad interpretation of the market-driven mandate of the treaties. The impact of European law – directly applicable and largely independent of the law of the member states – was one of EU's strongest weapons. That also explains why, for example, the EC's trade policy instruments were long regarded as far superior to those of GATT.[87]

Of course precisely this strongly binding quality occasionally led member states to put the international regulation of a problem in the hands of another organisation or to define the EC's legal standards less strictly in order to keep implementation comparatively simple.[88] It was the member states' consistent willingness to abide by collective decisions that allowed European law to have such a transformative impact.

Thirdly, finally, the EC commanded larger financial resources than other Western European organisations. The OECD's budget allowed for little more than funding its secretariat, a modicum of statistical research and a few expert commissions. Matters were little different for the Council of Europe, whose history is littered with insiders' complaints about the inadequacy of its funding. Its secretary-general Lujo Tončić-Sorinj remarked in 1972 that 'the greater part of our intergovernmental activities which go on very satisfactorily are prevented from enjoying greater success because of lack of funds.' Straight talk for an Austrian from a long line of diplomats.[89] The EEC, by contrast, possessed revenues of their own from 1970, while the ECSC had enjoyed the same since the very beginning. This made the EC comparatively independent of its member states, especially where spending decisions lay largely with the Commission and the Parliament. The arrangement was hard-fought; but once in place it granted the EC a degree of freedom its rivals could only envy.[90]

Together, these three factors propelled the EC into a position of primacy among regional organisations in Western Europe. Other factors also intervened occasionally, such as fortunate timing or the support of specific (lobbying) groups. This was not restricted to the above-mentioned business interests. The Action Committee for the United States of Europe, a transnational high-level group of pro-European politicians, for example argued in November 1959 for a fusion of the executives of the three Communities – long before this appeared on the official agenda.[91] The same applies to the role of prominent individuals. The charismatic personality, profound expertise, networks and (in)famous negotiating talents of Sicco Mansholt, the Dutch commissioner responsible for the Common Agricultural Policy, were crucial to its emergence as the EC's informal flagship within ten years after the Treaties of Rome.[92] These factors were of course not generally specific to the EC, much as they shaped the course of individual events.

At the level of the institutional structures, 1979 represented an important watershed. Now MEPs were no longer delegated but directly elected, which boosted their democratic legitimacy and self-confidence. Another aspect is frequently overlooked: until 1979 many of the same politicians also participated in the parliamentary assemblies of organisations like the Council of Europe and the WEU, which oiled the wheels of exchange and cooperation. From 1979 the EC became more autonomous, with its Parliament setting it apart from the other organisations.[93]

The EC's gradual rise is also reflected in the decisions of third states. Israel briefly discussed the option of joining the EEC in 1957, to the point of secret talks conducted between Jean Monnet and the young Shimon Peres, at that time director-general at the Israeli Ministry of Defence. The idea was quickly shelved, with a trade agreement signed in 1964 instead.[94] In the early 1960s the Greek and Turkish governments debated whether to look more strongly towards EFTA or the EC. In January 1960 Turkish foreign minister Fatin Rüştü Zorlu stated that both options had been considered: both Turkey and Greece had ultimately chosen to seek closer ties to the EC's Common Market, 'which corresponds more closely to their economic interests'.[95] That decision by Turkey and Greece launched a similar debate in Spain, which made a similar choice.[96] But the biggest success came in 1961 when the United Kingdom applied to join the EC, and offered to abandon its own competing model. Notably, the first international discussions about London's desire for membership were held in the Council of the WEU.[97] Even if the French veto ultimately shot down Britain's application, this represented an almost immeasurable symbolic boost for the EC. No wonder the EEC Commission rolled out the superlatives and declared the day the accession request was announced a 'turning-point in post-war European politics'.[98]

The press were rather slower. Leading media in Western Europe only began granting prominent status to the EC in the late 1960s and early 1970s; only now did the media as a whole begin to internalise the view long asserted by its glowing proponents, that the European Community was a creation *sui generis*, against which all other international organisations appeared secondary or even illegitimate. The EC was now increasingly equated with 'Europe' and in no country was the quality press more pro-European than in the United Kingdom.[99] *Times* editor William Rees-Mogg, for example, wrote in 1976 that it 'has always been wrong to be too impatient about the development of Europe'. The EC was evolving and there was no harm in that, as it gave people time to get used to it. Rees-Mogg drew up a comprehensive plan of action – and called for integration to be speeded up.[100] How times change, given his son Jacob's stance on the EU.

Altogether the EC's rise to become the primary forum of international cooperation in Western Europe proceeded in many small steps, and it only really got there in the second half of the 1980s. Even after that other organisations remained important or even decisive in particular policy areas. In transport, for example, the EU did not become a significant force until the 1990s;[101] in matters of external security it still plays second fiddle to NATO. Even in the realm of the economy – as its absolute core interest – the EC's leading role only dates back to the mid-1980s. As Laurent Warlouzet has recently demonstrated, even in the 1970s and early 1980s it was by no means clear to the member states which Western European organisation should be the central forum for responding to the economic challenges of globalisation. The EC ultimately filled that role only after a learning process in which first all conceivable alternatives for national policy-making and international cooperation were tried out, including GATT, OECD and ILO. Brussels may have been reminded of a saying attributed to Winston Churchill: that the Americans always do the right thing in the end – after first exhausting all other possibilities. Apparently the member states hewed to the same script.[102]

Primacy and Geometry

So what happened to all the international organisations the EC left behind as the years passed? Few were disbanded. Their members discussed and rediscussed their roles, and occasionally there were proposals to expand or deepen them. That is what Bonn proposed for the WEU in 1967 for example.[103] In that concrete case – and many similar such moments – not a lot actually happened because no consensus could be found among the member states. Often all that remained for representatives of organisations like UNECE, WEU or OECD was to join in the *cantus firmus* that the aforementioned Tončić-Sorinj sang for the Council of Europe. Radical downsizing was also a rarity, and few of these organisations were discontinued. In this respect international organisations share something in common with the institutions of ancient Rome, which often lived on after they had lost their original function. Some sank into obscurity; others like the OECD reinvented themselves. And occasionally one returned from irrelevance in a moment of crisis. That would be the WEU, for example, which enjoyed a brief last fling in the aftermath of the Cold War before its main functions were incorporated into the EU and its organisation wound up in 2011.[104] Shoring up the less successful pillars of the international system was part and parcel of the responsibility-sharing approach: reorientating rather than abolishing allowed states to keep options open, to which they could return if required. Alongside this strategic long game, another aspect is indicated by a German Foreign Ministry note from 1960. It argued that Euratom should be retained despite obvious problems, because abandoning the organisation would be tantamount to conceding that European integration had failed in that sector.[105] So occasionally organisations lived on simply as symbols of the will to cooperate.[106] Institutions also fought for self-preservation: seeking new tasks, building alliances with governments and interest groups, and highlighting their own symbolic significance. For all these reasons there is a lot to say for Austrian-American economist Gottfried Haberler's pithy observation in the 1970s: international organisations never die.[107] Indeed, the ruins of semi-functioning but never completely abandoned international organisations plaster the road to European cooperation to this day. And that is probably no bad thing.

For the EC itself, the journey to become the foremost forum of Western European cooperation was bound up with an apparently paradoxical countercurrent. At the very moment when it attained full-spectrum primacy, the centrifugal forces accelerated. These dynamics sometimes triggered processes of disintegration and dysfunctionality, but also led to a new phenomenon within the EC: it now became clear that only certain member states were willing or able to participate in certain projects. So primacy explains why there was now discussion about 'variable geometry', a 'multi-speed Europe' or 'Europe à la carte'. One reason behind this new trend for differentiation is that the questions at stake were increasingly portentous. Deepening and enlargement – like the EC's growing importance in comparison to other organisations – thus put the question of the limits of integration increasingly urgently on the agenda.

The tendency was not entirely new. Ever since the 1950s the treaties had placed particular geographical restrictions on the applicability of Community law. In 1957 Bonn insisted that trade between West and East Germany must remain a bilateral matter, and refused to treat East Germany as a third country outside the EC. The alternative would have been for Bonn to recognise the existence of the other German state, which was absolutely out of the question.[108] When the United Kingdom joined the EC in 1973 it also obtained special dispensations for New Zealand dairy products and Caribbean sugar.[109] But such arrangements were usually limited to specific transitional periods and represented comparatively minor inroads into the universality of Community law.

Such arrangements came in for increasing criticism from the 1970s as enlargement and deepening raised doubts as to whether all the member states were equally willing and able to sign up to far-reaching commitments. This process came to a head around the middle of the decade when the question of a common monetary policy appeared on the agenda. In view of the enormous differences in economic performance between the member states, former chancellor Willy Brandt proposed a 'gradation of integration':[110] the Benelux states, France and West Germany, whose economies were comparatively similar, would forge ahead on monetary matters; the others, especially Italy and the United Kingdom, would follow later. Building on these ideas, the Tindemans Report in December 1975 suggested that it was not necessary for all member states to complete all integration steps simultaneously. While Tindemans was even less keen on lasting differentiation than Brandt, his concern was to enable new joint initiatives to be launched while acknowledging the differences between member states.[111]

This early debate over differentiation unfolded at the intersection of three processes: firstly in the context of the first round of enlargement, which significantly increased the EC's economic heterogeneity; secondly in light of the idea of a monetary union, which would involve the integration process moving into a core sphere of state sovereignty; and thirdly against the backdrop of the collapse of the Bretton Woods system, to which we will return in Chapter 3.[112] Until the early 1970s Bretton Woods ensured that the EC had no need to play any significant role in this central field of international coordination, because a functioning mechanism already existed at the transatlantic level. The collapse of Bretton Woods opened up a yawning gap that the EC sought to close for its member states. As the Atlantic widened, the Western Europe context became both closer and more differentiated.

The responses from member states were initially largely negative. That only began to change at the end of the 1970s, and again monetary policy was an important factor. The European Monetary System (EMS) was established in 1979 to provide a substitute for Bretton Woods, following a number of false starts over the course of the decade. While all the EC member states formally belonged to the EMS, they did not all apply the Exchange Rate Mechanism. In the United Kingdom, the debate about joining the mechanism was particularly fierce. The more important the EC became, the harder it was to keep all member states on board in all projects, especially where accession talks with another economically weak country – Greece – were under way at the same time.[113]

Alongside monetary policy, justice and home affairs emerged in the mid-1980s as a second field where the EC discussed differentiation. In 1984 the European Council agreed to seek 'the abolition of all police and customs formalities for people crossing intra-Community frontiers'.[114] That was not, however, a practicable EC-wide objective: the resistance – again including the British – was too great. But the next year, building on a Franco-German initiative, France, Germany and the three Benelux countries (which were already cooperating closely in this area) agreed a corresponding programme. The Schengen Agreement – like the EMS, the EPC and the European Council – emerged outside the formal EC framework, even if it was always conceived and planned within it. This narrower group of five of the then ten member states joined together to dismantle border controls between them.[115]

This differentiation trend accelerated from the early 1990s. It has played a crucial role in shaping the debate about the EU ever since, further intensifying with the Common Foreign and Security Policy and the introduction of the euro, both of which were projects from which some member states abstained. For a long time politicians, researchers and the public tried to ignore the full implications of this development. Instead the discussion was dominated by an understanding of differentiation that was doubly short-sighted: on the one hand teleologically, assuming that everyone will ultimately reach the same goal, some simply more quickly than others. Only in recent years has an awareness surfaced that permanent differentiation is the most likely outcome.[116] On the other, the problem has been framed too one-sidedly in terms of progressive deepening and enlargement, making it harder to achieve homogeneity. While that is certainly correct, the EC's gradual rise to become the foremost forum for European cooperation is also relevant. One reason for the proliferation of differentiation questions within the EC and today's EU is that the existence of the EC increasingly closed off established arrangements for task-sharing among multiple international organisations.

The EC became the primary forum, but in the longer term this also makes it more vulnerable. If everything that matters is brought under one roof, the firewalls that once separated different organisations are lost. Crises in one policy area can now spark more easily across into others because they are now all handled in one and the same forum. Yet to this day the architecture of European integration bears little resemblance to the objective rationality of Bauhaus. It is an edifice that reflects its history, with round and pointed arches, with some windows bricked up and new ones broken through elsewhere, with extensions and conversions, ruins and follies.

Europe and European Integration: Résumé

Europe after 1945 was not just one experiment, but a whole laboratory with many different trials, the first of which were not even restricted to Cold War Western Europe, but reached beyond it. While the emerging Eastern Bloc treated integration principally as a matter of international division of labour among socialist states, organised through Comecon,[117] the West saw it more as a question of promoting economic growth by expanding trade. When the European Community formed it was a latecomer in an already densely populated field of international organisations. For much of its existence there was no inkling that the EC would one day acquire such a special status. Crises and new beginnings characterised the history not only of the EC, but also, for example, of the UNECE, the Council of Europe and the OECD. All these organisations repeatedly reinvented themselves, sought new responsibilities, enlarged and deepened. Governments and other actors possessed their own interests in institutional plurality, as this expanded their latitude and options. Talks over an issue frequently commenced in parallel in multiple forums, ultimately to end in just one or two. Over the course of time this was increasingly often – although by no means always – the EU, the decisive factors being its economistic logic, the power of its law and its financial resources. This only becomes apparent when one compares the different organisations and investigates their relationships.[118]

The EC did not become the foremost forum of international cooperation in Western Europe until the 1970s and 1980s. The three characteristics described above permitted it to move more comprehensively than other organisations into new policy areas of great importance, first and foremost monetary policy. Deepening was now joined by enlargement, with the EC defining success in terms of the successive assumption of new responsibilities for which other organisations were also asking, such as environmental policy. Paradoxically, it is also since the 1970s and even more the 1980s, when the EC became the foremost forum for all of Europe, that the calls for more differentiated integration and different speeds proliferated.

The EC was only able to gain such huge importance by the time the Cold War ended because the alternative models were increasingly running into their limits. That certainly applies to the classical nation state. While it is often forgotten how strongly

Western Europe's societies were already bound into a web of international cooperation even before the Treaties of Rome, the nation states always remained central actors. The economic policy experiments of the late 1970s and 1980s demonstrate that international cooperation was not the only way; nation-centred and nationalistic policies always remained an option. Another model was the historic empires that many Western European nations had built. In the 1950s many Europeans still thought in imperial categories, giving little credence to the idea that the era of empires was over.[119] That future was soon history, and this also contributed to the growing significance of cooperation within Western Europe. The same also applies to the external pressure generated by the Cold War. This was what actually made little Western Europe – grandly calling itself 'Europe' – into political reality. The same applies in relation to the United States, whose ability to guarantee reliable transatlantic structures eroded from the 1970s. Over the decades it also became increasingly important to underline a degree of autonomy vis-à-vis the Western superpower. For this the EC was a much more plausible option than, for instance, the OECD, where the United States was itself a member. The attrition of alternatives was thus one of the essential conditions for the gradual rise of the EC.

There was no master plan for any of this. The developments ensued from diverse historical processes with the typical twists and turns, learning processes, dead ends and new beginnings. In the parallel coexistence of the three Communities and the multitude of other organisations, one could recognise an expression of the supposedly deeply European principle of competition. But even that would presuppose a degree of intentionality that the processes do not bear out. The conflicting desires for organisational and institutional plurality and homogenisation were subject to a process of continuous rebalancing, and while the EC had become the central forum for certain questions by the end of the Cold War that certainly does not apply to all dimensions of international cooperation.

And that means that one cannot name a clear starting point or breakthrough for the EU's enormous gain in importance since the 1970s, especially where different policy areas developed at different speeds and altogether the coexistence of difference characterised the integration processes. For all its crises the EC turned out to be astonishingly robust and resilient. It never became what Jean Monnet dreamed of in 1950 when he wrote the Schuman Declaration. But it did become a growing reality. This is reflected – as the next chapter will explore – in questions of peace and security as the heart of what the EC sought to give Europe and the world.

2 PEACE AND SECURITY

For thirteen days the world stood on the verge of annihilation, as the Cuban Missile Crisis of 16 to 28 October 1962 brought the two superpowers to the very brink of direct military confrontation. In response to the basing of American medium-range missiles in Turkey, Moscow began constructing launch sites in 'America's backyard'. Washington saw this as an unacceptable provocation and imposed a naval blockade. As the crisis played out, both sides seriously considered using real military force, which would have triggered a spiral of violence and probably led to nuclear disaster. Today the Cuban Missile Crisis is regarded as the most dangerous confrontation of the Cold War.

The Cuban Missile Crisis was resolved in the end, of course. Secret negotiations played a decisive role, but the conflict played out before the eyes of the world. Newspapers published pictures of Kennedy, Castro and Khrushchev, photographs of warships and the suspected missile sites in Cuba, and both sides used the media for their own ends. Any moderately informed European knew that Europe would be one big battlefield if it came to war. The crisis was headline news across all of Europe – East, West and neutral. The Finnish newspaper *Uusi Suomi* wrote that 'the situation in Cuba has plunged the world into the worst crisis since the end of the Second World War'.[1] The Dutch *Het Vrije Volk* stressed that 'world peace' depended on whether 'Russia [sic!] realises that it cannot interfere in this region without starting a war with the United States. The coming hours, days and weeks will provide the answer.'[2] Eastern European newspapers, like the Polish *Głos Pracy*, reproduced Soviet statements blaming the

United States for the escalation.[3] *Le Monde* described in vivid terms the 'atmosphère de crise à Washington' and the *Frankfurter Allgemeine Zeitung* warned of immense potential consequences as East and West placed their armed forces on maximum alert.[4] Only the editorial in *Corriere della Sera* predicted confidently: 'War will not break out.'[5]

And how did the European Community respond? When the Council of Ministers met on 9 and 10 October, a few days before the crisis came to a head, the agenda was dominated by granular details of the emerging new Common Agricultural Policy. While the conflict between Washington and Moscow was already escalating, Brussels was discussing import regulations for fruit and vegetables.[6] By the next session, on 22 and 23 October, however, the agenda had shifted tangibly. The Missile Crisis was at its height and agricultural policy was pushed to the margins in Brussels. So what took its place? The EC's budget, including questions such as 'arrangements relating to the value of the unit of account and to the exchange rates'.[7] There was also a confidential part of the meeting – concerning matters such as the EC's relations with Turkey, Ireland and Iran.[8] Yet even if the Cuba Crisis was not noted in the official minutes, senior European politicians and functionaries did discuss the global confrontation playing out about 7,500 kilometres west of Brussels. French foreign minister Maurice Couve de Murville declared his country's solidarity with the United States, even if: 'they didn't consult us'.[9] But the deepest crisis in the history of the Cold War left no impression on the actual work of the EC itself. Instead the EC discussed problems such as the rules for exemptions from Article 17 of Regulation 19 on the development of the internal European trade in grain. The EC was much too busy to save the world from annihilation.

But in 1962 it was not only the EC in Brussels that was watching the Cuba Crisis from the sidelines. So for the most part were Bonn, Paris and the other member states.[10] When the West German cabinet met on 29 October, Chancellor Konrad Adenauer opened the meeting with a summary of the situation. He expressed his hope that it would soon resolve itself, but underlined 'the need to remain watchful and prepared'. Defence minister Franz Josef Strauß then listed measures to enhance the readiness of the West German armed forces: internal defence was being hardened, he said. West Germany stood on America's side but played no active role.[11]

The Cuban Missile Crisis as a whole casts a sharp and revealing light on the historic role of the European integration process in questions of war and peace. To date astonishingly little research has systematically addressed this issue;[12] the dominant narrative is essentially that cast by the protagonists of the integration process themselves. That version of events received very prominent accolades just a few years ago, when the 2012 Nobel Peace Prize was awarded to the European Union. The prize announcement highlighted how: 'The union and its forerunners have for over six decades contributed to the advancement of peace and reconciliation, democracy and human rights in Europe.'[13] There is a great deal of truth to that brief summary, of course; but it tells less than the whole story, especially if we look beyond the motives and intentions and focus first and foremost on the concrete effects. At the same time, all this also points to the fundamental problem of quantifying – or even just identifying – the role of politics in creating peace, not to speak of the question of defining what peace might mean apart from the mere absence of violence.

What I intend to lay out here is how the European integration process was initially much more a beneficiary of the European peace settlement, than shaping it in any significant sense. At the same time it is important to distinguish between different concepts of peace, above all between three dimensions: reconciliation between the member states and especially between the 'arch-enemies' France and Germany; the EC's contribution to peace in a world largely defined by the Cold War; and finally social peace within the member states. In security questions, moreover, the EC was late appearing on the scene at all and even then played a fairly subsidiary role: in this area the nation states remained decisive. The latter stand outside the scope of the present discussion, which concentrates on the question of the EC's search for an independent role.

Overall, the EC's contribution to peace and security should not be underestimated. Internally the Community preserved peace through its culture of compromise, through confidence-building, and through its contributions to securing social peace. It also lent a visible face to peace-making efforts, in a symbolic contribution that is not to be dismissed. From the 1970s, and even more the 1980s, it also contributed concretely to peace on the continent and in the world, and acquired rudiments of a security policy.

Cold War as the Frame

During the decades preceding the Maastricht Treaty relations between the member states were relatively peaceful. The same cannot be said for the global context, which is where we therefore begin. The greatest danger was presented by the possibility of global conflict between the two superpowers, which would have turned Europe into a radioactive desert. In fact, however, the EC played no meaningful pacifying role during the Cuban Missile Crisis or other phases of Cold War escalation. Quite the opposite: during the 1950s and 1960s it contributed to stoking the conflict between East and West.

This tendency can be traced right back to the 1940s, when the first plans for post-war European cooperation were drawn up. Like many inter-war initiatives, such as the pan-European visions of Richard von Coudenhove-Kalergi, most of these assumed a capitalist economic order which automatically lent them a decidedly anti-communist slant. The UNECE mentioned in the first chapter thus represented the exception that confirmed the rule. And it was quickly relegated to a relatively marginal position.

The Marshall Plan served as the standard-bearer. When US secretary of state George C. Marshall laid out his plans for reconstructing Europe in June 1947, he included the Eastern Bloc. Stalin was open to talks, and foreign minister Vyacheslav Molotov joined initial meetings in Paris. But the Soviet stance hardened after Moscow realised that the Plan was designed to establish an anti-communist bloc in Europe. Stalin rejected the conditions placed upon aid and ensured that the Eastern Bloc states followed suit. Although Washington was surprised that Molotov came to Paris at all, its intentions were less aggressive than the Kremlin asserted. As so often during the Cold War, overestimation of the other side's aggressiveness led to a spiral of radicalisation.[14]

The Marshall Plan set the scene for the role of Western European integration in world peace during the first decades of the Cold War. For a long time the EC's relations with the Eastern Bloc remained superficial and conflictual. In 1957 the Soviet Foreign Ministry criticised the EEC Treaty, which it said would lead to 'further deepening of the division of Europe and heightening of tensions within Europe'.[15] The Eastern Bloc frequently condemned the EC as a tool of US imperialism, German militarism or global capitalism (or as a combination of all three), contradictory as that stance was.

Especially in the 1950s and early 1960s, Moscow worried that the EC might threaten its grip on Eastern Europe. The EC's attitude towards the Soviet Union was similarly critical, although in this context 'Brussels' remained a great deal less influential than the member states and their respective foreign policies. Nevertheless, the EC's capitalist orientation and close ties with the United States and NATO served to deepen the Cold War divide.[16]

In this connection it is important to distinguish between peace and security. The EC formed one of many layers in Western Europe's security system. Together with NATO and other mechanisms, the Community stabilised Western Europe's external security – but tended to exacerbate the East–West conflict. In retrospect we know that the latter never caused war to break out in Europe – but at the time that was never certain.

One counterfactual thought is revealing in this connection. If the Cuban Missile Crisis had led to a third world war, and if any historians had survived it, Western European integration would have been regarded as a (subsidiary) factor stoking the superpower escalation and endangering world peace. So in terms of Europe as a whole it would be false to attribute the EC a peace-making role, at least for the first decades of the Cold War. To ignore that is to fall into the teleological trap of regarding 1989 as the inevitable end point of a process whose outcome was in fact open. And, to return from historical possibilities to the firmer ground of historical fact, not one politically neutral state joined the EC during the Cold War. Austria, Sweden and Finland waited until 1995 to take the plunge. When Austria (together with Sweden and Switzerland) applied for an association agreement in 1961, Vienna avoided any mention of the word 'association' so as not to ruffle Moscow's feathers.[17] Low-level economic relations continued (and intensified over the decades in the case of Austria), and Finland also grew closer during the mid-1980s, for example through collaboration on a high-tech project. But both steered clear of the highly symbolic step of full membership until after 1989.[18] Ireland represented a special case, joining in 1973; its Cold War neutrality had always been steeped in anti-communism.[19] All the relevant parties saw the EC as a party in the Cold War, not as a mediator, still less a neutral bloc.

European integration helped, as we will see in the following, to avoid a rerun of the last war. But in relation to world peace its role was much less significant. In the radically different conflict constellation of the post-war era it no longer had a significant role to play in containing the potentially greatest source of danger for Europe and the world.

Peace and Fragmentation in (Little) Western Europe

The EC's record on peace within Western Europe looks only a little better. If we take the Cold War as a given and ask to what extent the integration process contributed to peace in the world by strengthening Western Europe in the bloc confrontation, the answer remains ambivalent. The predecessors of the EU we know today emerged too late to contribute to peace through any real influence on the shape of the post-war order in Europe. The decisive actors in that process were the nation states, and at the international level a long series of negotiations and treaties that began while the Second World War was still in progress and were sealed at the conferences at Yalta and Potsdam. The pacification of Germany essentially meant loss of territory in the east, division of the remainder into zones of occupation, a massive occupying military presence, and from 1949 the Occupation Statute and internal liberalisation in West Germany, involuntary inclusion in the Soviet camp for East Germany. In Europe west of the Soviet Union the nation state was restored as the fundamental political form. In Western Europe the security role of NATO was complemented by a multitude of other organisations, as laid out in the previous chapter. The establishment of this arrangement, too, was well under way by the time the precursors of today's EU emerged onto the scene.[20]

A relatively stable peace – at least in retrospect – and a pre-existing network of international organisations and cooperation mechanisms in Western Europe therefore formed the starting point for European integration; in some respects it was in fact a necessary condition, but in no sense an ensuing effect. The central pillars of security in Western Europe were the alliance of the victorious powers and above all the United States, which became the benign hegemon through its role in NATO and its bilateral relationships.[21] Seen through the lens of the Cold War, NATO was the central guarantor of peace in the western part of the Old World, with Washington's security guarantee and massive military presence as its backbone. Paul-Henri Spaak, who occupied crucial positions in both NATO and the EC, put it in a nutshell in his memoirs: 'With the North Atlantic Treaty, I had contributed to securing peace in Europe, and I had also contributed to creating a united

Europe.'[22] For this 'father of Europe' peace was not essentially bound up with the idea of a united Europe.

So the EC had no need to create peace, nor would it have been able to. But was it at least able to meaningfully promote peace in Western Europe in the era of East–West confrontation? If we take Western Europe as a whole, that is not the case. In that context the EC was only one international organisation among many. In fact it weakened the Western camp's efforts to secure peace. If six states joined together economically and established common external tariffs and other protectionist measures, this reduced trade and other ties with neighbouring liberal democracies.[23] Ultimately EC integration did at least as much to divide Western Europe as it did to strengthen it.

The principal reason for this, it is pertinent to add, was to be found in the declared intentions of a string of Western European powers to pursue other forms of international cooperation. Organisations like the OECD and the Council of Europe were less important in this connection, because they incorporated the EC member states and as such did not represent direct competition. The most important alternative to the EC was the European Free Trade Association, EFTA. Founded in 1960 explicitly as a rival economic and above all trade formation, it brought together most of the Western European states that had not joined the EC. On account of their geographical position they were also referred to at the time as the 'outer seven' in contrast to the 'inner six' of the EC.

So Western Europe split into two camps, and found itself unable to address the Eastern Bloc with a single voice. This applied in the first place to the economic realm, but also had security implications, as all actors were well aware. In 1955, with the division of Western Europe already becoming apparent, Washington pressed for unity. Secretary of State John F. Dulles appealed to London, as the prime mover behind the EFTA project: Washington wished to avoid fragmentation, he said, and hoped 'that we can count upon your Government's support'.[24] The cajoling went largely unheeded. Economist Wilhelm Röpke was one of the sharpest critics of the division between EFTA and EC, deriding the EC as 'Spaakistan' (referring to its Belgian 'founding father' Paul-Henri Spaak).[25] The first president of the EEC Commission, Walter Hallstein, sought largely ineffectually to whitewash the problem, asserting that 'differenciation' in Western Europe was not the same as 'discrimination'.[26]

Map 3: EC and EFTA, 1960. © Peter Palm, Berlin/Germany

The East had its Council for Mutual Economic Assistance (Comecon), established in 1949 to bring together the states of the Eastern Bloc under Soviet leadership and at least in theory promote coordination and assistance between the socialist economies. In purely formal terms the East was more solidly organised than the West: the 'Six' certainly did not represent Europe as a whole, and not even Western Europe; they were nothing more than 'little Western Europe'. And that significantly reduced the EC's potential contribution to peace.

Peace as Motif, Peace as Motor?

This all leads directly to the question of the EC's contribution to internal peace within the Community. There can be no doubt that this was a core motivation behind the European integration process, especially in relation to Franco-German reconciliation as one of Europe's most significant achievements since 1945. The EC was strongly focused on this question, and in the immediate aftermath of two devastating wars it was highly optimistic to hope that the divided Germany would present so little in the way of threat. Only in retrospect are we reminded of the saying that 'Generals are always fighting the last war'. At the time preserving the peace within the Community had to seem a Herculean task, to which the EC was seeking answers from the very beginning.

This was already seen on 9 May 1950, when French foreign minister Robert Schuman proposed the founding of a European community for coal and steel. His proposal that 'Franco-German production of coal and steel be placed under a common "high authority"' was designed to ensure that 'any war between France and Germany becomes not only unthinkable, but materially impossible'. As such, Schuman tied cooperation in this sector, which is absolutely central to modern warfare, directly to the question of peace: economic matters were a means to an end. His proposal sought nothing less than 'the elimination of the age-old opposition of France and Germany'. But understanding between France and Germany after three bloody wars in the space of eight decades (1870–1871; 1914–1918; 1939–1945) was just the core of future cooperation. Schuman also invited other 'European nations' to participate in the project.[27]

In the following years, much continued to be made of the contribution to peace represented by the integration process and its institutions. The 1951 Treaty Establishing the European Coal and Steel Community took up Schuman's words and gave peace pride of place.[28] Six years later the preamble to the EEC Treaty chose a different tack, beginning with an affirmation of the determination 'to lay the foundations of an ever-closer union among the peoples of

Europe', moving on to name several primarily economic aspects before culminating in the intention 'to preserve and strengthen peace and liberty'.[29] The motif of peace runs through more recent treaties too, including those of Maastricht and Lisbon, and is also emphasised in many other contexts. The pithiest formulation is 'L'Europe, c'est la paix' – Europe is peace – as expressed many times by Mitterrand, Hollande and other leaders.[30]

So the EC's contribution to peace among its members and in the world has always been a big talking point. And what about the concrete effects? At the global level, as already laid out, these remained very modest in the 1950s and 1960s. While the motif of peace did guide the development of the Community from the very outset – and in particular Franco-German reconciliation – the effects should not be overestimated.[31] While peace between member states was celebrated in public speeches and formal treaties, other motivations were in fact equally or more important.

The research of the past thirty years underlines how strongly national interests and other factors influenced the integration process. The Schuman Declaration supplies a good example: the French government only resorted to that proposal after all other initiatives to contain Germany politically had failed, and plans for close cooperation with the United Kingdom had also been derailed. Economic interests frequently mingled with geostrategic motives. In this case, initiatives to modernise French industry had fallen short of expectations, exacerbated by structural problems in the coal and steel sectors. The broader idea behind integration in these two key sectors was to contain the stronger West German economy before it was able to unleash its full potential and restore German predominance.

The final trigger for Schuman's speech had to do with the attitude of the other two Western Allies. The United Kingdom and the United States wanted to remove the cap on West Germany's steel production – 11.1 million tonnes annually. The decision was to be made on 10 May 1950, the day after Schuman's speech. In view of the escalating East–West conflict – which was to lead just a few weeks later to the outbreak of the Korean War – London and Washington had decided to pursue rearmament, even at the price of strengthening Germany. Their proposals for watering down the Occupation Statute of 1949, which defined the rights of the three Western Allies in West Germany, also went in a similar direction.

Just five years after the defeat of Nazi Germany, the present threat of the Cold War was more important to Washington and London than locking away the demons of the past. With France fearing being left behind, all these reasons came together to move Schuman to make his Declaration. Of course he was also interested in preventing war, above all another war with Germany. But integration also represented an attractive and innovative instrument for securing French predominance in Western Europe's emerging post-war order.[32]

In other phases of the Cold War, too, peace between the member states represented but one of several driving forces in the integration process. It was accompanied, as Wilfried Loth demonstrates especially well, above all by three other motives: the question of how to deal with Germany; the search for prosperity in a globalising economy; and finally the desire for (Western) Europe to assert itself vis-à-vis the two superpowers.[33] Aspects of all these elements are found in the Schuman Plan. While it was not always possible to reconcile them harmoniously, it is safe to say that by 1950 peace was already far from being the sole or dominant motive driving action.

And if we turn to the effects, the ECSC's record on securing peace in the Community is rather mixed. Although it prided itself on preventing war between its member states, the ECSC became dysfunctional in important respects within just a few years. It aimed to remove tariffs and other trade barriers and to create a Common Market in coal and steel. But the ECSC plunged into turmoil within just a few years, as its member states responded unilaterally to the coal crisis of 1958. West Germany, for example, imposed an import ban that certainly contravened the spirit of the treaty, arguably also the letter. Other member states, like the Netherlands and Italy, ditched community preference and purchased cheaper coal from the United States. Changes in global markets and international politics trumped the rules of the ECSC, in a dynamic that was to repeat endlessly in the course of the integration process.[34]

That does not mean the ECSC achieved nothing. The coal crisis saw intense negotiations, but little in the way of results. As so often in the integration process, the ECSC diverted to other fields, where it made important contributions in the medium term – for example, in social housing and research policy. In its other central sector, the ECSC also helped to cushion the steel crisis of the 1970s and 1980s – even after an institutional crisis in the late 1960s when France for a time refused to obey agreed rules.[35]

All this had little to do with the lofty mission of securing peace within the Community through mutual control of coal and steel, as Schuman had envisaged in 1950. This led historian Klaus Schwabe to describe the ECSC as 'a kind of supranational investment ruin'.[36] His American colleague John Gillingham went a step further, arguing that the ECSC created the myth of supranational control over German heavy industry – but not the corresponding reality.[37]

Qualifying these critical findings a little, the Treaties of Rome were concluded just in time before the ECSC lost its conceived role. The relevance of the coal and steel sectors to war and peace was obvious; less so the Common Market and Euratom. Their peace-promoting role within the EC consisted primarily in their expression of ongoing interest in close economic cooperation.

Seeking Security

Failure was also the fate of the Community's attempts to stabilise or even create peace in Europe by producing dedicated security structures of its own. The most important project of the six ECSC states in this realm, the establishment of a European Defence Community, never got past the negotiation phase. The Korean War, which broke out just days after the first talks on the ECSC, catapulted the option of German rearmament to the top of the political agenda. The French government, which had blocked any such move for historical reasons, now conceded to American pressure. But Paris sought a path that appeared more politically acceptable than re-establishing West German armed forces under Bonn's command. In October 1950, building on Jean Monnet's ideas, prime minister René Pleven proposed the creation of a European army following the ECSC's organisational model. But after sticky negotiations the project was abandoned in August 1954. Ironically it was in France, which had been decisive in proposing the project, that the National Assembly declined to ratify the proposal. Alongside internal political uncertainties and problems, the burden of history lay over the debate: just a few years after the end of the war this was a step too far for most French parliamentarians. They were ready to accept West Germany as an equal partner in the ECSC, but not the idea of a military role, even one embedded in a European context. Here prior experience determined the scope of expectations. While the fears might appear exaggerated in retrospect, they were absolutely understandable in the contemporary context. Nevertheless ECSC president Paul-Henri Spaak felt the outcome of the vote was a 'very heavy blow for the supporters of a united Europe'; US secretary of state John Foster Dulles called the French decision 'a saddening event', a 'tragedy' with the potential 'to endanger the whole of Europe'.[38]

But the lamentations were soon forgotten. The European Defence Community may have failed, but no great hole appeared in Western Europe's security in the medium term. Instead it was quickly agreed to rearm West Germany in the NATO framework via the device of the aforementioned WEU. This represented the more plausible solution in military terms, and also came closer to Germany's hopes for completely equal treatment and influence in the Western alliance. Paradoxically, therefore, it was the French National Assembly's *non* that opened the door for West German rearmament under more sovereign auspices.[39] Not even the idea of a shared European uniform – which had been raised at the beginning – survived the debacle. Tellingly, the design of the new helmet issued when the Bundeswehr was established in 1955 was based on the American model, rather than a shared European one or the older German type. In other words, even a detail as small as the shape of the West German soldier's helmet reflected the manner in which peace through security remained largely outside the remit of the EC during subsequent decades, as primarily the responsibility of NATO.

At the same time, the existence of the ECSC as a Franco-German counterweight to West German transatlanticism made West Germany's admission to NATO more palatable to France. The different international organisations were like communicating vessels: while NATO tended to relieve the Europe of Six of security responsibilities, the counterweights and supports they created also played a role in stabilising NATO.[40]

There is one more reason why the EC's role in creating peace should not be overrated. Membership of the Community never deterred a Western European country from fighting wars with third countries. To select but a few from a long list, European integration prevented neither Belgian military interference in the Congo in the early 1960s, nor France's Algerian War of 1954 to 1962, nor the United Kingdom's 1982 war with Argentina over the Falkland Islands. In that sense, concentrating on what Western European integration achieved for peace means marginalising the global contexts, in particular decolonisation. Another reason to pause for thought before equating the EC too quickly with peace.

Peace through Trust

Relieved of the need to resolve the very largest questions, the EC did, however, make an important contribution to keeping the peace. Although its emergence was heavily influenced by the Cold War, the EC subsequently partially emancipated itself from that context. This was reflected in its scope of responsibilities, but also in the composition of its membership, which initially remained confined to 'little Western Europe'. This created a protected space, a cocoon, where the EC could initially concentrate on secondary problems. Anything else would have been too much for the emerging Community.[41] Reinforcing this process, from the early 1960s Europe tended to shift to the periphery of the Cold War after having played a much more central role during the initial years. Superpower détente, East–West rapprochement in Europe, a phase of unparalleled economic growth, and a relatively stable peace created circumstances where security issues could be put to one side for the moment.[42]

Concretely the EC contributed crucially to peace within its bounds by building confidence through cooperation and establishing a culture of compromise at the highest levels. Countries that had been at war just a decade or two previously now gathered round the table to seek solutions to shared economic and social problems. This brought especially the top politicians and civil servants of the member states into closer and more frequent personal contact than ever before. Of course the same also occurred via bilateral channels and within organisations like the Council of Europe and the OECD, but nowhere was the exchange as structured and intense as in the EC. For this reason the EC played an outstanding role at this level in Franco-German reconciliation and more generally in creating peace within the Community.

This approach was deeply ingrained in the Community's institutional arrangements. When it was established in 1958, the Commission of the European Economic Community comprised nine members from the six member states, who under the terms of the treaty were 'appointed by common accord of the Governments of Member

States'. Each commissioner headed a directorate-general, whose director-general always came from a different member state than the commissioner. These principles both embodied confidence in supranational cooperation and formed the basis for supranational confidence-building.[43] European issues were not only matters for heads of state and government and their ministers; in the member states hundreds and soon thousands of civil servants and politicians in the foreign, economics, agriculture and finance ministries and many other fields were soon in close contact with colleagues from other member states, often over significant periods. The same applies to lobbyists, journalists and other members of a growing transnational elite.[44] Luuk van Middelaar pithily sums up the effects of this web of connections: 'The "de-dramatisation" of European politics was a merit of the Community that cannot be overstated.'[45]

That is not to say that their dealings were devoid of mistrust and haggling. In 1959, for example, Bonn felt that Rome's candidate for the position of president of the High Authority of the ECSC, the Christian democrat Piero Malvestiti, was too lightweight for a post of that gravity. But after considerable toing and froing he was accepted in the end.[46] As well as governments, other actors were also involved in such bargaining. For example Jean Monnet – president of the Action Committee for the United States of Europe, but without an official position of his own during certain important phases – sought to pull strings in national governments.[47] Yet despite such interventions and conflicts, the decision-makers and multipliers knew each other well; this level of connectedness formed a 'soft' factor in the integration process – invisible but in no way to be underestimated – that helped to secure peace within the Community.

Especially given the frequency of conflict, it was regarded as an important outcome in its own right that all concerned worked to achieve compromise and consensus, and avoided subordinating Community projects to national interests. Negotiations often went to the verge of physical exhaustion and beyond. In the 1960s, when deadlines agreed in the treaties could not be met, the Council of Ministers simply decided to stop the administrative clock and meet in permanent session. These infamous meetings went down in history: the Sixtieth Session of the Council of the European Economic Community, for example, began on 18 December 1961. Important questions remained unresolved as the year came to a close, and the meeting ran on until 5.29 a.m. on

14 January 1962 before all decisions had finally been made. According to the *Frankfurter Allgemeine Zeitung* the meeting ran on 'a deadly mix of coffee, whisky and nicotine'.[48] Commission president Hallstein put it even more bluntly: 'Forty-five separate meetings, 7 of them at night; a total of 137 hours of discussion, with 214 hours in subcommittee; 582,000 pages of documents; 3 heart attacks'.[49] The new Europe was a creature of cooperation and compromise, trust and talk, with no place for national arrogance, ultimatums or political autism.

Many politicians and officials welcomed the EC with enthusiasm, none more so than the Italians, who often placed the good of the European project above their own national interests in the early rounds. But Italy, as the poorest of the six member states in the 1950s and 1960s, quickly found the other partners to be less altruistic. Nothing demonstrated this more clearly in the EC's early years than the Common Agricultural Policy: in 1963/64 Italy shouldered about 28 per cent of the agriculture budget, but received only 1.3 per cent back. West Germany, highly industrialised and much more affluent, paid in 28.2 per cent but did at least receive 5.2 per cent back. France contributed 25.6 per cent – and received a whopping 85.3 per cent. When the imbalance became impossible to overlook, the Italians hardened their stance. Within just a few years the tone became noticeably harsher.[50]

In the 1960s it was France that created the most trouble for the EC's compromise-driven model. In the decade after Charles de Gaulle became president in 1959, Paris became the EC's most difficult partner – not least on account of de Gaulle's criticisms of its supranational dimension. His juggling with ultimatums and vetoes was a significant factor worsening the atmosphere between the partners. Two low points came in 1963 and 1967, when de Gaulle unilaterally rejected British accession requests. Tensions ran even higher in 1965 when he paralysed the EC institutions with the Empty Chair Crisis. So ironically it was not Germany – as the wreaker of havoc in the first half of the century – that became the EC's most uncooperative partner.[51] Once again we see how little some of the EC's dynamics were predetermined by longer-term constellations.

In a discussion with his French counterpart, Olivier Wormser, in spring 1966, Rolf Lahr, permanent secretary at the West German Foreign Ministry, summarised the damage that had been done to mutual trust by the mid-1960s: 'My earlier optimism concerning the prospects of the EEC has faded'. In the meantime, rather than bold decisions and great advances: 'Brussels only delivers for cash, and gives nothing on credit . . . None of the delegations is willing to make a down payment on Europe's – unfortunately uncertain – political future.'[52] Lahr felt that the EC had degenerated into a shark tank whose everyday political and administrative routine was characterised by rigidity and bitterly fought compromises. The archives are so full of such sources that it is easy to forget that they actually continued talking and negotiating throughout. Cooperation remained close and intensified as time went on.

Ultimately the EC made a significant contribution to keeping and deepening the peace achieved between its member states prior to its founding, despite the many prophecies of doom. In every decade from the 1950s onwards journalists and politicians announced the EC's crisis or even collapse. In the early 1980s the *Economist* published a caricature with the EEC's gravestone.[53] The permanent contact between the Community's political, economic and administrative elites and the hard-won mutual trust were important for maintaining the peace. For example, the most recent research has demonstrated that de Gaulle frequently used theatrical rejection of the EC to tactical ends, but was actually well aware of the advantages of the integration process for France and therefore never allowed a crisis to escalate to breaking point.[54] Ultimately the EC offered benefits for all its member states. As much as it created a new forum for political ructions and made existing conflicts visible, so much it also contained them.

Stability within I

Peace was the objective and working for peace by building mutual trust was the programme. Economic questions served to lubricate the machinery. For example, the EEC Treaty laid out a twelve-year transitional period with detailed incremental arrangements for creating a Common Market. But several times in the course of the 1960s the Council of Ministers agreed to shorten the transition. The Customs Union for industrial products came into force on 1 July 1968, eighteen months earlier than originally planned; in the area of agriculture the Common Market had already come into operation for certain important products before this.[55] Terms like 'acceleration decision' may have sounded bureaucratic, but they reflected pride in the unexpected speed of the EC's establishment. The abolition of internal barriers and the establishment of shared rules for third states coincided with a phase of enormous economic growth which boosted the legitimacy of integration.[56] Another area where the EC was successful was the establishment of a common competition policy, which included a prohibition on monopolies and abuse of market power. Despite its many teething troubles this policy was celebrated as an important breakthrough.[57]

As well as serving to lubricate political negotiations, economic issues also had a stabilising effect within the societies of the member states, by contributing to social peace as the third dimension (alongside peace in the world and peace between the member states). This was predicated on welfare gains through integration, as elaborated in the next chapter. At the same time plans for a common social policy with harmonised welfare benefits never got very far and even more ambitious projects were never pursued in earnest at all, so European integration remained a rather intangible affair for the citizens of the member states. It did contribute to social peace, but without that becoming terribly visible.

There was one exception. Before the 1980s the EC was a tangible reality for one significant sector and the population working within it. This was agriculture. Here the process went further than for manufacturing industry: as well as abolishing internal barriers, Common Market Organisations were introduced: Brussels now set the prices for most agricultural products. We will return in due course to the problems of the Common Agricultural Policy (CAP), and of the EC's social policy.[58] On the positive side, the CAP helped to ensure that the historic transformation of the primary sector progressed largely free of major conflict in the second half of the twentieth century (whereas the same process in the first half of the century led to enormous political destabilisation). On paper the CAP pursued a whole spectrum of objectives, especially increasing production. In reality it served primarily as a covert social policy, introducing political measures to cushion the sector's utter transformation and the dramatic shrinking of its workforce. One should not overlook the paradox that farmers benefitted enormously from the CAP, but were more dissatisfied with the EC than any other group. Moreover, this approach to stabilising social peace worked well in member states with a comparably large agricultural labour force – which was the case for all of the original six member states, and most of those that joined later. The United Kingdom, with its history of a small farming sector, did not profit from this system and complained about the high costs. While contributing to social stability in most member states, the CAP became a continuous source of conflict with the United Kingdom. Historical experiences diverged too widely for a solution to be found. With the turn towards a more neoliberal policy during the 1980s under Margaret Thatcher, the CAP's redistributive approach and its idea of transnational solidarity came under even bigger fire.

Nevertheless, the CAP helped to nudge agricultural protest into peaceful channels. Farmers demonstrated in Brussels, but unlike in the inter-war years their protests rarely spiralled into physical violence or political extremism. In this sense the Common Agricultural Policy represented a tool of social stabilisation and pacification.[59] The EC's Regional Policy, established from the 1960s and especially the 1970s, played a similar role but was less controversial.

While contributing to social peace, the EC's role always had clear limits. It could not prevent the terrorism that affected many of its member states since the 1970s. Interior and justice ministries intensified their cooperation, and national governments learned from each other on questions of crisis management concerning terrorism. However, little joint action followed from these debates. If there were any positive effects with regard to social peace, they remained largely invisible.[60]

EC as Symbol and Synecdoche

The symbolic role that the EC assumed during the Cold War was perhaps even more important than its confidence-building and concrete political outcomes. For the European Community claimed a very special aura, as *the* European solution for the most important questions of the age. Even the most trivial technical decisions, such as setting export duties for wheat, were celebrated as manifestations of a peace-building cooperative system. For example in 1963 the French philosopher Raymond Aron lauded one such minor success as 'La victoire de l'idée européenne'.[61] Not that he was especially interested in market and trade issues; instead he saw the agreement in Brussels as one small step towards building a grand Europe. The EC became a symbol of Western Europe's political rebirth; it was a specific project, but one directed towards a much larger reality. In rhetoric, such a relationship between two phenomena is known as a synecdoche.[62] At a basic level the EC functioned as a synecdoche for a new era of peaceful coexistence in

Western Europe; and in this sense it became a projection screen for pro-European elites. Although the EC of the early 1970s still represented little more than a Common Market with a relatively sophisticated agricultural policy, it embodied the great ambition to create a new international solution after the catastrophes of preceding decades. In this sense the EC became the symbolic heart of all integration efforts, even if the political reality remained much more fragile and fragmented than the symbol might imply.

When, for example, in 1962 Charles de Gaulle and Konrad Adenauer met for the famous reconciliation mass in the Gothic cathedral of Reims, this embodied more than a new chapter in bilateral relations. The historically aware French president naturally spoke about the reconciliation between the two nations, but also pointed to 'the great European and global task that the Germans and the French still have to accomplish together'.[63] The international press reported the meeting in great detail and addressed its historical import for Franco-German relations. The *Washington Post* was not alone in seeing the 'symbolism' of the encounter as an expression of a new 'reality of European evolution'.[64]

Twenty-two years later François Mitterrand and Helmut Kohl were consciously following in their predecessors' footsteps when they held hands at the First World War battlefield of Verdun. This emotional moment quickly found its way into European politics, with the French Socialists using photographs of the event on their posters for the 1988 European elections:[65] EC meant Europe and Europe meant peace. Considering how little responsibility the EC actually held for peace, and the trail of havoc that is the history of the 'Old World' and its relationships with other parts of the globe, that is quite some claim to stake. The narrative could only gain traction because nobody was interested in the concrete details and effects of the integration process.

No other European or international organisation lent itself anywhere near as well to projecting such hopes for a peaceful and united Europe. NATO was much too much an instrument of the Cold War; the Council of Europe and the OECD were associated with technical cooperation.[66] So even if the EC played no meaningful role in establishing peace in Europe and was only a subsidiary factor in its preservation, it nevertheless became the symbolic heart of European understanding and reconciliation.

Figure 3: Adenauer and de Gaulle in Reims, 8 July 1962. AFP/Getty Images

Figure 4: Mitterrand and Kohl in Verdun, 22 September 1984. Marcel Mochet/AFP/Getty Images

Peace and Security in the World

Alongside these practical and symbolic dimensions in relation to internal peace, from the 1970s the EC gradually began playing a larger role in matters relating to peace – and even security – in the world. Two factors were decisive here. Firstly, the EC was now operating in a different European and global context, with new challenges of its own. And secondly, at the same time, a consensus emerged within the political elites that the EC required additional tasks and dimensions to address these challenges. Building new institutional structures played an important role for the latter, and over time these were increasingly filled with life.

To begin with the changing circumstances: the early 1970s witnessed the fragmentation of part of the cocoon that had enveloped and stabilised the EC. This was most obvious in the sphere of the economy. The historically unparalleled economic boom that had powered the integration process ended in the early 1970s. Economic stagnation, unemployment, rising state debt and high rates of inflation put the EC's achievements to their severest test yet. Worse still, the end of the boom tore holes in the institutional fabric in which the EC had been embedded. This applied especially to the Bretton Woods system, the post-war era's international monetary order with exchange rate bands and the US dollar as anchor currency. Without the reassurance of this established system Western Europe was faced with the task of creating its own monetary order. As well as deepening the economic crisis, the oil shocks of 1973 and 1979/80 demonstrated how dependent Western Europe had become on crude oil supplies from the Middle East.

This was also a time when the influence of the Cold War security system receded and a new, less predictable world emerged. Alarming conflicts flared, such as the Yom Kippur War between Israel and several of its Arab neighbours. At the same time, paradoxically, the superpower confrontation relaxed. Welcome as this was, it raised the unsettling question of how far Western Europe could still rely on the US security guarantee. The Cold War faded as a driving influence in European integration, as became very obvious in 1973 when the Conference on Security and Cooperation in Europe (CSCE) convened in Helsinki. Western Europe had to find positions for these bloc-transcending conferences, at which almost all European states were represented.

The EC states responded in different ways to these challenges. Above all new political instruments were created to enhance the new Community's capabilities. They all possessed dimensions relating to peace and security, without being dedicated exclusively to these. It was also conspicuous that the most important of the new mechanisms were not formally part of the EC and frequently emerged only gradually. Despite the EC's penchant for legalese, they began without even a clear basis in the treaties. Yet they granted the EC greater visibility and expanded its importance.

Concretely the EC states institutionalised their foreign policy cooperation with the establishment of the European Political Cooperation in 1970. The European Political Cooperation was a purely intergovernmental mechanism for detailed consultations on foreign policy, for which the EC had hitherto lacked a forum. Through it the EC states also worked to agree shared positions in order to exercise greater influence on global politics. Building on the Hague Summit of 1969, the EC heads of state and government held regular European summits from the mid-1970s: where previously they had convened only sporadically and for ceremonial occasions, they now constituted the 'European Council'. No longer would EC policy be left exclusively to the compartmentalised sessions of the Council of Ministers.

The emergence of the European Political Cooperation and the European Council reflected an awareness of a world of tough new challenges that demanded innovative forms of cooperation. And the EC appeared to be the appropriate organisation to host these formats, rather than the Council of Europe or the OECD. Such new departures were also facilitated by generational handovers in important member states: first and foremost Georges Pompidou as de Gaulle's successor in France and Willy Brandt in West Germany, whose governments played key roles in pressing for the establishment of the European Political Cooperation and the European Council. The EC also expanded its institutional and peace-promoting weight in 1973 with the accession of three new member states, above all the United Kingdom. Altogether the early 1970s saw important institutional changes that made the EC more capable and more relevant for questions of war and peace in the world.[67]

Security problems now began appearing regularly on the Community's agenda. Unlike in the 1960s, the EC now – through the work of the European Political Cooperation and the European Council – more frequently adopted a clear position and sought to influence international developments. This new self-perception is expressed in a declaration by the EC foreign ministers in November 1973, in which they outlined their ideas about a peace settlement for the Middle East. The document is notable for two reasons. It is the first time the EC adopts a unified position on a genuine security problem, and the Community itself offers assistance in restoring peace.[68] The *Document on the European Identity* adopted three months later had a principally transatlantic thrust and sought to enable the member states 'to achieve a better definition of their relations with other countries and of their responsibilities and the place which they occupy in world affairs'; one of the 'essential aims' is now 'to maintain peace'.[69] But the practical contribution of this and similar documents to peace in Europe and the world remained small. Neither the Middle East nor transatlantic relations looked any different afterwards, not least because member states frequently continued to indulge their egos. In neither of these questions did the EC succeed in agreeing a lasting joint position, and certainly not in having any real peace-making effect. But the documents did express a new confidence and a will to create new institutional structures to underline their peace-promoting ambitions.[70]

EC and Détente

In the second half of the Cold War the EC achieved greatest impact in external peace and security with the Eastern Bloc (as opposed to the Middle East, the United States or elsewhere). In the aforementioned CSCE context from the mid-1970s, the EC repeatedly succeeded in agreeing joint positions and speaking with one voice to become a factor in international politics over and above the sum of its member states. Mutual trust was able to develop through discussions about economic interaction and a closer form of all-European cooperation. The Kremlin also initiated phases of secret dialogue with the European Commission, in which the latter advocated Europe-wide cooperation. Although little in the way of concrete outcomes emerged, the dialogue itself had a peace-stabilising dimension. This was a striking difference to the first post-war decades, when Moscow identified the EC as an aggressor and refused to recognise it.[71]

This exchange laid important groundwork for the intra-European relations of the 1980s, when the member states worked to coordinate their foreign policies more successfully. This was, for example, the slant of a joint initiative by West German foreign minister Hans-Dietrich Genscher and his Italian opposite number Emilio Colombo in 1981. Two years later the Stuttgart Declaration of the heads of state and government of the Community refers explicitly to 'security' as a field where 'by speaking with a single voice ... Europe can contribute to the preservation of peace'.[72] And deeds followed words. As superpower tensions spiked again in the first half of the decade, Europeans on both sides of the Iron Curtain drifted further than ever before from the positions dictated by Washington and Moscow. The EC played a significant part in this, with trade cooperation in particular keeping lines of communication open (reciprocity by the Eastern Bloc states was naturally equally important). For example, in the aftermath of General Jaruzelski's imposition of martial law in Poland in 1981 the European Political Cooperation became a vital instrument of European policy. In this case the EC deviated a little from the US position. Like Washington, the EC imposed sanctions in February 1982, but kept them very mild.[73] Or to cite another example, in the early 1980s the EC states openly defied Washington's explicit request that they join the US embargo on supplies for a Soviet gas pipeline.[74] In all these cases concerns for peace and security were naturally not the only motive for upholding contacts with the East. There were also tangible economic reasons. Trade with Comecon was significantly more important to the EC states than it was for the United States. This seems to confirm Montesquieu's old idea of 'sweet commerce': close exchange serving as an impediment to Cold War escalation. At the same time human rights became overshadowed by economic and security interests.[75]

To this day there is no consensus over the causes of the end of the Cold War. But if one sees the collapse of the Eastern Bloc as more than merely an expression of internal developments within the Soviet sphere of influence or the effects of an American-led arms race, and instead accords détente a share in ending the conflict, this casts an interesting light on the EC. In the first half of the 1980s the EC made a tangible contribution to keeping intra-European détente alive (whereas in the 1960s each EC state still pursued its own policy towards the Eastern Bloc). The national level remained central, but in certain questions the EC now represented an additional collective actor. Above all the European Political Cooperation and the EC's Common Commercial Policy created instruments for speaking with one voice. They were not always able to agree on shared positions – but where they succeeded the EC became for the first time a factor in questions of war and peace (albeit still a secondary one).[76]

Global Politics in the 1980s

The idea of European integration as a peace project adapted successfully to shifting global political contexts, which were now much changed from the original situation at the end of the 1950s. This is illustrated very clearly by a conflict that occurred on the other side of the world, the Falklands War of 1982. I mentioned earlier that the EC did not prevent the United Kingdom from going to war, but here I must add an important detail: the EC clearly took the British side, and sharply criticised Argentina's invasion of the islands. And in April 1982, for the first time in its history, the EC agreed unanimously to impose effective economic and military sanctions on the basis of a UN resolution.

It was not, admittedly, the first time the member states agreed to impose sanctions on a third state. That was in 1965 against Rhodesia following a UN resolution. But despite agreeing the decision jointly, the individual member states implemented the measures differently. The use of sanctions remained highly controversial throughout the 1970s. For example, in 1977 the United Kingdom and France were unable to agree on EC sanctions against South Africa. Efforts to reform the European Political Cooperation therefore intensified in the early 1980s. On the basis of the London Report of October 1981, the European Political Cooperation introduced a new crisis procedure that permitted a rapid response to security emergencies.[77] About half a year later, as already mentioned, the EC imposed trade sanctions against the Soviet Union. Given that they did not take effect until 1983 this turned out to be a very blunt weapon. *Der Spiegel* commented that the Soviets were 'completely indifferent' towards the sanctions.[78] These were essentially symbolic moves, through which the EC states formally supported Washington's sanctions policy while working hard to avoid further escalating tensions with the East.

The case of Argentina two months later was different. This time the sanctions really hurt. In 1980 about one-fifth of Argentina's visible exports – worth about $4 billion – went to the EC. Europe also paid a price itself, as Buenos Aires retaliated by stopping payments on its $25 billion foreign debt. On top of the potential repercussions for European investments there was also a question over the legal position of about ten million Italian nationals living in Argentina. Despite the high stakes, the entire Community declared its political support for London and agreed to impose sanctions;[79] the US ambassador to the EC, George Vest, said in a confidential discussion that he had been 'very struck by the complete solidarity' in the Community of Ten.[80] In fact London had not been counting on such strong solidarity. A few days before the decision to impose sanctions the British Foreign Office reported that it was still 'doubtful ... how much support we will find in the Community'.[81]

The price of the hard line on Argentina quickly rose, and fractures appeared within the Community. The member states' original hopes that sanctions would prevent a full-blown military conflict were dashed. When actual fighting broke out in the South Atlantic a number of governments – including Dublin and Bonn – argued for the sanctions to be lifted. Ireland was no friend of British global ambitions and wished to preserve its political neutrality; West Germany was motivated more by economic considerations. Over the course of a few weeks the consensus on sanctions collapsed and a number of governments had already ditched them before the EC officially ended the measure on 21 June after the fighting ended.[82] In any case, British naval power was more important than European trade sanctions for restoring the peace and the *status quo ante*.

The Falklands War is nonetheless significant as the first time that a sanctions mechanism was applied – even for a few weeks – where trade and security objectives conflicted and the EC prioritised the latter.[83] This is especially striking given that even the tiniest cracks in the EC's united front were attentively noted in Moscow as well as Buenos Aires.[84]

Stability within II

By the 1980s the Community was also playing a significant part in securing social peace through its internal stabilising role, although it should be noted that the 'interior' was now very different from the early days. The social balancing and conflict-reducing role of instruments like the CAP and the Regional Policy was one aspect, even more important was the role of the EC in relation to the three states that joined the Community during the final decade of the Cold War, after a period of ever closer relations during the second half of the 1970s. Greece (entered 1981), Spain and Portugal (both 1986) were all emerging from periods of political turmoil. When they applied for membership in the mid-1970s, all three were young democracies newly emerging from right-wing dictatorships or authoritarian regimes. What that meant in relation to the Community's values is discussed elsewhere in this volume;[85] in terms of peace and security, accession was associated with stabilisation, both external and internal.

Let us consider the Greek case first: Greece joined the EC during an extremely tense phase of the Cold War. While Greece enjoyed enormous military strategic significance on NATO's south-eastern flank, its population was highly critical of the United States for supporting the dictatorship of the Colonels. Accepting Greece into the Community therefore contributed to strengthening the Western alliance. The EC also played a visible role in stabilising a democratic capitalist order. To that extent the issues encompassed both the security of the Western camp and the social peace within an enlarged Community.[86]

It was similar with Spain and Portugal. The 1974 Carnation Revolution in Portugal ushered in a period of political insecurity and economic and social turmoil in the Iberian Peninsula that lasted the best part of a decade. Under West German and French leadership the EC now served as a stabilising force, making a major contribution to social peace through the accession perspective and later membership of both states. Here the United States played a significantly smaller role than in other crises affecting the Western alliance. As in Greece, Washington was discredited in the eyes of large sections of the population, after maintaining overly close relations with the right-wing dictators. A US strategy paper in December 1975 outlined the problems the United States faced in the region and conceded that the EC could become a 'stabilizing factor' in the region.[87] Altogether the EC filled a strategic gap and became for many the symbol of a free and open future in peace and affluence.[88]

There was another peace-promoting dimension worth noting, even if its effects were often far removed from the most prominent political arenas. Apart from the central Franco-German conflict, there were other long-running bilateral tensions in many parts of Western Europe, often dating far back in history. Here just three examples must suffice. After the First World War, the Treaty of Versailles forced Germany to cede the small territory of Eupen-Malmedy to Belgium. After a brief period as part of Nazi Germany between 1940 and 1945 it was returned permanently to Belgium after the Second World War. Relations between Eupen-Malmedy and the rest of Belgium had never been easy, but gradually relaxed over time with Belgium and West Germany both being members of the EC.[89]

Even if the war in Northern Ireland was still to drag on for many decades more it is striking how little the troubles in this part of the United Kingdom complicated the EC's parallel accession talks with the Republic of Ireland and the United Kingdom in the early 1970s. London and Dublin often talked in a constructive mode that was unthinkable in connection with the Northern Ireland question. The British embassy in Dublin noted in 1975 that 'it is perhaps not impossible to imagine this wound to be healed in a developing European Community'.[90] While the statement is decidedly speculative it demonstrates a hope and a certain tendency, which were further deepened by later initiatives such as the European Parliament's Haagerup Report of 1984.[91]

A third example would be the dispute between Spain and the United Kingdom over Gibraltar, whose roots reach back to the early eighteenth century. Shared membership of the European Community helped to slowly defuse that conflict too, especially from the 1980s.[92] In none of these cases did the European Community achieve resolution. But cooperation in problem-solving and intense exchange of goods and persons did contribute to rapprochement and stability between the member states. These hidden positive effects were revealed recently when Brexit exposed the fragility of some of these successes.

Beyond the Cold War

The EC had an even more important role to play when the Cold War came to an end. Building on its successes in Greece, Spain and Portugal, it became one of the central institutional formats through which the fall of the Iron Curtain and German reunification were channelled into peaceful paths at the end of the 1980s. During the final dramatic months of the Cold War when events cascaded and the future appeared wide open, it was not immediately obvious that the European Community would step into such a role. The potential for conflict remained large, as underlined in particular by the attitudes of leading politicians. Despite decades of confidence-building and close cooperation in the scope of the Community and other organisations, Margaret Thatcher regarded German reunification as a great threat to peace in Europe. As late as September 1989 she told Mikhail Gorbachev that 'Britain and Western Europe are not interested in the unification of Germany'.[93] French president Mitterrand's position was initially at least ambivalent, and according to some sources similarly negative. In the end he argued that German reunification could proceed only within the EC framework, and that was also the position adopted by German chancellor Helmut Kohl.[94] In the end the obstructionism of Thatcher and co. was unable to block the road to reunification. The British prime minister was forced to concede; at a Special Meeting of the European Council in Dublin in April 1990 all the heads of state and government expressed their confidence that German unification 'will be a positive factor in the development of Europe as a whole and of the Community in particular'.[95] According to Kohl's foreign policy advisor, Horst Teltschik, the chancellor told his team after the closed meeting of the then twelve European leaders that the discussion had been 'super' – conveniently forgetting to mention that Thatcher was still expressing grave reservations.[96] The EC nevertheless became a stabilising factor, especially by virtue of its decision to integrate East Germany into the Community as part of the united Germany without preconditions or a separate accession process. In that sense 3 October 1990 was a key date in the history of the twentieth century, symbolising not only that Germany's division had been overcome, but also Europe's. The European Community had now expanded outside the Western Europe of the Cold War. One senior Commission official rightly called the process accession 'by the back door'. That is perhaps why the significance of the date for the history of the EC and Europe, and for the Community's internal peace, has always been underestimated.[97]

Above and beyond the German question too, the EC helped to ensure that Europe's transition into the post-Cold War era was able to proceed surprisingly rapidly and largely peacefully – in a situation where the future of Eastern Europe was initially pretty obscure. The EC had intensified trade relations with the Eastern Bloc states in the second half of the 1980s, culminating in their formal recognition of the EC in 1988/89. Once change was under way the EC also instituted economic aid programmes for the transforming states of the former Eastern Bloc, for example, through PHARE, a programme supporting economic restructuring by means of financial aid.[98]

Since the 1980s Eastern Central European intellectuals like Milan Kundera and Czesław Miłosz had dreamt of their societies 'rejoining' Europe. When they spoke of 'Central Europe' this also meant a rejection of the Soviet Union. It is noteworthy that they placed Europe at the heart of their thoughts and plans, rather than 'the West' or some other point of reference.[99] At the decisive moment Europe in the guise of the EC supplied political structures to ease the way for that 'homecoming' and direct it into stable channels. The EC was politically and symbolically central for making German reunification acceptable to Germany's European partners. The same applies to the end of the Cold War in Europe as a whole. Without the EC's prominent role in Southern Europe in the 1970s and 1980s that would have been almost unimaginable. At the same time, these developments enormously expanded the EC's role, which nobody would have thought possible twenty years earlier. Although the roots of the agenda that culminated in the Maastricht Treaty stretched back long before the end of the Cold War, the 1992 treaty ultimately represented one of the EC's initial responses to the geopolitical challenge presented by the end of the East–West conflict.[100]

Peace and Security: Résumé

Altogether we have seen how difficult it is to reduce the role of the European Community as producer or guarantor of peace and security during the Cold War to a simple formula. For a long time the EC profited more from relative peace in Europe than it contributed practically. Especially in the initial phase its active share in internal peace within the Community was narrower than often claimed, because some of its most important instruments quickly became dysfunctional. That occurred for example in the 1958 coal crisis, while the European Defence Community never even saw the light of day.

That does not mean that the EC played no role in internal peace. It did in fact contribute to peace and stability through its culture of cooperation, through the establishment of trust between elites within the Community. That applies especially to the Franco-German question, but also more broadly. At the same time causality is hard to establish at this level: trust only arose because there was peace anyway, of course, and as well as the EC there were others pushing in the same direction – even if the intensity of exchange granted the EC greater weight than other international organisations. At the same time this effect operated primarily at the level of the elites. Of course the EC also had a peace-promoting effect through its concrete policies, and quickly gave a face to the efforts to create a peaceful Europe. Its institutions made a decisive contribution to bringing the European peace narrative to life. From the 1980s the EC created additional instruments in order to cope with the demanding tasks it took on. These have subsequently been expanded, for example in the treaties of Maastricht and Lisbon.

In relation to peace in the world the EC expanded its arsenal of political options from the 1970s, especially in the guise of the European Political Cooperation and the European Council. The EC increasingly sought to contribute to peace beyond the bounds of its territory. Brussels produced a stream of publications on the question and a new self-confidence gelled. In line with its powers, the EC concentrated primarily on trade and trade sanctions, and here again one should not overstate their effect. Frequently they went no further than declarations and grand words, and the effects remained limited. The instrument of sanctions also illustrates how hedged any statement about the EC's contribution to peace must remain. In the case of the Soviet Union, the member states in fact regarded the mildness of their sanctions as a contribution to peace. For trade and security reasons they – unlike the United States – had no interest in further worsening the conflict with the Eastern Bloc. This interpretation implies that détente is the best means of securing peace: that view was contested, especially given that this course implied a realpolitik under which détente outweighed the human rights violations in martial law Poland. The case of the Falkland Islands is similarly complicated. EC sanctions were unable to prevent war, and although the British stance – and the EC's – originally enjoyed broad backing at the United Nations, their argument of international law possessed a formal legal dimension that ignored the longer history of British colonialism upon which Argentina based its claims. What peace meant and how it was best secured ultimately depended strongly on the observer's perspective.

For the two last decades of the Cold War it is also important to see the precursors of today's EU in the context of other organisations. To this day NATO is the decisive security instrument for most EU states and for the EU itself the real framework of power.[101] The eastern enlargement supplies the best example of this: Poland joined NATO in 1999, the EU not until 2004. The sequence reveals which appeared more urgent for the existential question of war and peace. Yet NATO was not even Poland's first bridge across the ruins of the Iron Curtain. It was accession to the Council of Europe in 1991 that opened the way for membership in other organisations. And in relation to peace and security the member states – especially the major powers France and the United Kingdom – placed more weight on their classical foreign policy instruments than on European integration. Sometimes they used the EC as a forum to discuss and act, but frequently they did not.

Perhaps even more important than the contributions to internal peace and peace in the world was the EC's contribution to social peace in the member states. Here too it is hard to isolate the EC's specific role from state-level policy and broader societal and economic processes. The Common Agricultural Policy, as a field where the EC possessed extensive powers, certainly played an important role despite its obvious deficits. The same applies with respect to the southern enlargement in the 1980s (Greece, Spain and Portugal) and the former Eastern Bloc after the end of the Cold War. A growing EC played a role in bolstering internal social stability under a democratic capitalist system, and guiding the fundamental transformations of these societies.

Altogether the EU has made important achievements in relation to peace, even if the overall picture is less positive than one might think. Its contribution to peace and security extends less far back than is frequently asserted, and often assumed different forms than generally believed. Peace in Western Europe cannot be causally attributed to the integration process, but was realised within that frame. At the same time there were several cases of hubris – for example in 1991, when Luxembourg foreign minister Jacques Poos declared that 'the hour of Europe has dawned' just as Yugoslavia descended into civil war and broke apart.[102] The EU proved ineffectual in the wars in ex-Yugoslavia; like the CSCE and the UN it failed in its efforts to bring about a lasting ceasefire and peace. NATO and especially the United States played a crucial role in ending the Bosnian War in 1995 and settling the Kosovo question in 1999, while the EU and Europe in general proved incapable of resolving these problems itself.[103] More recently too, the EU's record of action on securing peace in the world remains ambivalent. It failed to respond convincingly to the Arab Spring in 2010–2012, when the EU's institutions sent mixed messages and failed to consistently support the democratisation efforts. The Union was visibly divided over military intervention in Libya in 2011. And in the 2012–2014 negotiations for an association agreement with Ukraine it demonstrated little awareness of the geopolitical risks. Do not misunderstand me: Russia and the eastern Ukrainian militias it supports are responsible for the subsequent escalation in Ukraine and the spiral into war, not the EU. But there were certainly phases where the EU misjudged the wisdom of pulling a deeply divided country in a single direction – and underestimated the ensuing tensions with Russia. Especially in security questions, so many powers remain in the hands of the member states that it is often impossible to speak of 'the' EU taking a particular stance. So the EU today clearly possesses a peace and security role, but it should not be overstated. To date it has operated most effectively in conjunction with other organisations such as the UN or NATO, especially given that its instruments are fairly limited and remain strongly economic.

Nevertheless the scorecard is by no means negative, with much having been achieved especially in the second half of the period under consideration here. That is paradoxical, given that pro-European circles argue that during the immediate post-war era, it worked to mend the damage of the first half of the century. In fact the EU's part in this early phase was not terribly large – but all the more important in later decades, especially for its successively expanding internal space.

3 GROWTH AND PROSPERITY

The post-war era of rationing and scarcity was over. Many Europeans were now able to afford their first motor car, and most people owned and consumed more than their forebears ever had – despite working shorter hours. Now there was surplus in place of hunger. Recessions still occurred at intervals of course, but a burgeoning welfare state cushioned their impact as never before. Today the European Union is home to 7 per cent of the world's population, but produces almost one-quarter of its GDP. And it accounts for about half of all state social spending globally. No major non-European state spends a greater proportion of its GDP on social welfare than the European Union. Never in history has the average European been as materially prosperous and socially secure as in recent decades. Economically the EU is a giant.[1]

So is Europe a model for economic success? There has always been a lot of talk about problems and deficits, at both national and EU level (long pre-dating the financial meltdown of 2008). Many people see the European Union not as the solution, but as a source of economic dislocation and insecurity. And they pay no heed to the political leaders and captains of industry, who have always insisted that the Union promotes prosperity and represents the best response to the challenges of globalisation. Robert Schuman's Declaration of 9 May 1950, for instance, went beyond the question of peace. He also stressed that his proposal to establish a European Coal and Steel Community should serve to 'help raise standards of living', mentioning this aspect twice in his brief address.[2] The 1956 Spaak Report – the central preparatory document on the road to the Treaties of Rome – painted a gloomy picture, noting that the United States accounted for half of global production in almost all sectors. The states of the Eastern Bloc, it said, were growing at annual rates of 10 to 15 per cent, while Western Europe was falling behind. No Western European country on its own, the document argued, was strong enough to develop the very large and complex projects that were now crucial, for example to design and manufacture a large cargo aircraft. Asserting their place in the global economy would require the states of the European Coal and Steel Community (ECSC) to cooperate closely with one another, the document concluded.[3] Since the early post-war years European integration had concentrated primarily on the sphere of industry, and the wish for economic growth and material prosperity – understood here as rising GDP per country and per capita – formed a second central driving force of the integration process, alongside preserving peace.[4]

But what was the contribution of European integration to the economic history of Western Europe? The German news weekly *Der Spiegel* concluded in 1969 that the question was 'almost impossible to answer'.[5] And solid research on the economic effects of the EC is indeed thin on the ground.[6] There is little public awareness of such investigations, which have also been largely ignored in the research into the political history of the integration process. That is in itself enlightening, given the degree to which growth arguments were cited to justify integration. In 1953, for example, Max Kohnstamm, secretary of the High Authority of the ECSC, reminded Jean Monnet that 'the man on the street' expected two things from the integration process: firstly, peace, and secondly, 'Instead of stagnation, an improvement of living conditions. If this second promise remains unfulfilled, we will not have his support to do those things necessary for the first goal.'[7]

Whatever the pitfalls of seeking absolute clarity in this area, I venture in the following a closer examination of the economic implications and repercussions of the European integration process in the period bookended by the fall of communism and the signing of the Maastricht Treaty.

The *Trente Glorieuses*

The economic history of Western Europe during the Cold War can be usefully divided into two phases: an economic boom of dimensions the continent had never witnessed before began shortly after the Second World War and continued through to the early 1970s; by 1979 the economist Jean Fourastié had coined the term *trente glorieuses*.[8] This was followed by a succession of crises, which Anselm Doering-Manteuffel and Lutz Raphael characterise as a post-boom transition with low rates of growth and strongly fluctuating growth rates.[9] Although this periodisation has its critics, it does offer a useful frame for the present discussion.[10]

The *trente glorieuses*, Fourastié writes, brought France 'the successful realisation of its hope ... to free its people of the scourges that have traditionally haunted humanity (hunger, disease, poverty, misery and insecurity)'.[11] What Fourastié describes for France applies more broadly too. While Western Europe's GDP grew at 2 per cent annually between 1900 and 1950, the figure for 1950 to 1973 was a breathtaking 5 per cent.[12] It is worth reiterating: such strong growth over such an extended period – which coincides roughly with the beginnings of the European integration project – is without precedent in European economic history. At the same time, the states involved saw significant convergence in per-capita incomes and wealth. Not only were most people economically better off, but the differences between nations shrank as poorer countries tended to grow faster than their more prosperous neighbours. With trade expansion playing a role in reducing the gap between poor and rich, economic growth and convergence appeared to go hand in hand, at least for a period.[13]

So it comes as no surprise then, if French politician Pierre Pflimlin looked back very positively upon those first post-war decades. As he elaborates in an interview marking his ninetieth birthday in 1997: 'Everything went well at first. There was a period of great growth from 1945 to 1974, which has been called "les trente glorieuses". Since the Treaty of Rome was concluded on 25 March 1957, the average income in Western Europe has increased fivefold.'[14] After summarising the conventional economic success story, Pflimlin goes one small but decisive step further: he posits a causal nexus between integration and economic growth.

In fact, the assertion that European integration represented an immediate cause of rapid economic growth is highly questionable. Of course the six states that established the ECSC in 1951 and founded the EC a few years later were at the forefront of the post-war boom. Between 1950 and 1973 per-capita GDP in West Germany and Italy grew by 5.0 per cent annually. The corresponding figure for France was 4.0, for Belgium 3.5 and for the Netherlands 3.4 per cent. But it is enlightening to look beyond the bounds of the six states of the ECSC: Austria, which was not yet a member at this point, averaged annual per-capita GDP growth of 4.9 per cent; politically unstable Greece topped that with 6.2 per cent, while the Spanish and Portuguese dictatorships achieved 5.8 and 5.7 per cent respectively. On the other side of the Iron Curtain, it is perhaps even more astonishing to note that Bulgaria recorded 5.2 per cent, Yugoslavia 4.4 per cent and even the Soviet Union managed 3.4 per cent.[15] In view of the fundamental economic, social and political differences between these nations, it would seem that the boom in the EC states cannot in fact be explained solely or even primarily in terms of the integration process.

Moreover, the golden age of the *trente glorieuses* reached far beyond Europe. Corroboration for that assertion is found in contemporaneous developments in the United States and globally. In the United States, whose economic situation at the end of the war was incomparably better, growth averaged just 2.5 per cent, while the global average was 2.9 per cent. While the United States still dominated the global economy in 1950, Europe made up a great deal of ground over the course of the subsequent decades. The same incidentally also applies to Japan, whose economy grew even more rapidly than most in Europe: 8.0 per cent annually between 1946 and 1973.[16] So Europe possessed no monopoly over the golden age, even if it was regionally concentrated here – and even within Europe, its geographical reach extended well beyond the bounds of the contemporaneous EC. All this would strongly suggest that the integration process was not the principal driving force behind the boom.

Motors of Growth

The reasons behind the enormous vigour of the post-war boom in (Western) Europe were in fact complex, with the integration process touching on some but not all of the factors involved. We are dealing with a multitude of interpretations that cannot easily be reconciled. From the perspective adopted here, three sets of factors can be identified: firstly, the boom was driven by an interaction of short- and long-term economic trends operating largely independently of international cooperation and other primarily politically determined processes, first and foremost the pent-up demand accumulated over the three preceding decades. The period from 1914 to 1945 was associated with unusually strong isolation of national and macro-regional economic spaces. In comparison to the wave of globalisation preceding the First World War, this significantly impeded growth in Europe. At the same time, the images of cities turned to rubble burned deep into Europe's collective consciousness – but in fact they misrepresent the true economic situation at the end of the Second World War: especially in Western Europe, factories and infrastructure survived the war in better condition than the photographs would suggest, while repairing and replacing the damage that had occurred represented a growth factor in its own right. In Western Europe in particular, the underlying economy remained strong and infrastructure renewal became a motor of growth. Those who had survived the war got straight down to work, neither needing the state nor waiting for international cooperation.[17]

Secondly, efficient state-led allocation of resources played an important role, as did state structures promoting growth. Put in simple terms, labour market developments, technological progress, private consumption, state spending and private-sector investment all contributed. These aspects related primarily to processes within the respective societies or to the actions of non-state actors, and were not associated with international cooperation. In order to grow, industry needed labour. And fortuitously, this was the juncture where many agricultural workers became unemployed, as tractors replaced the horse, while new high-yield varieties and industrial fertilisers increased productivity. Rather than ending up on the street, many peasants and farm labourers quickly found employment in industry, and the same applies to workers shed by other shrinking sectors, such as charcoal burners and cartwrights. In many European societies this was actually the point where the transition to a post-agrarian society occurred, although the origins of the process naturally lay in the Industrial Revolution of the nineteenth century. Internal and transnational migration also played their part in satisfying the urgent and growing demand for industrial labour. Changes in the labour market thus coincided with technological innovation and rationalisation. All in all, therefore, the post-war era witnessed massive productivity gains. While an Italian worker's hourly productivity in 1950 was only 38 per cent of that of his or her American counterpart, for example, the figure had risen to 74 per cent by the end of the *trente glorieuses*.[18] An employer-friendly climate kept wage rises comparatively modest, allowing businesses to make good profits that were reinvested in plant and machinery. And the portion that landed in workers' pay packets quickly flowed back into the economy, to purchase food, a radio receiver, perhaps a motorcycle or even a motor car. Demand stimulated production. In Western Europe the state actively fostered social and economic consensus through a complex web of neo-corporatist structures, regulation and welfare state building – which also played a major part in driving growth.

The third set of causes lay in the field of international cooperation and trade policy, and it is only in this context that the EC played a role – alongside a string of other organisations and factors. Trade liberalisation, driven first and foremost by the United States, was certainly instrumental for economic growth in the post-war era. The preceding decades had seen trade barriers rising ever higher, with two world wars and the Great Depression. That now changed. Where the average level of customs duties in 1931 was about 30 per cent – and in 1944 much higher still – it fell to just 9 per cent by the mid-1970s. It is harder to put robust figures to the dismantling of the many non-tariff trade barriers that had accrued over the preceding decades and even centuries: technical norms and standards, red tape and import quotas to name but a few. Their inhibiting effects also diminished over the course of the post-war era, even if they initially remained significant.[19]

A Welcome Addition

So international cooperation did play a significant role in the *trente glorieuses*. But given that the boom began five years before the founding of the ECSC and a whole decade before the Treaties of Rome, on whose basis the Common Market was gradually established, it is impossible that the EC could have been exclusively responsible.

Instead we must begin by discussing the international organisations that were already promoting cooperation and trade before the ECSC came into being. Between 1948 and 1951 the Marshall Plan delivered $13 billion of aid to Western Europe. This time around – much more clearly than in the aftermath of the First World War – the United States committed to rebuilding the Western European economies. Although the older literature therefore interprets the Marshall Plan as an important motor of economic recovery, a different perspective has become widely accepted over the past thirty years. It is now argued that the direct economic effects of the Marshall Plan were rather smaller than previously believed, amounting to 0.2 per cent of GDP annually. More significant was its psychological impact; in contrast to 1918 and Versailles, the Marshall Plan symbolised a long-term US commitment to Western Europe and at the same time helped to accelerate processes of structural change in the targeted economies.[20]

More important in the long term was the Bretton Woods system created in 1944 to establish a new international monetary order for the Western world under American hegemony. The participating states agreed on a range within which their exchange rates were permitted to fluctuate against the dollar. But the economic problems persisted. During the immediate post-war years, trade within Western Europe remained negligible while strict currency controls impeded capital movements. Dollars were in short supply in all European states, which imported more from the United States than they were able to export back. An organisation known only to a handful of experts came to play a crucial role in overcoming these problems. The European Payments Union (EPU), created in 1950 by fourteen Western European states and the entire Sterling Area, promoted multilateral transactions and trade in Western Europe with the objective of achieving free convertibility of all participating currencies. Through multilateral clearing and a credit mechanism, the European Payments Union permitted its members to exchange directly without recourse to the dollar. This significantly eased trade between participating states. To some extent the EPU promoted and oversaw this process itself, but it also relied on the Organization for European Economic Co-operation (OEEC) that emerged from the Marshall Plan.[21] While the first half of the 1950s saw tensions between the global approach of Bretton Woods and the Western European EPU these dissipated from the mid-1950s, whereafter the different elements of Western monetary policy functioned more smoothly together.[22]

In one respect the EPU was rooted in the experiences of the 1930s and 1940s: it represented a lesson learned from the monetary problems of the inter-war years and was heavily inspired by the British economist John Maynard Keynes. Keynes in turn admitted that similar ideas to his had been espoused by Hitler's Reich Minister for Economic Affairs, Walther Funk, in 1940. Writing to Harold Nicolson at the British Ministry of Information in November 1940, Keynes noted that Funk's idea would be 'excellent if the name of Great Britain were substituted for Germany'.[23] Even before 1945 the economic necessity of free convertibility was recognised across the political and ideological spectrum.

On the other hand, the EPU with its complicated rules represented a precondition for getting trade moving again. The now largely forgotten European Payments Union thus created an important basis for a massive expansion of trade – and was later to become a necessary condition for the success of the EC. And because the EPU's membership was much wider than the six states that founded the EC, it formed a significant basis of the boom across Western Europe as a whole.

But what was the situation in the sphere of trade? Here too, the EC was by no means a pioneer of liberalisation, but instead built on a series of organisations that had emerged in Europe and globally since the end of the Second World War. One of these was the United Nations Economic Commission for Europe (UNECE) created in 1947 and operating across the East–West divide; another the General Agreement on Tariffs and Trade (GATT), also concluded in 1947. GATT was originally an agreement on international trade between twenty-three states, under which tariffs and other trade barriers were to be successively dismantled. Additionally, the OEEC also continued to work towards the same goal in the Western European context, even after the end of Marshall Plan from which it had emerged in 1948.

So the EC was by no means alone. The UNECE achieved a number of successes, for example in the fields of standardisation and transport integration. While these aspects are crucial for trade, their impact should not be overstated.[24] Even GATT remained relatively marginal for trade liberalisation in the 1950s; that was not to change until the Kennedy Round (1964–1967).[25] More important in dismantling intra-European trade barriers were the OEEC and its successor from 1961, the OECD. Not until 1949/50, when the OEEC's rules came into force, did trade within its region begin to race ahead of other parts of the world.[26]

The EC thus represented merely another Western European cog in the machinery of international cooperation, whose various components meshed increasingly better with one another. Nevertheless, it assumed an important role at the level of trade policy, because both the ECSC and the later EC were committed to dismantling tariffs and other non-tariff trade barriers. Economic analyses show that the costs of trade between EC member states did indeed fall significantly more quickly than those between other Western European countries, and also noticeably more rapidly than within EFTA.[27] In parallel to this, bilateral trade between member states grew more rapidly than their respective trade with third countries. Pre-existing business relationships with third countries were now partially diverted to partners within the EC. But growth in trade remained stronger than trade diversion. Tamim Bayoumi and Barry Eichengreen show that between 1953 and 1973 trade among the Six grew by more than 3 per cent annually more rapidly than would have been the case without the Common Market; for EFTA the figure was one full percentage point less.[28]

But how strong was the EC's influence on economic growth? There is no consensus among researchers. While Eichengreen calculated in 2007 that income in the EEC states grew by 4 per cent between 1959 and 1969 as an effect of European integration (equivalent to about one-third of a per cent per year),[29] Béla Balassa's pioneering study thirty years earlier reported additional GDP growth of about 0.5 per cent per annum.[30] For the entire period until 2000, Harald Badinger recently arrived at the same conclusion; in another study Eichengreen and Andrea Boltho, building on the work of Frankel and Romer, estimate about 0.6 per cent annually for the *trente glorieuses*.[31] Others are more sceptical. Daniel Landau finds almost no effect of the integration process on growth.[32] And Werner Plumpe and André Steiner, citing Balassa, ask provocatively whether there might not be a connection between the existence of the EU and the slow growth of its economies: might the institutional process have created more obstacles than stimuli?[33]

But we should remember that such calculations are always tricky, because they require contrafactual scenarios for how Western Europe would have turned out without the EC. Many of the older econometric studies assume a scenario where the factor 'EC' is simply zeroed while all others remain unchanged. But in view of the multitude of pre-existing regional organisations, it is plausible that other forms of regional integration would have partially compensated the non-existence of the Treaties of Rome. One approach of that type, building on a more complex contrafactual scenario than the older literature, is that recently published by Eichengreen and Boltho. Without the Common Market, they demonstrate, GATT would have had a greater impact – even though its influence on trade was weaker than the possibilities open to the EC. Altogether they argue that the integration process certainly had growth effects, but that for the period of the *trente glorieuses* these were rather smaller than in Eichengreen's earlier calculations.

Compared to the self-confidence of earlier econometric models, Eichengreen and Boltho have become much more cautious in their predictions and admit to sometimes using 'educated guesses'. They argue that during the *trente glorieuses* integration effects represented 'a welcome, if perhaps only limited, addition to living standards that were already growing very rapidly'. But the influence of political integration, they find, was always dwarfed by the impact of technological progress. And in light of the conclusions of the preceding chapter it is not without a certain irony that they conclude by referring to those scholars who argue that, ultimately, the EC's achievement was not so much economic but the establishment of lasting peace in Western Europe.[34]

Another relevant aspect is that many models take international cooperation as the starting point for their economic analyses – overlooking the fact that politics was merely catching up where market processes had already led the way. In fact trade relations between the future EC member states were already close long before the advent of formal cooperation under the auspices of the emerging EC, and their interconnectedness had been growing apace since the early post-war years, as Tony Judt pointed out a few years ago.[35] To that extent, rather than simply forming the starting point of an economically integrated Europe the EC channelled, amplified and institutionalised a trend that had been emerging for some time (especially since 1945).[36] Economic historian Werner Plumpe goes as far as to argue that existing economic integration made political cooperation imperative in the immediate post-war era.[37]

After the Boom

On 21 January 1972 the British *Guardian* wrote that there was 'bad news' from 'Europe the Growth Centre': 'The Community was booming in 1970, eased up last year and is still slowing down'. It was true, and this was far from the only report of 'Euro gloom' and 'stagflation'.[38] Research into the economic history of Western European has frequently characterised the 1970s in this way too, before the picture brightens a little in the 1980s. The central economic indicators were negative from 1973, with a multitude of factors underlining that the boom was over. A new wave of economic globalisation inflicted growing pressure of competition on the economies of Western Europe. Internal social unrest and anti-capitalist protest movements exacerbated tensions, while tectonic shifts in the international system caused grave repercussions. The collapse of the Bretton Woods system in 1973 had massive implications for the Western European economies, especially as it coincided with tensions in transatlantic relations on a scale unknown since 1945. The Cold War continued to thaw, giving rise to hopes of a more peaceful world but also generating new concerns. What if the superpowers reached a settlement over the heads of the Europeans? What were the economic and security implications of these changes? And what role did hitherto marginal actors play in the global power structures? The energy crises of the 1970s shone a spotlight on the Arab oil producers and the West's dependency on their black gold – and underlined the finite nature of fossil fuels and the ecological repercussions of human activity. What all these changes illustrated was that the golden years were over and old certainties had lost their power to guide action.

The weakness of growth in the EC is especially clear when contrasted with the *trente glorieuses* (see Table 1).

Per-capita economic growth slowed significantly after 1973 in the member states of the EC; in the founding six it roughly halved. The slowdown was even more marked in many of the states that joined later (with the exception of Ireland and the United Kingdom; the British economy had already been sluggish during the *trente glorieuses*). The decline in growth rates was particularly sharp when contrasted with certain East Asian economies. Western Europe, after rising like a phoenix from the ashes of war, now already appeared to have its best days behind it.

Fewer calculations of the effects of European integration have been put forward for this period of crisis than for the *trente glorieuses*. One of them arrives at a GDP growth effect for 1976 to 1985 of 0.6 to 0.8 per cent annually.[39] For the period from 1950 until the turn of the century another study arrives at a figure of 0.5 per cent per annum.[40] According to Nicholas Crafts, one of the leading researchers in this field, the effect of European integration during this phase can be summarised as 'useful but not spectacular'.[41]

Table 1 Growth in real per-capita GDP (per cent)

	1950–1973	1973–1992
Belgium	4.2	2.6
Denmark	3.8	1.9
France	4.9	2.5
West Germany	5.8	2.5
Greece	6.3	1.9
Ireland	4.0	3.8
Italy	5.3	2.4
Netherlands	4.1	1.9
Spain	6.4	3.0
Portugal	5.9	1.5
United Kingdom	2.9	2.0
Austria	5.6	2.4
Finland	4.6	2.4
Norway	4.3	3.2
Switzerland	3.2	1.5
Japan	7.6	3.2
South Korea	4.8	6.0
Taiwan	6.3	6.0
United States	2.7	0.9

Crafts, 'Economic Growth in East Asia and Western Europe', pp. 75–84, here p. 79. Figures adjusted to account for changing working hours.

Yet that laconic formulation conceals a finding that is all too easily overlooked. If we are to believe the econometric studies, the growth rates of the EC economies halved, but the EC's share of GDP growth remained largely unaffected at roughly 0.5 per cent per annum. In other words, the relative effect of European integration on economic growth grew significantly. Without the EC, the collapse after the boom would have been even more devastating.[42] It must be added by way of qualification, however, that several studies identify a very similar effect for EFTA during the same period. That could be interpreted as meaning that European cooperation was crucial, the specific form less so.[43] And at the same time, all these findings are based upon highly complex and not unproblematic calculations and counterfactual assumptions. They cannot be said to be truly watertight. It is nonetheless noteworthy that the existing studies for the 1970s and 1980s rate the influence of the EC so highly, and that the latter became even more of a stabilising factor for the economies of its member states.

Hidden Effects

So what can be the explanation for the integration process playing a relatively larger role during this phase than during the *trente glorieuses*? On the one hand it is obvious that the EEC Treaty only began to unfold its full trade-liberalising potential from the late 1960s. During the decade between the Treaties of Rome and the completion of the Customs Union in 1968, tariff reduction proceeded in stages with transitional periods. ECJ rulings also had trade-liberalising effects, with the crucial precedents on freedom of movement of goods – *Dassonville* in 1974 and *Cassis de Dijon* in 1979 – not coming until this post-boom phase.[44] This sealed the fate of a whole string of non-tariff barriers. The accession of six new member states between the oil price shock in 1973 and the Maastricht Treaty in 1992 also boosted trade and growth. The significance of the first enlargement round in particular is hard to overstate, in tangible as well as symbolic terms. In many respects this was the most important enlargement of all – even in comparison to 2004, when ten states with seventy-four million inhabitants joined the EU. The 1973 enlargement involved only three states with sixty-four million people between them. But in relative terms it expanded the Community's population by 33 per cent, 2004's by only 20 per cent. In terms of GDP too, the relative increase in 1973 was significantly greater than in 2004. The significantly expanded market stepped up the Community's growth potential, even if this was not immediately reflected evenly across all the member states.[45] Important developments also occurred in EC competition law, an area where the EC's powers were already especially far-reaching and largely supranational. Nevertheless, competition law was initially sidelined even within the Commission. Hans von der Groeben, the EC's first Commissioner for Competition, later related that nobody had wanted the brief, and he received it on account of his comparatively weak prior experience. Only from the 1970s and 1980s did EC competition law begin to effectively tackle state monopolies as obstructions to economic development.[46] In conjunction with national measures, this helps to explain why the member states' economies experienced especially strong deregulation during the 1980s.[47] Moreover, the EC began to develop a monetary policy of its own in the 1970s, essentially in response to the collapse of Bretton Woods at the start of the decade. Although the exchange rate system dubbed 'the snake' (from 1972) and the European Monetary System (from 1979) fell well short of expectations, matters would have been even worse without them. Finally the Community adopted its first reform treaty since 1957, the Single European Act of 1986, whose aims included completing the European Single Market by 1992.[48] Even before it had been fully implemented, the Act itself – and other reform initiatives of the European Commission under its dynamic president Jacques Delors – gave another boost to economic integration.[49]

On the other side a number of factors reduced or even reversed the potentially positive growth effects of European integration. The problems of the age went deeper than global economic turmoil and the specific, partly home-made, problems of the respective economies. For instance, economic history research has also demonstrated that the advantages of the Common Market were especially strong in its initial phase and for new members, but did not remain so permanently.[50] Altogether the growth-promoting potential of integration should therefore not be overestimated.

There was also one policy within the EC that tangibly reduced overall prosperity within the Community. Its origins lay in the *trente glorieuses*, but its full effect was not felt until the late 1960s, and even more so the two subsequent decades: the Common Agricultural Policy. Established from 1958 onwards in innumerable tiny steps, the CAP grew into the central pillar of the EC, consuming about 80 per cent of its budget by the 1970s. Initially regarded as the supranational beacon of European integration, the CAP became increasingly problematic from a growth perspective; it established high trade barriers against third states, while strong export growth was not matched by growths in imports. As such, the CAP obstructed global trade, with its protectionism harming producers in other parts of Europe and overseas. Within the EC itself the balance sheet looked little better. While the farmers – as the main beneficiaries – were frequently dissatisfied and regularly aired their grievances, the post-boom CAP mutated into an extremely costly beast. Its price-driven policies led to massive overproduction, the infamous topography of butter mountains and wine lakes, while all the products concerned could have been acquired considerably more cheaply on the world market. For example in 1969 a kilogramme of beef cost DM 4.80 in the EC, and just half that on the world market.[51] This state of affairs was tax-funded, and additional resources were required to dispose of the surpluses, either by destroying them, or selling them at subsidised prices on the world market. To that extent the CAP certainly cost taxpayers and consumers and reduced the GDP of member states – although to widely differing extents. As a new member the United Kingdom, for example, suffered more from the costs imposed by the CAP than France.[52]

This points to another important development during the phase following the boom. Strong economic growth during the *trente glorieuses* had tended to reduce inequalities between the member states. Now the effects diverged noticeably. In place of economic convergence, differences widened again.

The divergence is most marked among the states that joined since 1973. In certain cases membership was a success story associated with a noticeable increase in per-capita GDP. For Portugal the increase was a striking 16.5 per cent, for Denmark 14, for Spain still 13.7 per cent, but for Ireland and the United Kingdom significantly smaller at 9.4 and 8.6 per cent respectively. Greece experienced a decrease of 17.3 per cent, which was largely attributable to specific national economic and political factors such as clientelism and lack of industrial competitiveness.[53] Because the end of the boom coincided exactly with the first enlargement round, many of the (often unrealistic) hopes of prosperity through membership were to be disappointed. The convergence identifiable between various regions of the EU in the phase until 1973 also weakened thereafter.[54] The scepticism in significant parts of the population towards the integration process, to which we will turn in greater detail in the next chapter, can only be understood in that context.

The overall balance for the 1970s and 1980s is thus ambivalent. Some of the problems of the time were specific to the EC, such as costly agricultural surpluses and the persistence of trade barriers within the Common Market. But many had other causes. This brings us back to the observation that the *trente glorieuses* ultimately represent an unrealistic yardstick for growth and prosperity. No boom lasts forever. If growth rates fell from the mid-1970s, this represented merely a reversion to the mean. In the longer-term perspective it was the post-war boom – and not the subsequent two decades – that represented the exception in Western European economic history.[55] And even if the 1970s and 1980s saw regular soul-searching about stagnation and 'Eurosclerosis', the European Community was in fact now more significant in ensuring prosperity than during the supposedly glorious post-war era. If the economy grew at all now, this had more to do with the EC than ever before.

Fragile Knowledge

If we seek – as we have done thus far – the contribution made by the European integration process to growth in gross domestic product, we are using the same yardstick as the EC itself often has (even if this has done little to bring forth robust econometric analyses on the effects of European integration). But such a narrow and growth-fixated perspective excludes the social, cultural and wider economic implications.

First of all, therefore, we must shine a critical light on the instruments used to measure and compare societies. The use of data to monitor and manage societies proliferated during the post-war decades. Statistics on economic development and social questions had long been available, and by the inter-war period were already supplying increasingly frequent and precise comparisons of European societies.[56] But the post-war era witnessed two very significant new developments. Firstly, there was increasing availability of comparative statistics gathered using similar or identical parameters, and new criteria appeared. These included gross national product for quantitative comparison of economies, which only truly came into its own during the post-war era. At the level of international organisations this concept was initially propagated above all by the United Nations, but was soon taken up by others including the EC.[57] The EC itself produced ever more statistics to compare and illuminate social trends and standard of living in the member states. This revealed differences, convergence processes and diverging paths that had hitherto been invisible; in this sense comparisons played a role in constituting the very social orders they revealed.[58] The analyses covered not only the standard of living, but also topics such as consumer spending. In 1960, for example, the Statistical Office of the European Communities published a survey on the situation of working families that listed in detail 'the miner's spending' for the six ECSC states. It revealed among other things that spending on food was highest by far in Italy, while the sub-categories for fresh fruit and fresh vegetables varied little between the other countries.[59] Statistics also recorded the number of radio receivers, television sets and telephones, with one internal study in 1962 noting proudly that the trend in the EC states was 'more advantageous in certain ways than in the United Kingdom and Scandinavian countries'.[60] Such surveys were never simply descriptions of an economic and social reality; they also generated pressure, hope and frustration. Rolf Wagenführ, director-general of the Statistical Office of the European Communities, saw statistics as an instrument for 'equalising progress'.[61]

Statistical comparisons naturally looked beyond the member states too, becoming an instrument to calibrate the EC's achievements in global terms. By the 1960s the Community was already comparing data for its member states and the EC as a whole with the United States and the United Kingdom – and with Japan as the economic *miracle du jour*.[62] And that was not all. In 1965, for example, the Statistical Office of the European Communities reported that the Eastern Bloc was not growing as rapidly as had been assumed. In fact, it noted, the EC's industrial production had grown faster than EFTA's between 1958 and 1964 and was only marginally behind Comecon's.[63] Alongside rivalry with EFTA in Western Europe, the way the Cold War shaped the EC's self-image and public presentation serves as a reminder that the Soviet economic model was once regarded as a credible threat to the West. Even in the mid-1970s the *Yearbook of Industrial Statistics* published by the Statistical Office of the European Communities still contained comparisons with the Soviet Union where the EC was by no means obviously superior. A decade later such comparisons had been dropped. The Soviet Bloc was no longer regarded as an earnest rival, notwithstanding the series of economic crises experienced by Western Europe.[64]

At the same time it is conspicuous how little attention the EC devoted – in the many thousands of pages of analysis it churned out – to the specific contribution the integration process made to economic development. Not that there were no initiatives. As far back as 1952 the ECSC established committees to analyse and soon also forecast market developments. Under the Treaties of Rome this agenda was expanded beyond coal and steel to encompass the entirety of the EC's economic activity.[65] In 1960 the statisticians noted that 'the new stimuli attributable to the establishment of the Common Market will generate an increase in growth rates of 0.5 to 2 percent'.[66] The span was broad, however, and exclusion of the agricultural sector further reduced the forecast's reliability. Three years later Wagenführ commented on the first contemporaneous attempts to measure the integration effect, dismissing an EC-critical study by the

Hungarian–Belgian economist Alexandre Lamfalussy; his own analysis, he asserted 'supports very strong suppositions concerning the positive effects of the integration process'.[67] Breathtakingly vague coming from a statistician. Another three years later Wagenführ writes that statistics represent an instrument 'for identifying positive and negative effects of integration'.[68] But the questions he was now referring to were econometrically less challenging than the problem of the overall effect of European integration on economic development: matters such as the problem of measuring growth in trade as exactly as possible. In the meantime it had become apparent that great problems accompanied any attempt to determine the effects of integration more precisely. Wagenführ himself repeatedly emphasised that the methods of statistical recording at the national level had not yet been adequately harmonised. Any attempt to assess the EC's share in economic development was, he said, based on too many assumptions for it simply to be measured. Any attempt to do so would have opened the EC to political critique. As such, the statisticians retreated to a position of recording data that was comparatively easy to quantify. Only in the late 1980s, when the EC was pushing for an ambitious programme to realise the Single Market by 1992, were new attempts made to quantify the matter more precisely. A series of influential expert reports presented economic scenarios for implementation or non-implementation of specific reforms advocated by the Commission. This series of studies published between 1986 and 1988 bore the rather polemic title 'The Cost of Non-Europe' – considering that the question was to either preserve or deepen the present level of integration, not to abandon anything already achieved. But even these documents shied away from attempting to quantify the overall effect of European integration to date; for the future, they promised annual growth of 1 per cent.[69] Throughout the entire period there was virtually no public pressure to present a clear account of the economic achievements of the integration process. That is certainly astonishing, given that long before the Maastricht Treaty fractures were already appearing in the permissive consensus, as described in greater detail in Chapter 4, 'Participation and Technocracy'.

Happiness, Nostalgia and Other Effects

Alongside the vagueness of the findings at the statistical level, a more fundamental question is whether GDP, trade and other growth-led indicators are in fact the right measures for the effects of European integration. Fourastié was already aware of this conundrum when he coined the term *trente glorieuses*. The French economist possessed a clearer awareness than most of his contemporaries for the flip side of the growth cult. Western Europe had sought, Fourastié wrote in 1979, to generate 'happiness' through economic growth. That had proven to be extremely difficult and had ended in 'defeat'. Even Fourastié's *trente glorieuses* possesses a whiff of irony, playing as it does on the '*trois glorieuses*' – the three critical days of the July Revolution of 1830 when, as Fourastié put it, 'one despotism was replaced by another'.[70]

The price of the EC's growth-centred course was indeed high. Trade liberalisation and growing pressure of competition caused the loss of millions of jobs and the demise of whole industries. French agriculture shed 4.3 per cent of its workforce between 1960 and 1973, 3.4 per cent in the brief phase between 1973 and 1979, and another 3.3 per cent between 1979 and 1989. The corresponding figures for West Germany were minus 4.7, 5.2 and 3.1 per cent; for Italy minus 4.8, 2.5 and 4.2 per cent, and for the United Kingdom minus 3.2, 1.7 and 1.2 per cent.[71] With the exception of the United Kingdom, which traditionally had a small agricultural sector with comparably large units, this represented roughly a halving of agricultural employment over the period as a whole. And this was plainly something the protectionism of the CAP was powerless to redress. Behind the figures were naturally the fates of millions of human beings: people escaping harsh poverty and hard physical labour, and often finding secure employment in industry. But the changes also bulldozed lifeworlds dating back centuries. Farms that had been in a family for generations were abandoned, whole landscapes depopulated. When the historian Pierre Nora launched his ambitious project to catalogue France's *Lieux de Mémoire*, one of his absolutely central motives was the loss of the collective memory of the peasantry.[72]

Other sectors, such as the textile industry, also came under massive pressure to change and adapt. Europe had been the unchallenged global leader in textiles until the First World War. The British textile industry – the leader within Europe – had already begun to unravel between the wars; production in France, West Germany and the Netherlands slumped during the 1970s and 1980s, but hundreds of thousands of jobs had already been lost to rationalisation before that. Today Germany produces almost no clothing at all. The EC intervened much less in textiles than it did in agriculture, and there was no common textile policy.[73] Instead developments were characterised by dislocations in global trade, rising real wages and competition from cheaper producers in Southern and Eastern Europe and overseas, without the EC developing specific instruments to cushion the transformation.[74] It left this to the member states and even more so to the sometimes brutal forces of the market.

Leading politicians and officials at the EC level were certainly aware of these effects. Paradoxically, the EC sought to restrict, channel and amplify market processes through integration. The agricultural sector again supplies a good example: without the CAP the loss of agricultural employment would have been even more dramatic. So whereas the Common Agricultural Policy represented a protectionist impediment from a growth perspective, it appeared excessively market-driven to many producers. At the same time, preserving all existing agricultural employment through political intervention would have cost the earth for the member states or the Community. The CAP watered down the change wrought by globalisation and technological innovation and brought it – occasional farmers' protests notwithstanding – into the realm of the politically acceptable. As such it contributed to preventing the kind of rural radicalisation that exacerbated the crisis of many European democracies in the first half of the century. For all their protests – and incomes lagging persistently behind industry – farmers themselves knew what was good for them. Without the Community their situation would have been worse still. That goes some way to explaining why French farmers rejected de Gaulle's Empty Chair tactic: because it threatened the CAP. The Common Agricultural Policy ostensibly pursued a production-driven logic, but in its very essence in fact operated as a clandestine central pillar of the EC's social policy.[75]

Channelling and cushioning market processes was also a core motive of the ECSC; again the point was neither simply to freeze the sector nor to expand it through interventionism. Obvious evidence of this is seen in the reduction in the number of miners in Western Europe from about two million in 1950 to fewer than 150,000 in 1995.[76] From the outset Monnet factored in French steelmakers' 'fear of German industrial domination'.[77] He knew that concerns over growing competition would condemn the Schuman Plan to failure and therefore proposed supplying coal and steel at identical conditions in both countries. That still meant competition, but on a level playing field.

More broadly too, the EC repeatedly committed itself to forging ahead with economic liberalisation. Here integration functioned as a tool for bypassing national resistance. In fact one reason for the French government to support the Schuman Plan was that Europeanisation would expose outdated French operators to greater competition and give them a modernising shock. But Paris wanted the pressure to stay within controlled bounds; compared to sweeping liberalisation, a measured opening within the framework of a Common Market of six appeared to certain integration sceptics the lesser evil.[78] Italy even had its own term for this: many of the political and economic elites regarded the EC as a '*vincolo esterno*', an external constraint – and as a lever enabling otherwise impossible internal reforms.[79]

Others had much grander plans. In the letter to Monnet cited above, Kohnstamm underlines that a real 'revolution ... of the European economy' was required in order to create a 'truly expansive economy'. But that was no easy matter: 'What is needed is an education of not just the industrialists, but everybody; an education, even an indoctrination with the philosophy, yes, I feel inclined to say with the ideology of an expansive economy.'[80] Here Europeanisation serves as a means to overcome protectionist measures like cartels and trade barriers and boost growth through competition. Even if the motives and means diverged and further economic liberalisation by no means always characterised the approach, the EC's prime concern was to push economic development towards higher rates of growth.

This logic of growth and modernisation came under increasing pressure from the 1970s. In 1970, for example, futurologist Alvin Toffler identified a 'tremendous wave of nostalgia' in the Western world.[81] Confronted with rapid change in the present many people were harking back to a supposedly less complicated and more harmonious past, a boom in nostalgia succeeding the post-war economic boom.

The EC's fixation on growth has also been increasingly questioned since the 1970s, and in some quarters sharply criticised. To some extent this was driven by a left-wing critique of capitalism whose origins lay in the preceding decades; partly it reflected a growing awareness of the ecological harm associated with industrial mass production. Hopes of political change had turned out to be unrealistic and post-material values gained in significance. This altered cultural climate was exemplified by the Club of Rome's 1972 report on *The Limits to Growth*. The debate quickly reached the EC. Sicco Mansholt, initially Agriculture Commissioner and later briefly president of the European Commission (and a member of the Club of Rome himself), stressed in a letter to Commission president Franco Maria Malfatti that the environmental problems and the North–South question demanded 'a radical policy reorientation'. He argued for a new culture of self-restraint and hoped that the existing fixation on GNP (*produit national brut*) could be replaced by an orientation on *bonheur national brut*.[82]

This and similar calls went unheard. Instead the European Community adhered to the paradigm of quantitative growth – propagated in Western Europe even before the EC especially by the OECD.[83] Prosperity was still defined primarily in material terms. This approach was rooted in the same 'politics of productivity' with which the United States had shaped the world of international relations after 1945.[84] Only very recently has this begun to change a little. The Lisbon Strategy of year 2000 concentrated more on competitiveness than sheer growth, and included social cohesion and environmental protection among its concerns. After this ten-year agenda fell well short of core targets, its successor, Europe 2020, was launched with less fanfare. Even if both documents steer away from an exclusive logic of growth, to this day the broader public frequently identifies the EU with quantitative indicators.[85]

Social Policy EC Style

The benefits of growth are unevenly distributed. Understanding social policy as an attempt to paper over social fractures in times of both growth and recession, research on the EU frequently assumes that social policy at EC level remained marginal throughout the Cold War, and was always a domain of the nation states.[86] That is largely – but not entirely – correct. As already mentioned, the Common Agricultural Policy essentially pursued social policy objectives. More importantly: the conventional perspective reduces social policy to a redistributive model, which is ahistorical and overlooks the contemporaneous spectrum of ideas about insurance against life risks and market forces.[87] It also ties the discussion about social policy at EC level to the concepts and categories of the national welfare state systems, which fails to do it justice.[88]

The ECSC committed itself to a specific social policy approach, drawing on ideas originating from the inter-war ILO.[89] Concretely the

ECSC worked to improve health and safety and ran training programmes for the unemployed, as well as constructing housing for miners and steel workers. In other words, the redistributive aspects of this social policy remained small. Over the decades there were many attempts to change this, especially by social democrats, socialists and trade unionists. Gerhard Kreyssig, a member of the German Social Democratic Party (SPD) and of the Common Assembly of the ECSC complained in 1958, for instance, that the High Authority remained largely powerless in the field of social policy. And, he added, Parliament's attempts to change this had led nowhere.[90] Kreyssig advocated a redistributive approach, which to his mind was the only justifiable social policy option, and many others shared his view. But this current never gained the ascendent, and redistributive social policy remained a firmly national matter. Since the Second World War welfare had become a central responsibility of the national state, enhancing state legitimacy and fostering a loyal citizenry. And the fear that 'more Europe' would mean 'less welfare state' was always strong. Here the price of European solidarity appeared too high to most governments, be they conservative, liberal or socialist/social democratic.[91] Against this backdrop, the ILO approach dominated in the ECSC: seeking social progress primarily through economic cooperation rather than redistributive social policy. Growth and productivity were regarded as the best medicine for social inequality and conflict.

The measures developed by the ILO shaped the social policy of the Treaties of Rome even more strongly than they had the ECSC. This is seen especially clearly in the Ohlin Report, which was prepared in 1956 by a group of ILO experts and came to play an important role in the EEC.[92] In essence the question was whether welfare state standards could be harmonised internationally, and if so how. At the time this was also a hot topic in European labour movement circles. The ILO rejected such an approach as largely unrealisable. More important than a direct harmonisation of social standards, it argued, was the question of unit labour costs. This made market integration, productivity and economic growth the decisive instruments of social policy. In order to achieve growing prosperity leading to a gradual equalisation of social standards, ILO representatives argued, supportive measures were necessary, including vocational training, freedom of movement and occupational safety. While the French government in particular favoured a more strongly redistributive model, it was the ILO that ultimately put its decisive stamp on the Common Market.[93] Social housing – which the ECSC had taken on – was not among the EEC's responsibilities. And there was not a single word about European job creation schemes of the kind proposed by the League of Nations in 1931.[94]

The EEC Treaty of 1957 breathed the same spirit. Article 117 noted that living conditions will be improved and harmonised essentially through 'the functioning of the common market, which will favour the harmonisation of social systems'.[95] Redistributive social policy and protection against life risks and market failures remained primarily national political responsibilities – and it was only after the member states had firmly established domestic programmes of that nature that the representatives of the moderate left and their trade unions acquiesced to the EC's line.[96] The European Commission and other actors made repeated attempts to create a European social policy orientated more strongly on the national model, but such efforts never got very far.[97]

The EEC Treaty only adopts a rather more redistributive logic where it calls for equal pay for equal work for men and women. While these provisions did indeed have a certain effect, the treaty's influence should not be overstated. On the one hand many other actors were also pressing for gender equality, and a string of member states had already anchored the principle in law before the Treaties of Rome. On the other hand the objective remains unfulfilled to this day, and practices and outcomes differ markedly across the different member states, as the EU itself has frequently conceded.[98] So Wagenführ had a point in the mid-1960s when he cited the equal pay article as an example of the treaties containing 'ambiguous and fungible clauses'.[99]

Growth thus lay at the heart of the EC's approach to social policy, especially during the *trente glorieuses*. But that should not be confused with a truly free market policy: despite its anchoring in the EEC Treaty, for example, there were clear limits to freedom of movement. Movement of persons was liberalised and free movement of workers formed one of the four pillars of the EEC Treaty. But because the EC failed to insist on full mutual recognition of school and vocational qualifications, the impact on labour markets remained limited. Here the ball remained in the court of the member states, whose elites often understood European integration as a means to consolidate and expand the welfare state at the national level. They therefore had no interest in undermining social standards through excessive competition;

instead, the liberalisation always remained selective.[100] At the same time the founding members agreed in 1957 that workers who accepted employment in another EC member state would retain their health insurance and pension entitlements. This realised the ILO's logic of concentrating on growth and productivity, but without creating a supranational welfare state.[101]

The end of the boom stimulated criticism of this selective approach. The early 1970s saw a brief discussion about more strongly redistributive measures, and altogether the decade witnessed experimentation with Keynesian and neo-mercantilist initiatives. It was also during this period that the European Social Fund began to play a larger role, supplying benefits for workers to find new employment, retrain or seek work elsewhere in the Common Market. The extremely small budget on which it had survived until the early 1970s now expanded a little; but against the member states' own welfare spending it remained negligible. Unlike the CAP, where Brussels played the central role, the Social Fund was administered by the member states.[102] That decade also saw the first Regulation on the Application of Social Security Schemes to Employed Persons and Their Families Moving within the Community,[103] with the first Social Action Programme following in 1974. The EC's Regional Policy also acquired social policy aspects as it emerged from the CAP, in the sense of reducing the gap between poorer and richer regions of the Community.[104] But overall these activities remained subsidiary to the instruments of the Common Market and its objectives, and the same logic permeated the provisions of the Single European Act. Even if the 'social dimension' of the integration process was emphasised more strongly from the second half of the 1980s – and new initiatives emerged – the EC ultimately remained committed to an approach whose origins lay in the inter-war debates in the ILO, and now sought to overcome the crisis of the 1970s through deeper integration of markets.[105]

The British government in particular rejected more strongly redistributive elements in the field of social policy, and prime minister Margaret Thatcher herself frequently clashed with Commission president Delors over the issue. In one legendary speech to British trade unionists in Bournemouth in September 1988, Delors argued for a larger 'social dimension' in the EC – so to speak on Thatcher's doorstep.[106] However much trade unionists, sections of the European Parliament and even the Commission might have wished, a European social policy modelled on the post-war welfare states was not going to happen.[107] Even in the latter years of the Cold War, social policy proper remained a marginal concern in the Council of Ministers as the most important decision-making organ of the EC. Between 1978 and 1987 it generally occupied a halfway prominent place on the agenda at only two meetings per year, while policy areas like external relations and the CAP were consistently in double figures.[108]

Even if social policy never reached the heart of the European Community, the period did witness a number of notable developments. The differences between national systems narrowed noticeably during the course of the Cold War. While the respective systems retained their own characteristics, social spending and benefits in particular converged. Confluence in social policy should not be confused with an autonomous Community social policy, however. Additionally, in the 1980s inequalities between member states were shrinking – although soon to increase again. This process was not attributable exclusively to the EC, and also affected states that were not members at the time. Nevertheless, the changes are striking.[109]

A Neoliberal Europe?

Whereas social policy acquired a very specific meaning in the EC context and the set course was long adhered to, the EC's economic policy underwent great change between the 1950s and 1990s. Generally speaking, the Western European economies made a turn towards state regulation and intervention after 1945, which was reflected in a growing state sector and steadily increasing state budgets in most member states until the early/mid-1980s. As Table 2 shows, this effect was strongest in Belgium. There were naturally enormous differences between the various member states in the structure, measures, direction and effects of their economic policies, and everywhere there were major twists and turns. But at a more abstracted level they all shared the combination of domestic interventionism with external free trade – which became known as 'Keynes at home and Smith abroad'.[110]

A similar model, which one researcher refers to as 'qualified liberalism', dominated at the EC level well into the 1970s.[111] This meant that the Community prioritised dismantling tariff barriers within the Community but refrained from seeking a sweeping liberalisation of trade. Many non-tariff barriers also remained, and the general lack of

Table 2 State spending as proportion of GDP in Western Europe, 1960–1990

	1960	1974	1980	1985	1990
Belgium	30.3	39.4	59.0	62.4	54.7
France	34.6	39.3	46.1	52.2	50.4
West Germany	32.4	44.6	48.3	47.5	46.0
Italy	30.1	37.9	41.7	50.8	53.2
Luxembourg	30.5	35.6	54.8	51.7	51.3
Netherlands	33.7	47.9	57.5	59.7	56.3
Denmark	24.8	45.9	56.2	59.3	57.5
Ireland	28.0	43.0	50.8	55.1	44.5
United Kingdom	32.2	44.8	44.7	46.1	42.9
Greece	17.4	25.0	30.5	43.7	50.4
Portugal	17.0	24.7	25.9	43.4	41.7
Spain	n.a.	23.1	32.9	42.2	41.9
EC-12	31.8	40.7	45.9	49.7	47.8

After Tsoukalis, *The New European Economy*, p. 29 (as percentage of GDP).

recognition of foreign qualifications meant that labour market liberalisation remained only partial. Competition policy, where the EC already possessed especially wide-ranging powers, is especially instructive. This policy area was heavily influenced by German ordoliberalism, especially in the 1960s, but without being entirely tied to it; this frequently involved a specific interpretation of German law by the European Commission. The EC correspondingly concentrated on providing the market with a strong legal framework. In fact monopolies were not consistently challenged at first, which placed significant limits on the liberalisation agenda.[112] In the 1970s Keynesian and other more decidedly social democratic ideas also rose to the fore and with them the idea of managing demand for goods and services.[113]

For a brief period at the middle of the decade it even appeared as though the future of both France and Italy could belong to their reformist communist parties, which now distanced themselves from the Soviet Union under the banner of 'Eurocommunism'.[114] In effect the spectrum of political approaches tended to shift left at both the national and European levels, and the EC was in no sense clearly aligned with any one economic policy model. That applies even more if the Common Agricultural Policy is included in the discussion. Rather than liberalisation, it stood for central planning and a neo-mercantilist approach that sought to protect the Community's own producers using protectionist measures. Already in the *trente glorieuses* the EC's liberalisation agenda thus remained highly selective and its impact on the Community restricted.

At the end of the 1970s there were good grounds to believe that the nation states would reassert control over economic policy. For example, the French journalist Yann de L'Écotais asked in 1976 'if the European Community had been abandoned by its member states?'[115] The political responses to the economic dislocations of the decade did indeed suggest that the EC had passed the apogee of its influence in comparison to the member states. For example many countries, including France, Italy and Belgium, sought to promote 'national champions' using interventionist methods: firms under state control capable of surviving on the world markets. At the EC level, this approach and other Keynesian attempts to overcome the crisis tended to generate conflicts. At the same time the British government of Margaret Thatcher in particular challenged the *acquis communautaire* (the rights and obligations applicable to all member states). Centrifugal tendencies were certainly accelerating.

By the early 1980s the EC was in fact shifting increasingly towards liberalisation, in step with the Community's growing importance on the international stage and new powers vis-à-vis the member states.[116] As such, the Community found itself aligned with developments in many Western economies. Abandoning the trend to seek political interventions for all social problems, various governments now turned to supply-side economics and liberalisation. The United States under Ronald Reagan and the United Kingdom under Margaret Thatcher led the way.[117] But the U-turn was in fact most spectacular in France, where the left-wing experiment of president François Mitterrand was abandoned in 1983 after less than two years, for a *tournant de la rigueur* (austerity turn). A short phase of expanded state spending and intervention was followed – under pressure from the international financial markets – by a radical programme of cuts.[118] In the European Commission itself, the failure of a Keynesian reform programme in summer 1983 contributed to a similar reorientation.[119] The dismantling of non-tariff barriers now moved up the trade agenda, especially in the context of the Single European Act. The Commission now also pressed for privatisation of state-owned enterprises, and the EC as a whole increasingly pursued partial deregulation – alongside re-

regulation – although without this truly amounting to a consistent neoliberal policy.[120] If nothing else, the latter was precluded by the Common Agricultural Policy, which remained one of the Community's most significant programmes. The massive problems of past years were now addressed with cautious reforms, although these could not be said to be specifically liberalising. The milk quota introduced in 1984, for example, reined in overproduction – by enforcing a strictly interventionist approach.[121] To that extent liberalisation was merely a trend, and one that affected the different parts of the EC very differently. Neoliberal ideas played a significant role, but without being implemented across the board.[122]

There are many reasons why this occurred. The state interventionist experiments of the previous decade had turned out to be less than successful, and the political tide turned successively in many member states. For the EC itself, the effect of the shared European law also happened to be very important. As already mentioned, it now took hold and drove forward the liberalisation agenda.

At the same time these processes unfolded within clearly defined bounds. The Single European Act, for example, stood for liberalisation – but also embodied an attempt to prevent a race to the bottom by strengthening protections in areas like environment, health, consumer protection and working conditions.[123] And Commission president Jacques Delors – who came to be identified like no other with the liberalisation agenda – argued at the same time for a 'social Europe'.[124] He had certainly not shaken off his past as a socialist politician. Overall the shell of the EC was preserved while radically new content was injected.

Growth and Prosperity: Résumé

Over the years, much energy has been invested in grand speeches asserting or denying that European integration promotes growth and prosperity, but astonishingly little into investigating the claim. Among the few existing studies on the Cold War period those produced more recently are strikingly reticent to state anything definite. Nonetheless, it is possible today to identify an independent EC contribution to growing material prosperity in the member states during the Cold War, even if it apparently remained rather modest. It stayed well below half of one per cent additional GDP growth per annum, and as such lies in a similar order of magnitude to the Marshall Plan for the early post-war period. This comparison makes the Marshall Plan appear more economically significant than most research of recent years would have it, but also means that the economic role of the EC during the *trente glorieuses* should not be overstated. During the second half of the Cold War the Community had greater weight in relative terms: without it the slump would have been even worse. In other words, the EC ensured stability during the crisis of the 1970s and the recovery of the 1980s. That has been generally overlooked to date. The present situation where European integration largely governs the fate of the member states' economies, on the other hand, is primarily an effect of the 1980s and 1990s, including the Maastricht Treaty and ensuing changes such as the introduction of the euro.

Those aspects aside, the location of the economic within the integration process remained curiously vague during the Cold War. Economic integration was on the one hand an end in itself to promote prosperity; on the other it was always just a means to achieve overarching political objectives. In the interests of peace and reconciliation it was obvious to make compromises at the economic level; cooperation would have been impossible without a modicum of generosity. Instrumentalism in dealing with economic questions recurs in many sources. In 1964, for example, the West German Minister of Economics Kurt Schmücker admitted that he did not always understand the regulations he participated in creating.[125] European unity was more important than economic calculation and questions of detail.

But the economic side of the EC was also highly political for another reason, and this factor mitigated taking economic outcomes very seriously. Towards both the EC's own citizens and the Eastern Bloc, European integration was justified very much in terms of growth and prosperity. An economically strong and united Western Europe was regarded as the best bulwark against the Soviet Bloc – and against communist currents within. The EC therefore promoted a culture of comparison with other societies, above all within Western Europe; but in view of the Cold War also towards the Eastern Bloc and in the course of globalisation increasingly beyond.

Against this background nothing shaped the DNA of the European Community like the logic of economics. During the Cold War its institutions and powers concentrated largely on this area. Even social policy was principally conceived through this lens, and new policy initiatives were actually always rooted in economics and argued as such.[126] That was plainly the case with the ECSC; as Euratom faded from the 1960s the Common Market and the CAP moved to the top of the agenda. This economic focus was reinforced again in the second half of the 1980s when the Single Market project revitalised the EC.

A clear orientation on economic theory cannot be identified. The EC stood for trade liberalisation, sharpened competition and free market principles, but also for protectionism, regulation and in some cases even capitalist central planning. The specific balance between these elements shifted repeatedly and varied from one policy area to another. So the EC cannot be tied clearly to any one model, for example neoliberalism or German ordoliberalism. Of course certain policy areas, such as agriculture, exhibit great continuity in this respect. But altogether the EC has continuously adapted its economic theory alignments and its concrete instruments to each new situation and challenge. What it also demonstrates is how malleable a capitalist economic policy was, and how often political motives took priority over economic interests.[127]

Otherwise the economic debates remained largely national. This is reflected, for example, in the contemporaneous perception of the *trente glorieuses*. West Germans spoke proudly of the *Wirtschaftswunder* and Italians the *miracolo economico*; few were aware of the transnational dimension. In both countries state and society represented the decisive frames for understanding achievements and successes. That was a crucial aspect to the extent that in Western Europe at that time state legitimacy and national identity – like European integration – were essentially defined in terms of economic indicators. Incidentally, even Fourastié does not stray far from that line. While he devotes almost 300 pages to the *trente glorieuses* in France, the transnational causes and effects go almost unmentioned. Politics further reinforced these national explanations. The European project was often invoked in the abstract, but when it came to tallying up economic achievements the plus side mostly contained national rather than EC measures.

In 1970 two prominent American researchers, Leon N. Lindberg and Stuart A. Scheingold, argued that no truly reliable economic statements could be made on the EC's share of growth. 'Nevertheless, to the man in the street and even to the businessman the

Common Market is certainly associated with dynamism and growth.' And they went another important step further, arguing that 'the myth of the Common Market is in itself an important political factor'.[128] As such it did in fact come to shape events. During the Empty Chair Crisis, for example, French civil servants warned de Gaulle that France could not afford the economic cost of breaking with the EC.[129] And in the British accession debates of the early 1970s EC membership was regarded as crucial for the British economy.[130] Although these two member states were acutely protective of their own national interests, they were not actually able to cite truly solid, dependable facts to quantify precise prosperity gains through integration.

In fact economic growth attributable to the EC represented more than a myth – but also a smaller factor than often asserted. The contribution of integration to economic development always remained vague to the 'man in the street' and had little direct effect on the everyday lives of most Europeans – apart that is from farmers and a handful of others. To that extent the myth Lindberg and Scheingold describe certainly had its effect. At the same time many people also felt the EC to be remote and largely irrelevant. It is that complex relationship between the Community and its citizens to which we turn next.

4 PARTICIPATION AND TECHNOCRACY

It was such a simple trick: a pretty girl went to the border post and pretended to faint, letting the others sneak round from behind. While the border guards were distracted, 'the first group of European unification activists uprooted French border markers and demolished barriers'. Three hundred activists attended the August 1950 protest at the German and French customs posts at Sankt Germanshof/ Wissembourg. Their statement announced 'For the first time in history Europeans are marching to the border not to kill each other, but to demand removal of the borders.' They made a bonfire of border markers for their pro-European ideals – and made sure the press were out in force.[1]

The event could hardly have been more symbolic. The chosen location represented a strategically crucial section of the German–French border, and had witnessed many historical battles; it was heavily fortified, most recently with Hitler's construction of the Westwall.[2] The chosen number of demonstrators also possessed a deep cultural significance. As the leaflet continued, 'there were three hundred of us at Wissembourg and we burned the border markers, those awful symbols of national sovereignty',[3] echoing the three hundred outnumbered Spartans who resisted a huge Persian army at Thermopylae in 480 BCE: while the latter's heroism consisted in defending their frontier to the last drop of blood, the mission of their self-appointed successors was to abolish borders. Media coverage was supportive in the two affected states, and elsewhere too. The Dutch *Het Vrije Volk*, for example, proudly reported that the largest delegation had come from the

Netherlands.[4] For some of the participants these forms of pro-European protest were still relevant decades later: as German chancellor Helmut Kohl occasionally spoke about taking part in a border protest as a teenager.[5]

A range of forces drove European integration in the post-war era, with top-level negotiations between politicians and civil servants not necessarily uppermost. At crucial junctures European citizens spoke up to express support for or dissatisfaction with the EC, or addressed European affairs in other forums. Yet the process from which the EC and EU eventually emerged was always characterised by a degree of remoteness, and it is this tension between civil society participation and elite-centric politics to which we now turn.

The green flags with the white 'E' that activists waved in the early 1950s are long faded and forgotten, while border checkpoints lasted until the mid-1990s before they fell between many EU member states on the basis of the Schengen Agreement (only to be resurrected in places in 2015). So even very recently fences, barbed wire and watch-towers still symbolised the state of the integration process and marked its limits – geographically but also politically, legally and culturally. Lately demonstrations have returned to the borders. While refugee advocates and many civil society groups argue for freedom of movement, others demand tighter security and more border guards. Participation – understood in very general terms as public involvement in political discourse and decision-making processes – has both promoted and constrained the integration process. Even before the Maastricht Treaty of 1992, when the EC was supposedly still supported by a permissive consensus,[6] the relationship between citizens and their Community was often brittle. Consent to the integration process rested on much more fragile foundations than hitherto assumed.

Making Europe

Until well into the twentieth century 'Europe' played little role in most people's lives. It was not an idea or ideal that mobilised masses. Although some fairly solid concepts of 'Europe' had emerged by the second half of the fifteenth century, debates about unifying the continent politically, economically, culturally or socially remained largely restricted to a narrow circle of elites through into the inter-war period.[7] Some of the early modern intellectuals who are today occasionally celebrated as pioneers of European integration in fact remained forgotten for long intervening phases. William Penn's plan for European peace of 1693, for instance, circulated only in small editions and then gathered dust in a handful of libraries for almost two centuries, before it was rediscovered in the late nineteenth century.[8] Immanuel Kant's 'Perpetual Peace' of 1795 was similarly unknown to most people, still less that Kant's philosophy guided their actions.

Only after the horrors of the First World War and the Great Depression did Europe gradually become a meaningful category for broader circles, with ideas about political and economic cooperation entering the mainstream. The proponents of non-hegemonic European cooperation now networked transnationally, more than ever before. But the potential for mobilisation and opportunities for participation remained very limited: Europe was principally a project of elites who neither sought nor found broad public approval. One interesting case in this connection is the Paneuropean Union founded in 1922 by Richard Nikolaus Eijiro, Count of Coudenhove-Kalergi. On the one side, the Paneuropean Union took advantage of the modern means of mass communication and sought to mobilise on a broad footing. Coudenhove-Kalergi himself evoked the spirit of progress in the introduction to his Paneuropean manifesto: 'Europeans! Europeans! Europe's fateful hour strikes!'[9] In reality, however, he was much more interested in cultivating leading aristocrats, politicians and entrepreneurs. Tellingly, one late-1920s brochure devoted much more space to listing the organisation's 'personalities' and 'leading politicians' than to the perspectives and wishes of ordinary members. Accordingly, the Paneuropean Union never claimed more than a couple of thousand members in the whole of Europe.[10] The Union *douanière européenne*, which argued for a Customs Union, remained similarly exclusive.[11] In short, the elitism of most pro-European organisations was more in tune with the customs of the nineteenth century than those of an age of mass participation.

After a burst of pro-European enthusiasm in the first post-war decade, infighting grew as activism declined in the course of the 1930s. Now it was the far right that mobilised the masses.[12] In some countries they also instrumentalised the concept of Europe, although forms of excessive nationalism were almost always uppermost. Even the Nazis co-opted Europe into their propaganda arsenal: in November 1941 Reich foreign minister Joachim von Ribbentrop lauded the 'solidarity of our destiny' with which 'Germans and Italians, Finns and Rumanians, Hungarians and Slovaks, Spanish legionaries and volunteers from many other countries, speaking many tongues' joined together to fight the Soviet Union. They were, he said, a 'shining example of the already existing and constantly growing moral unity of Europe within the New Order that our great leaders have proclaimed and prepared for the future of civilized nations'.[13] Not that this had anything to do with cooperation between equals; the Nazi regime was driven primarily by racism and Aryan superiority. Such statements were propaganda, appealing only to small minorities in Europe.[14] But they do go some way to explaining why post-1945 pro-European slogans – especially when spoken by Germans – sometimes awakened bad memories in other countries.

Arguments for a very different approach emerged among the resistance to 'Hitler's Europe': Europe as the answer to the pre-war crises that had delegitimised established political models. Combat, for a time the most important group within the French Résistance, declared in June 1942: 'In place of a Europe enslaved under the jackboot of a power-crazed Germany, we will join with other nations to build a Europe ruled by laws and united liberty, equality and fraternity'.[15] Hopes of founding a united Europe directly after the war remained unfulfilled. Instead, reconstructing the nation states topped the political agenda; after the Nazi occupation most Europeans valued their national sovereignty even more than before, as examined in greater detail in Chapter 6, 'Superstate or Tool of Nations?' But even if Europe therefore returned to the nation state framework, this involved more than simply restoring the pre-war forms of statehood: the new political orders were now more closely integrated into international structures.

Alongside global and bipolar (bloc-aligned) approaches, various regional models were also discussed for Europe, such as closer cooperation in the North Atlantic region, among the Benelux states or in the context of the Nordic countries. In south-eastern Europe Yugoslav prime minister Josip Broz Tito briefly sought to create a socialist-leaning Balkan federation. While many of these debates built on long-established ideas, they now became tangibly more important.[16]

So that is how European integration grew from one marginal idea among many others into political option number one. In the new atmosphere of the first post-war decade numerous groups campaigned and mobilised for 'more Europe', building on transnational networks forged in the wartime resistance. The Union of European Federalists (UEF), set up in 1946 as an international umbrella organisation, recruited about 100,000 members in eleven Western European countries in its first year. This was a quantum leap compared to the inter-war period. The UEF called for a European federation, to form a regional section of the newly founded United Nations. The federalists wanted a united Europe with broad public support, created in a revolutionary constitutional act. They argued for a radical break with the continent's history and derived their legitimacy from the struggle against the Nazis.[17]

Alongside the UEF, a long list of other organisations were also arguing for closer cooperation. The United Europe Movement (UEM) founded by Winston Churchill in 1947 was particularly prominent. Unlike the UEF, the UEM sought cooperation between nation states and favoured the intergovernmental model over the supranational. Nor did the UEM seek broad public mobilisation, functioning instead more like a nineteenth-century assembly of dignitaries. In many countries individual members were not accepted at all, or only in limited numbers, with the organisation concentrating instead on recruiting prominent figures who also represented other organisations. Elsewhere, as in the United Kingdom, individual membership was allowed – although the UEM's British total never much exceeded 2,500.[18] Alongside UEF and UEM, a multitude of other organisations and groups advocated socialist, conservative/Catholic or primarily economic ideas. Together they covered important sections of political opinion in post-war Western Europe. In other words, there were many contesting ideas, rather than a single concept of Europe.

On top of such obvious distinctions, the various camps were also internally heterogeneous. The UEF, for example, brought together supporters of democratic republicanism with advocates of corporatist concepts. As before 1945, right-wing extremist groups also waved the European banner, for example the German journal *Nation Europa: Monatsschrift im Dienste der europäischen Neuordnung*, founded in 1951 by a former SS-Sturmbannführer. At the European level *Nation Europa* operated in the context of a far right alliance known as the European Social Movement.[19] The concept of Europe is so vague that any conceivable political current was able to claim it. What Europe actually stood for in organisational, political or economic terms thus remained unclear; it was certainly not directly identified with democracy, political unification or any particular economic model.[20] At the same time the debate about 'Europe' was more vigorous than ever before. For the first time the continent became a highly significant political and economic frame for broad sections of society.

In fact, 'Europe' now often meant no more than parts of Western Europe, as the Cold War took its toll in the second half of the 1940s. Initially many activists had hoped for a new beginning for the whole of Europe. One Polish underground newspaper argued in early 1942 for a united Europe comprising several federated regions. From this perspective establishing a 'central and eastern European confederation' was 'a necessary step' towards the overarching goal.[21] Such voices had been stifled by the end of the decade.

Nevertheless, the federalist vision of Europe was more than simply the West in the struggle against the Eastern Bloc. As Dutch activist Hendrik Brugmans noted in 1947: 'European peace policy requires a policy of independence. On both sides.'[22] Many others also sought to strengthen Europe as a 'third force' outside the emerging superpower polarity. Such ideas receded in the course of the late 1940s, squeezed out by the East–West conflict.

Even as the emerging Cold War shrank the Europe that might be unified, it also heightened the urgency of progress. One good indication is a survey initiated by Coudenhove-Kalergi in November 1946 among the approximately 4,300 Western European parliamentarians. Coudenhove-Kalergi asked them simply to say whether or not they supported 'a European Federation within the framework of the U.N.'

Several points about the survey are notable. Firstly, Coudenhove-Kalergi excluded parliaments in the Soviet sphere of influence, as he did not expect free and representative responses from the other side of the emerging East–West divide. That decision was controversial among federalists; some would have preferred to pursue a truly pan-European approach. Coudenhove-Kalergi also omitted Germany, as his initiative fell in the period before the founding of the two German states in 1949. Secondly, the timing of responses is interesting, and would appear in retrospect to justify the decision to exclude the Eastern Bloc: by January 1947 only about 10 per cent of recipients had answered. The number crept up over the following weeks, although interest still remained very modest. Coudenhove-Kalergi was undeterred and wrote again to all deputies who had yet to reply, enclosing interim results of the survey. This second round coincided with the Moscow conference of foreign ministers, which ended without agreement and the Cold War stepped up a notch. This motivated many parliamentarians to reply to Coudenhove-Kalergi after all, bringing the final total to 43 per cent. Thirdly, the result of the survey is interesting: 97 per cent of those who did respond said 'yes', which Coudenhove-Kalergi interpreted as absolute proof of support for a federal Europe. Fourthly, finally, there were significant differences between countries. Agreement was especially strong in Italy and Luxembourg (63 per cent of all recipients in both cases) and in Greece (59 per cent); there was also a majority in the Netherlands (53 per cent). Support was relatively strong in Switzerland (50 per cent), France (49 per cent) and Belgium (42 per cent). The figures in Scandinavia were much lower, with just 9 per cent support in Norway (and 11 per cent against, meaning that most did not answer at all); the figure for the British House of Commons was 28 per cent.[23] Different historical experiences with nation and statehood, international cooperation and external oppression left their mark on the debate. Support in Northern Europe was significantly weaker than in the rest of Western Europe; it was strongest in the states that were soon to join together in the ECSC (as well as Greece and Switzerland, which remained outside). The survey revealed meaningful trends, but these did not determine developments.

All in all, political circumstances explain why 'Europe' came to mean just Western Europe. Global political constellations turned out to be stronger than any preconceived idea about European unification. And even this 'little Europe' still had many gaps. The dictatorships in Spain and Portugal were excluded. In Northern Europe, ideas about Scandinavian regional integration proved more attractive than Western European projects. To that extent civil society engagement always moved within pretty limited geographical bounds.

Engagement and its Limits

Within this shrinking space the scope and intensity of engagement were nonetheless impressive. Alongside the border protest of August 1950 described at the beginning of the chapter, many other pro-European manifestations can be listed: protests at the Italian–French border near Nice in 1953; hundreds of pro-European youth summer camps; thousands of conferences and congresses; 40,000 pro-European demonstrators in Amsterdam in 1948; 520,000 Italian signatures for a united Europe; as well as pro-European publications whose total circulation amounted to millions.[24] Especially in Italy federalism acquired mass movement characteristics.[25]

Alongside these civil society actors, pro-European thinking was anchored in relevant parts of the Western European party-political landscape, including the French, Belgian and Italian socialists or social democrats. The role of the Christian democrats was even more important. For much of the 1950s Christian democrats governed all six states that set up the ECSC (and later the EEC), either on their own or in coalition. As well as promoting federalist goals domestically, these parties also worked closely together at the transnational level. Alongside a multitude of informal contacts, institutionalised networks operated openly and behind the scenes. One example takes us to summer 1954: just weeks after French objections had sunk the European Defence Community, Christian democrats from the ECSC states were holding intense discussions about possible new ventures and considering the idea of horizontal economic integration.[26] For all the differences over details, there was quite a broad consensus within the political class to pursue institutional solutions at a level above that of the classical nation state.

Ultimately, though, the civil society initiatives of the first postwar decade left astonishingly little impact and had scant influence on the emergence of European institutions. The creation of the Council of Europe in 1949 was a disappointment to many federalists, and they were no more enthusiastic about the ECSC or the EEC. Their Europe remained unrealised. Nor were the unification activists able to assert any real influence. The French Council of the European Movement declared in April 1950, shortly after founding of Council of Europe, that 'a cry of alarm must be sounded'. 'Thanks to short-sighted selfishness, vested interests and the timidity of governments', the unanimity principle was suffocating the Council of Europe.[27] This led many of their original supporters to distance themselves from the new emerging institutions. Paul-Henri Spaak, president of the Consultative Assembly of the Council of Europe, was booed and whistled in November 1950 because the new organisation did not go far enough for the several thousand well-dressed young activists.[28]

Figure 5: Students demonstrating in Strasbourg, 1950. Ullstein Bild/Getty Images

It was similar with the ECSC and EC. Italian federalist Altiero Spinelli argued that the Treaties of Rome did not represent true progress; instead they were part of a 'protracted and disappointing spectacle'. The real Europe would not simply appear out of nowhere, he said, so it was positive that in recent years a 'popular political pro-European opposition had emerged'.[29] But that quickly turned out to be an illusion. The eloquent Swiss federalist Denis de Rougement was similarly disappointed; in the EC context he insisted on putting the term *intégration* in scare quotes to clearly differentiate it from *notre idéal fédéraliste*.[30]

So why did these and other activists not enjoy greater influence? Several reasons are relevant: firstly, there were significant problems within the pro-integration camp. In the course of the 1950s the federalists suffered growing financial problems and infighting. The aforementioned Spinelli, for example, preached democracy but practised an authoritarian leadership style that riled many associates. While he stuck to his revolutionary guns, others were willing to adapt to the emerging realities, while a third group strongly dialled back its pro-European engagement. It is, for example, not widely known that until the mid-1940s Hannah Arendt advocated a federalist Europe. But by the end of 1945 she had already come to regard a European 'third force' as unrealistic and turned her back on the idea. At the same time, the steps that had already been taken went too far for the proponents of a strictly intergovernmental model, for example in the ranks of the United Europe Movement. Now, as Europe began to institutionalise, differences between the currents acquired sharper contours. And at the same time it became more difficult to acquire funding for pro-European campaigns, which appeared less urgent to business and political funders in view of the pace of institutional progress.[31]

On top of such organisational and ideological problems came, secondly, the still narrow social base of civil society activism. Although the idea of Europe mobilised considerably more people than in the inter-war period, the movers and shakers came almost exclusively from the upper (in particular educated) middle classes. At a time when only 4 per cent of school leavers went to university,[32] the border protest in 1950, for example, was organised by a transnational student organisation, the Union Fédéraliste Interuniversitaire, most of whose activists were also (male) students.[33] By the end of the decade sections of the federalist current were admitting that they had failed to represent their societies as a whole, and redefining themselves as representatives of the interests of a bourgeois elite.[34] For all these reasons, paradoxically, civil society engagement fell away precisely in the phase in which the precursors of the institutions of today's EU were founded.

This was closely associated, thirdly, with another factor, especially during the first two post-war decades: 'Europe' remained a highly controversial political option. For when it came to structuring a society's international relations, extremely powerful alternatives to European collaboration already existed.[35] The advocates of imperial and colonial models often rejected European integration. This was clearest in the case of the British, and the reason why London withdrew from continental integration efforts from the first half of the 1950s. If Winston Churchill nonetheless argued for a United States of Europe in his famous Zurich speech in 1946, this was a perspective he proposed for others, while 'Great Britain, the British Commonwealth of Nations, mighty America – and, I trust, Soviet Russia' would only serve as 'friends and sponsors'.[36] While some proposed combining empire with European cooperation, as analysed in Chapter 8, 'The Community and its World', the imperial option was frequently understood as the preferable alternative. The same also applied to the true believers in national sovereignty, who were found all along the political spectrum at this time. Of course it is unsurprising to find right-wing conservatives clinging to national autonomy and independence. But initially at least, the German Social Democrats were also sceptical towards Western European integration. In view of Germany's division, party leader Kurt Schumacher (from West Prussia, one of the territories Germany ceded to Poland in 1945) in particular prioritised national unity, while Chancellor Konrad Adenauer (firmly rooted in the western city of Cologne) advocated Western alliances. In the West German Bundestag the SPD voted against the Treaty Establishing the European Coal and Steel Community and against the European Defence Community.[37] In smaller member states, such as the Netherlands, widespread concerns over Franco-German dominance also mitigated against European integration.[38]

But empire and national sovereignty were not the only alternatives to European integration; Western Europe's far left also had other ideas. The French and Italian communists – who at times could rely on respectively just under and just over 30 per cent support – rejected all the early treaties and condemned the Treaties of Rome as a US-led capitalist conspiracy against the European working class and the Soviet Union.[39] Writing about the Treaties of Rome, *L'Humanité*, the central organ of the French Communist Party, emphasised that 'the United States is satisfied, the Vatican too'. From a communist perspective that said it all.[40] There were also free market criticisms that the EC was too protectionist, advocating instead a more globalised option.[41]

All these alternatives to European integration were argued more or less robustly, and some of their justifications overlapped. But altogether, through into the 1960s, European integration remained an exceptionally controversial question to which clear alternatives existed.

The way the integration process became increasingly detached from active public participation as it progressed is reflected especially clearly in the attitudes of young adults. In the early 1950s the young were the stalwarts of pro-European activism, leading the charge in spectacular actions like the storming of the border posts. The European Youth Campaign set up in 1951 brought together roughly 500 youth organisations from seventeen Western European states to work for closer European integration. The youth also played a central symbolic role during this phase, a fresh generation symbolising a new start for society, leaving behind the age of war and nationalism. Until it was wound up at the end of the 1950s after running into funding difficulties, the Youth Campaign proved quite effective.[42]

A good decade later the EC was already a force to be reckoned with in Western Europe. But it had largely lost the youth. Especially for the student movement of 1968, which now saw themselves as society's avant-garde, the integration process was a relatively marginal question. There was plenty of discussion about Europe, but almost none about the EC. There were also great differences of habitus to the activists of the first generation. Jeanette Luthi, the twenty-three-year-old student from Berne whose simulated fainting launched the German-French direct action in 1950, was a dapper and well-groomed young woman in a white blouse.[43] The student activists of 1968 and even more so those of the 1970s would have regarded her as the epitome of bourgeois conventionality. Many did see something positive in the Community, though: it ended the nation-centred phase of capitalism.[44] Tariq Ali, for example, a prominent left-wing leader of the British student movement, supported the UK's accession to the EC in 1972 on the grounds that this would accelerate the crisis of British capitalism and finally open the way for revolution from below.[45] This interpretation of Marxist crisis theory attributed the EC a walk-on role in the demise of capitalism; it never represented a positive point of reference. For most of the younger generation, their relationship with the EC was a non-relationship: the EC figured neither as a serious adversary nor as a crystallisation point for great hopes. In 1958 Walter Hallstein described the EC as a 'zoon politikon', a political animal; soon he was speaking for just a small minority of Europeans.[46]

This public disinterest contrasts to some extent with developments at the ideological and party-political levels where – in comparison to the first two post-war decades – the rivalry between European integration and alternative models faded from the late 1960s and especially the 1970s. As decolonisation swept the Global South the imperial option looked increasingly implausible. The influence of the nation-fixated far right also dwindled and Western Europe's Communist parties now showed increasing openness to the EC, welcoming some of its new political initiatives and starting to regard it as an alternative to dependency on the United States. All in all, the 'EC option' became less controversial during the second half of the Cold War – which does not mean it was of any special interest to its citizens.[47]

By now civil society engagement for Europe had sought other channels, with a string of transnational forums operating outside of the EC context. One such was the Centre Européen de Documentation et d'Information, a conservative elite circle working largely behind the scenes. Its activities occasionally coincided with those of the EC, but it also pursued very different priorities and connections, with the Franco regime in Spain playing a central role, for example.[48] Pro-European democratic values played a more prominent part in the town twinning movement. Building on early initiatives in the inter-war period, twinning was crucial in enabling and institutionalising contacts at the local level. Here again, this was a Europe not identical with the EC: in the first post-1945 phase, for example, West German towns twinned primarily with counterparts in Switzerland, the United States and the United Kingdom; continental Western Europe only figured significantly from the 1950s while partnerships with Eastern Europe took off in the second half of the 1970s. Much of this played out purely at the local level, through regional cross-border initiatives, or later at the state level. In terms of Western European organisations, the Council of Europe was for a long time more important than the EC in this field. While relations between wartime enemies were often slow to warm at the official level, close informal contacts were already developing in the 1950s through initiatives such as youth programmes. For example Colombes in France and Frankenthal in West Germany conducted a youth exchange for some years before concluding a formal twinning arrangement in 1958.[49]

Transnational exchange and Europeanisation outside the EC context were also enabled by Eurail, founded in 1959 by a group of European railway operators – not least in response to pressure from the European Youth Campaign. Its Interrail pass introduced in 1972 boosted international youth travel and tourism at a point where backpacking had already become a mass phenomenon. As well as adventure and self-discovery, international understanding was also a motivation. The Europe of Interrail was always larger than the EC. In 1972 – its first year, when 88,000 young Europeans bought an Interrail ticket – Yugoslavia was already on board. By 1979 the figure was 229,000, not counting thousands of young travellers from outside Europe using Eurail passes as well those travelling internationally on ordinary train tickets, by car, on foot and increasingly also by plane.[50]

It was not until the 1980s that the EC launched major international mobility initiatives of its own, such as the Erasmus student exchange programme and the Schengen Agreement – neither of which were to unfold their full effect until the 1990s.[51] In other words, the Europe of civil society engagement, of transnational contact and exchange, was a world apart from the EC institutions – and when the EC did intervene more actively it built on structures already created 'from below'. It was not the pioneer or foundation of civil society exchange between member states. This finding also reflects the composition of the member states. A significant proportion of early holiday travel was to Spain and to some extent Scandinavia, and thus to destinations that were not at the time members of the EC. Not until they joined the EC did the geography of international vacations become more closely aligned with the territory of the Community.

To summarise, the beginnings of the integration processes were not characterised solely by the interest of political and economic elites in reconstructing the European nation states, where integration was understood primarily as an economic instrument.[52] Instead civil society circles also demanded more Europe – and for reasons that were often more political and idealistic than those of the heads of state and government. But this never involved more than a small section of European civil society, and especially in the first two post-war decades the 'choice for Europe' was hotly contested.[53] The EC did not become the dominant forum for civil society contact and exchange between the member states and Western European countries more generally; instead such activities remained distributed across many channels.

At the same time, what Europeans wanted from Europe remained vague. Peace, security and economic growth are discussed in other chapters; the wish for greater mobility applied only to certain groups (especially in Italy because of the difficult labour market situation there). For most people, however, their own region or nation state remained the principal point of reference for education, training and work, and for questions of social participation and identity. At the same time transnational networking proceeded outside the EC framework, in initiatives like Eurail and town twinning. Altogether international civil society engagement concentrated on different crystallisation points than the European Community. This applied to peace groups as well as trade union work, religious engagement, the women's movement and human rights organisations – and from the 1960s also, for example, Third World groups and the environmental movements. Citizens in Western Europe were anything but passive, but their activity was directed into forums other than the EC.[54]

Technocratic Internationalism

So why was civil society engagement not more closely meshed with the new European institutions? As well as the reasons already mentioned, which relate primarily to the home-grown problems of the early Europe activists and their alternative models, this also has to do with an essential characteristic of the European integration process: its technocratic slant.

The concept of technocracy rose to prominence after the First World War, when the US sociologist Thorstein Veblen proposed that engineers would run the machinery of the state better than politicians.[55] A trend towards placing complex problems in the hands of experts had already emerged in the nineteenth century. This applied especially to issues at the international level and represented an alternative to classical diplomacy. That approach has been pertinently characterised as technocratic internationalism. This form of international cooperation relied on non-state transnational expert bodies and international organisations; it prioritised rational planning, efficiency and belief in progress. One prominent inter-war period technocrat described how he was 'struck by the logic of treating the production and distribution of wealth as an engineering problem'.[56] This model thus claimed to be superior to political process, democratic control and public participation.[57]

That said, technocrats were by no means unpolitical. While their spirit and self-image often were, the same cannot be said of their motives. Even in the nineteenth century they tied transnational infrastructure projects such as cross-border railway and telegraph networks to an explicitly pro-European course. In the inter-war period the Italian engineer Piero Puricelli argued for an all-European motorway network and injected his ideas into discussions – in the context of the League of Nations – revolving around reconciliation in Europe.[58] Such experiences were more influential for the EU than the philosophical lineage of thinkers like William Penn and Immanuel Kant.

Robert Schuman's famous Declaration and the road to the ECSC already possessed a strong technocratic moment. One reason why the speech by the French foreign minister on 9 May 1950 made waves was the absence of preparatory public discussion. Jean Monnet and a small group of staff had drafted the proposal for communitising coal and steel in secret; even the French cabinet only learned of it on the morning of 9 May. Schuman gave advance warning only to US secretary of state Dean Acheson and German chancellor Konrad

Adenauer, who just managed to inform his cabinet before Schuman gave his speech. In this respect the approach resembled classical cabinet politics where foreign policy is conducted without the participation of parliament. Schuman's original proposal was also technocratic in the sense that it relied heavily on expert-driven action and took up where the anti-liberal corporatist debates of the 1930s had left off. Monnet imagined a strong independent secretariat working closely with experts from the national ministries and establishing a depoliticised space where the experts could identify optimal solutions free of the constraints of everyday politics. Correspondingly, the original proposal had no parliamentary representation at the European level; this was only added after public pressure.[59]

In the subsequent phase too, Monnet, Schuman and Adenauer largely bypassed the parliaments. Only after the ECSC Treaty had been signed were the national parliaments asked to consider it.[60] And there was certainly no concept of involving wider civil society. Eugen Kogon, as one of the most prominent West German post-war federalists, warned in autumn 1950 that 'supranational hyper-bureaucracies' could develop within the ECSC and that it would be difficult to exercise parliamentary control.[61]

For men like Monnet – official Europe policy at that time being largely the prerogative of men of middle and advanced years – efficiency and outcome counted for more than democratic legitimacy or civil society participation. Much as the EC claimed to represent a completely new start, it stood in fact for an elitist understanding of politics and continuity with the manner in which economic and other questions of a technical nature had been regulated in Europe since the nineteenth century. Under this paternalistic and technocratic understanding of politics, decisions were best left to experts. Europe appeared both too important and too controversial for it to be left to the caprices of a fickle public.

In other words, the EC was born technocratic. And remained so, as seen in the work of the European Court of Justice: the discussions and votes leading to its majority rulings are always confidential, and judges are not permitted to publish dissenting opinions. In this respect the Court of Justice rejects the principle of judicial transparency that applies in many member states and in many aspects of international law. Already in 1960 the decisive German commentary on EEC law noted that the treaty had with good reason maintained the principle of absolute confidentiality already laid down in the ECSC Treaty.[62] The idea was to minimise pressure on the Court, for example from a judge's home country. Its rulings were to be monolithic and depoliticised, originating from the unassailable sphere of expertise. Since the 1950s there have been repeated initiatives to shake up and democratise the EU's legal system, but nothing has changed.[63] For decades the Court has also refused to open up its archives.[64]

This background was especially relevant as the Court of Justice frequently issued rulings of immense significance. The Treaties of Rome did not specifically state that the EC would have its own legal order overriding that of its member states: but it was only six years before the Court broke the accustomed bounds of international law, principally through the *van Gend & Loos* judgment. Another year on, in 1964, *Costa* v. *ENEL* created the doctrine giving Community law absolute precedence over the laws of the member states. Since then European law can override national law. Those were just two of the Court's most consequential rulings, which deepened integration more strongly than almost any single decision of the Commission or the Council of Ministers. Here experts decide how the Community is to be governed.[65] Citizen-orientated and directly democratically legitimised it is not. At the same time the achievements always remained fragile. In 1965, during the Empty Chair Crisis, core elements of the Treaties of Rome were up for debate. But even in this discussion and the process leading to the Luxembourg compromise, the opinions of the EC's citizens went unheard.[66]

In some cases the technocratic moment was amplified by outright mistrust. In post-1945 Germany, for example, Chancellor Adenauer – who had been driven out of office by the Nazis in 1933 – was understandably sceptical about the views of his own populace. But he also regarded the opposition SPD as notoriously unreliable. So the consultations over the Treaties of Rome largely bypassed parliament, even forcing the SPD to acquire information on the state of negotiations by circuitous routes, often via its European sister parties.[67] For the chancellor Europe was too important to risk major public debates.

The technocratic moment was quickly rationalised and legitimised by scientific research. Ernst B. Haas, German-American political scientist and groundbreaking early integration researcher, wrote: 'The emphasis on elites in the study of integration derives its justification from the bureaucratised nature of European organisations of long standing, in which basic decisions are made by the leadership, sometimes over the opposition and usually over the indifference of the general membership'.[68] So Haas and others lent normative legitimation to the actual; science gave the status quo its seal of approval.

Parts of the European Commission demonstrated rather more awareness. Even before the 1968 protests the Commission had expressed concern over growing disinterest among young people. Its response at the same time was symptomatic: in June 1967 it appointed a group of experts to analyse the attitudes of adolescents and young adults and investigate which media they used.[69] In the utterly transformed political climate of 1970 the Commission did organise a meeting with representatives of youth organisations – but excluded the radical left.[70] To that extent the approach to the problem and proposals for addressing it remained highly technocratic.

Of course the technocratic tendency was never absolute. There were always strong countervailing impulses. The supposedly apolitical experts in the High Authority of the ECSC acquired a strong counterweight in the guise of the Council of Ministers (requested above all by the Benelux states) and other forums.[71] And civil society critique was never silenced. In 1960, for example, the Dutch trade union leader Harm Buiter castigated the 'European technocracy' for requiring no more than 'an annual report to a select group of shareholders' rather than submitting to parliamentary control.[72] Especially harsh criticism from quite a different direction came a few years later when Charles de Gaulle called the Commission 'a technocracy, for the most part foreign, destined to infringe upon France's democracy in settling problems that dictate the very existence of our country'.[73] But even the moderate youth representatives at the 1970 meeting with the Commission insisted that the EC needed to reinvent itself if it was to offer a basis for real democracy.[74]

And there were certainly moves to seek openings for such a reinvention. The European Defence Community – had it succeeded – would have tangibly strengthened the parliamentary dimension.[75] And the European Parliament acquired growing clout over time. Even before the first direct elections in 1979 it was already more than a paper tiger. After 1979 it addressed the question of the EC's democratic legitimacy in depth, alongside concrete proposals on specific policy areas. More important than the institutional mechanisms were the actions of particular individuals who ensured that such questions remained on the agenda. One was the Dutch socialist Henk Vredeling, who bombarded Commission and Council with hundreds of written questions, and as such indirectly won Parliament a right of consultation. His nickname 'Vrageling' – from the Dutch *vragen* for 'to query' – was well earned.[76]

At the same time the limits to these developments should not be overlooked. If Vrageling and other MEPs succeeded in putting important questions on the EC's agenda, the effects were generally limited to the inner workings of the EC, remote from the highly visible public debates and major negotiations. A labour of Hercules, assigned to ordinary mortals. And that is why it is only the most recent research that underlines the importance of this dimension of the EC.[77] The introduction of direct elections to the European Parliament in 1979 also helped a little to bridge the gap between the Community and its citizens. But European elections still did not have the purpose of shaping and legitimising the EC's politics. Even if the European Parliament possessed certain powers analogous to those of national parliaments, it lacked the most important dimension associated with parliamentary democracy: even after 1979, the composition of the European Parliament still had no influence on the composition of the executive. Even after the introduction of direct elections in 1979, the contest still remained first and foremost a popularity test for national governments and was treated with concomitant disinterest by voters – as the turnout figures confirm.[78] Changes in the European Parliament expanded its formal democratic control of the EC and its institutions, but did little to improve its public image and legitimacy in the member states. The EC retained its technocratic aspect, creating an open flank for its critics that it was never able to completely close in the course of the following decades.[79]

EC as Adiaphoron

All this explains why the integration process left so many hearts and minds behind as it progressed. At first glance it might seem astonishing that approval ratings were so consistently high. In 1950, for example, a survey in twelve Western European states found 63 per cent support for the objective of European integration; in the six EC member states in 1970 it reached 87 per cent.[80] Even in later years the figure remained consistently above 60 per cent, although with tangible differences between member states. European integration was (and still is) always viewed through the filters of national and subnational cultures, alongside factors such as education, social class, age cohort and gender.[81] This is especially well researched for the phase since 1973, when the EC began conducting its own systematic opinion surveys.[82]

Knowledge of and interest in the European institutionalisation process, on the other hand, was considerably weaker. For example, most of the population responded with disinterest to the Treaties of Rome, which from today's perspective represented a quantum leap for European integration. In West Germany, according to a survey in January 1957, only 49 per cent had even heard of the 'Common Market' and the 'European Economic Community'. And only 17 per cent were able to give correct answers when asked what the terms meant. In January 1958 the corresponding figures were 56 and 21 per cent. Now, only 28 per cent were certain that the treaty in question had already been signed. West Germany was not alone in its ignorance: matters were not much better elsewhere. In France in May 1957 only 23 per cent were able to say what Euratom was, even though the French government was especially keen to establish a Community for the peaceful use of nuclear power.[83]

A survey in 1962 confirmed that strong approval need not necessarily correlate with knowledge: many people fundamentally liked 'the idea of European unification' but as soon as discussion turned to details their opinions became very vague. When asked to name concrete effects of the EC, 77 per cent of Italians were unable to name anything concretely positive, while nobody at all named anything negative. In Belgium, France and West Germany the corresponding figures were 59:97, 60:93 and 60:84 per cent.[84] By the end of the decade, when the Commission conducted a comprehensive survey, the situation was little better: 87 per cent approved more or less strongly of the integration process (27 per cent very strongly) but only 36 per cent were able to correctly name the six member states.[85] So saying 'yes' to 'Europe' did not mean knowing even the most basic of facts about the EC.

Approval was thus often no more than lip-service. People supported the integration process as long as it remained abstract and had little impact on their everyday lives. As soon as matters became concrete, approval ratings fell significantly. Nothing illustrates this better than surveys in the Netherlands, France, the United Kingdom and West Germany in the early 1960s. Again large majorities everywhere fundamentally supported European integration. But when asked about specific measures the figures often dropped by 10 to 20 percentage points – and were most consistent in the United Kingdom of all places (at that time an accession candidate).

'Negative' integration in the area of the economy – in other words dismantling of trade barriers – was one of the most popular concrete measures. Integration steps involving social redistribution and communitisation of foreign policy were less popular, even if they still commanded majority approval in many countries in this phase.

These trends continued in later years. If we consider the last decade before the Maastricht Treaty, there are several relevant findings. Firstly that the nominal support for the integration process remained consistently high,

Table 3 Approval for European integration (per cent)

	Netherlands	France	West Germany	United Kingdom
Adult Attitudes, 1962				
Overall Support	87	72	81	65
'Abolish Tariffs?'	79 −8	72 +/− 0	71 −10	70 +5
'Free Movement of Labour and Businesses?'	76 −11	57 −15	64 −17	52 −13
'Common Foreign Policy'	67 −20	50 −22	60 −21	41 −24
'Use "Our" Taxes to Aid Poorer European Countries?'	70 −17	43 −29	52 −29	63 −2
Youth Attitudes (13–19 Years), 1964–1965				
Overall Support	95	93	95	72
'Abolish Tariffs?'	87 −8	83 −10	89 −6	74 +2
'Free Movement of Labour and Businesses?'	64 −31	65 −28	75 −20	65 −7
'Common Foreign Policy'	80 −15	71 −22	74 −21	56 −16
'Use "Our" Taxes to Aid Poorer European Countries?'	82 −13	68 −25	72 −23	57 −15

After Inglehart, 'An End to European Integration?', pp. 91–105, who shows less interest in the differences.

although certain fluctuations can be identified and – more importantly – there was no clear upward trend across the period as a whole. The EC was not an immediate success snowballing popular support as it grew and developed. For that the EC would have had to develop more strongly into a transnational community-building forum.

The strong approval rates are notable nonetheless, if we remember that during this phase the EC grew from the original six to nine members (1973: United Kingdom, Ireland, Denmark), then ten (1981: Greece) and finally twelve (1986: Spain and Portugal) – and then acquired another sixteen million citizens in 1990 after German unification. That applies all the more given the

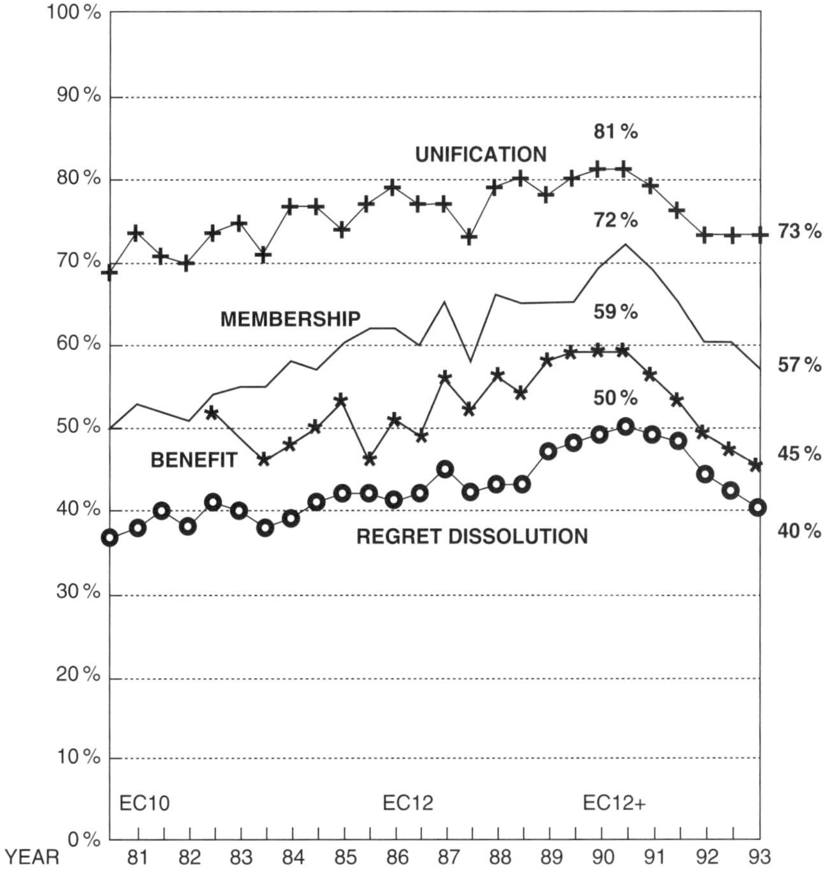

Figure 6: Support for European unification and for the EC, 1981–1993. Beck Publishers, based on *Eurobarometer* (40), 1993, p. 3

multitude of economic problems plaguing the member states from the early 1970s.

Secondly, it is conspicuous that there were striking gaps in this phase between general approval of European unification, approval of the interviewees' own country's membership, and personal affinity to the EC. The discrepancy was especially large between abstract support for integration on the one hand and concrete support for the EC on the other, as revealed by the crucial question of regret over its possible failure. If we examine this question at the level of the member states, the difference between the two figures was between 25 and 35 per cent in most countries across the period as a whole. Despite differences of degree, citizens everywhere identified considerably less with the EC than with the abstract objective of European unification.[86]

Two US political scientists, Leon N. Lindberg and Stuart A. Scheingold, interpreted this overall picture in 1970 as a permissive consensus, transposing a concept developed in US election research to the EC. The Community, they wrote, was 'a creature of elites': approval was widespread but not deeply rooted.[87] And they insisted upon this interpretation right through to the Maastricht Treaty.

In fact the relationship between citizens and the EC remained primarily a non-relationship. The Stoic philosophers of ancient Greece would have called the EC an adiaphoron, 'a matter having no moral merit or demerit'.[88] For all the support for 'Europe', that was the attitude of the overwhelming majority about the EC during the Cold War – and that perspective has repercussions to this day.

The EC as adiaphoron is also reflected in the targeting of public protests, which at that time rarely addressed the Community. During the period after 1984, for which systematic data is available, less than 10 per cent of public protests targeted the EC, more or less across the board. That was to change sharply in the late 1990s and even more after the turn of the century.[89] Not good, not bad – and not especially interesting: that is how most citizens in the member states (although not farmers) saw the EC, while they were much more interested in their own country's politics.

Such statistics never simply map social reality, but always also play a part in shaping it. This is true at multiple levels. From 1962 the European Commission conducted its own occasional surveys (which had previously been carried out by private institutes or national agencies, with some of the earliest studies even commissioned by the United

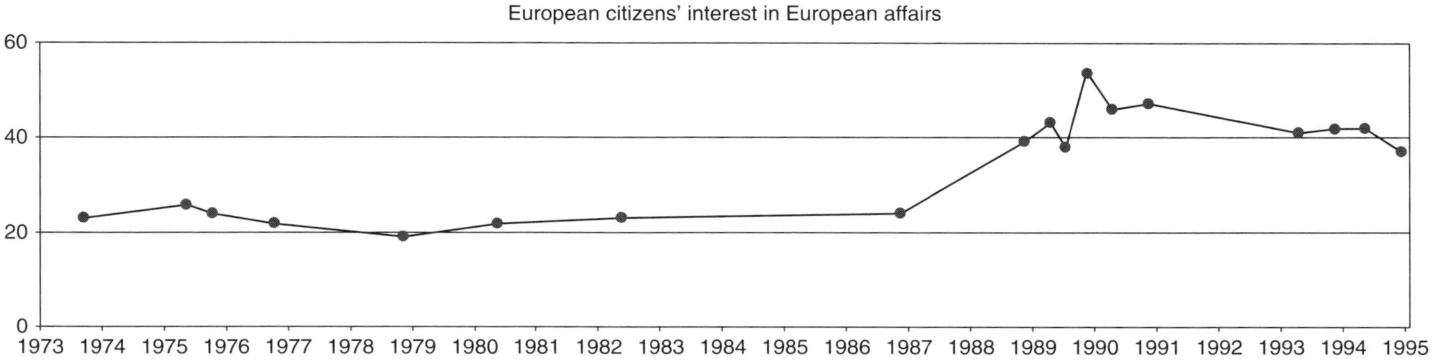

Figure 7: European citizens' interest in European affairs (in per cent). Beck Publishers, based on European Commission, *35 Years of Eurobarometer*, p. 13

States Information Agency).[90] As such the EC created its own direct opposite number in the population. Additionally, the surveys were never designed only to analyse but also to influence. By the 1950s statisticians were already correlating approval for the integration process with level of knowledge. This assumption of causality has driven the EC's information policy ever since.[91] In the process, criticism and disinterest were neutralised as communication deficits in a not always justifiable leap that persists to this day.[92] Strong approval rates were also instrumentalised to legitimise the integration process, including its technocratic aspects. The surveys often also possessed a prospective element, frequently asking what citizens thought about further integration steps. For example, at the end of the 1960s they wanted to know what people thought about establishing a European army, a shared currency and direct elections to the European Parliament.[93] Good results could be interpreted as a mandate to disseminate new proposals. In this way surveys became tools of information, evaluation – and power.[94]

Europe vs. EC

As integration progressed the question of what respondents meant when they spoke for or against 'Europe' or 'European unification' became increasingly pressing. The latter term was used for the Commission's Eurobarometer surveys, and is notable for its vagueness. It differs meaningfully from the comparably clear objective of a European federation, about which Coudenhove-Kalergi had enquired in 1946/47. Other early surveys also specified the form of collaboration more clearly. If the EC remained an adiaphoron during the Cold War, its concrete meaning also blurred. 'Unification' could also mean EFTA as a rival to the EC, or in early surveys even an all-European reconciliation encompassing East and West.[95] In such a situation the leading pollsters of the age had to console themselves with the idea that the datum of pro-European attitude was a 'floating referent' – without admitting that this significantly reduced the reliability and informative value of the surveys.[96]

The already low figures for interest in 'European affairs' need to be read in this light: they would probably have been even lower if the question had been worded more precisely to ask about EC/EU. The EC was never the whole of Europe back then, just as the EU is not today, and it never succeeded in monopolising the concept entirely. This terminological imprecision also made it so difficult to interpret pro-

European statements in surveys, simply because it remained unclear to which form of association they were referring. And if the question was repeated over a span of decades, this suggested greater support for 'Europe' than actually existed. That might in fact explain why such a nebulous term was chosen. At the same time its use succeeded in more strongly sidelining the alternatives: the liberal criticism was neutralised because the term 'European unification' says nothing unequivocal about openness or protectionism; nationalist objections were too, because the term (unlike 'federation') does not automatically imply supranationality as the guiding principle and is therefore understood as less of a challenge. Global historical shifts also overtook the empire models and the same increasingly applied to communism, whose pull evaporated over the decades while the EC increasingly appeared positioned to bring peace and order to both North–South and East–West relations. And the more open term had the advantage that it could also cover all the multitude of other forms of civil society contact and international cooperation independent of the EC, which citizens had often grown to appreciate more than the institutions of the European Community.

Bypassing the People?

The snapshot moments when voters are called to the polls also demonstrate how approval for the EU and its precursors always remained more fragile than generally assumed – and than suggested by the concept of the permissive consensus. But first of all, it is striking how rarely that occurred before the Treaty of Maastricht: many of the shifts in the integration process discussed during this period were never laid before the populations of the member states. That applied to the British accession applications in the 1960s, the Luxembourg compromise of 1966, and the establishment of the European Political Cooperation four years later. Nor were significant Community initiatives in areas like monetary, environmental and cultural policy, or the stronger orientation on human rights, since 1970s ever put to a vote. Here again we see the technocratic element.

There were, however, parliamentary votes and referendums over various membership applications and on the Single European Act. The results were not always in favour of further integration, although most referendums and parliamentary votes in the period before the Maastricht

Treaty did produce clear majorities for the EC. That applies to the referendums held in 1972 on the first enlargement round in France (68 per cent), Ireland (83 per cent) and Denmark (63 per cent), and to the British membership referendum in 1975 (67 per cent) as well as the Danish and Irish referendums on the Single European Act in 1986/87 (56 and 70 per cent respectively). But there are also important exceptions. In 1954 the French National Assembly voted by a clear 319 to 264 to reject the European Defence Community. Integration research to date has interpreted this as a unique defeat, but that is not entirely correct. A last-minute Norwegian referendum in 1972 – after the entire accession treaty had already been negotiated – rejected EC membership by 53.5 per cent. Ten years later Greenland voted to leave the EC by a margin of 52 to 48 per - cent.[97] And while the Irish referendum ratifying the Single European Act appeared clear-cut, the complex backstory involved first amending the Irish constitution to accommodate the EC's new structures.[98]

Attitudes remained particularly critical in a number of states that were not among the original six founding members, a fact reflected in surveys even more clearly than in formal ballots. In 1973, for example, only 37 per cent of the British supported European unification, although the figure rose for a spell in subsequent years. In spring 1981 just 24 per cent took a positive view of EC membership; in Denmark the value was 30 per cent and in Greece 42 per cent. Between 1982 and 1985 approval rose noticeably (United Kingdom: 35 per cent; Denmark: 37 per cent; Greece: 47 per cent). In Portugal in 1978, shortly after the formal membership application, 60 per cent were unable to say whether EC membership was important for their country's economy.[99] Altogether these figures underline how fragile support for the EC was in some places, even in the 1970s.[100]

But dissatisfaction remained largely invisible because citizens were so rarely permitted to vote on important EC matters. Because – as described above – many knew very little about the Community and showed little interest, it was comparatively easy to mobilise powerful forces against it. The EC suffered defeats especially where – as in Norway 1972 – the pro-EC camp was overoptimistic and lacked prominent campaign leaders, while the opposition was better organised.[101] The EC could quickly crumble from adiaphoron to object of diverse and often diffuse fears, which frequently had more to do with internal social and political conflicts than concrete questions pertaining to the European Community. This kind of criticism not only prevented further integration moves,[102] but also had the potential to call into question the status quo.

So it came as a complete shock to the Danish establishment and the EC elites when a narrow majority of 50.7 per cent voted on 2 June 1992 against ratifying the Maastricht Treaty. The heads of state and government of the other member states were deeply disappointed and dismayed; only British ex-prime minister Margaret Thatcher congratulated the Danes on the result.[103] In the research this defeat for the pro-EC camp, along with the slimness of the French referendum majority (51.1 per cent) and the knife-edge ratification in the United Kingdom, is frequently regarded as a turning point. In the end the treaty came into effect in 1993 after Denmark was granted extensive opt-outs. It was certainly a turning point to the extent that public criticism of the integration process assumed previously unknown dimensions. As the discussion thus far demonstrates, however, the dissatisfaction this reflected was nothing new and in no sense the first break with a decades-old permissive consensus. But it was the first time that discontent had immediate political consequences, and highlights at the same time a fundamental problem of the integration process: while it was not realised against the explicit will of the majority it certainly did proceed in some isolation from forms of direct participation and with little democratic participation and control. And moreover, it occurred without the active participation and control of viable majorities in the countries involved.

Participation and Technocracy: Résumé

Altogether post-war European integration was driven by many motors. What was realised institutionally was primarily a project of the elites. Even if some of the few parliamentary votes and referendums held over EC matters during the Cold War achieved fantastic results, attitudes towards the integration process – even before the Maastricht Treaty – were much less robust than had long been believed. The idea of Europe shot to prominence in the 1940s and a multitude of groups propagated their unification proposals. But most of these organisations remained modest in size and were largely populated by the elites. Paradoxically, civil society engagement levelled off precisely during the phase when the EC became institutional reality.

During the post-war decades the EC remained an adiaphoron: no bearer of great passions, although no longer just one international organisation like any other, either. The reasons for this include the Community's economic focus, its technocratic aspect and its remoteness from everyday life. At the same time many people preferred to become involved in other things than the affairs of the EC, for example, in youth exchange programmes, town twinning or Interrailing around the continent and other forms of transnational tourism. For important questions that the public had in relation to Europe, the EC at the time offered no answers and no platform for civil society engagement.[104]

European cooperation EC style was based more on toleration than on genuine approval. Integration remained most popular where it had few tangible consequences for people's own lives. Citizens put up with technocratic aspects and were happy as long as they were otherwise left in peace; their attitude towards the EC was consumptive rather than active. Detachment from the citizenry was a central element of the integration process, notwithstanding the introduction of rudimentary European civil rights in the pre-Maastricht phase (which went largely unnoticed at the time).[105]

A third phase began in the 1980s, where disinterest remained widespread but scepticism at least occasionally generated sharper polarisation and criticism. That was seen, for example, in the United Kingdom, in Greece and Greenland, and in the early 1990s in Denmark.

At the same time it would be false to place the blame for the EC's technocratic tendencies on 'power-mad Eurocrats' in the European Commission. Frequently it was the member states that blocked greater accessibility, whether in the form of more direct participation or more democratic control. For example if Charles de Gaulle criticised Brussels as a technocratic behemoth that did not mean he had any interest in further curtailing national sovereignty by enabling more direct participation, civil society engagement and democratic control. Moreover his line on Europe was by no means always backed by clear majorities: surveys in France in the course of the 1960s showed a consistent majority for British membership. That did not stop de Gaulle from twice using his veto against enlargement.[106] In general terms many national politicians preferred to keep the EC at arm's length; to claim the credit for successes in the integration processes while blaming Europe for any problems. Brussels was painted black in order to allow the nation state to shine. That was also down to the media, which often paid little attention to the integration process. But at least when important decisions were on the table the press did report attentively, and occasional rudiments of a European public sphere did emerge during the Cold War. A pro-EC perspective predominated in most of the leading media.[107] That makes the public disinterest and the political duplicity of many national politicians all the more problematic. All in all the Community remained a blank on the radar of political attention and projection for most citizens. This also explains why the EU – despite many attempts (especially since the 1990s) to increase democratic legitimacy and opportunities for participation – retains a strongly technocratic element to this day.

5 VALUES AND NORMS

Valéry Giscard d'Estaing was an educated man, a product of some of France's best schools who had risen to become French president. In 2002, now in his seventies but sharp as ever, he was chosen as president of the European Convention. After neither the Maastricht Treaty nor the subsequent treaties of Amsterdam (1997) and Nice (2001) had succeeded in placing the EU on a new permanent footing, the Convention was expected to do so by preparing a constitutional treaty for the European Union. It was also the Convention's presidium under Giscard d'Estaing that proposed a quote to introduce the preamble and ensured that it remained in the official draft of the treaty; Giscard d'Estaing insisted personally. The passage in question delved deep into the treasury of classical education, quoting Thucydides in the original ancient Greek and in the respective languages of the member states: 'Our Constitution ... is called a democracy because power is in the hands not of a minority but of the greatest number.'[1]

This passage – along with the entire document – is already long-forgotten, the European Constitutional Treaty rejected in French and Dutch referendums in 2005 and replaced a few years later by the Treaty of Lisbon. Nonetheless, the Thucydides quote, where the Greek historian reports parts of Pericles' famous Funeral Oration, is interesting for two reasons. Firstly, these words from the fifth century BCE do poor service to a modern understanding of democracy, which represents a great deal more than the rule of the majority. A modern democracy is bound by checks and balances, fundamental rights and minority protections instituted to prevent 'government by the people' turning into the tyranny of the majority. It should also be noted that the *demos* of Pericles' time, the citizens entitled to vote, included neither women, nor resident foreigners, nor slaves. In other words, the concept of the majority in fact excluded most of the population.[2] Some scholars also suggest that Thucydides actually regarded the definition of democracy he attributed to Pericles as nothing but dangerous propaganda; elsewhere he describes Pericles' style of government as 'a government of the principal man'.[3] That would suggest that Pericles was merely adorning himself with the trappings of democracy. Either way, the quote is hardly an edifying testimonial to the continent's glorious past. Giscard d'Estaing's choice of quote was no more successful than the Convention altogether.[4]

In another respect the Thucydides quote points to a conflict that flared up over the preamble and led to the classical reference being dropped from the draft in summer 2004 under the Irish Council presidency, about a year before the European Constitutional Treaty was buried for good. The document generated a lively debate over the EU's values and norms. For example, there was controversy over whether there should be any reference to God, as demanded not only by the Churches, but also the Polish, Irish and Italian governments. Giscard rejected this in line with French secular tradition, and others also voiced grave reservations.[5] In the end it was agreed that the preamble would just include a general reference to 'the cultural, religious and humanist inheritance of Europe' and to 'the values underlying humanism: equality of persons, freedom, respect for reason'.[6] There was much haggling over the list; attempts to add 'respect for ... belief' or 'solidarity' to it were ultimately rejected.[7]

What the controversy reveals is that the stock formulations describing the EU as a 'community of values' or 'normative power' paper over a long history of conflicts about precisely these questions.[8] When it was created in the 1950s the EC was certainly not yet describing itself as a community of values. It frequently found it difficult to define its values and norms – and even harder to stand by them. This is reflected in the priority (not) accorded to democracy, but also in the treatment of civil rights in the sense of the individual's rights vis-à-vis the state, where a contemporary definition would, for example, add gender equality to the classical physical integrity and freedoms of belief, conscience and speech. Similar complications are found in the history of the EC's relationship to human rights. These overlap with the civil rights, but apply to all human beings, as opposed to just the citizens of a country. Neither category is static, as rights are subject to processes of historical change.[9] For example just a few decades ago sexual self-determination was not on the list of generally accepted civil and human rights. And when the EC began anchoring and protecting rights in the course of the 1970s, it addressed only a selection of the range of possibilities; in light of its scope and powers that principally meant economic rights.[10] But institutionally this was still a great leap forward for the EC. Now it was not only regulating or overseeing civil rights within its member states, but also their application to the EC itself and a number of closely associated third parties. This took the EC into realms untrodden by normal international organisations.

That does not mean that values and norms played no role in earlier stages of the integration process. At the beginning of the 1950s these questions were already hotly debated, and the value-orientation is clearly reflected in the way European integration was very much understood as a contribution to securing peace.[11] To that extent, the European project is actually inconceivable without the values that grounded and legitimised it; values and norms shaped the EC's institutions and informal practices at very fundamental levels. But without a legally binding framework they initially remained fragile and vulnerable. And legally anchored civil and human rights and democratic guarantees were not the foundation upon which institutional cooperation was built. Instead these sneaked in by the back door. Especially in the early days the centrality of values was by no means obvious, and certainly contested. The search for a specific institutional ethos only really became significant in the course of the 1970s,[12] not least in order to consolidate the integration already achieved and guarantee the force of EC law, but also to expand the legitimacy of the integration process. To that extent the line on values was astonishingly instrumental. Today's EU was definitely not born as a community of values; instead it grew into one in a fascinating, decades-long process characterised by ambivalence and contradiction. The process was driven by the relationship to national courts and at EC level to the European Court of Justice and with certain caveats the European Parliament. But even more than interaction with the member states or rulings of the ECJ, it was the relationship to a specific group of third states that for a long time shaped the course of developments. While the literature often analyses these two strands separately (and frequently concentrates on civil rights without giving equal attention to the question of democracy), in the following we will bring together both these dimensions in all their facets.

Division of Labour as the Starting Point

In the post-war division of labour among international organisations in Western Europe, responsibility for civil and human rights fell in the first place to the Council of Europe. One of its purposes was to protect citizens from possible abuses by their own nation state. This set of issues was already on the agenda at the 1948 Hague Congress, which initiated the creation of the Council of Europe. Article 3 of the 1949 Statute of the Council of Europe underlined that all the member states recognised human rights and fundamental freedoms. In 1950 the Council of Europe also drafted the European Convention on Human Rights, which not only confirmed such rights but also sought to undertake 'the first steps' for their 'collective enforcement'.[13] On this basis the Council of Europe also created the European Commission of Human Rights and its own Court of Human Rights in Strasbourg.[14]

Even if the Council of Europe was to subsequently play the lead role in Western Europe, it was far from alone. In the global context the Universal Declaration of Human Rights of 1948 set the tone; even the long-forgotten Brussels Pact of the same year – the military alliance that was later to turn into the WEU – explicitly committed itself to human rights.[15] Yet none of that should be exaggerated. In this period human rights were not obviously on a fast-track to universality. The European Commission of Human Rights, as a vital organ of the Council of Europe for implementing this agenda, was not able to begin its work until 1954; the Court of Human Rights in Strasbourg even later in 1959. Institutionalised commitments to the protection of fundamental values and norms did not prevent Council of Europe members like Great Britain and France from savaging human rights in their colonial wars in countries like Kenya and Algeria. France even brought the violence home to its own capital city: on 17 October 1961 police killed more than 200 Algerian demonstrators in the centre of Paris.[16] So these questions were considerably less central in the 1950s than they were to become in later decades.[17] At the international level the formal rules safeguarding democratic standards and civil rights within states were weak at least until the international covenants adopted by the United Nations in

1966. In practice the principle of non-interference in internal affairs – as laid down in the United Nations Charter of 1945 – usually took precedence even after this. For all the fine words, democracy and civil and human rights were never terribly deeply rooted in Western Europe; they were frequently treated more as devices in the context of Cold War rivalry than as values and norms actually requiring action.[18]

Despite the narrow practical limits under which the Council of Europe and other organisations operated, the contrast to the EC is nevertheless striking. The precursors of today's EU initially possessed no mechanisms for securing democracy and human and civil rights; they were absolutely one-sidedly economic – and this aligned with general trends in international law during this period. In the post-war decades the sovereignty exercised by international organisations was not generally regarded as a legitimacy problem, and they were therefore not seen as threats to democracy and human rights. And for protecting such values in a positive sense the Council of Europe was responsible, not the EC.

That is seen, for example, in the ECSC: given its economic remit a strong concentration on values and norms would have appeared odd. In the subsequent period the governments of its founding members considered addressing that aspect in the scope of the European Political Community. The draft EPC Treaty referred explicitly to the Council of Europe's Convention on Human Rights and even provided for the EPC to intervene in the event of violations by a member state. But this ambitious project was stopped in 1954 – along with the European Defence Community – by French objections that had more to do with military issues than civil rights. At the same time this put an end for the time being to high-level civil society debates about fundamental rights in the EC framework.[19]

Henceforth the European Community took a different path. The Spaak Report of summer 1956 – as the central stepping stone to the following year's Treaties of Rome – exercised conspicuous restraint over such questions of principle.[20] The same applies to the EEC and Euratom treaties themselves. Here – as with the ECSC Treaty before them – there was no clear commitment to democracy as a fundamental principle and membership criterion, and no mention of civil or human rights. In the preamble to the EEC Treaty the member states agreed only on a very general reference to 'liberty'. Otherwise there were only subsidiary provisions that affected the civil rights situation: Article

119 of the EEC Treaty, for example, confirmed the principle of equal pay for equal work for men and women.[21] Symptomatically the provision applied to the field of labour relations, entirely in keeping with the Community's economic outlook. The same also applies to the four fundamental freedoms spelled out in the EEC Treaty: freedom of movement for persons, goods, services and capital.[22] In other words, civil rights appeared not in a political context but as an aspect of economic liberties. In the division of labour between regional organisations in post-war Western Europe the emerging EC's priorities quite simply lay elsewhere.

After the failure of the EPC project, the Fouchet Plans of 1961/62 represented a second juncture where a change of direction could have occurred. The French proposal for expanding cooperation between the EEC states in the area of foreign policy also named defending human rights and democracy as an objective. The other five were less enamoured with the inevitable upshot: disempowering the Commission and reining in supranationality. What the Plans do demonstrate is that even proponents of the Gaullist principle of intergovernmental cooperation placed the question of values and norms on the European agenda. Be that as it may, the failure of the Fouchet Plans also ended this attempt to involve the EC more closely in the sphere of values and norms.[23]

So who, aside from the Council of Europe, was responsible for questions of civil rights? The answer was obvious and simple: the member states' national constitutions and other legislation. This model of functional task-sharing is also reflected in early rulings of the European Court of Justice in Luxembourg. In 1958, for example, it was asked to rule on a case brought by a German coal wholesaler against the High Authority of the ECSC. One of the complaints was that the High Authority's actions had violated 'the inviolable right to the free development of his personality and to the free choice of his trade, occupation or profession' as guaranteed in Germany by the German Basic Law. But the Court of Justice in Luxembourg found that the High Authority was only competent to apply the law of the Community, meaning that neither the High Authority nor the Court possessed the authority to rule on this question.[24] Other early decisions of the Court of Justice also shared this spirit of modesty and self-restraint.[25] The EC was not accountable for protecting fundamental values and norms; its tightly circumscribed remit concentrated on technical questions in the economic field. At the European level the Council of Europe remained responsible for overseeing the application of civil rights in the nation states.

Integration Danger

This classical division of labour between member states and the Council of Europe on the one side and the EC on the other was brought crashing down in the mid-1960s by two rulings of the Court of Justice that created the principles of primacy and direct effect of Community law: *van Gend & Loos* (1963) and *Costa* v. *ENEL* (1964).[26] From this point on, EC law could override national law – implying that national constitutions could no longer necessarily comprehensively protect civil rights. This created potential for conflict and a problematic legal vacuum. The latter was exacerbated by a development that acquired enormous symbolic force from the 1970s, as protecting human rights – above and beyond the constitutional civil rights that each state guaranteed its own citizens – became one of the central pillars of political legitimacy at the global level.[27]

Italian and above all German jurists pointed particularly vigorously to this legal problem. For historical reasons the Italian Corte Costituzionale and the German Federal Constitutional Court both possessed especially far-reaching powers, with strong protections for civil rights being regarded as the lesson of Fascism. That was not necessarily the case in other member states: the Dutch constitution, for example, gave international treaties precedence over national law under certain circumstances.[28] In West Germany, on the other hand, jurists like Wilhelm Wengler and Hans Heinrich Rupp – both of whom had personal experience of Nazi injustice – insisted on constitutional protections.[29] In 1964 the association of German constitutional law professors discussed the issue,[30] and it also appeared on the agenda of the European Parliament. Here an important role was played by the Belgian delegate and law professor Fernand Dehousse, who had already fought for civil rights to be protected under the EPC Treaty in the early 1950s. Now he called on the European Commission to prevent Community law eroding civil rights and stressed its precedence over national law.[31] But essentially this was a discussion among experts. Questions of civil rights remained a niche issue in the broad scope of the integration process, and the EC concentrated largely on matters economic. Nonetheless, within just half a decade of the Treaties of

Rome the tenor of the debate had shifted significantly. Civil rights no longer lay outside the remit of the EC, but integration was seen as a threat to democracy and human and civil rights rather than their guarantee.

The dimensions of the problem became apparent at the beginning of the 1970s in *Internationale Handelsgesellschaft* v. *Einfuhr- und Vorratsstelle für Getreide und Futtermittel*. At first glance the case was as technical in nature as the names of the two protagonists would suggest, and yet it was to prove enormously important for the path of integration. The story was as follows: a German trading company (the 'Internationale Handelsgesellschaft') wanted to export maize, which under EC law meant applying for an export licence. That in turn was conditional on depositing a security that would be lost if the export deal fell through. That is precisely what had occurred, leading Internationale Handelsgesellschaft to sue. The administrative court in Frankfurt am Main ruled in favour of the plaintiff, interpreting the law of the Community as a restriction on freedom of trade incompatible with the German Basic Law.

The firm wanted almost DM 20,000. For the EC the stakes were existential, with the administrative court challenging the precedence of Community law over German law. The administrative court in Frankfurt, which was generally a hive of activity in matters of European law, referred the case to the ECJ.[32] The latter ruled in December 1970 that no basic right had been violated in the concrete case. But more importantly, the Luxembourg judges emphasised that Community law took precedence over national law, with 'the observance of basic rights' representing one of the legal principles the Court of Justice had to uphold.[33] As such, the ECJ was continuing a course it had set with two rulings in the late 1960s (*Van Eick* and *Stauder*), and consolidated with *Nold* in 1974.[34] The Court now underlined the centrality of civil rights for the Community's actions, in rulings that diverged strikingly from the decisions of the early 1960s. Legally the court was now treading on thin ice, especially as it neglected to supply any clear definition of civil rights or to name the legal sources upon which it drew. The *Stauder* ruling of 1969 refers at one point to 'unwritten Community law deriving from the general legal principles of the member states'.[35]

With these and similar verdicts at the beginning of the 1970s the ECJ not only created its own facts through decisions that went far beyond purely interpreting the law. It also contributed to constructing a myth: the myth that the legal principles of the member states could easily be reduced to a common denominator and – even more importantly in the long term – that protection of civil rights had always been part of the integration process.[36] In this narrative, insistence on civil rights was the lesson of the era of the world wars and represented a specifically European heritage. Yet if we review the Community's legally binding texts, their interpretation and the political practice, those conclusions turn out to be rather questionable. Really the Court's superbly trained jurists could have been expected to know that.[37]

Internationale Handelsgesellschaft was not satisfied with the ECJ's ruling and took the case to the German Federal Constitutional Court in Karlsruhe. The Constitutional Court highlighted the absence of a catalogue of fundamental rights in the EC, and noted the European Parliament's lack of direct democratic legitimation. In the event of conflict, it ruled, the German Basic Law therefore took precedence. In the best German legalese the Federal Constitutional Court concluded that it could exercise control itself, 'as long as the Community's integration process has not reached the point where Community law also contains a catalogue of valid basic rights adopted by a parliament, equivalent to the [German] Basic Law'.[38] Ironically, the framework of the Basic Law – which was regarded as a stopgap until the division of Germany could be overcome – appeared more dependable than the EC's ostensibly permanent legal community.

So while West Germany is often portrayed as the perfect European in this period,[39] it was the Germans who in fact ensured that the EC's role in civil rights remained tightly circumscribed. But the German Federal Constitutional Court's 'Solange' ('as long as') judgment of 1974 – which also came in for heavy criticism in West Germany – contained the seeds of its own reversal: if the EC altered its position on parliamentary controls and a catalogue of fundamental rights, the German court would reconsider its objections. That is precisely where the plot now led, with the Federal Constitutional Court's 'Solange II' judgment of 1986. Although the EC still lacked a formal catalogue of fundamental rights of its own, the German Constitutional Court regarded the ECJ's accumulated case law as offering meaningful protections essentially equivalent to the German Basic Law. If this remained so, it stated, there was no need for a separate scrutiny by the

German Federal Constitutional Court.[40] Complicated conditional clauses and a heavy dose of casuistry were required to persuade the West Germans to follow the example of the Italian Corte Costituzionale and accept the EC as guarantor of their civil rights. The German Federal Constitutional Court's Maastricht ruling of 1993 then took another new turn, but that falls outside the period covered by this volume.[41]

The Spanish Litmus Test

As well as the internal dynamics of European integration, relations with third states were also already placing the questions of values and norms on the Community's agenda by the early 1960s. This strand of the discussion thus had very different roots from the ECJ's, while sharing a decisive aspect: again what the EC did *not* do was crucial.[42]

Concretely, we are talking about the conditions the Community placed upon third states seeking membership. The EEC Treaty stated baldly that 'Any European state' could apply for membership of the Community, without tying this to any specific values and norms. The only additional condition highlighted in the authoritative German commentary was compatibility with the level of economic integration already achieved.[43] In early 1958 EEC Commission president Hallstein similarly described the enlargement question as a primarily economic one.[44] Such comments not only corresponded to the character of the EC; they must also be seen in the context of the Cold War, representing as they did an implicit rejection of states with socialist economies. At the same time we also see here the full weight of the economic logic that so fundamentally shaped the integration process.

The question acquired concrete significance in the early 1960s, in connection with particular accession applications. To the United Kingdom, Denmark and Ireland, which lodged formal applications in summer 1961, it applied only marginally. Nor did questions of human rights and democracy play any major role in connection with the multitude of former colonies with which the EC was establishing relations in this period; here a different set of rules plainly applied, as examined in greater detail below.[45]

Where things became interesting was in February 1961 when General Franco's Spain expressed a wish for closer relations with the Community. In a letter to Commission president Hallstein the Spanish ambassador to the EC expressed 'the desire of my government that

Spain participate in the European integration movement'.[46] The deliberately vague formulation could be taken to mean full membership, or some other form of association; either way it posed the question of how the Community should relate to a European dictatorship. At this juncture Spain was working hard to break out of the political isolation in which it had been trapped since the end of the war. Madrid was after more than just new economic ties; a close relationship with the EC would also have won enormous prestige for Francoism – especially given that the Council of Europe had turned Spain down in August 1950 and made the possibility of membership conditional on a democratisation process. In the meantime, however, Spain had succeeded in joining first a number of UN agencies and finally the United Nations itself. Although Spain had already overcome its pariah status at the international level, the EC remained especially significant.[47]

The governments of several EC member states responded relatively positively to the Spanish request, including the French and the German; Paris welcomed senior Spanish officials for a series of discussions intended to prepare the ground for possible accession to the EEC.[48] The European Commission also appeared open to the idea. From their perspective, the Cold War supplied strong grounds for closer economic and security ties. Given that this was little more than fifteen years after the end of the Second World War, far right ideology naturally also played a role, occasionally borrowing the language of the East–West conflict to conceal political affinities. In summer 1962 Hans-Joachim von Merkatz, German Federal Minister for the Affairs of the Laender, declared in Madrid that Europe would lose its identity without Spain, which belonged to the continent on account of its history, faith and understanding of honour.[49] During the Nazi period Merkatz worked for a time at the Ibero-American Institute in Berlin, whose director, Wilhelm Faupel, testified to his 'clear, dependable National Socialist attitude'.[50] Whatever his exact motives, civil and human rights were not among them.

In the end it was principally resistance from the European Parliament and civil society groups that ensured that Spain achieved neither membership nor association. Criticism proliferated in the European Parliament, which set up a working party on questions of enlargement and association. Its rapporteur was the German Social Democrat Willi Birkelbach, who heavily influenced its December 1961 report.[51] According to what came to be known as the Birkelbach

Report, the EC was fundamentally open to other states. But association and membership were subject to criteria that extended beyond the economic sphere. Instead the report saw 'the existence of a democratic state in the sense of a liberal political order' as an essential condition of membership, defining the standards in terms of the 'principles ... that the Council of Europe has laid out as its own preconditions for membership'. The report did not derive this orientation from legal norms or specific articles in the treaties, although the latter in particular would have represented the customary approach. Instead, foreshadowing the approach taken a few years later by the ECJ, it justified its line in terms of the political orientation of the Community and its existing members, which was also an 'integral component of the Western treaty system'.[52] In other words, the European Parliament sought to make closer relations conditional on democratic standards. While this was not legally convincing, it did express a clear political stance.

The Spanish government and sympathetic EC governments were initially undeterred by the report. Shortly after its publication in February 1962 Madrid requested the opening of an association process and even went as far as airing the question of later full membership. Spanish foreign minister Fernando María Castiella noted 'Spain's European calling, confirmed so frequently in the course of its history'.[53] Castiella, incidentally, belonged to the current of Francoism whose aristocratic anti-liberalism and deeply traditional Catholicism radicalised even further in the course of the 1930s, and had advocated ultranationalist expansionism during the Second World War. In 1940 he was still dreaming of a new global empire for Spain; now his nation's European calling took centre stage.[54] He plainly had no difficulty accommodating the new realities of international politics in the era of the Cold War.

So Paris and Bonn were certainly open to Madrid's request, not least because just a few years earlier they had thrown their weight behind Spain's successful applications to join the OECD and a string of other international organisations. It was the Dutch government that led the ethical opposition,[55] and emphasised the 'irreconcilability' of Spain's political regime 'with the democratic parliamentary views in the countries of the EEC, and the parliamentary controls that are also laid down in the EEC Treaty'.[56] At the same time, civil society resistance stiffened. Above all forces on the left in the European Parliament, the member states, the trade unions and other groups urged the

Commission and the Council of Ministers to reject the Spanish application, arguing that values should come first.[57] In the European Parliament, for example, Birkelbach argued that the EEC 'would cease to be credible' if it entered into this kind of relationship with Spain.[58]

After several months of discussion the opponents won the day. Rather than rejecting Spain's application, the EC postponed it indefinitely. Although the discussion simmered on quietly, the Franco regime was never granted association, still less full membership. The EC did, however, conclude a trade agreement with Spain in 1970, in an attempt to strike a balance between economic interests and values. A similar solution was also found two years later for Portugal, which also sought closer ties to the EC in 1962. But because Portugal was heavily economically dependent on the United Kingdom, whose membership was blocked by de Gaulle in the 1960s, the EC was spared explicitly answering the same question for the Salazar dictatorship.[59]

In the case of Spain, European politics burst the bounds of secret diplomacy; public pressure made it impossible to pursue interest-driven realpolitik. This is especially striking because the European Parliament possessed very few formal powers and played no official role in questions of accession and association. To that extent the decision represented a victory not only for the primacy of values and norms, but also for the European Parliament itself, whose representatives were by now working on all fronts to expand their institution's political clout. For the European Parliament the decision thus represented an obvious gain in influence. But there were clearly defined limits to the expansion. The Community still lacked binding rules on civil and human rights and on safeguarding democracy.

Unlike the European Parliament, the member states did not actively press for commitments on norms and values. Instead this was wrested from (or forced upon) them by the European Parliament and civil society pressure. One reason for the failure of the realpolitik line is the commitments generated by political rhetoric. Leading national politicians had simply too often lauded the integration process as an expression of peace and reconciliation. For example Chancellor Konrad Adenauer said in 1951 in London: 'The process of integration and the formation of larger communities of nations serves to preserve the Western Christian values that lend meaning to our lives.'[60] The Community now had to live up to the values it had so often invoked. In a different context the political scientist Frank Schimmelfennig describes how 'rhetorical entrapment', in the sense of the binding force of their words, ultimately makes it impossible for the proponents of realpolitik to defend their positions, while a value-led camp can deliberately exploit this to open the way for policies orientated on democracy and civil and human rights.[61]

This was a long, slow process. The EC's vacillation did little to improve its public standing in the member states or to lend it a positive image at a time when human rights questions were gaining in significance especially on the left.[62]

Inspiration from the Council of Europe

The question of how values and norms should be applied to third states remained highly relevant. The debate flared up again in April 1967 when a military coup put the Colonels into power in Greece. The EC's 1961 association agreement with Greece was highly symbolic: it was the first the EC concluded, leading EEC Commission president Hallstein to remark on its signing: 'We are doubly happy to conclude this Agreement with Greece, a country so close to every European's heart as the cradle of European culture and the source of spiritual currents that have indelibly shaped the continent's personality.' It also went further than most similar agreements in specifically mentioning the perspective of full membership at a later point, as noted in almost identical formulations in internal documents of the German and French foreign ministries, which had been decided at the time 'in light of political considerations'. In other words, seen through the Cold War lens, association played a role in cementing Greece into the Western camp.[63]

When the Colonels suspended democracy and violated human rights the EC was forced to take a position. Unlike Spain, this was not a hypothetical case of possible association, but the consequences of dictatorship for a relationship that already possessed a firm institutional and legal framework. The Council of Ministers and the Commission initially decided to wait the matter out. While some governments wanted to clearly distance themselves and others feared that silence would be misinterpreted as acceptance of the new status quo, France and Germany again counselled against condemnation on the grounds that Greece was too important to NATO. It was the Cold War geopolitical and security perspective that tipped the balance, causing Brussels to avoid a clear official response.[64]

Again the European Parliament led the opposition to realpolitik. And again socialists such as the German Walter Faller and the aforementioned Belgian Dehousse played an important role in the debate. But others also played leading roles, such as the Italian Christian democrat Edoardo Martino and Wim Schuijt of the Dutch Katholieke Volkspartij. In the end the EC decided in early June 1967 to freeze relations with Greece, in which state they remained until the dictatorship was toppled in 1974. This was a significant blow for the Colonels, especially as it blocked any chance of full EC membership. In a situation where neither NATO nor the United States took any effective public steps against the junta, the European Community's decision carried special weight.[65] Its implications were felt, for example, in the British accession process at the time: in 1972 the British government stated that it was interested in a 'good working relationship with the regime in pursuit of national defence and economic interests' but not prepared to sacrifice 'important British objectives within the Community ... for the sake of relations with Greece'.[66] In this way the member states' distancing from Athens also affected third countries in the accession process – even where these were heavyweights like the United Kingdom.

One aspect has largely been overlooked to date: the debate within the EC was heavily initiated and influenced by developments in the Council of Europe with its more strongly culturally and ethically driven approach. Greece joined the Council of Europe straight away in 1949, during the final throes of a bloody civil war accompanied by massive human rights violations. Its ongoing membership reveals that the Council of Europe did not always take its trumpeted values and norms entirely seriously. Security arguments were the decisive aspect for membership; furthermore, unlike Portugal and Spain, Greece did at least possess parliamentary institutions. But in the subsequent period Greece failed to develop into a stable democracy.[67] In view of its full membership of the Council of Europe and the organisation's special focus on human rights, the 1967 coup urgently demanded an adequate response. The Council of Europe's largely toothless substitute for a parliament placed Greece on its agenda just a few days after the military coup. That was an obvious move, after the junta provoked great consternation by placing some of the Parliamentary Assembly's Greek members under observation. Karl Czernetz, a Council of Europe delegate from the Austrian Social Democratic SPÖ who had spent the Second World War in exile in London, proposed a resolution criticising the situation in Greece in the name of the Socialist group. In the end, less than a week after the putsch the Parliamentary Assembly adopted a rather watered-down resolution insisting on the observance of human rights. This Order 256 immediately became the point of reference for national debates, and for the EC, especially its Parliament. One reason for this was that the European Parliament convened immediately after the Parliamentary Assembly of the Council of Europe – also in Strasbourg – and there were close contacts between the members of both bodies. As such, the Council of Europe played a crucial role in pushing the EC towards a value-defined position.[68]

That said, Greece was in no way representative of the EC's new stance, as illustrated by the latter's dealings with Turkey during roughly the same period. In 1963 Turkey, already a member of the OECD and NATO, concluded an association agreement with the EEC. Like the deal with Greece two years earlier, the Ankara Agreement, as it came to be known, offered the prospect of full membership. That was in itself notable, given that a military coup in 1960 had suspended Turkish democracy, causing the talks to be interrupted for a year 'on account of internal political developments in Turkey'.[69] President Cemal Gürsel, under whom the Agreement was ultimately signed, had been one of the coup's leaders but subsequently worked to introduce a new democratic constitution. So Turkey had stabilised by the time association came into effect, although death sentences had been carried out against former members of government shortly beforehand. Questions of human rights and democracy played an absolutely marginal role in the negotiations and no major one in the association decision. Instead the principal motivation was strengthening pro-Western forces in the country in view of Cold War pressures and economic considerations (not least in light of Soviet offers of aid).[70] The EC acted similarly in 1971 when the Turkish military again seized power. This did not prevent the Community from further deepening the Ankara Agreement with an additional protocol two years later. In 1980, though, the EC responded differently when Turkey experienced its third military coup within the space of two decades. This time – again two years later – the Community suspended the association agreement (although it must be said, Turkey had already done so unilaterally in 1978).[71] In 1987 Turkey submitted a membership application, which the Commission rejected in December 1989. Now the principal stumbling block was the Community's ability to absorb a nation the size of Turkey, and the country's economic problems in general. But the European Commission also noted that the human rights situation in Turkey had not yet achieved 'the level required in a democracy'.[72] While they were not spotlighted, values and norms did feature as a yardstick, even if they were not to attain truly unequivocal status until 1993 with the Copenhagen criteria, and even more so the Treaty of Amsterdam of 1997.[73]

Human rights and democracy thus left an identifiable mark on the Community's external relations, although to a lesser extent than one might have expected from today's perspective. In the early 1960s the EC saw no problem in concluding association agreements with Greece and Turkey offering the perspective of membership, despite those countries' questionable human rights records. In the case of Spain and a few years later also Greece, however, norms and values became the lever that ultimately blocked closer ties. The Greek case was especially significant, because the EC was seeking to influence the internal affairs of a third country. That contradicted the post-war principle of non-intervention and presaged the global shift to primacy of human rights over state sovereignty that accelerated from the mid-1970s. It was not, however, a real watershed, because suspending the association agreement did not prevent member states like West Germany and France from continuing to supply arms and materiel to Greece bilaterally; the United States initially suspended military exports, but resumed them in 1970 even though the junta remained in power.[74] In February 1975 the French Foreign Ministry also noted internally that suspension of the association agreement 'has not prevented the further development of existing economic relations between Greece and the EEC'.[75]

In the case of Portugal the EC and its member states avoided compromising themselves principally because Portugal was not seeking a close relationship. In the case of Turkey, finally, we see the EC punishing behaviour in the 1980s that it had still been prepared to tolerate in the 1970s.

Turning Point 1970s

The decisive discussions that paved the way for a harder line in the 1980s, where a number of new factors joined the ECJ and external relations in the debate, played out during the preceding decade.

In the 1970s the European Parliament took an increasing interest in questions of values and norms, not least building on the discussion about Greece. Its first big debate about the rights of the citizens of the member states came in 1973. Rapporteur Léon Jozeau-Marigné from France reminded his fellow MEPs that many people had little interest in civil rights: the constitution of the Fifth Republic did not spell out a legal categorisation of the kind found in the German Basic Law. Taking up where earlier interventions, like Dehousse's, left off Jozeau-Marigné's report pointed out the lack of civil rights safeguards in Community law and urged their development.[76] The *Document on the European Identity* published in December the same year did contain a vague reference to the member states' 'cherished values of their legal, political and moral order'.[77] The Tindemans Report of December 1975 saw more comprehensive protection of civil rights – as well as consumer and environmental safeguards – as an important step towards bridging the gulf between the EC and its citizens. The same objective was served by the proposal, based on *van Gend & Loos*, to give individuals the right to bring cases before the ECJ directly. That was certainly a notable development aiming to expand democratic legitimacy. In fact, however, *van Gend & Loos* had already created a direct legal relationship between the EC and its citizens, one that was without equivalent in international organisations like NATO and the OECD. Only in the EC did private individuals have immediate recourse to the organisation's law through the courts.[78]

In a second notable development, the debates reflected a growing sense that the EC should also apply the standards of democracy and human rights to itself. In other words they should not just apply throughout the territories of its member states, as in the case of the Council of Europe, but also to the EC's own institutions. That meant scrutinising the conformity of all the Community's actions with its values and norms, and went a good deal further than other international organisations, including the Council of Europe. The self-understanding reflected here corresponded more to that of a sovereign (or constitutionalising) political order, and reflected especially clearly the EC's ambition to assert significantly greater sovereignty than other organisations.[79]

Up to this point the European Parliament had been the driving force alongside the ECJ; in the 1970s sparks increasingly jumped across to the intergovernmental level of the integration process. The Davignon Report of 1970, which supplied the basis for the member states to institutionalise their foreign policy cooperation, acknowledged civil rights and democratic values, drawing not least on the debates about how to deal with the Greek junta.[80] Even more important was the role of the EC in the East–West deliberations of the Conference on Security and Cooperation in Europe, which culminated in 1975 in the Helsinki Final Act. Here the EC states worked in concert to ensure that human rights guarantees were included in the document. First they had to persuade their NATO partners, including the United States and then the other participants. At this juncture almost nobody believed that Helsinki would ever have tangible effects on the Eastern Bloc – yet within just a few years the Final Act had become a touchstone for dissident movements across the Soviet sphere of influence.[81]

Developments within the EC institutions increasingly entered public and academic debates from the 1970s, giving them a grounding in civil society and driving them forward. Academic, public and political discussions thus melded to give the EC a new self-confidence and even the rudiments of a sense of mission. Although these discussions revolved primarily around the EC's place in the world, values and norms played an important role that would have been unthinkable just twenty years earlier. In 1972/73 François Duchêne, a close advisor of Jean Monnet's and at this point director of the London-based International Institute for Strategic Studies, published two widely read texts about the 'civilian power Europe'. The EC, he argued, had to make the best of its 'inner characteristics', which were: 'civilian ends and means, and a built-in sense of collective action, which in turn express, however imperfectly, social values of equality, justice and tolerance'. These values, he said, needed to be promoted not only internally within the Community; the EC had to become 'a force for the international diffusion of civilian and democratic standards'.[82] Duchêne contrasted 'civilian power' with traditional (military) power; values and norms – and not just the EC's economic potency – nevertheless played an important role. The British journalist Richard Mayne, another of Monnet's close associates, now dreamed of an EC that was 'democratic, efficient and not merely a cumbersome monolith'.[83] Already in 1970, the pro-European intellectual Denis de Rougement was also arguing in a widely read book that European unification had long ceased to be the crux of the matter. One could 'live very well *à l'américaine*, a little less well under the fist of the *Parti communiste*'. Europe had to be built nonetheless, namely, 'to live our liberties'.[84] In this line of argument Europe, and European institutions, derived their *raison d'être* from their defence of specific values – whether or not one shared the Swiss philosopher's anti-communist and rather anti-American views.

While many of these statements remain rather vague,[85] they do underline how the debate became increasingly less restricted to the institutions of the EC. The reasons behind the expanding scope of the discussion were not only that the EC itself took an increasing interest in the subject, but also the dramatically different social and geopolitical context in which the EC was operating from the early 1970s: a phase of Cold War détente, doubts over the US security guarantee, economic turbulence as the *trente glorieuses* came to an end, but also the global rise of the human rights debate and civil society liberalisation trends, together with growing criticism of the way power in international relations was defined primarily as military strength: all these factors contributed to directing greater attention to values and norms, and to the questions of what role the European Community should play in securing them and how the unification project itself should be justified.[86]

These public debates fed back into the EC, and the Community found itself issuing increasingly frequent commitments to civil and human rights. This occurred very prominently in the Joint Declaration on Fundamental Rights adopted in 1977 by Parliament, Council and Commission, where all three institutions underlined 'the prime importance they attach to the protection of fundamental rights'.[87] When the European Parliament approved the Draft Treaty Establishing the European Union seven years later, human rights again played an important role. This was ensured not least by Altiero Spinelli, the responsible rapporteur. Although the Draft Treaty was never ratified, it underlines yet again the central role of the European Parliament in the debates, especially from 1979 when the European Parliament became the only formal Community institution possessing the democratic legitimation of directly elected representatives.[88] Especially in its first directly elected term the European Parliament contained many political heavyweights whose intellectual horizons were much broader than an interest in market organisations and customs regulations: names like Willy Brandt, Altiero Spinelli and Simone Veil. One issue taken up by the European Parliament was abolition of capital punishment, sparked by its abolition in France in the early 1980s. Given that the legal systems of half the EC's member states still had the death penalty in 1986, the debate ground on for many years. In this way democracy and basic rights crept in many tiny steps from the margins ever closer to the heart of the debates about the Community's purpose and orientation. And again the issue was their application not just across member states, but also within the Community itself. The new confidence of the European Parliament after the 1979 direct elections played an especially significant role in the development that saw the EC explicitly understanding and positioning itself as a community of values.[89]

A New Sense of Mission

Despite the growing weight of these discussions, with their intra-institutional focus, relationships with third states remained the most important context in which questions of democracy and rule of law appeared on the EC's agenda in the second half of the 1970s and into the 1980s. But the focus now shifted considerably. Whereas the Community was initially very cautious about committing to values and norms, these now became increasingly central to its self-understanding and its interactions with a series of third states.

The accession question returned to the agenda from the mid-1970s for Greece, Spain and Portugal, and again became the heart of the debate over democracy and human rights.[90] All three states had only recently shaken off authoritarian regimes when they applied for full membership. Greece applied in 1975, just a year after the end of military rule. The application rather took the member states by surprise, and democracy and human rights were not always uppermost. Again economic interests were flanked by security calculations, as described in greater detail in Chapter 2, 'Peace and Security'. Values and norms were by no means irrelevant, and for the first time the EC presented itself as an international force whose enlargement would make a meaningful contribution to safeguarding them. That interpretation was also encouraged by the Greek government. When prime minister Konstantinos Karamanlis informed the ambassadors of the then nine member states about the application in June 1975, he underlined that his country was taking this step not 'for reasons that are uniquely economic in character. Our demand rests in the first place on political reasons, reasons which concern the consolidation of democracy and the future of the nation'.[91] The European Commission batted back a declaration that the 'consolidation of democracy in Greece . . . is a fundamental concern not only of the Greek people but also of the Community and its Member States'.[92] For Karamanlis this argument was certainly a tactical asset in the complex accession talks: while underlining his own irrevocable loyalty to the West and its values, he also stressed the fragility of the democratisation process, for whose success he argued a speedy accession was vital. The function of this norm-based language, which proliferated within the Community at precisely this time, was to create a unifying instance aloof of economic and technical challenges.

For West Germany, which supported Greek accession more forcefully than any other, geopolitical and security aspects were uppermost. While Paris as a whole was rather more cautious, president Giscard d'Estaing saw stabilising democracy as a more important motive than many German leaders: the 'mother of democracy must not be excluded from the European union'.[93] Dutch prime minister Joop den Uyl saw things similarly, overriding resistance from cabinet members concerned about economic and other problems associated with Greek membership.[94] As in all other cases, 'rhetorical entrapment' and genuine support for the young democracy melded with other strands, with the strongest support for Greek membership coming from the Council of Ministers rather than the Commission (itself a striking development). Altogether commitment to specific values and norms played a more central role here than in any previous major decision of the European Community.[95]

The same applies to Spain and Portugal, which both submitted membership applications in 1977, two years after Greece. In 1978 the Commission issued a statement on all three applications that reiterated the high priority accorded to consolidating democracy and noted that 'three countries have entrusted the Community with a political responsibility which it cannot refuse, except at the price of denying the principles in which it is itself grounded'.[96] Despite the self-righteous tone – and although economic motives naturally also played an important role – it is certainly the case that the governments of all three countries saw accession as rewarding a successful transition to democracy, and as a means to expediting the same.[97] The EC now became identified with democracy and human rights because – ambivalences aside – it had already been applying stricter standards than for example NATO or the OECD. Given that the United States had backed the Colonels, the EC appeared an attractive partner to many Greeks.[98] After promoting democracy and human rights had played such a prominent role in the Greek accession, it was obvious to enable Spain and Portugal to join too.

A new tone also gradually crept into existing relations from the second half of the 1970s. Questions of democracy and human rights originally played no role in the association arrangements for the member states' former colonies: the Yaoundé Convention of 1963 was largely built around the principle of non-intervention in the internal affairs of sovereign states. That slowly began to change with the Lomé Convention of 1975. Where, as in Uganda, unexpected human rights violations occurred on a scale attracting global criticism the EC restricted its development aid. In the negotiations for Lomé II the European Commission and the British and Dutch governments in particular pressed for relations to be made more strongly conditional on human rights, but this was rejected by the other states. Lomé III in 1984 cautiously mentioned human rights for the first time; and their role expanded further in Lomé IV in 1989. Institutionally speaking, democracy and human rights remained weakly anchored, however; the words changed but the political practice lagged behind until the end of the Cold War – even if there were now instances of conditionality in relation to human rights questions. The Maastricht Treaty and above all the Cotonou Agreement of 2000 ushered in further changes at this level, granting democracy and human rights a fuller role in shaping the association relationship and development cooperation, without making them completely conditional. Even if standards plainly varied depending on the context, important gradual shifts occurred here too.[99]

Such debates ultimately impacted back at the level of the treaties. The preamble to the Single European Act of 1986, the first fundamental treaty document since 1957, underlined the determination of the member states 'to work together to promote democracy'. This was based on their respective national constitutions, the Council of Europe's European Convention on Human Rights of 1950 and the 'fundamental rights … notably freedom, equality and social justice' recognised in the Council of Europe's European Social Charter of 1961.[100] While this formulation is uncannily similar to the battle-cry of the French Revolution, it turned out to be problematic in two respects. On the one hand the actual provisions of the Single European Act fell well short of those lofty ideals. Like the Joint Declaration on Fundamental Rights of 1977 this was in the first place a verbal affirmation of values and norms, but not concretely legally binding. On the other hand the three terms represent values rather than rights. Those concerned were plainly still finding their way in the vocabulary. The Maastricht Treaty represented an important step forward. Now the member states confirmed 'their attachment to the principles of liberty, democracy and respect for human rights and fundamental freedoms and of the rule of law' and expanded upon them. With these and similar formulations Maastricht played a part in consolidating the myth that the EC had been committed to this agenda from the very beginning, in the sense that this was supposedly only a form of 'confirming' the 'attachment to the principles of liberty, democracy and respect for human rights and fundamental freedoms and the rule of law',[101] whereas in fact the treaty finally created a little clarity.[102] In this way each new legal step helped to further the myth of the long backstory, both papering over the lack of values and norms in the early EC and interpreting broader European history one-sidedly and extremely selectively through the filter of this ethos.[103] At the same time the Maastricht Treaty – and a few years later the Amsterdam Treaty – expressed the growing importance of the orientation on values and norms.

In the entire debate, from the 1970s and even more so the 1980s, the EC consistently referred to the Council of Europe's Convention on Human Rights. This was easy where all the states were members of the Council of Europe – even if the EU itself never signed the Convention.[104] Such a move frequently came up for discussion, revealing the different legal traditions and expectations in the various member states. While the French and German delegations were very keen, the United Kingdom and Denmark argued against. The British Foreign Office spoke of this question as a 'sleeping dog which we are most anxious not to stir'.[105] In 1994 the ECJ ruled that the Maastricht Treaty did not grant the powers required to join the Convention. And because that would have meant amending the treaties – by unanimous decision – the German Council presidency proposed creating instead the EU's own Charter of Fundamental Rights.[106] So while the Council of Europe figured as an important point of reference, the process also highlighted the tendency for the EC/EU to establish its own competing rules.[107]

Whereas the ECJ had always cited the Council of Europe and its documents as an important source of inspiration for its own jurisprudence, the EC/EU ultimately created an increasingly separate legal sphere – also to underline its claim to autonomy and independence. All these factors and developments come together in the concept of the 'community of values': the Union could hardly regard itself as the prime protector of values if it understood itself as a component of a broader regional and international context for the protection of human rights.[108] So in 1999/2000 a European Convention drafted a Charter of Fundamental Rights of the European Union, much of whose substance was orientated on the Council of Europe's Convention on Human Rights as well as national documents; the Charter was solemnly proclaimed at an intergovernmental conference in Nice in December 2000.

The negotiations over the Charter fell precisely in a phase where the values question was preoccupying the EU as never before. In early 2000 the Austrian People's Party (ÖVP) formed a coalition including the far right Freedom Party (FPÖ) under Jörg Haider, who was infamous for his xenophobia, racism and historical revisionism. The other fourteen member states (the EU-14, as they were referred to at the time) issued an unprecedented response, restricting their respective bilateral diplomatic relations with Austria (only the Austrian veto precluded joint EU sanctions). The tone towards Vienna was sharp. Yet what initially looked like a triumph for value-driven politics ended in resounding defeat half a year later: after consulting three 'wise men' the EU-14 lifted their sanctions in September 2000 without having achieved any noticeable change in Vienna. The report of the three wise men expressed criticism on individual points, but concluded that the Austrian government backed shared European values and that the legal situation corresponded to other EU states. The Austrian case thus demonstrated what was at stake if one sought to enforce value-driven policies within the EU: as long as the Freedom Party's problematic views were not reflected in the actions of government, the EU had no grounds to intervene. Altogether the EU came out looking bad, especially given that it responded much more leniently towards Italy in 1994 and 2001 when Silvio Berlusconi formed governments with the participation of an extreme right-wing electoral alliance. As well as complaints over the impotence of value-driven politics there were also accusations that little Austria – then a new member state – was being judged against stricter standards than its big southern neighbour.[109]

Finally, to return briefly to Giscard d'Estaing's search for a quote and to bring us up to the present: the Charter was soon to face a much larger challenge. First and foremost its content was celebrated, and the Convention process it had tested quickly became the model for the Constitutional Convention mentioned at the beginning of the chapter. The original plan for the Charter to acquire its legal force as part of the European Constitutional Treaty had to be abandoned after the failure of the latter. After further negotiations most EU member states declared the Charter legally binding in the Lisbon Treaty of 2007, although the United Kingdom and Poland insisted on 'opt-outs'. At the same time, in certain respects the preamble to the Lisbon Treaty, the valid EU treaty today, actually goes further than the draft European Constitutional Treaty of 2003. But wisely without the aforementioned words of Thucydides. Nor any other classical quote.

Values and Norms: Résumé

Altogether the consolidation and protection of civil and human rights and democracy in the European Community proceeded in fits and starts, with important markers laid down in the 1950s, steady growth in importance from the 1970s and – after the end of the Cold War – even more strongly from the 1990s.

These developments fit into a general pattern of growing concern for human rights and the hope – especially from the 1970s and 1980s – that an increasing number of societies were moving towards democracy. This shift was not restricted to the authoritarian dictatorships of Southern Europe and the Eastern Bloc, but was global in extent – for example concerning political developments in Latin America.[110] For the EC four specific factors turned out to be decisive. Firstly, for proponents of a federal Community the search for an ethos represented an important objective in its own right – as well as a powerful lever for building a supranational Europe: if it was now the Community, rather than the nation state, that guaranteed these values and norms, a very significant step had been taken towards a United States of Europe. By the beginning of the 1950s the soaring expectations placed upon the Council of Europe had already turned out to be unrealistic. And after the European Political Community went down in flames in 1954, European politicians like Altiero Spinelli placed their faith in the EC instead, hoping to nudge it gradually towards constitutionalisation.

Creating representative parliamentary institutions and codifying civil rights, perhaps even human rights, were central milestones on this road. Federalists therefore saw the question of the Community's values and norms as intimately bound up with the question of the final destination.[111]

Ultimately, however, the other three reasons were to prove more important for the course of developments. The second is that from the 1960s and even more so the 1970s the EC increasingly expanded beyond the sphere of the economic and technical. And this made the problem of legitimation of the integration process into a matter of quite some urgency. The idea was that securing values and norms would help to justify the Community – morally as well as constitutionally – in a period where dissatisfaction was beginning to grow.[112] This naturally applied both within the member states, where the Community was now frequently criticised as undemocratic, and, with the EC increasingly assuming responsibilities on the international stage, also towards third states. This momentum grew further as the promotion of civil and human rights rose up the agendas of international organisations. Nevertheless the EC stood out in this area from the 1970s, as it increasingly began to respect such rights itself, very much more so than normal international organisations.[113]

Thirdly, the Community was forced to anchor civil rights institutionally in order to maintain and protect the level of legal integration achieved by the mid-1960s. This problem arose because of the direct application of European law and its precedence over national law. Simply preserving the *acquis* required the EC to secure fundamental values – for if it did not do so, the precedence of European law would have created an unacceptable legal vacuum. The alternative would have been to roll back European law. So essentially the question was to defend the sphere of Community law against other legal systems, above all those of the member states. Thus the EC's commitment to observing the fundamental norms of liberty and democracy underpinned the autonomy of its own legal system. To that extent there were phases where the insistence on values and norms was more an instrument of institutional self-preservation than an end in itself. And the EC was willing to go to almost any lengths to preserve what it had already achieved. In this sense the commitment to values and norms represented an unintended consequence of the existence of competing legal orders.[114]

Fourthly, finally, came the normative force of political rhetoric. All the EC's founding states were more or less stable democracies, whose pro-European elites often justified the project in terms of shared values and norms. And this made it increasingly difficult to ride roughshod over human rights, as became especially clear in relation to Spain and Greece. From the late 1960s increasingly vocal public criticism demanded that the EC's stance towards third states be brought into line with its public statements.[115] In various member states the left in particular campaigned on value-driven policies. Governments and their representatives in the EC found themselves increasingly forced to pay heed to these dynamics. Public debates, political action at national and European level, and its legal codification became more and more closely interconnected.

At the same time the commitment to guarding democracy and civil and human rights in the EC's external activities never fully determined political decisions. In relation to third states this was most relevant regarding authoritarian regimes in Western Europe and in the Western camp more broadly; even into the 1970s it had much less impact on the former colonies and other third states. But even in relations with countries such as Spain, Portugal and Turkey there was always a tension between civil and human rights and other criteria, above all those relating to economic and security concerns. Human rights–driven policies were never more than one option among several. The non-intervention principle of the UN Charter also mitigated towards caution in this respect. More importantly, the Cold War context could not be overlooked when the issues involved questions such as securing a NATO flank or cooperation with a right-wing authoritarian regime to suppress communist or socialist activity. The motivation of protecting capitalist property relations and trade regimes should not be underestimated either.

Security-driven realpolitik and humanitarian interests were not simple opposites, however. They sometimes stood in a dialectical relationship to one another. This is seen especially clearly in the EC's relationships with the United States and with NATO. The latter frequently prioritised security, with the Greek junta a prime example. When the EC decided to place a little more emphasis on values and norms this represented more than a functional division of labour; it also earned the EC prestige and influence. This applied especially in the 1970s when the United States appeared weaker than at any previous phase of the Cold War and the Eastern Bloc was exhibiting centrifugal tendencies. These two factors created a policy void that the EC sought to fill, partly by placing the human rights question on its agenda with the Eastern Bloc. When the global political dynamic shifted again during the 1980s, the process within the EC did not grind to a halt. By this point it had gained much too much momentum for that to occur.

The relationship between capitalist economic interests and the values question is also a good deal more complex than one might at first think. Even after the ECJ created the possibility for ordinary citizens to bring cases directly under certain circumstances, that remained a comparatively rare occurrence. Much more often it was large companies that sought redress through the European instance, instrumentalising the language of values to press their interests. The *Internationale Handelsgesellschaft* case was symptomatic, and the sum of DM 20,000 not so small after all.[116]

The diversity of motivations and interests also disproves the assertion that it was primarily post-dictatorship societies – first and foremost West Germany and Italy – that pushed for a Europeanisation of human rights in order to stabilise their domestic political situation.[117] While representatives of both countries did play an important role in the debates, this argument underestimates the contribution of actors from other member states. At the same time the West German government, for example, long avoided pursuing a value-driven stance towards Spain or Greece. The field was much too complex and contradictory to be able to isolate clear national positions determined by domestic politics and historical experience.

The question of civil and human rights and democracy revolved largely around the question of whether *third* states abided by these standards. It was a long time before the EC itself introduced strong shared monitoring and control mechanisms for violations of democratic standards within its bounds, although the situation with civil rights did begin to improve from the 1970s. One reason for this is that some differences always existed between the member states over the precise meaning of civil and human rights and the definition of democracy. It was always easier to say what they disapproved of than to agree a positive definition of shared values and norms. When it came to complex questions of democracy and human rights – over and above a minimal consensus – the EU for a long time refrained from adopting firm joint positions (for example on abortion or freedom of speech) not least because these remained outside the sphere of its authority. So each state's legal understanding still remains largely characterised by national traditions. The adoption of concrete norms has the potential to divide rather than unite.[118] At the philosophical level this points to a fundamental problem with the concept of values. They are virtually impossible to pin down, and pluralism of values is at least as characteristic of a democracy as a canon of values. According to Herbert Schnädelbach, values are by definition vague; one can only abide by norms, which are sufficiently binding in nature.[119] Another problem is that civil and human rights and the understanding of democracy are themselves subject to continuous change. The field of social rights turned out to be inherently malleable, and the extent to which they fell under the umbrella of civil rights was always a matter of controversy. Taken together, these factors also explain why the EC itself never became a paragon of democracy. Ralf Dahrendorf – the German-British sociologist and liberal politician – summed up this paradox: 'If the EU were to ask to join itself, it would have to be refused on account of its lack of internal democracy'.[120] On the basis of their stated rules today's African Union in fact possesses stronger means of internal enforcement than the EU.[121]

Despite its regular verbal commitments to democracy and human rights, what role the EU actually wishes to play in relation to its member states remains contested to this day. That also explains why there is no consensus on these questions in the EU today. To understand why that is the case one must know the longer history since the post-war era.

6 SUPERSTATE OR TOOL OF NATIONS?

The signing of the Treaties of Rome in 1957 is one of the few moments in the EC's history that is still occasionally remembered today. Less widely known is what the representatives of the six parties actually put their names to: what we see on the photographs is in fact a stack of blank sheets; only the one with the signatures was real. The reason for this? Negotiations over a string of details had continued into the morning of 25 March.[1] Just as odd is the Italian postage stamp issued to commemorate the twenty-fifth anniversary in 1982. It correctly reproduces the twelve signatures, but unfortunately names the wrong date: '24 – III – 1957' was the day before the 'trattati di Roma' were signed. So does the EC hold the fates of its member states in its hand? Or is it really just a symbol?

Brussels has often been criticised as a bureaucratic monster, a supranational juggernaut, a new empire. While the terms leave much room for interpretation, they all present the EC as a threat to the political order of its member states. Margaret Thatcher in the 1980s, for example, feared a 'European super-state exercising a new dominance from Brussels', where 'an appointed bureaucracy' made the decisions, as she lectured the EC in no uncertain terms in her (in)famous Bruges speech in 1988.[2] In later years she insisted that the EC was 'synonymous with bureaucracy'; 'government by bureaucracy for bureaucracy – to which one might add "to", "from" and "with" bureaucracy if one were so minded', and well on its way to becoming a 'bureaucratic European superstate'.[3] About twenty years earlier, in 1953, Charles de Gaulle was similarly forthright, calling the plan for a European Defence Community 'that artificial monster, that robot, that Frankenstein which … is called the Community'.[4] While the

Figure 8: Italian postage stamp marking the twenty-fifth anniversary of the Treaties of Rome. Archive of the author

Dutch queen Beatrix and de Gaulle's immediate predecessor as French president, René Coty, visited the ECSC in the 1950s,[5] de Gaulle himself would never have dreamed of paying such tribute to the Community institutions; that would have granted undeserved symbolic recognition to 'Frankenstein'. On 14 January 1963, when de Gaulle announced his veto against British accession, the Council of Ministers was meeting in Brussels. But the French president spoke in Paris, making his speech not just a substantive affront to London, but a symbolic snub to the Community institutions.[6] Two decades later Thatcher could not afford to stay at home, as the European Summit now gave the heads of state and government a direct role in the EC.

But did that confirm or constrain the dominance of Brussels? There is no simple answer. Unlike Thatcher and de Gaulle, whose polemics helped to ensure that their nightmare scenarios never became reality, many scholars note the persistence of the nation states in the integration process.

Here we are going to look beyond the rhetoric of de Gaulle and Thatcher, ignoring misdated postage stamps and treaties on blank paper, to examine what the EC really became. The member states have received countless mentions in the preceding chapters, through the actions of heads of state and government, ministers and civil servants, institutions and civil society actors. So why not have a separate chapter on the member states? The reason is simple: they are so central to the integration process that they appear throughout the story. That is not to suggest that Brussels simply represented an extension of their interests.[7] It is true to an extent, yet in the course of time the integration process also fundamentally transformed the member states. But there was no need for a gigantic Brussels bureaucracy to subjugate or substitute the member states. The mechanisms involved, as I intend to demonstrate here, were much more subtle, and for a very long time went largely unnoticed. In the following we will consider how the relationship between the EC and the member states developed over time, and what this can tell us about the character of the Community.

In 'everyday affairs', Max Weber observed, 'the exercise of authority consists precisely in administration'.[8] That aspect is highly relevant, as European integration created growing and increasingly interwoven administrative connections between the EC and its member states. This did not mean that the European and national levels mingled; they remained formally separate but cooperated increasingly closely, initially in regulation, later more and more in administration too. Community law also played a vital role in transforming the political systems of the member states. The scope and form of the *acquis communautaire* – the rights and obligations applicable to all member states – changed dramatically over time, with crucial shifts occurring especially in the 1980s. At the same time, the concrete effects varied between member states; connection, intertwining and change should not be confused with homogenisation. Yet ultimately the differences between the political systems, including bureaucratic customs and political cultures dating back centuries, proved to be stronger. So while great change occurred at the political and administrative levels, it appeared to make little difference to the everyday lives of ordinary people – who in turn showed little interest in these processes. And by the time the effects finally became somewhat more obvious the basic foundations had already been laid, making it difficult to 'turn the clock back'.

Most people find the questions examined in the following dry as dust. And that was central to European integration and its transformative effect. Whether or not you choose to believe the author (or sneak a peek at the conclusions at the end of the chapter): if you have the patience to read on you will learn why comitology has nothing to do with comets, how French blackcurrant liqueur washed away trade barriers, why Eurocrats were compared to the 'Mexican army', and how one could make a mint from revolving beef exports. And of course why one cannot afford to ignore the subtle and transformative effects of European integration.

Comfort and Security

In the 1960s it was Charles de Gaulle who led the opposition to any move towards a European superstate. But even without the eloquent French president, there would have been no United States of Europe. Most other governments and large parts of the population showed insufficient interest in the EC, and even less enthusiasm for relinquishing the nation state. In that respect the widely cited theory of integration 'rescuing' the nation state invites misunderstandings. In political terms the nation state did not need saving after 1945; it was more broadly accepted in Western Europe than ever before, while the idea of a supranational Europe always remained marginal. The border protests of the 1950s – described in Chapter 4, 'Participation and Technocracy' – involved a few hundred participants, and marches for the European ideal never exceeded tens of thousands. State and nation mobilised the masses on quite a different scale. When Juliana was crowned Queen of the Netherlands in 1948, hundreds of thousands came onto the streets and the head of *Newsweek*'s London office spoke of 'the greatest show in postwar Europe'.[9] Interest in the coronation of Queen Elizabeth II four years later was greater still; even in the United States and Canada it was the television event of the year.[10]

The lesson most Europeans drew from Nazi tyranny and the age of catastrophe was that they needed a strong nation state to protect them against external interference. After the French, Belgian and Danish democracies had been unable to stop Hitler, for example, the conclusion was to rebuild them all the more robustly. As a result, the bulk of the era's intellectual, political and administrative energy was channelled into creating strong and viable nation states. While borders were redrawn and millions displaced east of the Iron Curtain, the foremost process in Western Europe was national reconstruction. West Germany represented an exception in this context. Regarding its political system as a stopgap awaiting reunification, the Federal Republic presented itself as a break with the past (although it did hark back to earlier periods).[11] So the Second World War had shaken Europe's societies to the core and even if activists like Altiero Spinelli hoped to build a federal Europe on the *tabula rasa*, most Western Europeans craved the comfort and security of the nation state. Corresponding as it did with the plans of the victorious Western Allies, this current was to largely shape developments.

Statehood came to assume quite new forms, however. State planning – hitherto the instrument of the Soviet Union and right-wing dictatorships (and wartime exception elsewhere) – became increasingly prevalent in democracies. Drawing the lessons of the pre-war crises, planning was supposed to reduce economic risks and make people's lives more secure. Europeans yearned to pursue personal happiness, which demanded a dependable political framework. The Commissariat général du Plan that de Gaulle established in France in 1946 embodied that spirit. And who headed the Commissariat in its early years? No less a figure than Jean Monnet. Before becoming the architect of European integration, he played a leading role in rebuilding the French nation state. The state intervened massively in the economy, especially in the immediate post-war period. France nationalised a string of major companies, including carmaker Renault; and everywhere the expansion of state bureaucracy proceeded apace.[12]

These developments were not restricted to the economy, as a systematic expansion of the welfare state provided pensions, healthcare, social housing, improved access to education and much more. 'The state' now meant more than just government and legislation, tending instead towards penetration and regulation of all areas of life. Of course there were still great differences between countries and fields; planning also had a tendency to be more a panacea than a consistent guide for political practice. Nonetheless, never before in peacetime had people's lives in Western Europe been so heavily influenced by their own state.

That is also reflected in the striking expansion of the state in this period, where we find a strong overall trend with certain national differences. The proportion of public employees in the Italian workforce rose from 10 per cent in 1951 to 12 per cent in 1961, 19 per cent in 1971 and 22 per cent in 1976; in West Germany the figures increased from 10 per cent in 1950 and 1960, 12 per cent in 1970 and 13 per cent in 1980; in the United Kingdom from 27 per cent in 1951 to 24 per cent in 1961, 28 per cent in 1971 and 31 per cent in 1981; and in Denmark from 12 per cent in 1950 to 15 per cent in 1960, 21 per cent in 1970 and 32 per cent in 1979. State spending also rose strongly, as described in greater detail in Chapter 3, 'Growth and Prosperity'. In brief: it grew in Italy from 25 per cent of GDP in 1950 to more than 45 per cent in 1980, in West Germany from 37 per cent to more than 50 per cent; in the United Kingdom from 35 per cent to 46 per cent and in Denmark from 22 per cent to more than 60 per cent.[13]

Of course the states were embedded in larger structures. To most Western Europeans in the immediate post-war era, however, this meant not the world of international organisations, but the empires that gave many nation states a global role. When Juliana was crowned in 1948 she became queen not only of the Netherlands itself, but also of the much larger Dutch East Indies (today Indonesia) and other territories. On the day after her coronation *De West* published a 'home story' describing her as 'queen and mother of the nation' – *De West* being the local paper not of Zeeland or Groningen, but the Latin American colony of Suriname.[14] Belgium, France and the United Kingdom also still possessed global empires. The coronation gown worn by Elizabeth II in 1952 bore not only the symbols of England, Scotland, Wales and Northern Ireland, but also the emblems of all the states of the Commonwealth including the wattle of Australia, the Indian lotus flower, the South African protea and the Canadian maple leaf.[15] Alongside little Luxembourg, defeated Germany stood out in Western Europe for its lack of colonies.

Even if these empires were already disintegrating, they still shaped the way Europe saw the world. For example, Juliana's coronation address mentioned the people of Suriname and the Netherlands Antilles, for whom she asserted that 'liberty, equality and independence' were an 'inalienable inheritance' – but within the confines of 'the new kingdom'.[16] The decolonisation of Africa and large parts of Asia gained momentum after 1945, with formal independence achieved by the early 1960s in many cases. But in some places, like Suriname, colonial rule persisted; the mental and informal legacy lasted much longer, as examined in greater detail in Chapter 8, 'The Community and its World'. At the same time the end of empire reinforced the nation state as the obvious political framework.

Where the Western European nation states did encounter limits was in fulfilling their promises of prosperity and security. International cooperation was seen as a way out, especially where the costs of programmes at the national level threatened to bankrupt national budgets.

That applied, for example, to French and Dutch agricultural policy in the 1950s. When Alan Milward writes in this connection of 'The European Rescue of the Nation-State', his argument possesses a convincing economic core.[17] That dimension of European integration is discussed in other chapters; here we concentrate instead on transformative effects and limits of European integration as the project progressed.

Modest Origins

Like its ideals and identity, the EC as political and administrative reality remained fairly marginal in the post-war decades. Even the launch of the ECSC was very modest: its High Authority was initially accommodated in an unassuming grey building in Luxembourg vacated by the railways administration.[18] Improvisation was required again when the EEC set up in Brussels, as the Belgian state struggled to keep up with the demand for office space.[19]

Contrary to certain stereotypes that persist to this day, the EC's organs remained astonishingly small and compact. This is illustrated most clearly by the example of the Commission, which was also conspicuously homogeneous especially at the highest levels. As far as size is concerned, the figures might seem to suggest a different conclusion, as the Commission's growth was certainly rapid. The number of grade A (policy-making) officials grew from 982 in 1960 to 2,565 in 1975 and 4,727 in 1990, with the fastest relative growth in the early phase.[20] In 1967, before its fusion with the Commissions of the other two Communities, the entire High Authority of the ECSC comprised a staff of about 1,000.[21] In 1972, just before the first enlargement round, the Commission of the three Communities employed about 5,700 officials, rising to 8,700 in 1980, 10,000 in 1985 and 13,000 in 1992. Pre-Maastricht expansion was uneven, with especially strong growth in DG I (External Relations), DG VI (Agriculture) and DG VIII (Development). Agriculture remained one of the EC's central activities during this period, while the significance of external relations grew. Stagnation in other policy areas was reflected in personnel trends. This applies especially to DG VII (Transport). It took until the 1990s for the member states to permit Brussels to expand its influence in this field.[22]

But these absolute figures tell only one side of the story. In 1988 personnel costs accounted for only about 4 per cent of the EC's total budget, and in terms of its size the Commission was on a par with the French Ministère de la culture or the British Lord Chancellor's Department and smaller than Amsterdam's city administration or Madrid's Comunidad autónoma.[23] But the EC was responsible for much larger sums of money than those municipal authorities: by 1989 the EC budget represented almost 4 per cent of the total state budgets of its member states.[24] From that perspective the Commission was anything but large.

At the same time the Commission remained astonishingly homogeneous in terms of educational background and career, especially at the very top. Almost half the commissioners who served in the period between the first and third enlargement rounds – from 1973 to 1986 – were lawyers. About two-thirds had acquired political experience before joining the Commission, mostly as parliamentarians and frequently also in national governments. Many belonged to the war generation, with former officers of the German Wehrmacht working side by side with forced labourers, collaborators with resistance fighters and members of the Allied armies. All vowing: 'never again!'[25]

The top level was homogeneous in another respect too. About 44 per cent of officials in the 1970s and 1980s were women, but the distribution was very lopsided: they never exceeded 10 per cent in grade A but dominated the more junior functions.[26] The top Commission posts initially remained an exclusively male preserve; the first female commissioners were not appointed until 1989, with the Greek Vásso Papandréou and French Christiane Scrivener. It was to be another ten years before the ECJ appointed a female judge, with the Irish Fidelma Macken. Male dominance of the executive levels made the few exceptions all the more conspicuous, most notably Margaret Thatcher as British prime minister and Simone Veil as a prominent and long-serving member of the European Parliament (and its president 1979–1982).

To return to the question of the size of the organs: the other EC institutions were also anything but overdimensioned. The European Parliament had 518 members at the end of the Cold War; after the first enlargement in 1973 it was 198, in 1958 142 and in the ECSC era just 78.[27] Here again absolute growth appears rapid, but that cannot be the only yardstick. Significant differences in rights and responsibilities make comparisons with national parliaments problematic. For perspective, however, it should be noted that the Twelfth German Bundestag (1990–1994) had 662 members while the 518-member European

Parliament at that point represented the electorates of ten member states.

So the EC did not produce a bureaucratic Frankenstein, a Goliath or any other kind of monster. Instead we are left wondering how institutions of such modest size were able to accomplish their wide-ranging tasks at all, and what that meant for their relationship with the member states.

So how did the Commission function internally? Here decisions made in the High Authority era turned out to be crucial.[28] Its first president, Jean Monnet, established it as a small and highly cohesive elite group. Whereas NATO, the United Nations and other international organisations largely had to make do with delegated, seconded and temporary staff, the EC created its own high-level bureaucracy, where temporary and external staff only played supporting roles. The Commission staff were characterised by their high level of education and a rigorous selection process. In comparison to other bureaucracies the Commission was always 'top-heavy', with relatively few officials at the lower grades (B to D) and many at the policy-making grade A. In the Commission itself scurrilous comparisons were occasionally drawn with a 'Mexican army': more generals than soldiers.[29]

The Commission wanted its officials to be able to operate autonomously and independently of their respective country of origin. At the same time the Commission's administrative structures and culture were heavily influenced by the French model, without copying it directly: the German Foreign Ministry and the Tennessee Valley Authority of New Deal America also served as templates for particular elements. Emile Noël, the Commission's *éminence grise* and long-serving secretary-general from 1958 to 1987, played a major part in ensuring adherence to the French model of strict formal hierarchies complemented by flexible informal practices. According to one Spanish Commission official, Noël embodied 'French intelligence in action'; one Italian official became even more lyrical, calling Noël 'the Callas, irreplaceable, unique: the top official who France lent to Europe'.[30] Throughout the period French remained the lingua franca, and even officials who knew one another well used the formal *vous* in line with the hierarchical administrative culture.

Of course many changes occurred over the decades. For example, the High Authority of the ECSC was initially characterised by a less hierarchical and more informal style than the later EEC

Commission. Enlargement also modified the composition of the institutions, not least on account of the existence of an informal system of national proportionality. Experience of the Second World War, which was originally formative at all levels, also faded, with those born after 1945 starting to appear in senior positions by the 1980s. In comparison to the early years and the 1980s, the Commission developed few successful policy initiatives of its own in the 1970s; in that decade's politically troubled climate upholding the status quo was the priority. Nevertheless, in relation to their size the Commission and EC were astonishingly potent.[31]

Quietly Effective

The secret of the great leverage acquired by the EC's small but highly effective bureaucracy was the way its institutions increasingly opened up to, connected and later even intertwined with those of the member states. The EC's administrative practice had centripetal effects, increasingly drawing personnel from the member states into its orbit. As its powers expanded it involved growing numbers of national politicians, civil servants, experts and others in its work, not only at the top ministerial level. The same applied in the informal context too: if Brussels enjoyed growing clout, it was obvious for at least part of the lobbying business to move there. So 'Brussels' was ever less a separate political sphere outside of the political and administrative activities of the member states. This began at the level of preparatory planning, continued in formal decision-making, and was felt throughout the field of policy implementation and evaluation, with the dynamic affecting regulation earlier than administration. The process was noticeably more intense in a field like agricultural policy, where the EC was enormously influential from the 1960s, than, for example, in transport policy (or still less security). Nevertheless, in an increasing number of policy areas and problems the EC interwove itself ever more with the political and administrative apparatuses of the member states, by drawing on their personnel and expertise.[32]

Official EC institutions like the Commission and the Council of Ministers were only able to function in the regulatory sphere by virtue of the groundwork of a multitude of committees. The Committee of Permanent Representatives is comparatively well known, often under its French acronym COREPER. But even COREPER, which prepared the sessions of the Council of Ministers, was not enough to supply the millions of details required. These were provided by working parties for the different fields. The Commission also surrounded itself with a sophisticated system of committees composed of representatives of the member states. They increasingly supported, advised and monitored the Commission, and in some cases oversaw the implementation of EC decisions in the member states. In the new EC jargon this system of committees revolving around the Commission became known as comitology. A third type of committee contributed expertise without exercising formal control functions.

Without this cosmos of committees the EC would never have been able to make and rapidly implement meaningful decisions. For example in 1970 when the EC was negotiating a Common Market Organisation for wine, the committees were responsible for preparing specific definitions for table wines, exceptions for sparkling wines, quality standards and much more. Their staff and expertise came from the ministries of the member states. Obviously questions such as specifying permissible grape varieties for each wine-producing area demanded extraordinarily specialised knowledge that even the comparatively large Directorate-General for Agriculture in Brussels did not possess.[33]

The number of individuals from member states involved in Commission committees and working parties represents an area of impressive growth. It grew from under 7,000 in 1965 to 11,000 five years later and 16,000 by 1984. For diplomats, financial experts, lobbyists and many others the EC became increasingly important.[34]

The way such bodies shaped processes and procedures is illustrated by the example of the Council of Ministers. By 1962 its agenda was already distinguishing between A and B items: A items had been clarified in advance in the committees and could usually be simply agreed without debate at the beginning of the meeting; only the B items had to be discussed. Yet, if the ministers' meetings in Brussels failed to generate excitement, this was even truer of the work of the committees. The EC epitomised the de-dramatisation of political conflict through integration, linkage and increasing interconnection.[35]

Like the Commission, the Council of Ministers also underwent fundamental transformations over the course of the decades. As the representation of the member states it met – and still meets – in different formations depended on the policy area under discussion. In view of the limited powers of the early EEC, this initially meant principally the foreign, economics, finance and agriculture ministers. By the 1990s that had changed fundamentally; now it was hard to name a policy area that was entirely untouched by the EC. The Council was meeting in thirty-seven different formations by the mid-1990s, with the proportion of meetings accounted for by the four aforementioned 'traditional' ministeries falling from 80 per cent in 1967 to 42 per cent in 1995.[36] And the Community ran into some interesting puzzles. For example, when the EC culture ministers met for the first time in September 1982, several member states were left wondering who they should actually send. West Germany had no federal minister of culture, and the answer was by no means obvious for the British either.[37] As Lutz G. Stavenhagen, secretary of state at the Foreign Ministry in Bonn, noted in 1986: 'Integration has moved beyond the originally affected ministries, and now reaches into almost all departments.'[38]

The deliberations of the Council of Ministers often revolved around naked national interests. Margaret Thatcher's insistence on reducing the British budget contribution, which even many outside observers regarded as overblown, is one prominent example from the 1980s; another the campaign by Greek prime minister Andreas Papandreou for special status and a larger share of the Regional Fund, where Papandreou explicitly emulated the hard-nosed British strategy.[39] Despite the impression created by frequent retelling of these and similar cases, there was more to the process than merely pursuing national interests at the European level. This was seen especially clearly in agricultural policy. In the early years the agriculture ministers and sectoral lobbying organisations worked together to mould the CAP despite differences in their national positions. But when, in the second half of the 1960s, it became apparent that the costs of the Common Agricultural Policy were spiralling out of control, resistance formed especially among the finance and economics ministers. Agriculture ministers and lobbying groups quickly understood that they were on a hiding to nothing if they continued to pursue isolated national interests. Gradually a transnational common front emerged – national agriculture ministers held together by transnationally co-operating lobbyists – opposing all initiatives to reform the CAP. A producer-friendly pro-farmer stance now became more important than national loyalties. This again underlines how strongly the political systems and power structures of the involved European societies were changing.[40]

That does not mean, however, that the EC had the same transformative effect in all areas. The Empty Chair Crisis, for example, buried the Commission's lofty aspirations for a rapid expansion of its powers – which would lead to even deeper penetration into the member states. But even in core areas the Commission occasionally encountered limits or had to live with ambivalent outcomes. One area where this occurred in the early phase was the area of competition law, which was to become one of the EU's strongest weapons in the medium term. In this case the problem was not a lack of powers but a shortage of personnel to apply them effectively. The EEC Treaty prohibited 'All agreements between undertakings, decisions by associations of undertakings and concerted practices which may affect trade between Member States and which have as their object or effect the prevention, restriction or distortion of competition within the common market'.[41] But many procedural details remained vague until Regulation 17/62 supplied greater clarity five years later. Under the Regulation, which was adopted in February 1962, 'agreements, decisions and concerted practices' could be permitted if they were properly notified to the EEC Commission.[42] By April 1963 Brussels had received 36,000 notifications, underlining the Regulation's significance for businesses in the member states. But in 1964 the Directorate-General responsible for competition law (DG IV) had only seventy-eight officials to process all these cases. That was obviously impossible – and also left the Commission lacking the resources to actively search for violations. In order to be properly effective it would have needed a considerably larger apparatus. Thus on the one hand competition law stood for strong centralisation with sweeping powers for the Commission, which did not have to rely on national competition authorities for enforcement. On the other, the process was exceedingly complex and time-consuming, with a lack of personnel imposing tight constraints. This demonstrates again: the EC had the strongest administrative impact where it melded with the member states. This theory is confirmed by a glance at later developments. In 2003 the EU annulled the 1962 Regulation. Its replacement, Regulation 1/2003, sliced through the problem by decentralising the enforcement of competition law.[43]

The Microphysics of Law I: An Alcohol Problem

Alongside interconnection with national administrations, European law turned out to be an effective lever for the EC to bring

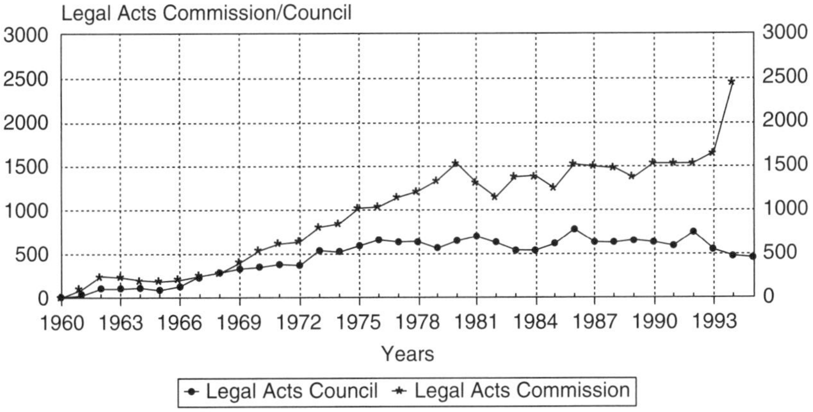

Figure 9: Legal acts adopted by Council and Commission. Beck Publishers, based on Wessels, *Die Öffnung des Staates*, p. 202

about change within the member states. Correspondingly large was the number of legal acts adopted by the Council of Ministers, and from the late 1960s increasingly frequently also the Commission. The bare number is not necessarily terribly revealing, however, as it lumps together trivial rules affecting minor details with regulations with great impact.

The significance of early ECJ decisions, above all *van Gend & Loos* and *Costa* v. *ENEL*, has already been mentioned in earlier chapters.[44] In the following we take a rather closer look at the role of law in relation to the Common Market as the heart of the Cold War era EC. Here we are looking at developments that also played a central role in transforming the political systems of the member states.

The impact of EC decisions was especially strong in the case of 'negative' integration, which played a central role in the establishment of the Common Market. Here 'negative' refers to the process of removing trade barriers, as opposed to the 'positive' (in a value-neutral sense) creation of shared policies.[45] The relevance of this is that while 'positive' integration – such as the aforementioned Common Market Organisation for wine – required a multitude of detailed rules that had to be thrashed out and then implemented, reducing tariffs between member states as provided in the EEC Treaty offered greater impact for considerably less political and administrative effort. The 'negative' and 'positive' approaches were thus rooted in quite different concepts of integration; the former involved the implementation of European legal norms couched as individual rights, whereas 'positive' integration was characterised by a desire to create policy.

For a long time therefore, 'negative' integration was no cakewalk. Tariff reductions effected under the EEC Treaty and decisions of the Council of Ministers were only the start. Integration became a great deal trickier when it came to removing non-tariff trade barriers, because states had been using health, safety and environmental norms and standards to regulate and restrict trade for decades, indeed centuries. Some of these measures were justified and served to protect the public; others stemmed from protectionist interests – and rarely was it easy to differentiate the two. In this area the debates in the Council of Ministers were noticeably tougher and often torpedoed by the unanimity rule. It is against this background that a series of key rulings by the European Court of Justice came to play a crucial role in advancing integration.[46]

While the EEC Treaty prohibited in fairly general terms 'quantitative restrictions on importation and all measures having equivalent effect',[47] it was left to the ECJ to put this into practice. One of the most significant examples was its *Cassis de Dijon* ruling in 1979. West Germany had prohibited imports of the French blackcurrant liqueur, on the grounds that its alcohol content was less than the 25 per cent by volume required for fruit liqueurs under German law (the Branntweinmonopolgesetz). In *Cassis* the ECJ ruled that the West German ban restricted freedom of movement of goods in a manner that breached the treaty. Barriers to trade between member states created by differences in national regulations, the judgment spelled out, were acceptable only where they were indispensable for public welfare. The case at point, it ruled, failed that test: the West German government's argument concerning public health was 'not decisive' because 'the consumer can obtain on the market an extremely wide range of weakly or moderately alcoholic products'.[48] This sober legalese could have been stated more bluntly: cassis contained less alcohol than many beverages that were legal in Germany (and was diluted to consume). If the German state had been earnestly concerned about the health of its citizens it would have had to ban all the much stronger German schnapps too. The Court's decision opened the German market to the French blackcurrant liqueur, which went on to become Germany's fashionable long drink of the decade under the name Kir Royal: cassis mixed with sparkling wine or champagne.

More seriously, the ruling on liqueurs had repercussions elsewhere. *Cassis* cemented the principle of mutual recognition:[49] any product that is legally traded in one member state may be also sold in another, even if it does not necessarily satisfy all the technical regulations there. The ruling blew the market wide open. It enabled free movement of goods without harmonisation of national regulations, and as such impinged heavily upon the sovereignty of the member states. In effect the law of one member state could now apply in the territory of the others. In legal terms *Cassis* was based on the ECJ's *Dassonville* judgment of 1974, which was actually even more radical.[50] But in the subsequent period it was *Cassis* that had the greater impact when it came to removing non-tariff trade barriers. From 1979 the European Commission frequently cited this ruling in its efforts to promote liberalisation, emphasising its implications beyond the area of alcoholic beverages.[51]

But the real breakthrough did not come until the mid-1980s. The struggle against trade protectionism is always a labour of Sisyphus, and by this point the situation had escalated visibly. For all their lip-service to liberalisation the member states responded to the recessions of the early 1970s by introducing new protectionist measures, especially non-tariff barriers. Immediately after its inauguration in 1985, the new European Commission under its enormously effective president Jacques Delors exploited the mood of crisis to argue for change. The resulting work programme was ultimately to culminate in the Single European Act that massively advanced the deepening of the EC in the economic sphere. At the technical legal level the Commission used *Cassis* as a lever, especially under the eccentric British Internal Market Commissioner Lord Arthur Cockfield. The Commission's white paper of 1985, as a central milestone on the way to completing the Single Market by 1992, referred in its almost sixty pages just once to *Cassis*, but its thrust depended heavily on the ruling.[52]

At the same time the Commission's public presentation of the programme outlined in its white paper was highly effective. While much of the document was very technical, its conclusions in particular deployed emotive language, asserting that Europe stood 'at the crossroads': 'We either go ahead – with resolution and determination – or we drop back into mediocrity.'[53] The ambitions were expressed in terms of realising a Single Market – distinct from the existing Common Market – by 1992. Legally speaking it was questionable whether the new term actually meant anything larger or different than its predecessor. Similarly, the deadline of December 1992 was sometimes presented in almost chiliastic terms; in fact it was psychologically and politically relevant, but not legally.[54] In this manner the EC created a new vision for itself, injecting drama and symbolic significance into largely technical questions in order to broaden its appeal.

The Commission enjoyed the support of business circles such as the European Round Table of Industrialists – representing the interests of multinational corporations – and the pro-European Ligue Européenne de Coopération Economique.[55] The governments of a number of member states also threw their weight behind the white paper's agenda, first and foremost the British.[56] In contrast to other EC questions – and contradicting the clichés – the Thatcher government campaigned hard for greater integration in the area of the Single Market and worked closely with the Commission, whose plans coincided with British government's. In fact, London went as far as arguing for the Single Market to be complete by 1990. An internal Commission document noted during the white paper's preparatory phase that the British request should not be taken 'too seriously', as it represented the stance of just one member state. Of all governments, it was particularly the British under Thatcher who pushed for deeper European integration in relation to the Single Market.[57]

So, from the late 1970s state sovereignty was eroded by a viscous liqueur. Market opening was executed via the jurisprudence of a proactive Court of Justice, while the member states' governments initially did little. What they did do was accept Community law and, as we will discover below, that was not to be sniffed at. Community law was especially effective in connection with *Cassis*, because it focused largely on 'negative' integration, whose implementation involved considerably less bureaucracy than its 'positive' counterpart. Under this approach the EC was able to keep its apparatus comparatively small without sacrificing impact. Until the Maastricht Treaty the Common Agricultural Policy, which relied more heavily on 'positive' integration, represented the most important exception to the rule. At the same time the European Parliament, and even more so the Commission, studied ECJ judgments like *Cassis* very closely, and were soon using these cases to legitimise further integration steps.[58] That was the technical foundation upon which the Single European Act was ultimately to lead to a significant deepening of European integration.

The Microphysics of Law II: The New Approach

European law had a still more subtle effect in another context. Here we are dealing not simply with 'integration by law',[59] but with even more complex processes of negotiating the role of the law in which the member states had an important say. This case, again, concerned the EC's Common Market and developments in the 1980s. And again the measures were aiming to reduce the multitude of non-tariff trade barriers and thus promote 'negative' integration. But this time legal harmonisation of safety standards was also involved, which takes us into the sphere of 'positive' integration.

If we want to understand these mechanisms, we will need to venture even further into the weeds of dry and technical legal minutiae. *Cassis* was naturally important, but it certainly did not determine all subsequent ECJ judgments; sometimes the Court even pulled in the opposite direction and curbed market opening. One such example is the *Wood-working machines* decision of 1986. Anyone who has talked to an older carpenter or joiner knows how dangerous such machines were. Hand injuries caused by circular saws and other wood-working machinery used to be an even greater occupational hazard than they are today; it was nothing unusual for a carpenter to lack a finger or two. In the concrete case, the Commission lodged a complaint against France for banning the importation of such machines from Germany on the grounds that Germany's safety standards were too lax. In a clear defeat for the Commission, the ECJ ruled in France's favour and confirmed national trade restrictions based on occupational safety.[60] Where product safety was at stake member states were able to resist market opening, at least as long as there was no agreement on shared norms and the respective safety concepts and cultures (although not necessarily the actual level of safety) differed. But harmonising Community-wide product standards turned out to be extremely difficult, as long as this required unanimity in the Council of Ministers. It would also have meant agreeing almost impossibly detailed rules and would have overtaxed the abilities of the law. The tangle of objective grounds for different standards and essentially protectionist arguments was virtually impossible to unravel.

In the end even this challenge found its solution. On 7 May 1985 the Council, following the Commission's recommendation, decided to cease tackling technical barriers to trade using detailed norms and regulations. Instead 'legislative harmonization' was now restricted to 'the adoption . . . of the essential safety requirements' in what came to be known as the New Approach.[61] From now on, a product only had to satisfy relatively general requirements in order to be traded in another member state. The details of technical norms, on the other hand, were regulated through non-binding standards issued by European standardisation bodies. The New Approach opened up new possibilities and allowed the Single Market to deepen without overburdening it with excessively complicated rules or creating a bureaucratic monster. But it also generated problems of its own: for example, whether the standardisation bodies adequately represented consumers as well as producers, or the ecological implications. Even more importantly: this was a largely technocratic approach, whose democratic legitimation could legitimately be doubted.[62]

Legally speaking, the 1985 Resolution and the New Approach in general relied on a combination of European and national law. Their hybrid approach differed from *Cassis*, which had brought forth a unified European law. All that the New Approach strove for was to standardise basic health and safety requirements rather than maximising legal harmonisation. Even more than *Cassis*, the New Approach made it difficult for the member states to impose restrictions and regulate their own national markets, because this brought them under suspicion of hindering access. Nevertheless, the member states retained ultimate responsibility for environmental and health and safety questions, which kept the Commission's workload small. But again in this case, the law lastingly transformed the relationship between the Community and its member states, changing the character of statehood and tending to reduce national sovereignty.[63]

Even if the New Approach was largely identified with the Commission, many other actors were also behind it; together they formed a broad coalition for more market liberalisation. Academics played a role, along with various export sectors and individual governments, including the British (even if London was to reverse its stance a few years later).[64] Representatives of the European Parliament were involved too: German MEP Karl von Wogau, for example, wrote to Commission president Delors in April 1985 demanding 'improvements in the conditions for creating joint European norms'. This meant 'transforming the standards institutes CEN and CENELEC into an autonomous European standardisation body', whereby new products should be subject to common European norms rather than national ones.[65] The standardisation bodies Wogau referred to did play a central role in the New Approach; but it was problematic that the technical nature of their work meant that public control was weak.

Initially all the New Approach did was to open a door, and it remained unclear how much of its potential would be realised. The aforementioned *Wood-working machines* judgment fell in a phase where the New Approach already existed, and followed the older line of detailed harmonisation. The ECJ remained restrained in its rulings. So the victory of the New Approach was initially by no means resounding.[66]

That was soon to change. Barely a year after the Council Resolution on the New Approach the member states adopted the Single European Act, the first major treaty reform since the Treaties of Rome. Under Article 100 of the original EEC Treaty, 'acting unanimously on a proposal of the Commission', the Council shall 'Issue directives for the approximation of such provisions laid down by law, regulation or administrative action in Member States as directly affect the establishment or functioning of the common market'. In practice this often meant the cumbersome route of seeking full harmonisation. The Single European Act boosted market opening with the new Article 100a, under which 'measures for the approximation of the provisions laid down by law, regulation or administrative action in Member States which have as their object the establishment and functioning of the internal market' could be adopted 'by a qualified majority'.[67] Although it excluded taxes, freedom of movement and labour rights, the arrangement significantly deepened integration in all other areas. While the principle of mutual recognition opened markets, Article 100a also initiated the process of re-regulation and thus mitigated towards 'positive' integration.

While that might sound rather technical, the implications were enormous. Many of the politicians involved in bringing Article 100a into being understood it as nothing more than a minor administrative tweak and underestimated its effects. This perspective was encouraged by the member states' insistence on preserving the Luxembourg compromise; on paper vital national interests continued to enjoy priority. But in the subsequent period majority voting became the norm, not least because Article 100a raised the bar to invoking the Luxembourg compromise: in order to assert vital national interests and use a veto, a member state now had to convince half the other governments to invoke the 1966 compromise. This significantly reduced the sovereignty of the member states in a core area of European integration. Again the EC was able to hugely expand its influence without having to create a bureaucratic monster.[68]

The medium- and long-term effects of these legal rulings in the 1970s and 1980s were immense. Initially *Cassis* and the New Approach were applied almost exclusively to goods. But from the 1990s they and their legal successors also found their way into other areas, such as the service sector, where they functioned as a lever to expand market opening. This in turn provoked massive public resistance, as seen, for example, in the fuss over the so-called Bolkestein Directive (the Services in the Internal Market Directive of 2006) and the ensuing admission of cheap labour from Eastern Europe ('Polish plumbers').[69]

These later conflicts were only partially connected with the legal essence of *Cassis* and the New Approach. But they do point to the problems that were already associated with the initiatives to deepen market integration using legal channels in the 1970s and 1980s. The question of the extent to which consumer, labour and environmental interests were represented alongside producer interests always remained relevant. At the same time the market opening programme increased the pressure of competition and – especially in weaker economies – produced many losers who were unable to withstand it.[70]

The objectives of the New Approach and the Single European Act were not revolutionary; in fact they were covered by the original EEC Treaty. But they possessed great leverage, especially as they departed from the European Commission's centralised approach. At a microphysical level the law was more diverse and drew on various strategies: on a proactive Court, as in the case of *Cassis*, but also on the active participation of the member states and their readiness to accept majority decisions. These various transmission belts transformed the structural relationship between Community and member states, with the latter's national sovereignty experiencing significant transformation and further curtailment during the fifteen years before the Maastricht Treaty. Even if this was still largely invisible to ordinary citizens – who showed little interest – the integration process began to exert considerably more impact than in the preceding decades. And when the citizens did begin to notice how deeply the EU affected their lives in the 1990s and 2000s, they frequently asked who had decided this, when, how and why.

The Beef with Beef

The 1985 white paper stressed that all the 'Community's political and legislative efforts to create an expanded home market for the people and the industries of the Community, will be in vain if the correct application of the agreed rules is not ensured'.[71] As such, it pointed to a problem that was particularly pressing for a supranational formation like the EC – and leads us from the sphere of regulation into the realm of administration.

Susceptibility to fraud became one of the EC's greatest challenges: the bulk of its spending consisted of subsidies, especially in the realm of the CAP, whose Guarantee Section accounted for between 60 and 80 per cent of the EC's total budget in the 1970s and 1980s.[72] Sums of that magnitude attracted crime like bees to a honeypot. Cases of abuse were revealed with increasing frequency from the 1970s, with the figure peaking in 1985. One especially popular target for criminal activity was agricultural exports to third states, which received financial support through the aforementioned Guarantee Section. In a so-called carousel fraud (missing trader fraud) goods were exported from the Community and corresponding export subsidies collected. Then the goods were reimported – and in some cases the procedure began again with the very same goods. In the most 'environmentally friendly' version, only the freight documents actually made the journey, maximising the illicit gains. In 1985, for example, the EC paid export subsidies on twice the amount of butter than was actually exported.[73] Other forms of fraud targeted other EU funds. A European Parliament report in 1987 estimated that at least three billion ECU were lost to fraud annually, a shocking sum in relation to a total budget of thirty-six billion ECU (revenue).[74] Research about the 1990s, where more reliable figures are available than for previous decades, suggests that up to 10 per cent of the EU budget was wasted on fraud and other forms of abuse; a lack of precise data lies in the nature of the problem.[75]

One contributing factor was the Commission's reliance on the member states' administrations to spend its budget funds (as for all other administrative functions too) and especially in the early days its lack of anything more than rudimentary control mechanisms of its own. Although the Treaties of Rome already provided for financial controls of the Community's revenues and spending, the auditing rules initially remained vague. Even in 1973 the relevant audit committee had fewer than three dozen members, while bearing responsibility for a multitude of questions. In 1977 the EC founded its own independent European Court of Auditors, which by 1987 had ten times the personnel of the audit committee in 1973.[76] Nevertheless the loopholes remained enormous, with the Court of Auditors noting in its 1987 annual report 'with concern' that a trader that had been investigated in 1985 for export refund fraud in one member state had shortly thereafter received a payment of twelve million ECU in another EC state without being subject to any special controls.[77]

At the same time, the labyrinthine nature of the EC's rules was an invitation to abuse. The rules for export refunds for beef, for example, differentiated between chilled and frozen meat, between hindquarters and forequarters, male and female animals, and pure and mixed breeds; for beef alone there were eighty classifications, in agriculture as a whole more than 1,200. Customs checks involved immense effort, and were in practice often impossible. This played into the hands of criminals.[78] Given the lack of controls, different prosecution thresholds and differences in regulations between member states, the risk of successful prosecution for fraud or improper use of EC funds remained small.[79] The situation was exacerbated by the rules governing the relationship between the Commission and the member states: under a Regulation from 1972 the member states could be required to reimburse the Commission for the costs of fraud, which did nothing to encourage them to report incidents to Brussels.[80]

At the same time, one should not think that fraud and abuse were exclusive to the EC. Again agricultural policy supplies the best examples. Many member states had established their own protectionist measures before the CAP was set up, in some respects anticipating the EC's approach, and these had already been subject to subsidy fraud on a grand scale. In Germany the concept of carousel fraud was established long before any European agricultural policy existed. At the end of the 1950s, for example, there was a string of prosecutions for carousel fraud with eggs in the Oldenburg region, with the media distinguishing between variants like *Eierwäscherei* (washing off the date stamp and reselling) or trade in *Lufteier* (non-existent eggs).[81] To that extent, certain forms of crime simply migrated from the national level to the European. But the problems expanded too, as the complex structures of the EC meant that the loopholes for criminal activity were larger than in individual states.[82]

Thus even as the relationship between the Community and the organs of the member states intensified in the course of the post-war decades, the fraud cases spotlight the losses associated with the process. Consequently, the Community's credibility was at stake. But seeking a solution to the problem would have meant a much closer degree of harmonisation than the member states were willing to accept. In other words there was a price to pay for Brussels remaining so small.

The Challenge of Implementation

Even leaving fraud aside, whether and how Community law applied in the member states became a relevant question. Implementing decisions taken in Brussels across differently structured political systems presented significant challenges. Political cultures, institutional structures and also the inherent logic of specific policy areas all shaped the integration process.

Nevertheless, generally, the member states did seek to implement the decisions made in Brussels.[83] Considering the degree to which the EC challenged, transformed and constrained state sovereignty, levels of compliance and implementation in the period before the Maastricht Treaty were altogether high. A culture of lawful action – sometimes involving renegotiations, recourse to higher instances and suchlike – characterised the approach of governments and administrations. While the public rhetoric was occasionally sharp, open non-compliance was rare.

This is all the more notable given that the EC possessed no independent administrative organs of its own, with which to implement decisions across the territory of the Community (or even just to closely monitor observance). It also lacked policing powers of its own to investigate violations (and still does today). It was therefore relatively easy to boycott decisions made in Brussels. As in the aforementioned preparatory processes, national, regional and local instances played central roles in implementation in the member states. Without always realising it themselves, they increasingly operated within a framework shaped by the EC.

Successful implementation of decisions was an absolutely crucial aspect for the Community's legitimacy. But it was vital in practical terms, too, especially in the Common Market. If certain member states had failed to implement measures, an uneven competitive playing field would have resulted. To that extent national instances and individual market participants also possessed an interest in full and complete implementation, alongside Brussels itself. At the same time the mode of implementation differed depending on the type of legal act. EC regulations and decisions took effect directly, whereas directives had to be transposed into national law.[84] That made matters a good deal more complicated, especially if we consider the dimensions: by the end of 1969 – about a decade after the Treaties of Rome – the EC had adopted almost 150 directives. Ten years later the figure reached about 950, in 1989 it passed 2,000 and just five years later hit about 2,860.[85]

One good example illustrating the challenges of implementation and its potential to transform the status quo is found in the area of the EC's transport policy: the tachograph, commonly known as the 'spy in the cab'. Through a series of legal acts beginning in 1969, the EC restricted the hours HGV drivers were permitted to spend behind the wheel and insisted that tachographs be installed to verify compliance.[86] The original background to the measure was principally the desire to equalise conditions of competition in the transport market between member states and between road and rail. These EC rules were, however, implemented not by EC organs but by the member states. In most cases the national transport ministry was responsible, but other parts of the state apparatus were also affected. Roadside checks, prosecution and sentencing guidelines were also national responsibilities. From the minister of transport through the police authorities to the courts: all were now heavily affected by the EC. The same applied to lorry drivers, trade unionists and business owners, as well as, for example, researchers investigating the impact on competition, later also on road safety and the environment. Through such channels the tachograph brought the EC another step further into daily life in the member states. It is notable that this occurred in a field – transport policy – where the pre-Maastricht Community possessed comparatively few powers.[87]

The tachograph story illustrates the type of difficulties potentially associated with implementation. When the EC first developed its policy it comprised just the six original member states, where the tachograph was already widely used. It was much less common in the United Kingdom and Ireland when they joined the EC in 1973, but London and Dublin naturally had to implement decisions made in Brussels both before and after accession. At the end of the decade the Commission accused the United Kingdom of violating its commitment and failing to pursue implementation properly. The case came before the ECJ, which ruled for the Commission.[88] Although considerably poorer, Ireland experienced no such difficulties, leading London to comment condescendingly that Dublin was adhering 'slavishly' to the installation timetable from Brussels. Cheap jibes were the response when a former colony mastered a challenge better than the British themselves.[89]

While they may have been limited, the Commission did possess certain legal tools to monitor implementation in the member states and to enforce compliance by judicial means if necessary. An infringement procedure before the ECJ was the strongest weapon in formal terms, but was notoriously slow in practice and frequently induced negotiating processes on the political plane. To that extent its impact should not be overestimated. Otherwise the Commission possessed rights of information and investigation, and could also seek to pressure states to observe the rules through publicity. Alongside the Commission as the 'Guardian of the Treaties' and the ECJ, the European Parliament and the Court of Auditors played a growing role in insisting on observance. In comparison to a nation state, the EC thus possessed comparatively few enforcement tools – but those it did have were strikingly powerful in comparison to other international organisations like the Council of Europe or the OECD.

While the legal and administrative details are not of interest here,[90] it is worth noting that the number of officially registered treaty violations grew significantly over time. That is not exactly surprising if we

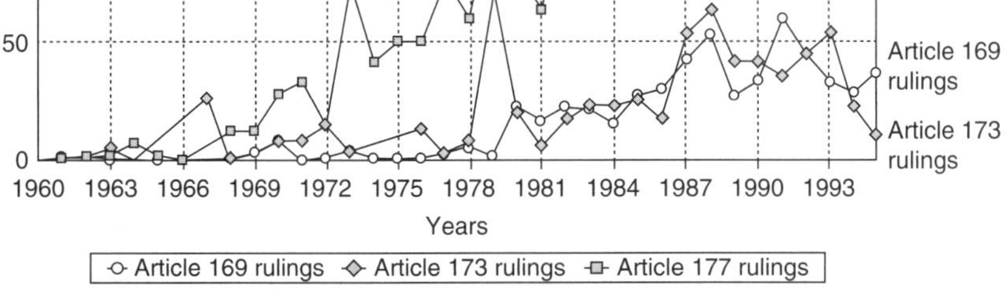

Figure 10: ECJ rulings against member states. Beck Publishers, based on Wessels, *Die Öffnung des Staates*, p. 245

remember how strongly the *acquis communautaire* expanded during the period. The growing number of directives offers a good example: the burden they placed on the administrative capacities of the member states made friction inevitable. This applies especially to the Single Market Programme, which encompassed about 300 individual measures. While progress seemed impressive at the legal level, the member states struggled to implement measures within the stipulated timeframe. By 1991 the twelve member states had only implemented about 65 per cent, although the figure had reached 95 per cent by the December 1992 deadline. Implementation demanded time and effort.[91]

The Value of Black Sheep

What were the reasons for the member states' problems? The most important finding is that there is no simple answer: for example, that fundamental rejection of the integration process cannot explain all of them. Systematic research on this question, incidentally, only began in the 1980s and quickly revealed how complicated the problem was.[92] One early overview already listed more than 300 variables relevant to explaining questions of implementation,[93] and since then it has become even clearer that there are many potential reasons for a state to implement an agreed decision late, inadequately or not at all.[94] Those who stood out of line were not necessarily black sheep, but might sometimes have had good reason.

One factor frequently mentioned in legal and political research is the compatibility of EC law with existing national rules. Where, to return to the example cited above, tachographs were already the norm in many member states and a legal requirement in some, EC law was easier to implement than where this was not the case, as in the United Kingdom. At the same time the Irish example demonstrates the limits of an explanation that concentrates on conformity with the legal status quo in a particular member state.

Another closely related reason is the absence of institutions and administrative resources required to implement EC law in a member state. Among the original Six this is especially clear in Italy, which traditionally found it most difficult to implement EC directives in national law – and attracted the most infringement procedures. Yet Rome generally pursued a pro-EC course, which at least at first glance jarred with its implementation problems. A good part of the contradiction is accounted for by the country's political instability and comparatively weak administration. One challenge was presented by a mechanism originally conceived as a democratic safeguard. After liberation from Fascism the Italian parliament was granted unusually extensive powers. With all new legislation requiring a majority in both chambers and no mediating instances between them, draft bills sometimes shuttled endlessly between Senato and Camera. This 'perfect bicameralism' looked wonderful on paper but was unwieldy in practice; it hampered the orderly legislative process as much as the unstable and often short-lived governments of the post-war decades. Until 1990 the lack of a specialised agency or coordinating body for EC matters further complicated implementation. The central problem was not Euro-scepticism, but the home-grown problems of Italy's political and administrative system.[95]

Conversely, France was able to achieve a high rate of implementation for EC legislation because Paris was especially successful in influencing decisions made in Brussels. This naturally made them easier to implement. What this reflects is the strength and clarity of French policy on Europe, and its administrative substructure led by the Secrétariat général du Comité interministériel pour les questions de coopération économique européenne (SGCI) founded in 1948. Despite its rather complicated-sounding name, the SGCI was from the 1960s a highly efficient inter-ministerial coordinating body that enjoyed a very good reputation within the EC – and was feared for its influence. In later years it served as a model for many other countries including the United Kingdom and Denmark.[96] In Germany and Italy on the other hand, coordination of European policy always remained difficult for institutional reasons – with potential repercussions for decision-making in the Council of Ministers and for implementation. Ministerial particularism frequently weakened West Germany's position in Brussels; and when it came to implementation the West German federal system created challenges of its own, with the *Länder* frequently required to implement decisions they had otherwise played no part in.[97] The Danish case is also interesting: Copenhagen's representatives acquired a reputation as tough (even pedantic) negotiators in the Council. But once a legal act had been adopted, implementation in Denmark often proceeded very smoothly.[98] In certain questions the EC established special budget lines to expand the possibilities for the member states to realise agreed goals. That applies, for example, to the European Regional Fund established in 1975 and the European Social Fund created in 1958.[99] To that extent the road to implementation was influenced not only by the specifics of the implementing member state, but also by the origins and nature of the legal act itself.

This brings us to the most important reason why EC legislation was so consistently implemented despite the problems: because these were legal acts decided by the member states themselves. The principle of unanimity applied in many cases, and where it did not the Luxembourg compromise was always at hand. The upshot was that the representatives of the member states almost always agreed on that to which all of them could subscribe. This is why, for example, security questions were excluded for so long. At the same time this process expanded the weight of the rulings of the Court of Justice, the New Approach and Article 100a, serving as a counterweight to the member states' control over the direction, intensity and form of integration.

As well as support from the member states, as manifested in their legislative activities, there was also another last factor. On the basis of *van Gend & Loos* the Community's citizens played an increasingly important role in applying European law and using the courts and state instances to insist on its observance. Now they were able to appeal directly to the fundamental freedoms, regulations and other parts of EC law and have these enforced by the courts. This applied, for example, specifically to environmental impact assessments on the basis of the 1985 directive. Such a degree of public participation in legal matters was unheard of in organisations like the OECD or NATO. This special public mobilisation behind EC law also promoted successful implementation.[100]

While the discussion to date has flagged distinctions between member states, recent research demonstrates the limits to such an approach: sometimes the pace of implementation varied so strongly within a single policy area in a single member state that one cannot even generalise on that scale.[101] After thirty years of research there is a broad consensus that there is no magic formula for determining the process and outcome of implementation; to that extent it represents a field where there are still more questions than answers. That also remains true where some directives suffered legal flaws that hindered their implementation. All these aspects together pose the question: is completely uniform enforcement possible at all? Rather than seeking an ultimately unrealistic comprehensive uniform law, the point is to continually redefine the bounds of acceptable pluralism.

And, more importantly: a purely legal/political perspective concentrating on the original legislation itself or its implementation in national law tells us little about whether the measures in fact achieved their planned objectives. In other words, formal implementation should not be confused with the actual application of rules by administrations, businesses and citizens, and still less with their effectiveness. For example, a directive prohibiting gender discrimination in pay came into effect in 1975.[102] One could pursue the question of whether and how the member states legally implemented these and subsequent rules applying the principle of 'equal pay for equal work'. Or one can simply note that more than forty years after the 1975 directive, reality in the EU still falls short of that goal. This relates to a further point: in the pre-Maastricht era the impact of integration on the member states' political systems – and to a certain extent their administrations – was transformative, but the influence on public discourse was much weaker and therefore went widely unnoticed. That was not to change – building on the developments of the second half of the 1980s – until the period after the end of the Cold War.

Superstate or Tool of Nations: Résumé

First off, Europe's post-war integration process did not produce a bureaucratic monster, and the EC never came anywhere near abolishing the nation state. Quite the opposite: in many respects the Community was outcome and instrument of national interests. At the same time, in order to function it required stable, predictable and dependable member states – and it copied their fundamental mode of operation, which was based on laws and bureaucracies.

But in the long term European integration had even more far-reaching effects: the EC level increasingly networked with state structures and processes, initially in the sphere of regulation, later increasingly in relation to administration. Administrations are integral to the modern state. By making use of these structures, the EC made itself even more ubiquitous.[103] And these processes stabilised the European Community; one could say it actually emerged through a process of increasingly melding with the administrations of the member states. This in turn engendered a transformation of existing state structures, especially from the 1980s onwards. The process political scientist Wolfgang Wessels describes for West Germany also applies to other EC states: membership of the EC opened up the Western European state like no other Western European international organisation. The OECD and the Council of Europe also made moves in the same direction, but their impact remained much weaker.[104]

Not only did Brussels become a crucial point of reference for politicians, civil servants and administrators, as well as experts, lobbyists and an ever growing spectrum of others. The rights and obligations also changed noticeably. This was not solely due to the content of the *acquis communautaire*; it also resulted from the procedures associated with the *acquis*. Because the member states were principally represented by their governments in Brussels, the integration process strengthened the executives vis-à-vis the parliaments and in federal systems, the national level over the regions. Direct elections to the European Parliament from 1979 and the (moderate) consideration given to regional entities in the Single European Act represented efforts to correct those problems, but were unable to truly resolve them.[105]

An even more important factor was the almost invisible effect of European law. After a round of landmark rulings in the early 1960s, this applies in particular to the 1980s, with a proactive Court of Justice, the New Approach and the expansion of majority voting with the Single European Act. A quantitative comparison best underlines the accelerating penetration in the second half of the 1980s: from 1958 to 1987 the average number of new directives and regulations introduced annually was 789. It rose to 1,645 between 1988 and 1992, falling back to 1,311 in the subsequent five years.[106]

All in all the law turned out to be a highly flexible tool for connecting and melding the states of the Community and their shared institutions. It permitted transitional phases and exemptions, for example, realising the Common Market in a series of stages and granting farmers in tiny Luxembourg exceptions from the Common Agricultural Policy.[107] But above all it was the far-reaching inclusion of the member states' political and administrative apparatuses that gave the EC such an impact. This is seen especially in the implementation of the Community's legal acts, which was a highly decentralised process. There was no telling when implementation would be successful, when it would not. Much depended on degree of compatibility with national regulatory and institutional traditions, and on party-political preferences and civil society pressure. At the same time it was crucial how contested the EC proposal was and whether interest extended beyond the legal level of implementation to include the really relevant question: the consequences of the legal acts for the economy and society. So there were clear limits to interconnection, and as always the devil was in the details.

Nevertheless, what the historian Charles S. Maier once called 'territorial purity' – the growing congruence of the space of economic activity and political identity with the political space defined by the modern state and its central government apparatus – was increasingly eroded by European integration.[108] What emerged was a post-classical form of sovereignty – states cooperating in a partially supranational framework – that some experts believed presaged a process of constitutionalisation.

But such developments should not be confused with a homogenisation of the member states. It was – and remains – a matter of contention whether ultimate legal power resides at national level or has migrated to the Community. Often, moreover, an independent legislative shaping and implementing policy on the ground was absolutely necessary. In fact, directives and common policies did not just mitigate towards gradual convergence, but also exposed or even exacerbated existing differences between societies. This is reflected both in the British jibes about Ireland's 'slavish' implementation of EC decisions and in Italy's conspicuous implementation problems.

The Italian postage stamp illustrated at the beginning of the chapter embodies all these developments. It shows the signatures of the representatives of the six founding states. The member states – sometimes referred to as the 'Masters of the Treaties' – are visually prominent. The name of the issuing state, the value in the corresponding national currency, the issuing institution and the name of the artist give the stamp a national touch.[109] And the symbolic presence of another international organisation also relativises the weight of the EC. The French abbreviation CEPT in the top left corner stands for the European Conference of Postal and Telecommunications Administrations. Because the European Community lacked the authority to issue postage stamps of its own, this commemorative issue required a joint initiative by the EC states in the scope of CEPT. And still, the stars of the Community stand out among the signatures. The twelve gold five-pointed stars on a blue ground were not to become the official symbol of the EC until 1986, and nobody could yet imagine that they would be omnipresent in the member states twenty or thirty years later. But the real basis for this was laid in the 1980s, especially the second half of the decade. Despite its misdating, this little stamp told more about the future than one could have imagined in 1982.

Until the end of the Cold War, connection and transformation through European integration seemed at first glance to affect only the state apparatuses. Ultimately, in fact, they generated effects penetrating deep into the societies. But there was little public awareness of this, and consequently no critical discussion of the changes. In the first place the measures affected economic policy and the economic realm: questions in which most people had little interest as long as the consequences appeared not to affect them directly. While dissatisfaction arose sporadically over changes to the familiar nation state framework,[110] this was ultimately outweighed by disinterest, and there was virtually no discussion about European identity or the pros and cons of integration. Monster or not, Brussels appeared to have little to do with daily life. In much of continental Europe, dissatisfaction with the EU – like serious public support – was not to find any real expression until the 1990s.

7 DISINTEGRATION AND DYSFUNCTIONALITY

Frustration over national and European politics had been building for some time among the island's citizens. A referendum cleared the air: the population voted by a small majority to leave the European Community. Three years later they were already out. In the run-up to the vote the island's political leader declared that his country possessed very special features 'in terms of language, culture, economy and social structure'; it was necessary to leave the EC 'to preserve the particularity of the country'.[1]

So what else did the islanders do in parallel to their exit process? Jonathan Motzfeldt, the leader of the exit camp quoted above, also worked hard to acquire the status of an associated overseas territory of the European Economic Community instead. In future the territory would not be bound by the EC's laws, nor would it profit in full from its subsidies and other benefits. But it would continue to enjoy privileged access to the Common Market and other concessions.[2]

This episode – describing Greenland in the 1980s – illustrates a number of points. The most fundamental is that European integration has always been reversible, and that it was possible to leave the EC during the Cold War. As well as contradicting widespread preconceptions, the event is also notable because the 1957 Treaties of Rome made no provision for withdrawal: the Community was explicitly established as a permanent institution.[3] The 1953 proposal for a European Political Community went even further, describing it as 'indissoluble'.[4] But it was never to be ratified, torpedoed instead a year later – together with the European Defence Community – by the French National Assembly. An exit mechanism was not introduced until 2007, with the now infamous Article 50 of the Treaty of Lisbon.[5] Greenland's path out of the EC points to another significant aspect too: there is no longer a sharp dividing line between European integration on one side and sovereignty and full independence on the other. Today societies are so interdependent – economically, socially, legally and politically – that the question is only the degree and form of cooperation. In a globalised world untrammelled sovereignty has become unaffordable, and no state thinking about leaving the European Union can have any interest in cutting all ties.[6]

This applies especially strongly in the case of Greenland. The world's largest island with a population of just 50,000 joined the EC in 1973 as part of the Kingdom of Denmark. Yet in the Danish referendum of October 1972 – where a majority of the population as a whole voted to join – 70 per cent of Greenlanders voted 'no'.[7] Seven years later Denmark made Greenland an autonomous dependent territory, which was the precondition for Greenland to leave the EC in the early 1980s without separating from Denmark. The biggest criticism of the EC was the unfairness of the Common Fisheries Policy: boats from other member states were able to fish in Greenland's bountiful waters, while the handful of Greenland fishermen saw little benefit in privileged access to Cromarty, Forth, Tyne or Dogger.[8]

The consultative referendum of February 1982 produced a small but clear majority of 52 per cent for leaving. Motzfeldt's wish was fulfilled. His island left the EC, but simultaneously became an associated territory. The economic consequences of this apparently paradoxical two-step were massive and lasting. Formally speaking, Greenland is now less closely tied to Brussels than it was between 1973 and 1985 – although only in certain areas. A series of protocols negotiated in parallel to the exit itself preserved the EC's comprehensive fishing rights in Greenland waters and maintained close relations in other areas.[9] The compromises were hard-fought, with West Germany in particular insisting on the *do ut des* principle: Greenland had to keep its waters open in exchange for advantageous association terms.[10] Indeed, ties actually deepened following the exit. Today Greenland is one of the EU's Overseas Countries and Territories, meaning that large parts of EU law apply there but local residents have no say in making them. This has been especially true since a deepening of the partnership in 2006, under which Greenland continued to receive funds from the EU and in return kept its waters open to EU fishing vessels. Integration has made such enormous advances since the 1980s that the island's ties with the Union are in many respects even closer now than before it left. For example, in trade: in 2014 84 per cent of Greenland's imports came from the EU and 64 per cent of its exports went there. So leaving the formal structure has certainly not separated Greenland's economy from the European Union. The forms of connection and dependency may have shifted in certain respects, but they remain very strong. Ironically, there is also a tendency in Greenland today to move closer to the EU again – as an instrument to achieve greater independence from Denmark. All in all, the fronts have shifted markedly since the 1980s, and little remains of Motzfeldt's original agenda.[11]

And how did all this look from the perspective of those who remained in the Community? The 1982 referendum caused quite a stir at the time. Behind the scenes Copenhagen was working to keep the renegade islanders inside the Community – in an absurd constellation where EC law required the Danish government to negotiate a withdrawal it opposed. Ironically it was the government of Margaret Thatcher – scourge of Brussels' Eurocrats – that enquired informally in Copenhagen whether anything could be done to persuade the Greenlanders to remain. Copenhagen advised against, as this could backfire. But Brussels and various national governments were still concerned; London and Bonn worried that Greenland's departure could encourage centrifugal tendencies in other parts of the Community.[12] In view of the United Kingdom's often harsh and nationalist tone under Thatcher, London's line was especially surprising. Bonn fretted about the consequences for the German deep-sea fishing fleet, which relied on the waters off Greenland for 45 per cent of its catch (and accounted for most of the EC's catch there).[13] Alongside this economic argument, the German Foreign Ministry – as in so many questions of that era – viewed the matter through the Cold War lens and feared a weakening of the West.[14] That was not entirely absurd in light of Greenland's geostrategic importance, and goes some way to explaining Thatcher's stance too. The European Commission also regretted the decision, stressing that 'there has been insufficient awareness and understanding of all the Community has done for Greenland'. All in all, the rest of the Community grudgingly accepted the Greenlanders' decision to leave, but treated them rather like ungrateful children.[15]

The EC tended to play down the significance of the event in its public statements. Many experts at the time also emphasised that Greenland's decision was an absolute exception with no systemic consequences whatsoever, and represented no trend towards disintegration.[16]

Disintegration is thus nothing new historically, and is certainly not as simple as just restoring national sovereignty. And the relationship between disintegration and dysfunctionality within the unification process is a good deal more complex than one might think at first glance. At the same time it is astonishing how little attention these processes have attracted to date, with researchers tending to blindly follow the 'stop-and-go' narrative preferred by the protagonists of the unification process themselves. This is most vividly expressed in a witticism attributed to the first president of the Commission of the European Economic Community, Walter Hallstein: 'Integration is like a bicycle. You either move on or you fall off.'[17] In this way of thinking, there is no going back: bicycles may be versatile, but what they cannot do is reverse. While certain abandoned initiatives have found their place in the narratives and memoryscapes of European integration, there is no place for reverses or setbacks, which is a very good reason to examine those here.

Algeria: Departure by Degrees

Another country left the EC about twenty years before Greenland, and that disintegration story is even less known.[18] Algeria parted ways with the emerging EC in 1962. With its roughly eleven million inhabitants, Algeria had joined the Community in a similar way to Greenland: as part of a European nation state, in this case France. When the Treaties of Rome were signed in 1957 Algeria still belonged to France's global empire, along with large parts of Africa. In formal terms, however, Algeria – unlike, for example, Tunisia or Senegal – was not a colony but a part of France itself, constituting several of its *départments*. In reality, Algeria was a colony of a French state that defined itself in negation of its colonial status.[19] Article 227 of the Treaty Establishing the European Economic Community therefore treated Algeria not as an associated territory but as a part of the Community itself (although subject to certain special terms).[20] Algeria only left the EC in 1962, when it separated from France after its bloody war of independence. Occurring barely five years after the Treaties of Rome, the event left hardly a trace in the history of integration; the implications for the EC were always overshadowed by the much greater impact of Algeria's independence from France and the broader decolonisation process that was rapidly gaining momentum at the time.[21]

So what did Algeria's Motzfeldt do in this situation? The charismatic Ahmed Ben Bella, Algeria's first post-independence president from 1963 to 1965, had been one of the key leaders of the uprising against France. He fought for France in the Second World War and was decorated several times, receiving the Médaille militaire from Charles de Gaulle in person. Subsequently he became one of the most vocal adversaries of European colonialism. Ben Bella looked to Gamal Abdel Nasser's Arab socialism in Egypt, and sought backing from the Soviet Union, which was to award him its highest distinction a few years later.[22]

Ben Bella took a correspondingly critical stance towards European integration. Addressing Algeria's Constituent Assembly in September 1962 he lauded his country's hard-won independence from a 'colonial domination of 132 years' and stressed that the free Algeria intended to participate in the construction of African union. He made a point of mentioning the threat posed to the Maghreb and African countries by the EC's emerging agricultural policy. It must not be allowed to obstruct agricultural reforms in Algeria, he argued. Instead, cooperation with France must be subordinated to 'the interests of our farmers'.[23]

On Christmas Eve 1962, almost exactly three months after this bold speech, Ben Bella wrote in his capacity as president of the Algerian Council of Ministers to Walter Hallstein, the president of the Commission of the EEC. So what did Ben Bella want? In rather oblique terms but wasting no time on niceties, he asked for the EC to maintain Algeria's special status. In other words, Algeria should continue to be treated as if it were still part of the Community, even after leaving. However sharply it contradicted the idea of independence and hard-fought sovereignty, Algeria's leaders had quickly recognised that this option would best serve the country's interests. Preserving the de facto status quo relationship would help to cushion the economic effects of the formal break with France and the Community.[24]

Astonishingly the EC accepted the proposal. A secret document of the EC Council of Ministers noted in mid-1963 that Algeria would be treated 'as a de facto member state of the Community'.[25] The extent to which Article 227 (2) could continue to form the basis of the relationship was certainly controversial. It was in fact France that pushed for the closest relationship, despite the fiasco of its colonial war there, which cost hundreds of thousands of lives and left French international power and prestige in tatters. Surprising as this might at first glance appear, this actually fitted into the broader picture of bilateral Franco-Algerian developments during the post-independence period. France saw continuing close relations as a vehicle of national influence and prestige. President Charles de Gaulle himself continued to advocate close cooperation for economic, cultural and above all political reasons. The idea was that this approach would open doors for France in the emerging 'Third World' and as such serve its desire for national *grandeur* and independence from the two superpowers. Algeria's leaders, for their part, sought a tricky balancing act between confrontation and cooperation: for all their revolutionary rhetoric, their country's predicament certainly produced an interest in close relations with the former colonial power.[26] Within the EC, Rome in particular pulled in the opposite direction. Italy opposed treating Algeria differently than other third countries and saw it as unnecessary competition for its own Mediterranean agricultural products. Initially, however, it was French high politics that determined the Community's course.[27]

Trade barriers were raised slightly in the following period, above all Algeria's obstacles to imports from the EC. While Algeria exhibited new self-confidence, neither side was prepared to see relations rupture.[28] When the member states lowered their internal tariffs by about 10 per cent at the beginning of 1965, the arrangement also included Algeria: France's conciliatory stance again prevailed over Italy's rejection. That said, the decision posed a serious problem for the EC. The Commission noted internally that 'such a measure does not in the slightest prejudice the future stance of the Community. The arrangement applied provisionally to Algeria by the Six is uncertain, lacks any legal basis, and cannot remain in force indefinitely.'[29] Not only were the six EC member states ignoring the letter and spirit of their own nascent Common Commercial Policy, according to which Algeria would have had to fall under one of the EC's predefined relationship types, but each member state also interpreted the Algeria rule differently.[30] In 1968 the EC noted internally that its relationship with Algeria continued to lack a clear legal basis; in terms of trade policy Algeria remained in a legal limbo.[31] One Algerian expert writing at the time saw matters similarly, describing the situation concerning the EEC as 'both accidental and paradoxical'.[32] So even several years after Algeria left the Community, the disintegrative effects remained astonishingly minor and the actual situation obscure.

From Soft to Hard Exit

From 1966 onwards, however, matters deteriorated for Algeria. The strides made by the EEC's Common Market, and its stiffening external customs borders, increasingly obstructed Algerian producers' access to the internal market. When the six member states again lowered their internal tariffs at the beginning of 1966, Algeria was excluded. Algeria's original privileges faded and it instead increasingly found itself facing the same trade barriers as normal third states. For some time already the Algerian government had been seeking to place its relations with the EC on a new footing. While exploratory talks were held in 1964, Brussels subsequently refused to pursue serious negotiations. One reason for the delay will have been the paralysis affecting the Community during the Empty Chair Crisis of 1965. But another factor was more important: the member states were unable to agree on a common position. France remained the most open to Algerian wishes, while Italy – motivated primarily by commercial interests – represented the opposing pole and was already treating Algeria de facto as a third country. One argument put forward by Rome was that the EC was already producing surpluses of some Algerian products, and if Algeria were granted favourable market access they would grow still larger. The other states adopted positions in-between the two poles. The Commission consistently pressed for an agreement with Algeria, but failed to bridge the diverging positions.[33]

So Algeria found itself at the mercy of disputes between the member states. The emergence of the EC's Common Market during the same period steadily eroded the astonishingly privileged position Algeria had enjoyed immediately after independence. In contrast to 'normal' third states, there was no solid legal basis for the Community's future trade with Algeria. For the moment the arrangements were comparatively favourable for Algerian producers, but uncertainty over future developments is always deadly in matters of trade. The EC's procrastination also left Algeria unable to apply for the associated status normally granted to former colonies. Thus after leaving, Algeria initially remained a privileged de facto member only to see its situation degenerate on account of internal Community politicking. At the same time the trading relationship remained highly asymmetrical, with the EC largely dictating terms. Algeria had become a political football with little influence on the outcome of negotiations.

The effects of growing trade discrimination were most marked in the wine sector, the mainstay of Algeria's exports. European settlers had been making wine in Algeria since the 1880s, primarily for sale in France. Within just a few decades the sector experienced breathtaking success, and by 1960 Algeria was the world's largest wine exporter (and fourth-largest producer); wine accounted for more than half of Algeria's exports. But there was a downside to the export miracle: it represented a typical case of colonial monoculture, dedicated to the needs of France and other European markets. As a largely Muslim country, Algeria itself consumed little wine.[34]

Nevertheless, the new Algerian leadership placed great hopes in the wine sector during the immediate post-independence era. Ben Bella saw strengthening the agricultural sector as 'our first battle'.[35] Yet the wine industry was already in trouble, for two principal reasons. Firstly there were home-made difficulties. Until 1962 almost all vineyards had been owned and run by European settlers. Indeed, the Algerian Front de Libération Nationale (FLN) regarded them as a symbol of colonial oppression. In 1957 the French army reported that 12.5 million vines had been destroyed in the conflict, many of them deliberately uprooted by independence fighters.[36] After targeting the wine sector during the anti-colonial war, the new independent government nationalised it in 1962. However, the dramatic loss of expertise caused by the flight of most European settlers coincided with local mismanagement to create serious difficulties for wine production and export.

Alongside the problems attributable to war and independence, certain decisions by the EC also helped to tip the Algerian wine industry into existential crisis. During the founding phase of the Common Agricultural Policy there was initially no Community-wide market organisation. France then saw the opportunity to create new barriers against Algerian wine, not least to boost opportunities for its own producers. Algerian wine was generally poor in quality, and the vintners of France proper were keen to substitute their own products.[37] In 1970 the EC did then create a Common Market Organisation for wine. New tariff barriers virtually excluded Algerian wine from the Common Market, especially after the rules were tightened in 1976.[38]

The Algerian government complained about the EC's attitude in 1972, arguing in what was an unusually sharp tenor for an official memorandum that the country had been forced to produce wine during the colonial era. In response to increasing discrimination in European markets, the document noted, they had already destroyed thousands of hectares of vines since 1965, but this was still not enough to prevent overproduction. The EC was 'forcing a developing country to shut down its most modern agricultural sector, which employs more than two-thirds of its entire agricultural workforce, in order to allow a group of developed countries to preserve a backward sector'.[39] According to a separate letter from the Algerian government to the European Commission, the EC was 'turning its back on dialogue and making unilateral and arbitrary decisions that demonstrate nothing but contempt for the even most elementary interests of our country'.[40] *El Moudjahid*, the official organ of the FLN, also complained that this was an 'arbitrary act'.[41] But the EC's member states remained unmoved by such criticisms.

Alongside home-made problems stemming largely from nationalisation and the Algerian government's inability to find substitute markets quickly enough, the EC thus contributed to the decline and fall of the Algerian wine industry. The negotiations were further complicated by entanglement between arrangements for Algeria and those for Morocco and Tunisia. Within the space of just fifteen years Algeria's wine production trickled away; today the country produces almost no wine at all. The clock has turned back to before 1880, and Algeria's great century of wine is long-forgotten.[42]

Disintegration had enormous repercussions for Algeria. Initially the effects remained minor, partly on account of concessions made by the EC member states, partly due to their inability to agree on a new arrangement. That internal discord also explains Algeria's export problems in the subsequent phase, starting in 1966 and even more so from 1970, when the EC's actions came to be characterised by insecurity and trade protectionism. The economic problems were unmistakable, and strikingly seen in the wine sector, in particular. The Algerian government responded with a typical move for a left-leaning ex-colony during this period: it tried to sell its wine to Comecon. As such, wine became a Cold War bargaining chip. In 1969 the government signed a seven-year deal with Moscow, and the Soviet Union became the main purchaser of Algerian wine. But the trade remained too small to compensate the loss of Western European markets: Moscow's interest did not extend that far. Ultimately, at least in the economic sphere, Algeria's new sovereignty did not come with clear gains in autonomy, independence and power.[43]

Disintegration had massive consequences for the EC too. Despite the dramatic power asymmetry between the Community and Algeria, the ex-colony was certainly not alone in feeling the impact. Its withdrawal contradicted the objective of the Treaties of Rome 'to confirm the solidarity which binds Europe and the overseas countries'.[44] Even if France exhibited more generosity than Italy during the initial years, Paris still cared more about vintners of the Midi, Burgundy and Bordeaux regions than those in Tlemcen, Oran and other Algerian wine-producing centres. Producers from less well-known and lower-quality regions of mainland France, in particular, had been criticising Algerian imports since the late nineteenth century, and their protests found a growing hearing after Algeria became independent. By this route aspects of the protectionism that had characterised French policy towards Algerian wine imports since the first half of the twentieth century ultimately found their way into the Common Market Organisation (CMO) for wine of 1970, for example, quality requirements and restrictions on planting vines. In other words, some of the EC rules contained the legacy of French colonialism. Article 26 (4) of the Regulation prohibited blending of EEC wines with imports, and was aimed directly at Algerian imports. As well as having significant regulatory consequences, protectionism at the EEC level also created new openings for wine producers in the member states.[45] These rules go a long way to explaining the famous 'wine lake' that the CAP produced in the 1970s, alongside the better-known butter mountain.

The great French intellectual Albert Camus died in 1960, and was therefore spared these developments. Camus was born in 1913 into a settler family of mixed French and Spanish origin in Mondrovi (today Dréan) close to Algeria's border with Tunisia. His father was a wine-shipping clerk. Camus had a very different vision of the future after the Second World War: a federal Algeria, Europe and world. His vision was a multi-ethnic Franco-Algerian federation in which the Arabs, French, Berbers and others would live together in peace. At the same time he wanted a united Europe, as part of a world without nations and nationalists and instead governed by treaties, federations and other forms of international cooperation. The first part of his dream was blown away by the Algerian War. A European federation remained a pipe dream too. What did emerge in the western half of the continent were shared institutions designed to shape a peaceful coexistence. But against Camus' hopes, this process excluded Algeria, his former home.

The year 1976 saw a small improvement in economic relations, with the EC and Algeria concluding a bilateral cooperation agreement. Now the Community supplied a certain amount of financial support to the ex-colony, trained experts and helped with infrastructure development. An association agreement in 2002 further deepened cooperation, and soon thereafter even closer cooperation began under the European Neighbourhood Policy established in 2004.

Even if independence from France did not by any means lead to complete isolation from the EC, trade tailed off significantly in the medium term. Certainly, the EC/EU has always remained a crucial trading partner for Algeria, which today sources almost half its goods imports from the EU (although the EU ranks only seventeenth for Algerian exports). But in the 1960s and 1970s the EC occupied a much more central place in Algeria's foreign trade, with figures between 80 and 90 per cent in both directions. Conversely, Algeria has never been terribly important for the EC/EU. Today, for example, Algeria accounts for only between 1 and 2 per cent of the EU's total import and export volumes.[46] After a relatively mild transitional period, Algeria has paid a very high economic price for independence from France – and the EC. That distinguishes the Algerian experience from Greenland's.

What connects Greenland and Algeria is that neither joined the EC as a sovereign state, but in both cases within the context of European colonialism. To that extent some of the conditions differ significantly from Brexit. But the further European integration progresses and the more strongly the Union closes itself off, the stronger the economic case for remaining within it – however much one might like to do otherwise for other reasons.

At the same time, these two examples demonstrate that leaving the Community is not a new challenge associated exclusively with the unification process in the early twenty-first century. Especially given that a third case can be added to the list. In 1975 the United Kingdom held a referendum on its membership of the Common Market. Just three years after joining, the idea of leaving again was being discussed. None of the other member states raised any formal objections: long before the Treaty of Lisbon the idea that a full member might withdraw from the organisation was widely accepted. In the end the June 1975 referendum produced a clear majority for continued membership (although the British government had made preparations for the eventuality of the vote going the other way, which cannot be said of the 2016 referendum).[47] Nevertheless, it is worth noting that long before Brexit the idea of the 'ever closer union' and continuous enlargement was encountering tangible resistance.[48]

Disintegration and Dysfunctionality as Political Normality

But actually leaving the Community represents only one extreme form of political disintegration. Disintegration and dysfunctionality appear less visibly and spectacularly in those places where they result from asynchronicities and disequilibriums in the unification process. In this connection it is worth taking a brief detour into the history of integration theory, as the phenomenon described here is closely related to one that underlies the neo-functional take on integration, but stands the theory on its head.[49]

Since the early post-war era there have been attempts to explain European unification through neo-functionalism, where the 'spillover' mechanism plays a central role. In the classical definition by Leon N. Lindberg this involves 'a situation in which a given action, related to a specific goal, creates a situation in which the original goal can be assured only by taking further actions, which in turn create a further condition and a need for more action, and so forth'.[50] In this theory spillovers result from pressures arising out of functional relationships between different parts of a complex structure, such as the political and economic order of a community. In order to preserve the functionality of aspects already integrated, further steps towards European unification are required. For example, communitising the coal sector only made sense if the same applied to steel, as the two were so closely interconnected. Research conducted over recent decades has shown that political practice by no means always obeyed this academic theory. Otherwise there would have been a common transport policy from about the 1960s. Not only was this explicitly mentioned in the Treaty Establishing the EEC (Articles 74 to 84); many good reasons also existed at the functional level, as a fully functioning Common Market presupposes the removal of protectionist measures – such as different freight tariffs – in the field of transport. Obvious as the spillover effects would have been and hard as the European Commission worked towards them, they simply refused to occur.[51]

There has been a tendency to overlook the full implications of moments where member states decided to defy the logic of functionalism.

Where policy areas and sectors are so closely connected, the absence of spillover effects can lead not just to 'standstill', but in fact undermine and dissolve aspects that have already been integrated. Lindberg spoke of preservation of the 'original goal' demanding further actions. This also applies to absolutely concrete policies, and not just to more or less abstract goals. While that has generally been overlooked to date, it is not actually particularly surprising. Because neo-functionalism appeared to explain the strategies of post-war politicians like Monnet and Schuman, and was quickly put to use by the pro-European elites to legitimise their own actions, one should therefore not be surprised about the lack of critical distance to the narratives produced by the actors themselves.[52] Disintegration was made 'unspeakable' to keep it outside the realm of the possible.

The point here is not to propose a negatively neo-functionalist disintegration theory. But it is revealing that the phenomenon described here can already be identified in the 1960s – shortly after integration under the auspices of the EC began in the first place.

The best illustration is offered by the Common Agricultural Policy. The CMOs created in the 1960s defined prices for agricultural products produced within the Community and for imports from third states. CMOs formed the central instrument dividing the internal market from the world market (where some prices were considerably lower). Because the member states each possessed their own currency, the Council of Ministers initially agreed to define the prices of market organisation products using the Community's gold parity unit of account. This fictitious currency corresponded to the gold-backed US dollar and soon became known in Community jargon as the 'green dollar' on account of its importance for the agricultural market. That sounded like a sensible and pragmatic solution.

When the Council of Ministers agreed on this in 1964 nobody imagined the enormous repercussions. EC law now stipulated that if a member state devalued its currency its domestic prices had to increase correspondingly in order to preserve the relative level of prices agreed within the Community.[53] Any change in the valuation of a state's currency therefore created major problems. For example, when France devalued the franc by 12.5 per cent in August 1969, producer prices in France should have risen by the same amount. But at a time when overproduction of agricultural goods was already a growing problem, the increase would have given producers enormous windfall profits and created incentives to further expand production. The other alternative, devaluing the unit of account by the same amount as the French franc, would have penalised uninvolved farmers in all the other member states. By mid-August the Council of Ministers had agreed to temporarily decouple French prices from the CAP system. The figure chosen for the reduction – 11.11 per cent – reflected political compromise more than economic rationale.[54]

So just one year after its much trumpeted birth, the common agricultural market was de facto suspended again. Free movement of goods between France and the five other member states ceased, and the Fifth Republic now had a national agricultural market with European rules. This was especially significant because France accounted for more than one-third of the six-member EEC's agricultural production at that time, and the CAP formed the very heart of the Community. Günther Harkort, state secretary at the German Foreign Ministry, wittily described it as an 'interment of the European agricultural market by common pricing' – where the tombstone had deliberately been set so squint that the deceased would hopefully soon come back to life.[55]

The striking thing about this story of burial and hopes of resurrection is, firstly, how poorly prepared the Community was. Parity adjustment is a routine monetary policy matter, but now acquired far-reaching implications within the Common Agricultural Policy. Yet the franc devaluation took the Community unawares, and it responded with a hastily cobbled-together compromise. Secondly, it reveals the complexity and interconnectedness of the integration process. The CAP stumbled not over any inherent problem, but an apparently unrelated issue. The currency problem became existential because integration progressed unevenly, with the CAP functioning as the spearhead of the unification process. Harmonised agricultural prices required fixed exchange rates between the member states. But these could not be guaranteed where economic and monetary policy remained national prerogatives. Thirdly, we see here again that concrete negotiations will not necessarily always end in standstill or a further step towards integration. Here, instead, a genuine step backwards occurred – and was discussed as such by the press.[56] The problem only worsened a few weeks later when West Germany floated the deutschmark in response to economic problems, and introduced import levies and export refunds at its borders. For a number of weeks then, strictly speaking, the common agricultural market was reduced to just four members, until France and

West Germany returned to the fixed exchange rate system.[57] At the same time, everyone now agreed that exchange rate fluctuations were deadly for the CAP.

The inadequately considered implications of agricultural integration were now glaringly obvious: a situation where one country dropped out could be tolerated perhaps, but all concerned agreed that if two or more did so for any length of time this would threaten the market principle. The EEC's agricultural policy, as its administratively most advanced field of activity and flagship, turned out to be highly trouble-prone. Without at least coordination – or still better integration – of economic and monetary policy there could be no lasting and sustainable resolution of the CAP's problems. Otherwise – interventionism aside – unintended paradoxical effects would recur, as in 1969 when the system put France (as the biggest producer of surpluses) under pressure to increase its producer prices while – to complete the paradox – Germany (as the biggest importer) was required to lower its own.

Just a few years later those problems looked like warm-up exercises. In the early 1970s large dollar inflows placed European currencies under increasing pressure. The member states sought to defend their fixed exchange rates, motivated as during the late 1960s in no small part by concern for their agricultural policy. In the end, Germany and the Netherlands were forced to adjust their exchange rates in May 1971. Just a few weeks later US president Richard Nixon took the US dollar off the gold standard. In December 1971 the Group of Ten (Belgium, Canada, France, West Germany, Italy, Japan, the Netherlands, Sweden, the United Kingdom and the United States) sought to salvage what they could, agreeing new central exchange rates with clearly defined fluctuation ranges. However, this failed to stabilise the currency markets more than temporarily, and the Bretton Woods system collapsed for good in 1973.[58]

The international monetary crisis had grave repercussions for the CAP. After monetary pressures had disrupted the EC's agricultural market in 1969, this latest development cemented the new parity fluctuations. Subsequent attempts to reinstate the shared market were stymied by persistent monetary policy problems at the end of the Bretton Woods era. As in 1969, an apparently unconnected economic and political issue upended the common agricultural market. It made trade within the Community considerably more complicated – and turned the border adjustments, upon which the fates of many farmers depended, into a bone of great contention. This inadvertently produced a sweeping renationalisation of the common agricultural *market* – but not of the Common Agricultural *Policy*. While the downsides for farmers, consumers and taxpayers were obvious, the CAP itself as the flagship of the then EC remained largely untouched. That also explains why the whole business has been largely forgotten, why the narrative of progressive enlargement and deepening has completely obscured a history of disintegration and dysfunctionality.

The situation was similar for the Common Market as a whole, which was also put to a severe test by the monetary crisis. Whereas the CAP involved the establishment of a joint and partially supranational policy, the Common Market project concentrated more strongly on 'negative' integration in the sense of dismantling trade barriers, without moving straight to joint price-setting and CMOs. Monetary problems were especially visible and virulent in the area of agriculture, but they also caused disintegrative effects within the Common Market.[59]

The relationship between the Common Agricultural Policy and Common Market on the one hand and monetary policy on the other thus generated increasing problems, with the policies already existing within the EC tangibly restricting its monetary policy options: the CAP in particular represented one of the obstacles to moving towards a permanent policy of floating exchange rates.[60] At the same time, the monetary challenges accelerated moves to provide the EEC with new powers. The Werner Plan of 1970, a reform proposal prepared under the auspices of Luxembourg prime minister Pierre Werner, for example, pointed out that: 'These part elements of an economic union [created by the CAP and the Common Market] could not be held together if one did not implement also the principle of integration right in the economic decision centre constituted by the monetary system itself.'[61] The plan therefore proposed a monetary union with a single currency, to be established by 1980. A number of steps were in fact implemented during the subsequent period; for example, in 1972 the member states set up an exchange rate system, which achieved short-lived fame as the 'currency snake' (aka the 'snake in the tunnel'). Of course, there were also other factors behind this attempt to reduce fluctuations in member states' exchange rates, aside from preserving the level of integration already achieved, such as the fall in the value of the dollar and the consequences of the Community's first enlargement of 1973.[62] But the structural problems could not be solved by this and similar approaches, such as the European Monetary System (EMS) that replaced the snake in 1979. This was not to change until the Treaty of Maastricht and the euro it created. Disintegration thus became an integral component of integration; measured against their own objectives, the Common Market and CAP remained partly dysfunctional, and the same applies to the monetary policy initiatives of the 1970s.

Karl Marx agreed with Hegel that 'all facts and personages of great importance in world history occur, as it were, twice' – but added: 'the first time as tragedy, the second as farce'.[63] Today, the long-term fate of the euro is unclear. There can, however, be no doubting that the disintegrative element has also infected the euro: while the shared currency has had certain positive market effects, it is inherently challenged by the lack of a broader economic union. At the same time the potential macroeconomic effects are – because of the depth of integration achieved and the growing number of member states – considerably more serious than in the 1960s or 1970s. In structural terms, however, the problem can be traced back to the early phase of European integration.

But let us return to the historical analysis. In broad terms, an apparently unrelated question became the stumbling block for the CAP and the Common Market. It led to a real step backwards from the level of integration that had already been achieved – a sacrilege. Knowing how hard-fought the existing achievements had been, this must have left a bitter aftertaste for the protagonists.

So why were such problems not anticipated more clearly? In the case of the green dollar those involved apparently failed to foresee the full implications of their actions. Yet in many other cases they were fully aware of the irresolvable internal contradictions. Peter Jay, who served as British ambassador to Washington for several years in the 1970s and subsequently pursued a media career in the United Kingdom, recalled in 2012 a conversation that occurred exactly sixty years earlier. At the age of fifteen, he had overheard his father, a senior Labour politician, speaking with Jean Monnet. According to Jay, Monnet argued that Europe had to be built in little steps 'by zig and by zag', until finally the United States of Europe came into being under French leadership. Jay interpreted this as a conspiracy of federalist elites: the faults and imbalances in the integration process resulted not from a lack of foresight or the vagaries of future developments, but were part of a dangerous plan – the compelling need for further integration to save the achievements already accomplished serving as a strategy to create a federal Europe against the wishes of the majority.[64] As Jay saw it, doubling down in response to crisis was part of a cunning plan. His polemics basically represented nothing but a mirror-image of the neo-functionalist approach. Monnet and other European leaders did indeed regularly argue that crises should be grasped as opportunities to expand European integration. Monnet had always believed that 'Europe would be built through crises, and that it would be the sum of their solutions';[65] Hallstein stressed that integration should be sought first of all 'in those spheres which stir up fewer emotions and where the practical reasons for fusion are compelling and obvious', before proceeding from there towards the ultimate objective of federation.[66]

The influence of such positions has largely evaporated since the 1960s, and no proof was ever found for the kind of conspiracy Jay claimed. The crux of the matter lies elsewhere: the process of finding compromises between the member states is often so fraught that the outcomes are necessarily less than perfect. And these outcomes have repeatedly turned out to be astonishingly durable, frequently later forming the starting point for further integration steps. But that has not always been the case, especially where no new consensus could be found – neither to overcome the existing problems nor to push on with integration. To that extent the strands of resistance against neo-functionalist politics and Monnet's 'by zig and by zag' have always remained strong. That is another aspect explaining why integration has so frequently been associated with disintegrative and dysfunctional manifestations.

Beyond Teleology

Disintegration and dysfunctionality have characterised the history of integration in other respects too. Both were at work in the Empty Chair Crisis of 1965/66, a turning point in the history of the EC that is today almost unknown outside expert circles.[67] Essentially, the government of de Gaulle boycotted meetings of the Council of Ministers for about half a year to underline French displeasure with the slow progress of integration in the field of agriculture, as well its criticism of the Commission's attempts to carve out a larger role for itself and for the European Parliament at the expense of the member states. The effect was to paralyse the Community's institutions.

The resulting inactivity left the Community dysfunctional in certain important respects. Late in the night of 30 June 1965 French foreign minister Maurice Couve de Murville declared that the agreement promised for that day would not be reached. The deadline had been set several years earlier and the French in particular had attached great importance to it. But the Council of Ministers had already failed to meet several similar deadlines. The five other delegations proposed simply continuing the debate later in the month at a special summit. Couve de Murville rejected this 'frostily' and engineered a rift between France and the other member states.[68] Paris withdrew its representatives from the Council of Ministers – even though Article 5 of the EEC Treaty obliges member states to 'Take all appropriate measures, whether general or particular, to ensure fulfilment of the obligations arising out of this Treaty or resulting from action taken by the institutions of the Community'.[69] The question now facing the remaining five member states was whether to proceed *sans France* or to postpone all outstanding issues until the conflict could be resolved amicably. Following intense consultations the five chose the latter option and thus avoided a further escalation.[70]

Many facets of the Community remained completely unaffected throughout the Empty Chair Crisis. Existing legislation remained in force, it was only impossible to make new decisions. That was bad enough, given that the Common Market, the CAP and many other projects were just being established. Along with many other countries, Algeria, as outlined above, waited in vain for the EC to move. To that extent the stalemate certainly extracted a high price. It was only the judicious stance adopted by the five that contained the conflict and prevented broader disintegrative effects.[71]

The crisis did have a more strongly disintegrative influence in a different respect. It occurred during the transitional period between ratification of the EEC Treaty and full implementation, with measures designed to establish the Common Market incrementally. During the first stage the member states made almost all decisions by consensus, but the treaty provided for an expansion of majority voting with each future stage. Majority voting implies that a country can be outvoted, and that in the extreme case an overwhelming majority might override a vital national interest. The essentially supranational logic of the EEC Treaty assumed a successive deepening of the integration process. Alongside a number of specific issues, the crisis revolved not least around this commitment to future changes. In the end, pressed by de Gaulle, the member states agreed to disagree. Still, the Luxembourg compromise gave every member state a de facto veto over issues where 'vital national interests' were at stake. The crisis was overcome and business as usual resumed – but the future had changed.[72]

To put it in abstract terms, the EC's integration model had until this point been based on a sequenced teleological timeline. The Community's voting modalities were supposed to shift in stages to a more strongly communitised model. To that extent – beyond technical questions such as trade preferences and intervention prices – the process was always also about the utopia of 'ever closer union', which was ultimately rooted in a supranational logic. De Gaulle thoroughly dashed those hopes in 1965. But the five other members successfully resisted any radical counter-proposal, such as renationalisation. Nonetheless, the outcome was a tangible strengthening of the intergovernmental principle, where the Community as a whole was defined as a hybrid system with a mixture of intergovernmental and supranational elements. In fact such a hybrid state was originally planned to exist only during the initial transitional phase. In place of a linear timeline forging by definition towards deeper integration, a more open approach with a less definite schedule now came to the fore. To reiterate the point: the status quo remained unaltered. What the Luxembourg compromise represented in comparison to previous plans was a heavily stripped down utopia; the future was to be considerably less integrated than originally planned.[73]

Taken together, these two dimensions – the Empty Chair Crisis and the Luxembourg compromise – represented an important turning point in the history of integration. France's inactivity made parts of the Community's mechanisms dysfunctional for a time. And the Luxembourg compromise pulled the Community back from integration expectations that were firmly mapped out in the treaties.

Disintegration and Dysfunctionality: Résumé

Since the 1940s pro-European elites have embedded concrete steps towards European integration within a narrative that the member states were on the road to an ever closer union. The unification process was posited to be unidirectional and irreversible, resting on the twin motors of ever progressing deepening and enlargement. This federalist thrust ultimately shaped many official documents and statements. The legal machinery largely retained this slant until the Treaty of Lisbon introduced provisions for a regulated withdrawal in 2007. Nevertheless, Algeria still managed to leave in 1962, as did Greenland in 1985. And even attentive observers may have missed another such event: in 2012 the French Caribbean island of Saint-Barthélemy altered its status to become an overseas territory of the European Union. Previously it had been part of the EU itself; its relationship to France – as an overseas collectivity – remains unaffected by the change.[74] As such the Saint-Barthélemy case bears a resemblance to the Greenland withdrawal; in both cases an entity on the outermost periphery distanced itself from Brussels without seceding from the motherland.

In other, indirect ways the narrative of the 'ever closer union' had already been called into question long before the Treaty of Lisbon: the Luxembourg compromise of 1966 ditched an integration step laid out in the treaty and instead adopted hybrid decision-making; Algeria and Greenland withdrew, and the United Kingdom seriously considered leaving in 1975. The absence of spillover also explains why even existing policies occasionally became dysfunctional.

A plethora of small and tiny changes also accumulated to disintegrate existing achievements or make them dysfunctional. As already outlined, the Coal and Steel Community was largely non-functioning only a few years after its establishment.[75] And the member states quickly pruned the powers of its High Authority so heavily that its leadership considered resigning en masse in 1959. In the end they resigned themselves to the status quo instead.[76] The German news weekly *Spiegel* rightly commented: 'The treaty instrument is blunt, and can function, if at all, only in normal times – when it is largely superfluous anyway.'[77] The alternative would have been accelerating integration of a kind unwanted in many member states. A politician like de Gaulle clearly recognised this trend, thus explaining his resistance to the insatiable logic of the integration process.

Thus far, we have discussed disintegration and dysfunctionality exclusively on the political/administrative level. Many other processes that can be described in the same terms can also be identified at other levels. For example, if we understand disintegration as the thinning or fracturing of existing economic relationships, we find the political unification process to be accompanied by a multitude of such phenomena.[78] This has been associated above all with the Community's external protection, as integration has always meant joining together in differentiation from others. This has had a huge impact on pre-existing relations with nations outside Europe, as described in greater detail in Chapter 8, 'The Community and its World'. The same phenomenon can also be identified within Europe, for example, towards the former Eastern Bloc, where 'European integration' at least temporarily deepened differences and dissolved existing ties.[79] The same applies to Western European states that (initially) declined to join the Community. Denmark offers a good example, remaining outside the European Community until 1973. From the 1960s Danish agriculture in particular began to suffer under the protectionist provisions of the CAP. While Denmark – jointly with the Netherlands – was the leading agricultural exporter in Western Europe at the end of the 1950s, it was overtaken by all six EEC members in the course of the subsequent decade.[80]

Even if we confine ourselves to the realm of the political, integration and disintegration processes frequently went hand in hand even before the Treaty of Maastricht. Disintegration and dysfunctionality are part of the political normality of the integration process. They are produced by the treatment (or non-treatment) of complex problems and knock-on effects of the integration process itself. The trend has strengthened further since Maastricht. The unification process achieved a depth and breadth that made it considerably more vulnerable than the much smaller post-war Western European community with its technical projects in the field of economics. Unsanctioned violations of jointly agreed rules – or their problematically vague interpretation – belong in this context, be it the Maastricht convergence criteria or unilateral suspension of the Dublin Regulation. The same also applies to the withdrawal of member states, for example, in the form of Brexit. Nevertheless, none of these things are actually fundamentally new. All that is new is that they are shaping the debate over the European Union more strongly than ever before.

8 THE COMMUNITY AND ITS WORLD

In the second half of the 1970s officials at the European Commission joked about the long-serving French development commissioner: what is the difference between God and Cheysson? God is everywhere, Cheysson everywhere except Brussels. There was a grain of truth to it. The 1970s witnessed a noticeable increase in shuttle diplomacy by senior representatives of the Commission, taking them ever further from the member states and Western Europe. Claude Cheysson played a pivotal role in creating an agreement with former colonies in Africa, the Caribbean and the Pacific in 1975. His German colleague Wilhelm Haferkamp, responsible first for energy, later the internal market, drew public criticism for costly trips as far afield as the United States and China. Their wanderlust was topped by the British Commission president Roy Jenkins, who regularly visited the capitals of the member states, but also Greenland and Ghana, Senegal and Sudan, Yugoslavia and Japan, the United States, Egypt and many other countries.[1]

But how did the Community actually interact with states and regions outside Europe, and what global role did it play? For all the thousands of miles travelled by Jenkins and colleagues, the pre-Maastricht EC never acquired the power to alter the fate of global politics. But in a lesser fashion it did exert influence – via other channels and in other forms than one might perhaps have expected. This is seen especially clearly in relation to the three regions upon which I focus in this chapter: the United States, as the hegemonic power in Cold War Western Europe and the model from which the EC sought to differentiate itself; the countries of Africa and more generally the Global South, with which Western Europe had long maintained close – and highly problematic – ties through its colonial empires; and finally East Asia, with Japan and China.[2] We will also take a very brief detour to Latin America, which remained marginal throughout the period. Although the Middle East appeared on the agenda for a brief phase in the late 1960s and early 1970s, the EC never really managed to escape the constraints of US hegemony and play an effective role of its own.[3] In the three regions of principal interest, trade policy – as the Community's oldest instrument for shaping its external relations – played a special role, although other policy areas such as agriculture and development cooperation were also of relevance.

The West

In the beginning was America. During the Cold War the United States represented far and away the most important overseas point of reference for the integration process. If the European Community was at least partly product of the East–West conflict, this was to some extent because it was so closely allied with the United States.

America deeply influenced European integration from the late 1940s, both in relation to the EC's interactions with the rest of the world and – at a much more fundamental level – in the thrust and direction of integration itself. Indeed America's influence on the post-1945 integration process was so central that it is this we must address first, before moving on to examine its effect on the EC's role in the world.

I have already outlined the extent to which European cooperation and integration were tied to the United States from the second half of the 1940s, for example, in the scope of UNECE and OECD.[4] The Marshall Plan played a crucial role here, channelling billions into the economic reconstruction of Western Europe. The OEEC was originally founded in 1948 to implement the Marshall Plan, charged with distributing US aid, coordinating planning and projects in the receiving countries, and working to remove obstacles to economic growth. Much more than before, Washington now believed that the nations of Western Europe should work together to tackle their economic problems. The US planning elites also had clear ideas about the model for future cooperation in the Old World: the United States itself of course. As such, they were working towards nothing less than the establishment of a strongly supranational United States of Europe.

Washington's stance was itself a product of the emerging Cold War and thus an outcome of global political shifts in the immediate post-war period. In 1935 Minnesota senator Thomas Schall told Congress: 'To hell with Europe and the rest of those nations!'[5] Positions of that ilk were largely sidelined during the Second World War of course, but they never disappeared entirely. When the war ended, the initial US stance was that of the recently deceased president Franklin D. Roosevelt: the United States, the United Kingdom, the Soviet Union and China should act as the four 'global policemen' to create a new – and peaceful – global order. That plan saw no autonomous role for continental Europe. Instead the prevailing attitude in Washington was to maintain a comparatively brief presence in Europe, commit as few resources as possible, and leave the representation of Western interests there largely to the United Kingdom.[6]

In 1947 Roosevelt's successor, Harry S. Truman, initiated a reorientation in US policy towards Europe. In the meantime it had become clear that London was unable to play its assigned role, and Paris unsuited to replace it. With the Marshall Plan as the most visible expression of the shift, Washington now worked towards the broadest possible unification of Western Europe as part of its strategy of containing the Soviet Union and stopping Moscow's supposed expansionism. A strong united Western Europe was seen as a counterweight to the emerging Eastern Bloc.[7]

While this argument arose out of the logic of the Cold War, the lesson of the first half of the twentieth century supplied a second security consideration. In Henry Kissinger's words, Washington realised that 'unless America was organically involved in Europe, it would be obliged to involve itself later under circumstances far less favorable to both sides of the Atlantic'.[8] This line quickly prevailed over isolationist currents that sought in particular to stabilise Germany as Europe's fragile centre. What this meant was a strong West Germany as a part of Western European and North Atlantic structures, rejecting positions seeking a united but neutral Germany or a fragmented and permanently weakened one. After decades of exploring different approaches, this policy towards Europe reflected Washington's new global engagement and underlying sense of mission, while its German components in particular pointed clearly towards the Cold War constellation. These two ultimately connected security motives explain the rather paradoxical approach, where the US superpower worked to create another major power by integrating Europe.

These security-driven considerations were accompanied by economic motivations. The Americans saw both the Marshall Plan and the later EC as economically strengthening Western Europe and thus enhancing its attractiveness as a market for US goods and capital. The United States sought to create an economic and political alliance to bring the American model – a global economic and trade order built on liberalism and multilateralism – to the Old World. In other words, a reinvigorated Western Europe was needed to support US global policy. Economic integration of Western Europe was the necessary precondition for a fairer sharing of burdens.

It took quite some time before Washington realised that organisations like UNECE, OEEC and the Council of Europe had little to contribute to these lofty objectives, and that the United Kingdom was not open to renouncing aspects of sovereignty to create a supranational organisation on the US model. Once it had, the Americans increasingly directed their hopes towards the EC. Although it was less supranational than Washington might have wished, it came closest to the US strategy: the pragmatism of the possible.

Washington therefore supported the 1950 Schuman Plan, of which US secretary of state Dean Acheson learned two days beforehand. Sceptics suspected that the French merely wanted to create a huge European steel cartel, but their doubts made little impression in Washington. Fundamentally Schuman's ideas aligned with American wishes, as the Plan aimed to recognise the young West Germany as an equal partner, open markets and strengthen militarily crucial sectors of the Western Europe economy. So Washington backed it – and even worked to block British interference – despite the tendency of the emerging ECSC to contradict American economic interests.[9] Foreign policy and security trumped such concerns. The United States also left its mark on the concrete shape of the ECSC, for example, in the area of competition rules where transatlantic expert networks played an important role.[10]

In the case of the plans for a European Defence Community, US support again quickly outweighed initial misgivings. And the negotiations supplied an important lesson about the possibilities and limits of American engagement in Western Europe. In December 1953, as French resistance to the project grew in advance of the parliamentary vote, Acheson's successor, John Foster Dulles, threatened an 'agonising reappraisal' of US policy towards Western Europe. But this pressure, bordering on open blackmail, had the opposite effect. It was one of the reasons why the French National Assembly blew the project out of the water the following summer. Subsequently the United States learned to be at least more discreet and subtle in its support for European integration.[11]

Not that that meant any change in Washington's fundamentally pro-European stance. In the negotiations for the Treaties of Rome the United States supported both Euratom and the EEC, even though both projects involved economic disadvantages from the American perspective. Dulles underlined the primacy of overarching political goals, where Washington was especially interested in the supranational component. In many respects European integration appeared not as a challenge to the Atlantic partnership but as an integral part of it.[12]

European leaders took a similar line, fostering a constant coordination process and flow of information across the North Atlantic. In April 1956, for example, Jean Monnet warned in confidential discussions that Washington should not advocate too publicly for Euratom, because otherwise 'the public might conclude that pressure was being brought to bear on Europe by the United States in order to cause Euratom's coming into being'.[13] When the talks were over, Secretary of State Dulles wrote to his Belgian colleague Paul-Henri Spaak that he was 'highly gratified' about the outcome; an internal US document shortly afterwards called the conclusion of the treaties 'a truly historical event'.[14]

Sometimes Washington seemed to be better informed about the positions of the member states' governments than they were about each other, simply because US diplomats and business representatives consulted so closely with their European partners through bilateral channels as well as forums like the OEEC and NATO. As the EC institutions in Brussels took shape in the course of the 1960s, the United States Mission to the European Communities also began to acquire increasing importance; its establishment in itself represented a sign of American support for the EC.[15] Europe was certainly worth putting effort into: the files in Washington are full of lunch and dinner invitations to European partners, with detailed accounts of the discussions sent back home.[16] Contacts of this kind built on relationships already established by Monnet and others during the inter-war years.[17] So it is no surprise if Alfred Mozer, the Dutch–German head of cabinet at the Directorate-General for Agriculture, and Oscar Zaglits from the US Mission chose the informal 'Du' form when they corresponded in German in the early 1960s.[18] And no wonder if Washington was unsettled by public accusations concerning the Nazi past of one particular high-ranking German diplomat in Brussels: the man was one of their best sources, occasionally – and illegally – passing 'his complete working file' to the Americans.[19]

Empire by Integration

That is not to say that the relationship remained without conflict or that the United States consistently played an important role in all aspects; there was no 'golden age' of the Atlantic alliance. Neither the ECSC nor the Treaties of Rome were based on American ideas. The initiative for the Schuman Plan in 1950 came from Jean Monnet and was disseminated via the French Foreign Ministry; one of the motivations behind it was to pre-empt an American change of course over Germany that would have contradicted French interests. The initiatives for European integration, which matured between 1955 and 1957 and ultimately led to the Treaties of Rome, were advanced principally by the Benelux states.[20] And just as Washington was unable to force through the EDC in the early 1950s, it failed again a decade later to ensure British accession against French resistance.[21] Occasionally there were even blunt threats and trade conflicts, for example, in the 'Chicken War' of 1961 to 1964, when the United States sought to overturn the protectionist effects of the Common Agricultural Policy.

There was also open public debate about the transatlantic relationship and its implications for European integration. Jean-Jacques Servan-Schreiber's *The American Challenge*, criticising American dominance and arguing for deeper European integration, sold more than half a million copies in France alone and became an international bestseller.[22] In the ongoing debates over strategy and transatlantic burden-sharing, Washington almost always supported the European Community through its benign attitude, informal networks, material support and willingness to make concessions – without insisting dogmatically on its own priorities.

There is also another reason to regard the United States as a benevolent hegemon: if Washington had had fundamental objections it could easily have put a stop to integration, which was always a matter of controversy within Western Europe. That applied especially to the

EC's protectionist agricultural policy, which remained a persistent thorn in the side of the American farming lobby. The mantra of White House and State Department was to point to the overarching political benefits of European integration. They negotiated hard over the issues, but ultimately exhibited willingness to compromise and sought multilateral solutions.[23] In this respect Washington's stance was very different from the one adopted by Westminster in the 1950s. For President Kennedy, in view of the global challenges faced by the West, the question 'Is the Grand Alliance going to founder on chickens?' was never a serious one.[24] Benevolent hegemony should not be confused with rigid dominance.

At the same time, one must note that US support for European integration did not mean a blank cheque for European global politics – especially at crucial junctures in the 1950s when individual Western European states sought to secure their overseas empires. In such situations Washington usually refused to supply assistance – as in spring 1954 (in the decisive weeks before the EDC vote) when US forces failed to come to the rescue of French troops besieged at Điện Biên Phủ. This sealed France's defeat in the First Indochina War.[25]

The French and British received an even greater humiliation with Washington's response to the Suez Crisis in autumn 1956. After London and Paris responded to Gamal Abdel Nasser's nationalisation of the Suez Canal Company with a military invasion, Washington withheld its backing and forced them to evacuate. No other moment better illustrated the Western European powers' loss of influence at the global level.

From a different angle, Suez also reveals how denial of US support shaped the integration process. When the crisis broke out negotiations over the EEC and Euratom were struggling. The Suez debacle represented a significant factor persuading the French government of Guy Mollet to place greater hope in Europe. On 6 November, German chancellor Konrad Adenauer was on a special train to Paris, hoping to inject some movement into the talks on the Common Market and Euratom, when he received the shocking news that Khrushchev was threatening to bomb Paris and London if they failed to withdraw their forces from Egypt. Adenauer continued his journey to the French capital. While he was conferring with Mollet and foreign minister Christian Pineau, the news arrived that the British prime minister Anthony Eden had succumbed to US pressure and agreed to an immediate ceasefire.

According to Pineau, Adenauer commented that for the European powers there 'remains only one way to play a crucial role in the world – to unite in order to create Europe'. There was no time to be lost.[26]

As we see, during the phase of its creation the EC's place in the world was shaped not only by support from the United States, but also by the weakness of the Western European nation states and the denial of American backing for their global ambitions. Shortly before becoming the first president of the Euratom Commission, Louis Armand joked that 'we [should] erect a statue to Nasser, the federator of Europe'.[27]

What emerged was a form of hegemony that inserted the European Community into the Atlantic community but left the Western European states a great deal of leeway.[28] The Norwegian historian Geir Lundestad has described this as an 'Empire by integration', where after 1945 the Western European states repeatedly invited the United States to take the leading role in and for Western Europe.[29] That might be mildly overstated, especially as American influence was frequently less overt in the day to day business of European integration. Nevertheless Lundestad puts his finger on an important truth: with its security umbrella and the NATO framework, the United States created one of the central conditions for the possibility of European integration. And beyond that, through its contributions to the negotiations for the EC, it also shaped its conditions and repeatedly opened up concrete opportunities for European and transatlantic cooperation. It was only by virtue of Washington's willingness to make economic concessions for overarching reasons of security that the EC was able to develop influence internally and increasingly also towards third parties. To that extent ex-Commission president Walter Hallstein was right when he commented in 1972 that for the United States 'European integration was not only sought, welcomed, and encouraged. It was also jointly defended.'[30]

From Bad to Worse?

During the early 1970s noticeable tensions arose at the transatlantic level, especially during the presidency of Richard Nixon. In comparison to its overwhelming economic and military dominance in the immediate post-war period, the United States now found itself significantly weakened and mired in deep moral crisis over Vietnam.

After three decades of growth and integration Western Europe was in a considerably better situation than in the 1950s, but, like the United States, found itself struggling with significant economic problems. The deterioration in relations between the United States and Western Europe culminated in Washington's unilateral termination of the Bretton Woods system, the US-led international monetary regime of the preceding three decades. Until this point monetary policy had been a central pillar of transatlantic cooperation, upon which the Common Market also rested. Now the EC found itself both forced and encouraged to seek its own monetary arrangements, which unsurprisingly simply deepened the rift between New and Old World.[31]

Growing challenges developed in the field of security too. This might appear paradoxical in a time when the Cold War had lost some of its edge. But now it became apparent how strongly the conflict had functioned as the external brace for the transatlantic relationship. Détente raised the pressing question of whether Europe could still rely on the US security guarantee. France in particular had been attempting since the 1960s to create a European defence block outside of NATO. While these efforts were ultimately unsuccessful, they still strained the transatlantic relationship.[32]

European integration now tended to become a stress factor, rather than a stabilising influence in relations between the United States and Western Europe. Economic crisis and global turmoil led the Americans to prioritise their own economic interests more strongly again, and other parts of the globe became relatively more important in American global strategy. While Washington still gave verbal support to European integration, the truth looked different behind the scenes: swelling disinterest and open rejection. The relationship reached a low point in 1973 when Nixon remarked in a closed meeting that the EC could become a 'Frankenstein monster'.[33] On top of this, on the European side the EC was increasingly becoming an actor with independent political structures and global ambitions. This shift is reflected in the *Document on the European Identity*, in which the European Community emphasised its independence of the United States on the world stage and increasingly portrayed itself as a distinct political model.[34]

The relationship deteriorated further in the late 1970s; Lundestad has characterised the phase from 1977 to 1984 as 'From Bad to Worse'.[35] As at the beginning of the decade, economic troubles exacerbated political tensions. A renewed intensification of the Cold War notched up the stress, with the Community declining to fully support America's policy of hard confrontation.[36]

But that was only one aspect. The renewed confrontation between East and West also brought the Western partners closer together, while European integration progressed with the southern enlargement and a series of reforms. US support for the EC increased noticeably in the second half of the 1980s, with the advent of perestroika and glasnost in the Soviet Union. By 1977, for example, the United States had already accepted that the Commission could be represented by its president at G-7 summits, making it the only international organisation to enjoy direct representation at these high-level meetings. Washington backed and promoted a significant role for the EC in the Helsinki process that was to shape the overall European situation. Now the Western alliance and European integration were again seen more strongly as synergetic. This was also a product of internal changes within the Community: Washington very closely followed the emergence of the Single European Act, and a few years later the efforts to create a Common Foreign and Security Policy – with a degree of scepticism and criticism, but always under the premise that the EC was a serious partner. And when the Eastern Bloc collapsed in 1989–1990, the United States perceived the European Community as a central factor for shaping the new Europe. Such an attitude would have been unlikely in the early 1970s.[37]

So the United States left its mark on the integration process throughout the period. The European Community always remained embedded in overarching transatlantic structures that turned out to be elastic enough to weather crises and absorb diverse processes of exchange and exclusion. The Community was much more than a marionette or a function of the transatlantic relationship, increasingly developing into an independent actor in its own right. But even in that process it remained closely orientated on the United States.

An Actor by Trade

What, then, was the effect of the transatlantic bond on the EC's role in the world? In the context of its relationship with the United States, the European Community became an actor on the global stage principally through trade matters. In no other policy area did the pre-

Maastricht Community play such a significant role towards third states, as witnessed especially in the context of GATT as the negotiating forum for world trade. This first became clear in the Kennedy Round from 1964 to 1967, which sought to reduce obstacles to trade by reducing tariffs. The talks involved sixty-six (largely Western) nations from all continents, accounting for 80 per cent of world trade. On the basis of the EEC Treaty the Commission represented the entire Community vis-à-vis the GATT partners, first and foremost the United States. So at the talks in Geneva the EC member states were represented by a single delegation led by Jean Rey, Commissioner for External Relations and later Commission president; this task represented one of the Commission's central sources of power.[38] Of course Rey made his decisions on the basis of a negotiating mandate and in close consultation with the governments of the member states. Yet in central questions of external trade policy the EC spoke with a single voice and became an autonomous factor as far as the rest of the world was concerned. That had not yet been the case in the previous GATT talks, the Dillon Round of 1960 to 1962, when the Community had still been establishing its structures. So in this crucial arena of international politics, the European Community emerged from the Kennedy Round as an actor the like of which the world had never seen before.[39]

At the same time this development can only be understood in the context of transatlantic relations. While other GATT states complained that the trade provisions of the EEC Treaty were incompatible with GATT and discriminated against third states, Washington refrained from criticism. The overarching political reasons to succour the EC were weightier. Without Washington's backing the Community would have found it very much harder to become a trade policy actor.[40]

The transatlantic relationship was also significant for the way Washington and Brussels pulled in the same direction over some questions but not on others, and for the consequences these shifting constellations had on the global stage. There was little transatlantic conflict concerning international tariffs on industrial products, with Washington and the EC both pressing for substantial reductions. Sharp conflicts did arise, in agriculture, where the European Community sought to preserve its protectionism against American demands for liberalisation. Washington was very critical here, with an internal document in September 1966 stating that the 'success of the negotiations will depend in large part on the substantial improvement by the EEC of their very meager initial agricultural offers'.[41]

Finally, the relationship between the United States and the EC played a decisive role in the overall outcome of the Kennedy Round. The United States set the tone on industrial goods, with EC backing, and the Kennedy Round brought a significant reduction in tariff trade barriers. On average tariffs fell by 35 per cent, in two-thirds of cases by 50 per cent. The limits to tariff reduction were set by agriculture, where the European Community stood its ground despite criticism from the United States and others, and insisted on strong external protections. As the Dutch Foreign Ministry noted after conclusion of the talks: on agriculture 'the results have remained small'.[42]

This shows two things. Firstly, that the US government chose not to use all means in its power to enforce its own economic interests, for the sake of a greater strategic goal. If Washington had applied the thumbscrews, the EC member states would have struggled to maintain a common front. Washington had it in its power to demolish the EC as a collective actor on the world stage. Instead it tolerated the EC's stance in order to avoid endangering the unity of the Community – and ultimately of the West. Secondly, the outcome of the agriculture negotiations in the Kennedy Round underlines how serious the six member states really were about integration: any concession would have endangered the nascent CAP with its hard-fought and delicately balanced compromises.[43]

This also explains why the EC now operated with a strange mixture of economic policy stances at the international level, advocating a liberal approach for manufactured goods but a solidly protectionist line on agricultural products (and for certain politically less central sectors such as textiles). We will return to the consequences for other regions of the world below, when we examine the EC's relationship with Africa and East Asia. But the EC's new role also had immediate impacts within Western Europe: for example, Switzerland would have stood little chance of upholding its strong agricultural protections against American demands for liberalisation had it not been able to hide among the protectionist skirts of the much more powerful European Community.[44]

The EC also continued to pursue this mix of economic policy approaches in the subsequent GATT Tokyo Round (1973–1979). Not until the Uruguay Round of 1986 to 1994, which fell in the transformation phase at the end of the Cold War, did the EC demonstrate any willingness to extend liberalisation to agriculture. This was to be the last round where the overall outcome was heavily shaped by the United States and the European Community.[45]

The transatlantic relationship was systemically central to global trade relations through into the 1990s, with the initiative for new GATT rounds always coming from the United States, and the United States–EC tandem largely determining process and outcome. For example, the entire GATT machine ground to a halt in the second half of 1965 while the EC was paralysed by the Empty Chair Crisis. A few years later transatlantic tensions during the Nixon presidency hampered progress in the Tokyo Round, which only achieved its breakthrough after the European partners were able to work with his successor, Jimmy Carter.

The great extent to which the EC had become an independent actor and factor is underlined by a summit meeting in London in May 1977, where Commission president Roy Jenkins laid out the EC's position on GATT to the most powerful leaders of the Western world. He spoke – as the transcript of the meeting shows – as an equal among equals, and was treated with concomitant protocol.[46]

At the same time one should not overstate the role of the EC. Even in the crisis-riven 1970s and early 1980s – despite signs of emancipation extending beyond the transatlantic context – the European Community never openly challenged America's leading role. The partnership between the Community and the United States remained unambiguously hierarchical and strongly focused on economic and especially trade questions, while security or culture, for example, remained primarily the responsibility of other organisations, like NATO, or consigned to the bilateral or civil society levels.

Altogether the United States was extremely important in the process of the EC becoming a significant actor first within its member states and later beyond, and for the form in which the Community interacted with the rest of the world. This process of asymmetrical partnership was always accompanied by prophecies of doom. Every decade of the Cold War saw talk of a crisis in relations with the United States. It was precisely this dialectical mix of basic support, degrees of ambivalence and frequent crises in the transatlantic relationship that over time turned the European Community into a rather important actor in questions of economic policy and especially trade.

Eurafrique

In the beginning was Africa. And Africa was no strange faraway continent, but intimately connected with the Europe of the early

EC. We have already examined Algeria's path into the Community and back out again,[47] and the colonial dimension of European history played a crucial role throughout the early years of the EC. Integration was by no means restricted to the internal aspect of relations between the member states, even if that is what public debate and research have largely concentrated on. Instead the early European Community also represented a forum where the colonial powers could consider the future of their empires, and from the 1960s a tool for coping with the political and economic aftermath of decolonisation.

This contradicts an interpretation that posits the EC as the Old World's response to the end of centuries of global dominance; that decolonisation represented a necessary condition for a European Community of equal democratic partners to emerge.[48] Even as their empires crumbled, the metropolitan political elites were not yet willing to accept this in the 1950s. They clung to their colonies – in the case of the continental European states heavily concentrated in Africa – even at the expense of immense resources and the application of violent military force.[49] In France especially, it was hoped that Europe might serve as a means of saving the colonies under a concept known as 'Eurafrique'. To that extent European integration in the 1950s was not simply an inward-directed post-colonial movement with an unsullied relationship with the Global South. In fact, especially for Africa, it was steeped in the problematic past – a past that was still far from over in the 1950s.

The significance of the Eurafrique idea is exemplified by a little-known passage in Schuman's May 1950 Declaration: 'economic unification' would, the French foreign minister said, allow Europe to 'pursue the achievement of one of its essential tasks, namely, the development of the African continent'.[50]

Here Schuman was alluding to older debates. Whereas the colonies had been understood primarily as national projects throughout the nineteenth century, from the 1920s Eurafrique became a touchstone in the debate about Europe's place in the world.[51] In 1923 Richard von Coudenhove-Kalergi emphasised that his Pan-Europe would also include the colonial possessions of the continental European states.

Europe, Coudenhove-Kalergi wrote, had been gravely weakened by the Great War. The United States and the Soviet Union were becoming global powers to rival the British Empire. Europe's only chance to survive was to integrate, including its colonies: 'By unifying

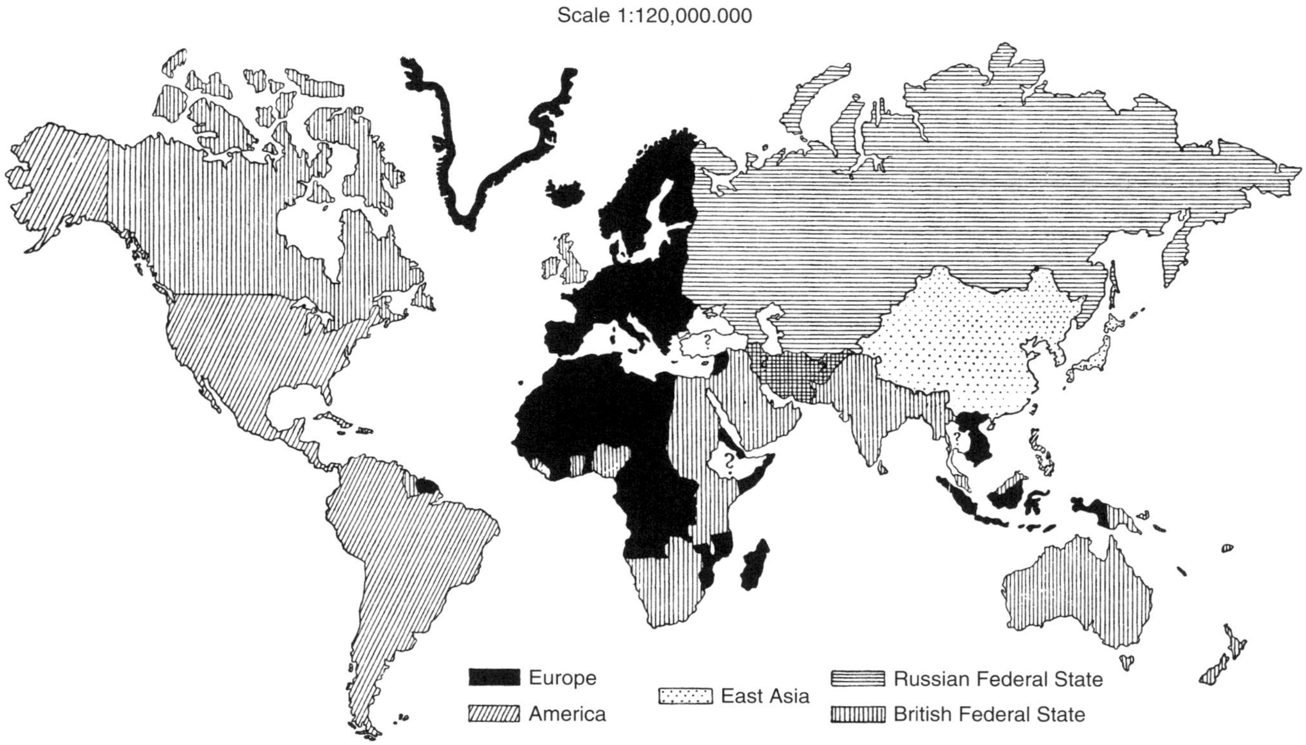

Map 4: Coudenhove-Kalergi's World Map. Redrawn, based on Coudenhove-Kalergi's *Pan-Europe*, 1923

its organization and rationally opening up its African colonial empire … Pan-Europe could itself produce all the raw materials and foodstuffs it requires'.[52] Only with Africa would Europe be truly viable, he concluded. But equal cooperation between Europe and Africa is not what he was proposing; he saw Europe exploiting Africa's economic resources and sending its purported population surplus there. This would seem especially surprising coming from Coudenhove-Kalergi, who was actually a cosmopolitan. His mother was Japanese and in the 1920s and 1930s he campaigned against the spread of anti-Semitism in Europe. Yet a sense of superiority – rooted in racism and deeply embedded in modern European culture – also shaped his thinking.[53]

While Coudenhove-Kalergi saw his Eurafricanist Pan-Europe above all in the context of rivalry with the United States, the Soviet Union and the British Empire, from the late nineteenth century others had been pointing to the rise of Japan and China – the 'Yellow Peril' – as an argument for European unity. In many cases, such as the French politician (and briefly prime minister) Albert Sarraut or the German architect Herman Sörgel, this again meant a Europe that included Africa, and again the discussion was frequently rooted in racism. Altogether European integration was not simply an internal process but driven in a meaningful sense by the perception of global developments and a fear of cultural and economic decline. Even if it was almost forgotten just a few years later, the problematic heritage of the European belief in expansion and superiority was deeply embedded in this debate.[54]

The Eurafrique idea remained marginal during the inter-war years, more a vague space of dreams and projections than a clear political concept of any meaningful relevance.[55] But from the 1940s it gained in significance and acquired clearer contours as the European power base in Asia crumbled and Eurafrique appeared to offer a realistic fallback for waning global influence. In fact, not only were France, the Netherlands and Belgium still colonial powers in 1957 when the Treaties of Rome were signed. Even Italy still retained a piece of Africa, where its former colony Somaliland remained a UN trusteeship under Italian administration until 1960.[56] Other factors also contributed to the rise of Eurafrique: the United States and the Soviet Union appeared even more powerful than in the 1920s and 1930s; globally Europe had never been weaker in modern history. And it was only now that 'Europe' appeared as a political factor potentially representing more than the sum of its states and empires. Consolidating the Old World as an independent factor in the emerging Cold War: that is what Eurafrique meant in the new global constellation after 1945.

Eurafrique now increasingly became associated with the idea of development, which rose to enormous international prominence during this period. Much more strongly than in the inter-war years, this now also meant improving the living conditions of the non-white majorities in the colonies. This appeared to be a promising route to stabilise the colonies politically and socially – and to relegitimise European rule in an era of growing anti-colonialism after the founding of the United Nations boosted the idea of national self-determination.[57] At the same time the proponents of Eurafrique hoped it would simplify the negotiations about European integration: according to this line of thought the shared objective of developing Africa would facilitate the process of balancing interests within Europe and increase the global weight of the Old World in political and economic terms. The Russian-French philosopher Alexandre Kojève, a French senior civil servant with a past as a Hegel researcher, spoke paternalistically of a transition from 'taking' to 'giving' colonialism.[58] His German correspondent Carl Schmitt asked himself whether 'Europe might not become a convincing provider of homogenous development aid'.[59] The urgency of such an approach was heightened by US and Soviet moves to promote their own versions of development in Africa. Occasionally there was veritable rivalry over the best concept for catapulting Africa into the modern age.

Just how strongly ideas of white superiority continued to characterise the relationship with Africa is illustrated very well by the history of the Council of Europe. Before the EC had even been established, the Council of Europe was the most important forum for the Eurafrique debate.[60] When the Council of Europe adopted its Convention on Human Rights in 1950, the colonial powers – at the request of Belgium, France and the United Kingdom – retained the right to choose whether to extend its protections to their colonies. In other words, universal human rights existed from the outset within a tight territorial corset based on racism.[61] Representatives of the Global South railed against the decision, and the protests of non-white delegates representing the colonies at the Strasbourg meeting reached the European centres. Alongside appeals criticising double standards, the Cold War also served as an argument. This position was taken, for example, by the Senegalese poet and politician Léopold Sédar

Senghor, who joined the Parliamentary Assembly of the Council of Europe as a member of the French National Assembly. He pointed out that although communism despised liberty, it promised to defend equality and condemned racist discrimination. If the colonies were excluded from the Human Rights Convention, he said, the African delegates would have nothing to counter communist propaganda at home. Europe had already 'let the hour of Eurasia slip'. Would it now also 'fail to grasp the opportunity of achieving Eurafrica?'[62] Such appeals went unheeded. Instead, even in the Council of Europe racist criteria decided who would be permitted to enjoy human rights.

Associating Africa

After the Schuman Declaration, Eurafrique also shaped the institutional context that was ultimately to lead to the EC. The issue gained further momentum in the course of the 1950s, after the failure of both bilateral efforts to deepen cooperation on colonial questions and the attempt to agree an effective development policy for the colonies in the Council of Europe framework.[63] The discussion was also influenced by the Suez Crisis, growing unrest within the colonies themselves, and the economic situation in the ruling nations, which increasingly suggested that the colonies were a burden.

Association was the keyword under which these debates eventually made their way into the EEC Treaty. After long and difficult negotiations the member states agreed to seek association with 'the non-European countries and territories which have special relations with Belgium, France, Italy and the Netherlands' to cite the euphemism used in the treaty.[64] What this meant concretely was a close trading relationship and an investment fund for eighteen African countries to be administered by the EEC Commission. The investment fund made Africa the largest destination for EC development aid, without the recipients receiving any direct role in the Community's relevant decision-making organs. The associated states were also included in the EEC's tariff system and were required to reduce their tariffs on imports from the EC in the same timeframe as the EC member states among themselves, while their external tariffs towards third states remained unchanged. The effect of this was to create a free trade area in which the (ex-) colonies received privileged access to the EC market, but on conditions dictated by Brussels.[65] Questions of values played no explicit role in the agreements, in line with the Council of Europe's course of territorialising universal values to a specific European space. Altogether the Treaties of Rome were rooted in a paternalistic understanding of politics under which Africa had to be secured for Europe – and Europe for Africa – and all on European conditions.[66]

In the negotiations over the corresponding article of the EEC Treaty the French government in particular had argued for the non-European countries and territories to be tightly integrated. Paris hoped to offload part of the enormous cost of administering its colonies onto its partners – and even the burden of its colonial wars. The latter was quickly dismissed, with the Netherlands and West Germany especially criticising the French ideas and their own proposed contributions to the joint fund. In public debate, too, Eurafrique was occasionally discussed as an instrument of French power and of neo-colonialism.[67] But even in these two member states many fundamental supporters of Eurafrique could be found. The Dutch social democratic prime minister and foreign minister Willem Drees declared, for example, in November 1956, that he could agree to the idea of a binding system for trade between the EEC and the overseas entities, but had to reject any 'coupling of that arrangement to the establishment of an investment fund for these territories'.[68] A mixture of fundamental openness and criticism of specific proposals also characterised the public debate outside elite political circles. For example, Anton Zischka, an Austrian non-fiction author who was enormously successful in post-war West Germany, published a book in 1951 entitled *Afrika: Europas Gemeinschaftsaufgabe Nr. 1 (Africa: Europe's First Shared Task)*. Eurafrique was certainly not just a French project, and in none of the Six was it uncontroversial. Even if it was sometimes interpreted as anti-colonial, it breathed the spirit of late colonialism.[69]

Association agreements were similarly controversial within Africa. Ghanaian president Kwame Nkrumah was especially critical, even though his country as a British colony was not directly affected and Ghana gained its independence less than three weeks before the signing of the Treaties of Rome. Nkrumah feared that Eurafrique would stymie his plans for pan-African cooperation and lead to economic discrimination against his country and other British (ex-)colonies.[70] He noted in 1961 that the Treaties of Rome 'can be compared to the treaty that emanated from the Congress of Berlin in the 19th century; the latter treaty established the undisputed sway of colonialism in Africa; the former marks the advent of neo-colonialism in Africa'. In other words, six rich European countries had multilateralised their previously bilateral dependencies and in the process quasi-annexed many of the poorest and most helpless African countries.[71]

Also in countries that were directly affected by the association offer as (ex-)colonies of the original six EC states, there were many critical voices. The aforementioned Senghor, who became president of Senegal after independence in 1960, complained about the lack of influence granted to the African states in the treaties. Even after independence the economic and political leeway available to most of these countries was too small for them to feel able to reject the offer of association. Even more importantly, their governments and economic elites hoped to derive benefit from the new arrangement.[72] At the same time the EC sought to tie the states of Africa to itself in order to consolidate its global role. From the French and Belgian perspective this built on the existing model of dominance, while many German sources speak of the danger that African countries might otherwise turn to the Eastern Bloc.[73]

Development à la Yaoundé

Eurafrique's heyday was over by the early 1960s. That had less to do with the EC itself than with a development in which successive African states gained their independence and the original arrangements therefore had to be reviewed. Where the EC's association policy was born out of the spirit of late colonialism, it now increasingly transformed into an instrument for shaping the consequences of decolonisation.[74]

The Yaoundé Agreement of 1963, revising the existing arrangements, reflected this changing context. Now the eighteen African states (fourteen of them former French colonies) represented themselves in the talks. Even if their governments were now formally equal and able to play a more active role, the Agreement cemented the structural advantage of the developed European economies. The investment fund, for example, did little to promote local industries; instead, priority was given to complementarity with products from EC states and avoiding unwanted competition. To that extent the relationship remained strongly asymmetrical and characterised by a paternalism that never for a second forgot the interests of the European economies.[75]

From here on, the Eurafrique tradition ceased to play any meaningful role in Europe's self-image and collective memory. The principal reason for this is that the association agreements were flexible enough to respond and adapt to the new post-colonial constellation. Now the motive of development rose to the fore, no longer understood just as a means to enable progress for Europe but more strongly borne by the idea of a partnership. That fitted the times, with the United Nations declaring the 1960s the 'development decade', relegating older concepts and placing development cooperation between the EC and African states in a global context.[76] This new perspective was to shape relations in the subsequent period. Because Yaoundé granted the African states continuing access to European markets, the African political elites had little interest in recalling the late colonial roots of the association process.[77]

On many levels it was France that shaped the EC's policy on development through into the 1970s. This was seen most obviously in the person of Jacques Ferrandi, a former French colonial official, who served first as director, later director-general of the European Commission Directorate-General for Development (DG VIII) and represented the *éminence grise* in this policy area. No wonder that a disproportionate share of the investment fund went to the former French colonies.[78]

But that was only one side of the coin. The Commission also developed ideas that explicitly departed from the French model. For example, its approval practice for investment projects was extremely selective and set a high bar; planning also became longer term and development management more professional. All these changes relativised the importance of clientelist networks, for example, from the late colonial era. And perhaps even more importantly, trade policy in the Yaoundé context was orientated on the ideas of the German and Dutch governments. They sought a liberalisation to open the associated countries to the global market – directly contrary to the French perspective of enabling a gradual transition to world trade through market quotas, price stabilisation and other interventionist instruments. As Martin Rempe has demonstrated for Senegal, this policy of liberalisation turned out to be more important than the investment fund; to that extent the continuities of French colonialism in the EC should not be overestimated.[79]

At the same time this changed nothing about European predominance in relations with Africa. One reason for the EC's occasionally almost autistic tone in negotiations with third states can be found in its severe internal conflicts of goals: if the member states actually managed to agree on something among themselves, it was too much to ask of them also to consider the perspective of their African partners.[80] This applied all the more if one also wanted to reach agreement with the Americans in the GATT context; then the Global South was often squeezed out completely.[81] This became especially tangible as the Common Agricultural Policy emerged in the course of the 1960s, as its protectionist slant made it increasingly difficult for African products to access the Community's markets. Senegal's peanuts – whose oil was found in almost every French kitchen – now had to compete with other oil plants for which the EC adopted a market regulation in 1966. Senegal had market access, but still suffered noticeable disadvantages. France would actually have preferred a more generous arrangement for peanuts, but was forced to accept the logic of the EC's rules.[82]

These policies of the European Community came in for criticism from various quarters in the 1960s. The associated countries themselves complained that the arrangements disadvantaged them, all the more so because the EC applied a double standard. The Yaoundé countries were denied the accession perspective offered to Turkey and Greece, they said, because the EC distinguished between association leading to accession and association for development, with the dividing line determined by security policy, economic considerations and racism.[83] Attacks also came from elsewhere, including GATT and the United States, not to mention the even harsher verdict of the Eastern Bloc. All these objections acquired additional weight through the United Nations, which now offered a global forum where criticism could be articulated.[84]

That said, the impact of such hostility remained limited, not least because the EC presented itself as a fresh new start. Altiero Spinelli, for example, wrote that the coming European federation 'will not possess the colonial past of some of its member states, and will be able to seek a new form of association and cooperation with the peoples of Africa'.[85] But south of the Mediterranean such lofty formulations sounded pretty hollow. A more important factor was the power gap between the Community and the associated states. Also, although the EC was enormously important for trade, it remained irrelevant in areas like security and secondary even in the context of development cooperation, where the bulk of funding always remained in the hands of national governments and an early attempt by the European Commission to entirely communitise development came to naught. The proportion of funds supplied by the EEC in comparison to individual states (whether EC member states or third states like the United States) varied between recipient countries but in almost all associated states ranged between 15 and 30 per cent of the total volume;

altogether the share from the EC amounted to about 20 per cent of what these states received in the form of bilateral and multilateral aid.[86] In the field of development the European Community was not the first instance, but in many Francophone countries in Africa at least the second.

There is another reason why the Yaoundé Agreement was important for the EC's role in the world: now there was a decision of principle in favour of a permanent association policy, whereas the original arrangements had been limited to five years. In this manner the EC became a development actor with a profile of its own. This applied all the more given that Yaoundé theoretically opened up the association policy to all African countries and other societies of the Global South. Here again the Community distanced itself from the late colonial roots of its development policy in order to present itself as a credible partner.[87]

Lomé's World

After an initial extension brought little change to Yaoundé's thrust, the follow-on agreement concluded in February 1975 in the Togolese capital Lomé involved clearer modifications. France had essentially argued for an extension of the Yaoundé arrangements, but lost the debate. Building on initial amendments at the beginning of the 1970s, Lomé reflected the accession of the United Kingdom and an opening beyond the circle of former colonies. And it was also affected by another dramatic change in the global context: alongside the EC's enlargement in a further decolonised world, the negotiations also reflected the weakness of the United States after Vietnam and Watergate. There was a third crucial factor too. Some of the countries of the Global South possessed important resources such as oil, which noticeably enhanced their negotiating position after the recent oil shock. Moreover, it was during this brief phase that the post-colonial states were most successful in bridging their internal differences and presenting a common front.[88]

In the end the Agreement covered no fewer than forty-six African, Caribbean and Pacific (ACP) states, as well as the EC. The Guyanan and Nigerian delegations played an outstanding role in ensuring that the negotiations were conducted on equal terms. The outcomes included a stabilisation mechanism to help the developing countries to compensate fluctuations in export revenues – representing a certain counterweight to the previous course of trade liberalisation. Equally importantly, the EC now abandoned reciprocity of trade preferences in response to demands from the Global South. The ACP states enjoyed free access to the EC market without having to grant the same conditions themselves. Finally, the development fund was reformed and its volume more than tripled; instead of economic growth and infrastructure, satisfaction of basic needs was given greater priority and the receiving countries were given a slightly greater say in planning, selecting and implementing projects.[89] The process was also characterised by broader debates on reforming international economic relations between the industrialised countries and the Global South, discussed at the time under the label New International Economic Order. While these new departures were important, one should not overestimate their significance: the tripling of funds was matched by an almost equally large expansion of the circle of recipient states; and satisfaction of basic needs often remained a fine-sounding but ultimately empty political promise.[90]

On the EC side the aforementioned Claude Cheysson embodied these changes. An Anglophile French Socialist, development commissioner from 1973, and one of the architects of the Lomé Agreement, Cheysson sought transparency and partnership with the ACP states, and hoped to overcome the clientelist system established by Director-General Ferrandi. At the insistence of the ACP states, the Lomé Agreement stood for a rhetorical rejection of the term 'association' and its paternalistic connotations. Instead the two sides now spoke of partnership and cooperation, as did Commission president Sicco Mansholt, who wished to grant the countries of the Global South fairer economic relations.

But Cheysson's dedicated shuttle diplomacy could never have achieved this outcome without the acquiescence of the governments of the member states. New ideas were also surging in the societies of the EC member states: the rise of a left-wing alternative culture with its concern for the 'Third World', the experience of post-war immigration from the ex-colonies, and social democratic or socialist-led governments in a string of member states can explain at least gradual shifts. This was associated with a wish to positively distance oneself from US development policy and propose the EC's own model for the future of the Global South. One sign of the new times and the EC's changed course was that even the Italian communists approved Lomé, after previously always rejecting association.[91]

Lomé thus amounted to a geographical, symbolic and substantive recalibration. After the expansion to the ACP states this was no longer just about Africa (still less Eurafrique), but large parts of the entire Global South. Even more so after the EC, building on Lomé, signed cooperation agreements with a series of Mediterranean and Arab countries in the second half of the 1970s.[92] On the one hand, the institutional roots of the ACP arrangement lay in the late colonial system; on the other, globalisation permitted the development and trade policy that the EC had established by this point to overshadow the late colonial roots. To that extent Lomé was highly symbolic and aimed to position the EC squarely as a post-colonial actor, including the countries of the Global South as equals. Lomé was also highly symbolic in a second sense. Despite enlargement and the difficult economic circumstances of the 1970s, the Agreement demonstrated the EC's viability; it was an actor in the world.[93]

Like its predecessors Lomé I was valid for five years. But it marked a rather brief interlude. The follow-up agreements Lomé II to IV between 1980 and 1990 expanded the ACP system to states like Cape Verde, Angola, Namibia and Haiti. Moreover, new developments overtook the Agreement of 1975. The ACP states were no longer able to agree on joint positions as they had in the Lomé I talks. This heterogeneity, fostered by growing economic discrepancies and diverging political paths, weakened their negotiating position. In view of the pre-existing power gap, changes within the EC itself turned out to be even more consequential: escalating economic problems in the member states in the second half of the 1970s, the re-emergence of the East–West conflict in the following decade, the renaissance of transatlantic relations, the attention devoted to the Southern European countries accepted into membership in the 1980s, the influence of economic neoliberalism and finally the huge issue of coping with the collapse of the Eastern Bloc. In many member states and at EC level these pushed the relationship with the Global South into the background. Civil society pressure to tackle these issues was also on the wane. Rather than fighting poverty, the focus returned to economic growth and the EC moved closer to the line of other international organisations like the World Bank and made aid more strongly conditional.[94] And the Community reversed its market opening using non-tariff barriers such as the new environmental and standardisation rules (the United States and Japan deployed similar neo-protectionist measures). The situation was further exacerbated by the CAP, not just through its protectionist aspects, but also through dumping of surpluses, which created problematic dependency on subsidised EC agricultural products in certain developing countries. For all these reasons formal access to the EC was worth less to the ACP states than one might have thought at first glance, although the effects naturally varied from country to country and sector to sector. As a whole the EC tended to freeze the original Lomé Agreement rather than adapting its successors to new challenges.[95]

At the same time the EC somewhat expanded the role accorded to human rights questions from Lomé I and even more from the mid-1980s, not least on account of civil society pressure. But many ACP states regarded this as illegitimate interference in their internal affairs. So the two sides tended to grow apart. One indicator of the waning influence of the European Community in North–South relations was the fact that the EC played no major role at all in one of the crucial problems of the 1980s. The states of Western Europe preferred to discuss the debt crisis that plagued many developing countries through other channels than the EC, for example, bilaterally or in the scope of the G-7. The EC remained an actor in relations with the Global South, but its weight shrank.[96]

In this context the economic significance of the ACP countries to the EC states continued to reduce (but much less so in the opposite direction). This is seen particularly clearly in Africa: in 1958 about 10 per cent of the exports of the six member states went to Africa. By 1971 the figure had fallen to 6 per cent, and for the enlarged EC of 1985 just 5 per cent. For imports from Africa the corresponding figures were 12, 5 and 5 per cent.[97] But from the African perspective the situation was very different: in the early 1990s almost 50 per cent of all African exports went to the EC/EU. More than half of the development aid for sub-Saharan Africa came from Europe, 15 per cent from the EC, the other 85 per cent bilaterally.[98]

Development cooperation with states in Asia and Latin America – outside the ACP – began in 1976. Here negotiations were never with groups of states, but bilateral between the Community and the respective country. The rhetoric of partnership played no great role and in concrete development programmes the orientation was more on Yaoundé than Lomé: the EC was not granting these recipients an active role. The development relationship to Latin America, for example, thus remained largely unchanged from the 1950s through to the 1990s.[99]

Although the EC's development policy shed much of its late colonial baggage over time, its genesis was significant nonetheless. There was no global political or economic reason to treat Asia or Latin America differently than Africa; economically the former would have been more obvious choices than Africa in terms of development possibilities and economic complementarity. The outcome can only be explained in terms of a path dependency that stretches back to the old Eurafrique idea. And the colonial past of its member states is still present in the EU to this day, with possessions such as Spain's North African exclaves of Ceuta and Melilla, France's island of Réunion in the Indian Ocean, the Azores and other overseas entities that are either an integral part of a member state or maintain close ties to the EU as 'Overseas Countries and Territories'.[100]

To summarise the role of the Global South for the Community and its world: on the basis of a late colonial, Africa-specific policy the EC transformed over decades into a global trade and development actor in a post-colonial world. Leaving aside countervailing tendencies in Lomé I in the early 1970s, the EC's approach was always characterised by power asymmetries and by a desire to defend its hard-fought internal consensus on the international stage. The non-European states often found themselves facing a simple choice: 'take it or leave it'. Certain concessions were largely derived from colonial paternalism and the desire to bind the states of the Global South to the Western camp in the Cold War. The EC succeeded in speaking with a single voice to the associated countries and quickly became a comparatively influential actor in this context, although certainly without overshadowing the individual nation states (first and foremost France until the first enlargement round). Nevertheless Africa was initially quite important for the EC's world – above and beyond the phase of late colonial dreams and projections in the 1950s – and on that basis defined the EC's relationship to the Global South in general. From the late 1970s to the end of the Cold War, however, interest in Africa and other poor states of the Global South tended to decline. The EC spoke with a single voice – but in rather a whisper. These regions of the world, where Europe had often played a dominant role for many decades or even centuries, receded into the background and the EC concentrated on other questions.

Giant in the East

Finally we must turn to the meteoric economic rise of an East Asian power, one which from the 1970s became an increasingly important factor for the global role of the EC. This development took most Western European states by surprise; even in the 1950s trade with this country had been negligible. When its prime minister visited Europe at the beginning of the 1960s, de Gaulle referred to him disparagingly as a 'transistor radio salesman'.[101] A decade later nobody would have dared. By 1969 the *Spiegel* was devoting its title page to report that this country had pushed West Germany out of third place in the ranking of the world's industrial powers. Its prime minister, *Spiegel* reported, had recently announced there were currently 'two major global powers' – but he believed there was 'enough room for a third'.[102] One might suppose we were talking about China, but of course the discussion was about Japan.

If there was one East Asian economic power that played a growing role for the European Community in the decades before the Maastricht Treaty, that was Japan. This is reflected in the first place in questions of trade, which expanded enormously over the period. Nothing underlines this better than a comparison of the Japanese and Chinese shares of world trade. While Japan shot to meteoric prominence in the post-war decades, China remained absolutely marginal. Its rise only began in the 1990s – when Japan's star began to fade again, not least because its initial success built on analogue high-tech sectors that played little role in the digital world of the twenty-first century.

Whereas the EC was still fretting about 'the American challenge' in the mid-1960s, the Japanese challenge soon appeared even more pressing. From the late 1960s Japan presented dangerous competition

Table 4 Japanese and Chinese shares of world trade (exports) (per cent)

	Japan	China
1960	4.6	:
1970	8.9	:
1980	9.2	1.2
1990	11.9	2.6
2000	9.6	5.0
2016	5.2	17.0

Europäische Kommission, Außen- und Intrahandel der Europäischen Union, p. 12; for 2016, see https://bit.ly/316aBgm (accessed 1 July 2019).

not only in external markets, but above all within the Common Market itself, with increasing success in central sectors such as semiconductors, automobiles, electrical appliances and shipbuilding. As in the case of the United States – and unlike the Global South – the question here was less how the EC operated in relation to third countries in other regions of the world, but more about how it went about managing their impact within its bounds.[103]

Tariff barriers between Western Europe and Japan were still comparatively high in the 1950s, which protected the Common Market from Asian imports. During this period Washington called on its Western European partners to follow the US example and open its markets to Japanese products. Initially this was met with scepticism, coloured by the memory of East Asian dumping in the inter-war years and observation of current trends in Japanese–American trade. But in 1955 Japan joined GATT, and tariff barriers gradually came down over the course of successive negotiating rounds. The effect of GATT should not be overstated, however. During Japan's accession talks the states of Western Europe insisted on exceptions that permitted them to maintain some of their existing trade barriers. After the EEC had been established, its members made use of these to widely differing degrees, and as a result – despite the Commission's efforts to harmonise – the member states ended up having very different arrangements. Nor did the Common Commercial Policy, which was then still in the transitional period provided by the Treaties of Rome, do anything significant to change that.[104]

In 1970, when the transitional period ended, the Commission launched trade talks with Japan. This was the first case where the EC took the initiative, so important was the relationship now felt to be. The Commission sought – but failed to achieve – a uniform trade agreement. It argued for extensive trade liberalisation, but most of the member states insisted on protection clauses, and internal diversity of interests made it difficult to agree on a single line. The 1973 enlargement round, which fell in the middle of the talks with Japan, further complicated matters, and the same applies to the economic problems that erupted in autumn that year. Tokyo rejected protection clauses on the basis of negative past experience and was reluctant to accept the Commission as its central partner, seeing advantage in bilateral arrangements where it could more easily divide and rule. Unlike in the GATT context and with the ACP states, the Commission was therefore unable to operate effectively in this core sphere of trade policy towards Japan.[105]

This explains why trade relations between Japan and the various parts of the EC continued to develop differently. After the failure of talks in the early 1970s, GATT functioned as the lowest common denominator in dealings with Japan. Otherwise the EC member states pursued quite different paths. While France and Italy tended to favour protectionism and confrontation, West Germany and the Netherlands with their more competitive industries were stronger proponents of liberalisation. The British under Margaret Thatcher were even more enthusiastic about cooperation, with plants operated by the three big Japanese carmakers – Nissan, Toyota and Honda – coming to replace the dying British car industry. One important milestone in this connection was a cooperation agreement concluded in 1979 between Honda and the ailing, state-owned British Leyland. This step was especially attractive to Honda as it gained a foothold not only in the British market, but in the EC as a whole. Italy on the other hand continued to protect its car market and even in the late 1980s was still restricting Japanese car imports to 2,000 units annually. To that extent external market penetration coexisted with internal protectionism.[106]

At the same time the Commission continued to seek harmonisation. But it did not get very far. Anti-dumping complaints proved as ineffectual as attempts to improve European access to the Japanese market. Nor did a 1978 joint declaration by the EC and the Japanese government, in which Tokyo promised to reduce its trade surplus with the Community, produce results satisfactory to the European side. Continuous negotiations in the 1980s about limiting Japanese exports to the EC made slow progress and the Commission's frustration burst into the public sphere in March 1979 with the leaking of an internal document by Roy Denman, Director-General for External Affairs. Japan, he wrote, was: 'A country of workaholics living in what Westerners would regard as little more than rabbit hutches.'[107] Apart from precise statistics on Japanese business success, Brussels could apparently think only in stereotypes.

What this meant for the EC should be obvious. While Brussels was a significant factor in its own right in the GATT talks, in the transatlantic context and towards the former colonies and later ACP states, this was much less the case vis-à-vis Japan – at a time where the flood of imports 'made in Japan' was headline news. The interest and fears were not unfounded; after all it was estimated that imports from Japan had cost the EC more than one million skilled jobs by the early 1990s, while European consumers were queueing up to buy cars like the

Table 5 Trade between the EC and Japan

	EC exports (billion ECUs/euros)	EC imports (billion ECUs/euros)	Trade balance (billion ECUs/euros)
1960 (EU-6)	0.2	0.2	0.0
1970 (EU-6)	1.0	1.2	−0.2
1980 (EU-9)	4.6	12.3	−7.7
1985 (EU-10)	10.1	27.2	−17.1
1990 (EU-12)	22.7	46.1	−23.4
1995 (EU-15)	32.9	54.3	−21.4
2000 (EU-15)	44.9	87.1	−42.2

Europäische Kommission, *Außen- und Intrahandel der Europäischen Union*, p. 23, 25. Annual change was especially dramatic during the 1970s, see CMA, CM2, temporary LR 21360, EP Report, 666/78, esp. pp. 10–14.

Mitsubishi Galant and digital watches from Casio or Seiko. The EC's trade deficit with Japan also rose inexorably, while Japan did comparably little to open its own market for goods from the Community.[108]

Even if this meant that there was no big flagship deal, other factors should not be overlooked. Firstly, neither side had any interest in weakening the sophisticated systems protecting their respective agricultural sectors; so as well as conflicts there were also certain congruences. Secondly, the trade debates between the EC and Japan unfolded against the backdrop of a similar discussion between Washington and Tokyo, and even if the United States was a global power of quite a different calibre than the Community, the negotiations here too turned out to be complicated and by no means led to automatic American success. Thirdly, finally, the continuous negotiations between the Commission and the Japanese government (and the latter's minor concessions such as promising to restrict exports) gained time for the EC to make its own industries more competitive.

Ultimately, then, trade relations with Japan also had important effects on policy areas within the Community. In the 1970s and 1980s Japan was a central point of reference in the debates about Community industrial policy and research efforts. The same applied to the EC institutions themselves: between its first regular meeting in 1975 and the Single European Act eleven years later the European Council had Japan on its agenda more often than any other third country, eleven times in all.[109] The same also applied to non-state actors. For example, the Comité des constructeurs du marché commun, founded in the early 1970s to represent the European car industry, lobbied against the Japanese competition. For a time it was chaired by Gianni Agnelli. As well as occupying leading positions at Fiat, he and his brother Umberto were also among the decisive proponents of an EC industrial policy modelled on the ECSC and stood in close contact with the Commission. Fear of the Japanese was also a significant driver in the emergence of a research policy in the course of the 1970s.[110] So the EC's ability to speak with a single voice to Japan always remained below expectations; but at the same time important internal developments – above all the emergence of new fields of activity – cannot be understood without the Japan complex.

Little Brother

In comparison to the obvious importance of the United States, the long-forgotten relevance of Africa and the more indirect role of Japan, the relationship with China was always secondary, not least on account of the small weight of trade during this period. It is interesting nevertheless, not least on account of the political context. After all, China was a communist country, and in the 1950s had castigated the integration process as capitalist imperialist manoeuvring. In 1962, for example, the official *Peking Review* called the EC the 'economic arm of the aggressive NATO bloc'.[111]

By the 1970s Cold War slogans of that kind were few and far between. In 1975 the European Community and China opened diplomatic relations, after France had already normalised its relationship a decade prior; China had begun showing a growing interest in the EC since the late 1960s. With this move both sides hoped to step outside the Cold War confrontation. As well as fitting with the general atmosphere of détente, the process was also facilitated by the growing rift between Moscow and Beijing since the 1960s, as well as China's strategic interest in a multipolar world. Accordingly Beijing interpreted the Community's plans for monetary cooperation in the early 1970s as an expression of the 'desire of West European countries to get rid of superpower domination'.[112]

Yet Beijing's hope that the EC would become a new global partner outside the East–West conflict quickly turned out to be illusory; the Community was too closely bound up with the United States. What the EC was after was not a multipolar world but another opportunity to present the Community as a viable force both externally and internally.

That implied sidestepping the ideological factors and doing business with a communist regime. There was also an economic argument: amidst the crises after the end of the *trente glorieuses* the EC hoped that China would offer a new market; until the mid-1980s the Community ran a trade surplus. A trade agreement in 1978 led to noticeable growth, especially following a second agreement in 1985. Only now did the tables turn, with China beginning to develop a trade surplus with the Community. Otherwise China's principal interest was to import technology for purposes of modernisation: between 1981 and 1986 almost half of all Chinese technology imports came from the EC.[113]

Nevertheless, trade with China still lagged behind trade with Japan. In percentage terms China remained insignificant compared to the United States and Japan, and into the 1990s the EC imported considerably more from Switzerland than from China. That indicates how important intra-European – and even more so intra-Community – trade remained for the EC. The world grew in importance, but the Community still defined itself in the first place as an actor within its own space. The Chinese perspective was a little different. Here the EC was already a very important trade partner in the 1970s, in fact well ahead of the United States. In that respect the situation in China was similar to that across much of the Global South.[114]

Although there were also attempts to coordinate external policy towards China through the European Political Cooperation, trade remained the most important bridge between the two world regions, with the ideological contradictions having little influence. Questions of

Table 6 EC exports and imports

	Exports from the EC (share in %)			Imports to the EC (share in %)		
Year	United States	Japan	China	United States	Japan	China
1960 EC-6	9.2	0.8	0.9	14.0	0.5	0.5
1970 EC-6	12.8	1.9	0.6	15.5	2.1	0.4
1980 EC-9	12.5	2.1	0.8	16.2	4.5	0.6
1990 EC-12	19.5	5.8	1.3	19.3	10.4	2.4

Europäische Kommission, *Außen- und Intrahandel der Europäischen Union*, p. 23, 25; see also Eurostat, *External and Intra-European Union Trade*.

human rights only came to the fore after the Tian'anmen massacre in 1989. The European Parliament and the Commission quickly condemned the violent suppression of the protests and the Council of Ministers agreed to impose sanctions. But certain member states, including Italy, pursued a much more conciliatory line. By 1990 the Community – like Japan and the United States – was seeking to normalise the relationship again, and the economic relationship deepened considerably in the subsequent period. Here again we see the extent to which the EC's global role was defined through trade, even given the ideological contradictions in the case of a country like China.[115]

The Community and its World: Résumé

At one of his infamous press conferences Charles de Gaulle in 1964 outlined his ideas about the future of Europe. What he wanted, he said, was 'a European Europe' that 'exists in its own right, in the sense of pursuing its own global policy'.[116] The French president hoped especially that Europe would emancipate itself from the United States. Of course for de Gaulle 'Europe' meant not just the institutional framework of the EC, but in the first place the individual member states with their instruments of classical power politics, first and foremost France. Such ideas were always highly controversial in his own country and elsewhere, and ultimately the European Community of the Cold War era never developed clearly in the direction desired by de Gaulle. This is reflected most obviously in the transatlantic relationship, which despite many crises always remained much closer than the French president hoped.

At the same time an unmistakable rift opened up between ambition and reality. All in all, the European Community was only able to develop a moderately clear profile in specific issues and in relation to particular non-European regions – and at the same time it was remarkable that it even managed to accomplish that. There were several starting points, with relations with the United States and with the member states' (ex-)colonies turning out to be especially influential. In these processes the European Commission played a central role, always seeking new opportunities to wield influence. The Commission in particular embodied the Community's sense of opportunity, with the shuttle diplomacy of Jenkins, Cheysson and Haferkamp serving not least the desire to underline and expand their own role whenever the opportunity arose.

Through into the 1990s the EC's most important instrument for this was the Common Commercial Policy, as seen in the GATT context and also in the Community's interactions with the Global South. Especially in the latter case, the EC made itself into a very important partner in a manner inconceivable without the late colonial origins of the relationship. The negotiations with Japan, on the other hand, indicate that even in the sphere of trade the Community did not always succeed in becoming an influential actor, and encountered clear limits where the differences between member states were too large. Comparably close relations never developed at all with China. And where an intensification did occur despite the ideologically burdened relationship, this was again driven primarily by trade, small as its volume still was at this time.

In connection with the decolonising world and the Global South in general, development cooperation became increasingly important alongside trade, with the (primarily internal) Common Agricultural Policy representing a central factor for both policy areas. Against this backdrop the EC stood for a hybrid trade and economic policy with a liberal approach for manufactured goods and protectionism in the agricultural sector, the mix predicated primarily upon the complicated coordination processes within the Community.

The crucial role of fragile internal compromises created difficulties in the EC's interactions with other regions. It frequently gave the Community's actions a self-referential slant. What that meant in relation to Algeria was already described in Chapter 7, 'Disintegration and Dysfunctionality'. At the global level the Community played no leading role even in trade matters. Instead the EC often acted defensively, whether towards Japan, the United States or in the GATT context. Very often its difficulties reaching an internal consensus slowed progress in relation to world trade, as, for example, during the Empty Chair Crisis. One good example of the degree of introspection is supplied by an internal Commission paper prepared in 1977 for a trip to the United States by Jenkins. While underlining that the EC should emphasise its 'outward-looking character', the document also laid out why it was imperative to defend strong protections for the agricultural sector: aside from the issue of fluctuating global prices, the CAP constituted 'one of the few really "common" policies of the EC, with the political, social and economic importance which derives from that fact'.[117] When it came down to it a common policy was an end in itself, and more important than minor economic gains in relations with third states; the problematic CAP in particular was regarded as sacrosanct. Interestingly the United States, as forbearing hegemon, was generally amenable to this approach. To that extent a Europe existing 'in its own right', which de Gaulle intended as a badge of pride, also characterises the EC's self-referential leanings. For it was structures and priorities originally created primarily for internal use that shaped its interactions with other parts of the world.

This process was accompanied from the 1970s, as described in Chapter 2, 'Peace and Security', by attempts to play a greater role in security questions in the CSCE context. Whereas this permitted the EC to contribute to weakening the Iron Curtain, its security initiatives outside Europe were much less successful. Only in the Falklands War of 1982 did the EC briefly succeed in speaking with a single voice, as also described in the aforementioned chapter. Otherwise NATO and the nation states remained paramount in questions of security. 'Who do I call if I want to call Europe?': this biting comment attributed to Henry Kissinger in the crisis-ridden 1970s exposed the weakness of the EC when it came to problems of 'hard power' and 'grand politics'.[118] One did not need to be an avowed Gaullist to insist on the rights of the nation states, especially in the sphere of foreign policy. For a long time this remained unaffected by new established formats, first and foremost the European Political Cooperation and the European Council (the latter instead exerting greatest impact on internal dynamics within the Community). Even if there was much discussion about a well-defined autonomous external policy and a real global role, especially from the 1970s, this was more talk than reality.[119]

Yet the European Community's relationship to the world was not determined one-sidedly by national interests. At least in certain questions the EC was made into a player at the global level by external developments to which it was forced to respond, be they shifts and changes in the Cold War, decolonisation or the rise of Japan. Indeed, since the nineteenth century plans for deeper cooperation and integration in Europe had always been discussed against the background of global processes and fear of decline. While it is true that the member states' governments insisted on their sovereignty, at the same time they supported the Community's basic premise of relating to third states as a collective political order. This was important not only externally, but also internally for the functioning of the Common Market. Together with the Commission's proactive role, this created a momentum that the member states were not always able to control. Ultimately the tension between the postulated primacy of the member states and the inherent logic of the integration process transpired to be constitutive for the EC's global possibilities and perspectives.

Finally, we see here how the external and the internal were so closely interconnected that the lines between the two occasionally became blurred. In the post-war period integration meant more than just 'little Europe', but followed colonial ties to seek a much greater geographical reach. The effects of the Common Agricultural Policy were felt by peanut farmers as far afield as Senegal and South Carolina. And by the early 1990s Nissan was employing 3,500 workers at its plant in north-east England and sourcing components from more than 120 suppliers in the United Kingdom and a good half-dozen other Western European states.[120] At the political level too, the Japanese case demonstrates how a non-European third country was able to trigger significant changes within the Community, for example, in the area of research policy. At a much more fundamental level this applies to the United States too. All in all, one cannot understand the history of the EC without examining the global dimension.

EPILOGUE

You rarely get a second chance in politics, yet Maastricht did in 1991. On 9 and 10 December the city at the southernmost extremity of the Netherlands, known for its cheerful lifestyle and fine cuisine, hosted the decisive negotiations for the treaty that came to bear its name. A previous European Council in Maastricht exactly ten years earlier had ended in disaster, at least on the culinary front. A buffet for more than 1,000 officials and journalists was contaminated with salmonella, and more than half the guests came down with what one regional newspaper called the 'Eurosummit bug'.[1] According to press reports, a rerun of the debacle was only narrowly avoided in 1991: at the meeting of the heads of state and government themselves a spoilt cheese was only removed at the last moment.[2]

The Maastricht Treaty, which the leaders signed the following February after final revisions, came into effect in 1993 and has often been described as a turning point in the history of European integration. Indeed: the European Community became the European Union; the treaty stands for the euro, and is associated with many other integration steps. For all these reasons public debate and academic research frequently treat Maastricht as a turning point or watershed.[3]

Yet it is illuminating to take a look at the topics discussed at the long-forgotten Maastricht Summit of March 1981 (which even the hosting Dutch government did not regard as terribly significant).[4] Alongside the economic situation, monetary policy was high on the list, noting that dialogue with the United States needed to be intensified. The meeting also resolved to pursue a 'coherent energy policy' and to 'foster the development of high-technology and innovative enterprises'. The heads of state and government were satisfied with recent 'substantial progress' on the introduction of a European passport. And finally the meeting issued a string of statements on global problems from Afghanistan to Poland, underlining the Community's claim to a leading global role.[5]

So many of the issues we now associate with the Maastricht Treaty of 1992 had in fact been on the EC's agenda for years. And, in fact more significantly, even without the collapse of the Soviet Union and German reunification there would have probably been a significant step towards integration in the form of a new treaty. That applies especially to the Economic and Monetary Union. The popular German myth that Maastricht saw the German government forced to relinquish its dependable deutschmark as Europe's price for German reunification is just that: a myth. In fact talks over a common currency had been under way since the 1970s and accelerated in the course of the 1980s; the foundations of the Monetary Union had already been laid by the end of the 1980s. Of course the Maastricht negotiations over a European Monetary Union could in theory have failed – but that would have been rather unlikely. There were good and genuine monetary and economic grounds for such an outcome – not least in light of the Single Market project of the second half of the 1980s. The developments of 1989/90 simply notched up the level of urgency.[6] Nor was the Common Foreign and Security Policy completely new either. It built on the European Political Cooperation and its codification in the Single European Act, as well as widespread criticisms of the deficits of those arrangements, such as the Genscher–Colombo Initiative of 1981.[7] And, to cite a third example: before lauding the question of Union citizenship as a breakthrough of Maastricht 1991, one should perhaps take a look at the Council Conclusions from 1981...

Similarly, the new institutional arrangements agreed in Maastricht also built on informal developments over the course of the two preceding decades – quite apart from the obvious continuities to the existing treaties. A political theory has recently surfaced that it was Maastricht 1991 that established the European Council as the Union's dominant actor on questions of economic policy.[8] But closer analysis of the summits of the 1970s and 1980s raises question marks. Economic matters were central at the Maastricht Council of 1981 – and at most of the summits since the 1970s. And the heads of state and government not only were discussing with one another, but also heeding a sense of shared responsibility for the Community – as already formulated in 1975 by Valéry Giscard d'Estaing, Harold Wilson and Helmut Schmidt.[9] At the 1981 Maastricht meeting Giscard had reminded his colleagues that the European Council was not simply 'a super Council of Ministers': it had a duty to tackle overarching problems.[10] Altogether the role played by the European Council in the pre-1992 institutional framework is not to be underestimated. The 'new intergovernmentalism' that some today would class as a 'post-Maastricht' phenomenon can in fact be traced back to the 'pre-Maastricht' era. And even more importantly, the idea that only the intergovernmental approach has grown since Maastricht cannot be substantiated. In fact the EU's supranational side has been repeatedly strengthened too, for example, during the euro crisis when a series of intergovernmental negotiations were followed by supranational action. Overall the two integration approaches created a continuously rebalancing equilibrium. Maastricht represented no hard turning point in that respect.

In another respect too, Maastricht was not the absolute watershed it is often said to be. It was no breakthrough on responsibilities, institutions or membership catapulting the Union into the post-Cold War world. On the one hand, it was to be another dozen years before the first Eastern European states joined the Union in 2004. On the other, with the accession of the territory of the former East Germany, the first step east of the defunct Iron Curtain had already been made in 1990. And a year before that the European Council had created the PHARE Programme to assist economic restructuring of the transforming Eastern Bloc. In other words, important developments occurred before and after Maastricht. It was the same story with the euro, not only on account of the aforementioned background, but also with respect to subsequent developments. Maastricht wrote a timetable for the Monetary Union, but currencies, like railway services, do not always run to time. There were several later points where the euro experiment could have switched onto a different track, and at the beginning it was by no means clear which states would participate. Another reason not to overestimate the Maastricht Treaty, at least in terms of its immediate effect.[11]

From another angle too, the Maastricht Treaty itself was soon history. In terms of the mechanisms by which the Union developed, it falls into quite a different phase than the one we are in today. Maastricht was followed by long series of further reforms: the treaties of Amsterdam (1997) and Nice (2001), the ultimately rejected draft Constitutional Treaty (2004) and the 2007 Treaty of Lisbon. Like these subsequent agreements, Maastricht was already regarded as incomplete when it was signed, and fundamental reform efforts were moving on before the ink was dry. Maastricht thus stands for an era where changes at the fundamental level of the treaties were seen as the route of choice for developing the European Union. In retrospect the Single European Act of 1987 can be seen as the starting shot for a twenty-year series ending with the Treaty of Lisbon.[12] Today we find ourselves in a phase where a new comprehensive reform treaty must be regarded as an extremely remote prospect. As in the 1970s the Union prefers to muddle through. In the context of ongoing Brexit talks – when a departing member state could hold the others to ransom – it has little alternative. But more important than Brexit is the ultimately sobering experience with treaties over the past twenty years. Further very general factors include growing differences within the Union with its more than twenty member states and a lack of public support for such initiatives.

All in all, it transpires that the origins of some of what is often associated with the Maastricht Treaty are found in the 1970s and above all the 1980s, while other aspects only properly surfaced in the course of the 1990s. The new start cannot therefore be attributed exclusively to the treaty text. For all its real legal, political and symbolic significance, in many spheres slow, gradual changes proved more significant than the prominent negotiations. Even if one is interested only in the EU's post-Maastricht history, one still has to dig a good deal further back simply because the origins of many developments attributed to the treaty in fact began much earlier.[13]

Project Europe: Lessons

So what else can we learn from all this for the European Union today? Firstly, for a long time there was not just one Project Europe, but many – most of them conceived as alternatives to nation-centred forms of politics. It was by no means inevitable that the European Community would come to be the dominant forum of cooperation and integration in Cold War Western Europe. Not until the 1960s were there growing signs that the EC was on the way to becoming a different class of actor than, for example, the OECD. And even in the early 1980s its status was anything but certain. Only from the second half of the decade did it (and later the EU) come to quasi-monopolise European cooperation. So it would be altogether mistaken to project the European Union's undisputed contemporary status back into its early decades. In many respects the EU is a surprisingly young construct in which powers and processes are a good deal less entrenched than one might expect, given that it has been almost seven decades since the founding of the European Coal and Steel Community. That should teach us humility, but perhaps also forbearance.

It was above all the periods of turmoil that made the European Community into the central European project: for example, economic and political challenges as the *trente glorieuses* ended in the early 1970s, or about fifteen years later when the Eastern Bloc crumbled and collapsed. As much as the origins of the EC were shaped by the Cold War, it was now seen as the ideal forum for guiding Europe into the post-Cold War world. In that sense it partially emancipated itself from its own beginnings. While it had enormously expanded its relevance, its institutions and purpose had not progressed towards the objective of a United States of Europe as certain representatives of the founding generation had hoped. It was by no means inevitable that the EC would emerge strengthened from crises, and yet these phases did often turn out to be opportunities and were used productively.

This breathtaking gain in importance is also the main reason for a growing trend towards differentiated integration. With ever more states joining the Union and ever more important questions at stake, it is no longer possible to keep them all signed up to a central consensus. Some insist on opt-outs, while others seek even deeper cooperation. Aspects of this phenomenon have always existed, but it has grown considerably since the 1980s. Before the proponents of integration get too nostalgic about the apparently less complex world of a time gone by, though, they should perhaps remember that the division of tasks between different regional organisations often produced similar effects to differentiated integration in the EU today. It used to be thought that differentiation simply meant moving towards a shared objective at different speeds. Today it is clear that the participating states are pursuing different paths and heading for different destinations.[14] This understanding of non-linear differentiation has great similarity with the situation when the EC was merely one of several similar significant forums of international cooperation in Western Europe. Paradoxical as it might sound, precisely because the EU now occupies a dominant position in relation to European cooperation, legal differentiation represents the most important means for moving forward.

This incremental growth in significance has made the European Union vulnerable. On the one side the EU is now responsible for truly important matters and enjoys perceptible influence. Additionally, diverse synergies arise when so many questions and policy areas are dealt with in a single institutional framework that has long since transcended that of a classical international organisation. The European Union has become astonishingly resilient, in the sense that it is in a position to turn externally driven change to its advantage rather than merely rebuffing it.[15] This stems less from the idealism of the participants than the enormous inertia of established institutions, the diverse interests contained within them, and the general momentum of the integration process. On the other hand the task-sharing mode of international cooperation during the post-war period made it less easy for crises to flashover from one arena to the next. Of course the overall power of all international organisations was much smaller – to that extent the stakes were lower. The EU of our time is not only systemically more relevant than ever before. It is also more vulnerable to fundamental crisis. In such a scenario of cumulative crises – for example, exit moves, massive economic turmoil, subversion of European law and military tensions – it would be crucial to isolate the problems from one another and tackle them separately.[16] Otherwise that might be the end of the project.

At this juncture it is worth briefly recapitulating the various dimensions that have come to be increasingly associated with the European Community. Peace was the central argument for European integration in the post-war period. In the intervening years it came to be regarded as a problem solved, but has recently returned with shocking urgency. In the early phase, it is frequently asserted, integration was central to the pacification of Europe as the 'dark continent'.[17] But over the decades, the argument goes, the lesson that European integration brought peace had increasingly become forgotten because the hard-won peace simply became normality for subsequent generations. As a result, this motive had lost its power to justify European integration.

I demonstrated how dubious that argument is in Chapter 2. Especially in the early days the European Community had little practical impact in this sphere. In fact the EC was a secondary factor in the post-war peace settlement; more beneficiary than architect. The post-war order was already done and dusted when the Community emerged. So it was never actually able to make a major contribution to peace in the world, not even when it stepped up its efforts in this dimension in the 1970s. Only in the East–West context did its role expand in the 1970s and 1980s – contradicting the conventional view that its contribution to peace was most significant in the initial years. In terms of internal peace within the Community, as a second dimension alongside peace in Europe and the world, the EC certainly also played a role by contributing to reconciliation between former enemies, especially France and Germany. But other relevant factors should not be underestimated: the hegemonic role of the United States, the forces of the Cold War, bilateral ties and civil society forces without any direct connection to the EC. The Community was but one factor among others, although it did stand out as the public face of peace efforts. That symbolic level also goes some way to explaining why its peace-promoting effect is so frequently exaggerated.

The EC's role was most significant, finally, in securing social peace within the member states, in particular through the Common Agricultural Policy. As a form of covert social policy, the CAP helped to ensure that the deeply crisis-prone transformation of the agricultural sector remained a peaceful process: first of all in France, Italy and West Germany for instance, later also Ireland, Greece, Spain and Portugal. Despite the growing significance of its Regional Policy, the EU can point to no such role today (an equivalent could, for example, be offering new perspectives to the losers of globalisation and the digital revolution). So at this level a look back at the history is certainly instructive.

Later and differently than generally believed: that summarises the role of the EC in relation to peace in the decades of the Cold War. And today too we need a realistic assessment of the EU's possibilities in the dimension of peace and security. It is likely to be most effective in cooperation with the United Nations or NATO. Even more than during the Cold War, however, this means contributing to the functioning of these organisations at a juncture where they stand under massive pressure. At the same time the tensions in our own times remind us how precious peace is, and how much the institutions that promise to safeguard it deserve our attention.

At the economic level too, our review of the history tells a different story than the one generally circulated today. First of all it must be noted that the EC's contribution to prosperity cannot be exactly measured, and public and academic interest in the question has been astonishingly meagre. In fact, it has been largely overlooked that in relative terms the EC's effect tended to be larger in the crisis-torn years from the early 1970s to the end of the Cold War than in the twenty years prior.

The EC was born with a focus on the economic, especially as the EEC increasingly hogged the limelight from the early 1960s. The latter's business-centred capitalist logic was one of the main reasons why the EC was able to become the dominant forum of international cooperation in Europe. Seeing the world through an economic lens decisively shaped the EC and continues to do so today – for better and worse.

At the same time the attitude to the economic was often instrumental. The underlying premise of the post-war years was that the overarching political objective of European integration was a matter worth spending money on. That was doable as long as the historically unique economic boom persisted and the economic effects of integration remained secondary. Even the expensive CAP ultimately represented an annoyance but not a threat to the economic foundations of the member states. The history of the euro since the 1990s offers an example of how dangerous the primacy of the political over the economic can be when questions of systemic import come into play. One example would be the risky inclusion of Greece in the euro on the basis of dubious statistics – the repercussions of this decision being largely borne by the Greeks themselves. Another would be the general structural defects of the euro, which created a common currency without common bank regulation or common political structures.

The instrumental tendency in the treatment of economic issues has a long history. In view of the stakes today, this is now more dangerous than it ever was during the Cold War. I have already mentioned the possibility of the EU disintegrating through the impact of cumulative crises, with grave consequences for its member states. The structural instability of the Economic and Monetary Union presents a similar risk of fundamental crisis – in contrast to the curious but unexpectedly stable structure of the old EC. The euro is at particular risk if crisis strikes a large member state like France or Italy. Beyond this the opportunities and risks of economic and monetary decisions must be thought through more consistently and placed more strongly in the centre of public interest. Misrepresentations like the Brexit camp's claims about savings to the national budget would be harder to disseminate if the achievements and failures of European integration were presented more transparently and discussed more intensely. This is tied to the questions of whether prosperity is the best indicator of the success of the integration project, the ecological cost of focusing only on jobs and growth, and what the relationship should be between prosperity and solidarity.

The problem is made all the more urgent by the EU's failure to win the hearts and minds of many citizens in the member states. This finding is notable because well before the Maastricht Treaty the Community had already entered the economic and political arteries of the member states, and even then the attitude of most citizens to the integration process was more distanced and critical than had hitherto been thought. Project Europe was a creature of the elites with a strongly technocratic dimension. The reform treaties of the twenty years from 1987 to 2007 were conceived not least as an attempt to close the gap between the Community and its citizens, with but modest success. Instead the dominant mood is disinterest morphing into resistance in moments of crisis. For a long time most people generally took little interest in the European Community and assumed that it had little to do with their own lives. But as the effects of integration became increasingly obvious from the 1990s and even more the 2000s, many asked themselves how and when they had actually consented to these changes.

Alongside the feeling that one need not take the EC too seriously, other external braces for integration included Cold War anti-communism and to an extent anti-Americanism, and in the early years fear of loss of global influence through decolonisation. This found expression in ironic proposals to honour men like Joseph Stalin and Gamal Abdel Nasser as promoters of a united Europe. 'Europe' increasingly understood itself as a counter-project to these ideological alternatives and as a response to global challenges. In this reactive process the appellation transformed increasingly from a geographical/cultural reference to a term associated with a specific political/administrative reality. While Bismarck thought it was wrong to speak of 'Europe' in a political sense, John Pocock, as one of the twentieth century's leading historians of political thought, came to quite a different conclusion exactly 120 years later. The term 'Europe',

Pocock wrote, had something dynamic, indeterminate and hegemonial about it; it was 'tendentious and aggressive'. Pocock was actually writing about the Europe of the Early Modern rather than the EU. While one need not agree with him, it is certainly noticeable that in the post-war decades it became taboo to speak badly of Project Europe, unclear as it was what the project actually meant.[18] That has changed of late, as openly nationalistic tones rise again. More broadly, blurring of the distinction between friend and foe intensifies centrifugal tendencies: in parts of Europe, states that combine authoritarian politics with economic rewards for quiescent partners, like China and Russia, are increasingly regarded as an attractive alternative to the European Union.

The problem of participation in, support of and control over the integration process by the citizens of the member states or by institutions and procedures they accept is now even more urgent than in the post-war decades. This is because the EU today has an immensely greater and at the same time considerably more visible significance for weal and woe than it did in the 1970s and 1980s. At the same time a technocratic solution always remains an important option for the elites – as seen repeatedly during the euro crisis. But the growing desire for participation, democratic control and transparency makes such an approach more controversial than ever. Moreover, differentiated integration often represents the most practicable option but is problematic from the perspective of democratic legitimacy and control: differentiation makes the EU appear even more confusing than it is anyway, and tends to dissolve the project into many parts, each of which needs to be justified to the public. This further weakens the legitimacy of the project as a whole. A classical dilemma with no easy solutions.

The latest opinion surveys show greater support for membership than there has been in a long time, as well as the highest values since 1983 for the question of whether the respondent's own country profits from membership. But there is nothing to suggest that identification with the Union has grown simply with the sheer duration of its existence or that citizens' emotional and political bonds to the nation state have weakened over time. Instead, the growing politicisation of European problems has fostered dissension.[19] Today there is hardly a member state without a strong euro-sceptic party. In a world that has become a more dangerous place again and an economy that has recently passed through one of the deepest crises of modern times, support for the EU might remain strong but Project Europe is still exceptionally controversial.[20]

Its fragility is currently reflected not least in the sphere of values and norms. The EU is most often posited as a 'community of values' where it faces challenges from various quarters concerning basic and human rights or democracy and needs to take a stance. A glance at the history is instructive here. It goes without saying that an orientation on values has shaped the integration process since the beginning. But this initially remained largely implicit, while the Council of Europe was entrusted with safeguarding values. The status of norms and values in the EC was frequently extremely controversial, especially where third countries were concerned, and far from being the overt guide of political action. That applied even in instances of association and membership application, as in the cases of Spain in the 1950s, Greece in the 1960s and the so-called ACP states of the Global South in the 1970s and 1980s.

Since the early 1990s the EU has pursued the objective of promoting democracy, human rights and the rule of law with even greater emphasis, for example, in the scope of its Mediterranean Policy. But the EU's stance towards Egypt offers a good example of how such measures remain quite ambivalent and in case of doubt the EU may privilege realpolitik over value. Elsewhere too, the EU is willing to work closely with authoritarian regimes. For an actor that carries real clout on the global stage – at least in certain questions – concessions and compromises are practically inevitable. But they become a double standard if the 'community of values' banner is waved too high.

Internally too, the EC only began to formulate its own ethos in the 1970s – and struggled with the process. Interestingly, such measures tended to be orientated on securing the institutional status quo more than any genuine expression of dedication to values. Since the 1990s the status of norms and values within the Union has been boosted by the Copenhagen accession criteria of 1993 and the Charter of Fundamental Rights of 2000. These steps have not resolved the problem of effective protection, however. Historical analysis places the sometimes apparently enormous gap between wish and reality in perspective, revealing that the discrepancy is less new than it might appear at first glance. The EU has also been more convincing in insisting that third states observe norms and values than in safeguarding the latter within its own bounds – problematic as that may be. That awareness casts the current challenges presented by the Hungarian and Polish governments in a different light, and at the same time helps to explain why the European Union finds it so hard to effectively reject alternative value systems introduced from outside, for example, by Russia or China. If the EU often appears confused and weak this has not only to do with coordination mechanisms or questions of power, but also with the longer, complicated history of norms and values in the process of European integration.

European integration has always meant more than cooperation between sovereign states. National interests have deeply shaped the history of the EU, but have never been able to fully control the integration process. Instead integration linked, interwove and transformed the states themselves with their administrations and political processes. They became post-classical nation states that relinquish sovereignty in central questions in favour of international collaboration.[21] That does not say that this shift occurred in the same manner everywhere; the established state structures and the cultures and societies behind them were too strong for that. How policy on Europe was made and how the Community affected the state differed markedly, for example, between France, Ireland and Greece.

Various institutions on the European side drove the transformation processes. The European Court of Justice turned out to be especially important, along with the enormous potency of European law and – at a more general level – the influence of creeping change at the administrative and legal levels, whose effects only kicked in over time and only became visible to the broader public even later. *Cassis de Dijon* and the New Approach are prime examples.

Since the promises of prosperity and liberty associated with Project Europe turned out to be so fragile, resistance to the political and social transformations associated with integration – which many people perceive as outside domination by faceless 'Eurocrats' – has been growing.[22] The belief that compromise-based international cooperation represents a value in its own right no longer goes unchallenged. The same applies to the autonomy of the law, the argument that 'there is no alternative', the tendency to apply technocratic solutions and finally the strategy of effecting large changes in very small steps. Instead phenomena that appeared long overcome have resurfaced: the insistence on national sovereignty and putting the nation first (whatever that means exactly); charismatic, polarising leaders asserting imperatives and willing to act above the law; and finally the staging of apparently great authentic moments that renew the bond between leadership and followers. This trend is by no means restricted to the EU, and is also found in the United States, India and Turkey. But the European Union offers an especially rewarding target for populist currents left and right.

Against this background there has been increasing discussion of disintegration recently. This is not fundamentally new. For all the European Community's institutional robustness, membership and integration have repeatedly turned out to be reversible. If we know about Algeria and Greenland we will be less surprised by Brexit. Whatever the fundamental differences between their routes out of the Community and the situation of the United Kingdom today, their history holds valuable lessons for the present. Two in particular: firstly, in the second half of the twentieth century leaving the Community did not mean regaining full sovereignty. This is likely to apply even more so in the even more deeply networked and globalised world of today. Secondly, adapting the German football adage 'After the match is before the match': after the exit talks is before the next talks. The long-term relationship a departing state creates with the Union will depend only partly on the arrangements made at the point of separation. Currently all attention is directed towards concluding a deal between London and the rest of the EU. But that is unlikely to be so crucial for the relationship in twenty or thirty years' time.

Leaving aside the highly symbolic exit question, dysfunctionality and disintegration represent aspects of normality in the history of European integration rather than fundamental crisis. Only certain crises and setbacks have systemic relevance or touch on core competencies; many others are located at subsidiary levels. It is nothing unusual if certain responsibilities are returned to the member states under the subsidiarity principle officially sealed by Maastricht or if a country has difficulties implementing EU directives. The latter in particular has always been part of the normality of European integration and should not be confused with disintegration. Even dysfunctionality can only be cited in extreme cases.

It is quite a different matter if a member state argues it is not bound by a ruling of the Court of Justice of the European Union or otherwise fundamentally challenges the validity of the Union's legal system and the mechanisms by which it functions. That was the step taken by Viktor Orbán in September 2017, when he announced that the Hungarian government would ignore an ECJ ruling on the refugee question. The case could indicate a systemic crisis – or paradoxically it could ultimately lead to a strengthening of the supranational level in response to illiberal tendencies at the level of the member states. The last word has not been spoken. Beyond that, although recent years appear at first glance to have been turbulent and crisis-torn for the EU, there has actually been astonishingly little disintegration in the strict sense of the word. Brexit is a case in point. The euro crisis led to further integration. And while the refugee and migration question has seen progress blocked and rules ignored, there is at least as yet no clear evidence of lasting disintegration. The fact that such tremors have as yet left little mark on the foundations of Project Europe evidences its resilience. The horizon is darkening but the portents should not be confused with the status quo.

While the EU today is concerned above all with internal problems and often appears to have its work cut out with them, its relationships to the rest of the world possess more significance than ever before. For a long time interactions with other world regions were secondary and the EC was characterised by a rather self-referential and occasionally even autistic touch. After a compromise package had been finalised at enormous effort by the member states, it was not easy to undo it for a third party without undermining the Community's clout and ultimately its actor character. External relations are naturally always complex, and doubly so for the European Union and its predecessors. As benign hegemon, the United States long demonstrated considerable patience. And even if nobody would belittle the transatlantic turbulence created by President Trump, his critical stance towards the EU is not entirely unprecedented. In some respects it recalls the Nixon era. In retrospect the transformation phase at the end of the Cold War, when the United States and the EC worked closely together again, seems to be the period that actually demands explanation – rather than the longer trend of accruing conflicts. Partially hidden continuities and the power of memory should not be underestimated in relation to other world regions either. More than in the member states of the EU, where pretty much nobody has heard of terms like Eurafrique, the problematic late colonial origins of the relationship are still liable to be remembered today in Africa and other parts of the Global South. And it is no surprise that the EU's double standard on liberalisation for industrial and agricultural products was quickly identified and criticised in these quarters. This self-serving approach rather dented the friendly self-image that Project Europe wanted to send out into the world.

At the same time the relationships with the United States, with Africa and also with Japan and China indicate the centrality of the Common Commercial Policy with its strongly supranational elements for the role of the EC in relation to non-European world regions, not least because the EC always remained secondary or marginal in other spheres such as classical diplomatic foreign policy or military affairs. The treaties of Amsterdam, Nice and Lisbon have lastingly changed the shape of EU trade policy, expanding from trade in goods to cover complex issues such as services and investment. Also political and civil society criticism of the mainstream liberalisation credo has grown louder over the past twenty years. Even if the European Commission continues to play a central role, the tableau of actors has expanded considerably. For example, the European Parliament has noticeably more to say in this policy area today than it did before the Treaty of Lisbon. The member states also continue to play a significant role as was seen very publicly in the ratification cliffhanger for the free trade agreement with Canada in 2016, when a Belgian regional parliament wielded its veto for a time. Many levels and actors are thus involved, which is appropriate given the stakes. But it does make the internal processes even more difficult.[23] This growing politicisation of trade questions has both strengthened and weakened the EU's position, and here again one cannot identify a simple trend of growing importance. At the same time it has made the EU's stance less predictable, doing no good to its reputation. The same applies all the more in a world that has become so much more complex than during the Cold War. This too must be remembered when proposals are mooted to give the EU greater global weight, far beyond the realm of the economic.

Historia Magistra Vitae?

Learning from history is never easy. Cicero's assertion that history is the teacher of life turns out to be problematic. Historians cannot supply historical examples for timeless norms; we cannot provide knowledge codified in rules or analogies. The circumstances and contexts are too fluid for that: history is always open-ended.[24] What this volume has addressed are the questions of how and why developments occurred in the process of European integration and what effects they had on larger questions of European contemporary history. Ralf Dahrendorf, who interrupted a long career as scholar in the early

1970s to serve briefly and with modest success as a commissioner in Brussels, put it as follows: we can learn from history, but we cannot apply it.[25]

History teaches us how improbable and fragile our own time is; from the perspective of the past the present was but one of many futures (and potentially an unlikely one). That is the case for Project Europe too. Rather than proceeding as the implementation of a master plan, the EU we have today appeared in fits and starts. Above the level of detail the project set out to make the future more predictable. It was this hope that shines through all the treaties and directives, summits and compromises, plans and proposals. While many saw precisely that as a value in its own right, the idea of Project Europe as an attempt to contain the future is less certain again today.

Nobody knows what the future will bring for Project Europe. But one thing is certain: it will depend not least on the conclusions Europeans derive from its history.

ACKNOWLEDGEMENTS

Everything began with bitter disappointment. In spring 1982, a ten-year-old boy had developed such an interest in philately that he informed himself in advance about commemorative stamps the German Bundespost was about to issue. For May, it announced a stamp on the Treaties of Rome. Interested in Roman antiquity, he was thrilled, even if he did not know what these treaties stood for. The announcement itself simply sounded great. This child was already used to travelling the world through his stamps – just as Walter Benjamin had described during the 1920s. What a disappointment when the little piece of paper finally reached our boy's home in provincial south-western Germany: the stamp made no reference to the past grandeur of the Roman Empire. The Treaties of Rome commemorated by the stamp were barely twenty-five years old – and thus much more remote to the young lad than the times of Caesar and Cicero. Aby Warburg, a stamp collector as passionate as Benjamin, would have rejoiced: this kid felt closer to an imagined antiquity than to a past that was so much closer to his own days.

But what did the stamp feature? The plain postage stamp displayed several European flags and a text that did not make much sense to our young collector. Half a dozen kings and other heads of states had decided something. The stamp did not tell what, for the text was truncated at the decisive point. The composition was prosaic and boring in comparison to all the exciting, colourful stamps from Africa and Asia that his London-based uncle sent at regular intervals. And how utterly banal in comparison to his Roman gods and heroes! Confused, our boy

Figure 11: German postage stamp marking the twenty-fifth anniversary of the Treaties of Rome. Archive of the author

went to his mother, who told him what the 1957 Treaties of Rome were all about.

Our world is fundamentally different from the one of 1982. The Cold War is over. Germany is unified. The future of the EU seems less clear today than it did back then. These days, nobody would read a printed brochure on forthcoming stamps. And no normal kid collects stamps anymore. The stamp itself was strange, too: it did not feature the emblem we today associate with the EU, with the twelve golden stars on a blue field. This symbol was only introduced a few years later. Everything was different but also strikingly familiar: being confused, slowly making sense of things, and the profound question of whether this was yet another topic worth spending time on.

This is how my own sentimental journey towards studying what we today call the European Union began. This book brings together many of the threads by which I have worked on the history of European cooperation and integration over the past fifteen years and develops them further. It is not a mere synthesis of my earlier work but based on fresh research on a series of topics that were new for me, taking me to more than a dozen archives in several countries. Having said that, my earlier work on the EU and its history – as well as addressing completely different topics – was instrumental in choosing the approach for this book.

So did everything really start with bitter disappointment? Like every project, this one also had many more beginnings than one might think at first glance. Pierre Bourdieu warns of what he calls the biographic illusion – the tendency to read an (academic) life all too easily as a logical sequence of events that build upon each other. Bourdieu's warning has also rubbed off on the structure of this book. It does not analyse the history of the EU following a strictly chronological model. Instead, I chose an approach that keeps an eye on asynchronicities and changes as much as on continuities. The book thus offers an alternative to established histories that assert a clear starting point. This also holds true in the way my analysis embeds integration history into the broader context of European contemporary history. It assesses achievements and deficits more critically than is often the case.

Looking back, this project has important origins in my time at Humboldt University in Berlin, where I first started to work on this topic. Since 2006/07, when I was a Kennedy Fellow at Harvard University, interdisciplinarity has shaped my work in this field. This thread continued through the four years at the European University Institute (EUI) in Florence, Italy, my eight years at Maastricht University from 2011 to 2019, as well as most recently at Ludwig Maximilian University in Munich.

I would firstly like to thank my colleagues and students at these various institutions. I have also profited greatly from my affiliation with the KFG 'The Transformative Power of Europe' at the Free University of Berlin. *Vielen Dank* to its two directors Tanja Börzel and Thomas Risse, as well as to Wolfram Kaiser, with whom I ran several projects on the history of the EU under the auspices of the KFG. Moreover, I am very grateful for the invitation to the Gerda Henkel visiting professorship at the German Historical Institute London (GHIL) and LSE during the academic year 2014/15, when the real work on this book started. Particular thanks go to Andreas Gestrich and Piers Ludlow, but also to the whole team at the GHIL and LSE's International History Department. *Un grand merci* to Sciences Po in Paris, where I was visiting professor in January/February 2017, especially to Marc Lazar and Jakob Vogel. I would also like to thank all my colleagues in the still rather small field of research on the history of the EU, most importantly those in the Groupe de liaison des historiens auprès de la Commission des Communautés Européennes, first and foremost Wilfried Loth and Antonio Varsori. The same holds true for the members of the Arbeitskreis für Rechtswissenschaft und Zeitgeschichte at the Academy of Sciences and Literature in Mainz, particularly Hans Christian Röhl. Together, we organised the 2017 annual meeting on the history of European union. In Maastricht, *hartstikke bedankt* to my colleagues in the Research Group Politics and Culture in Europe for things big and small. With Sophie Vanhoonacker, I did not just experience the ups and downs of academic administration during my Maastricht years; occasionally, we also found time to jointly research and teach the history of the EU. Similar things hold true for Wolfgang Wessels and Jürgen Mittag, with whom Sophie and I cooperated in the framework of a Jean Monnet Centre of Excellence. *Grazie tante* to Federico Romero and Ulrich Krotz. In the context of my Maastricht Jean Monnet Chair, I have worked with these two EUI-based scholars on the history of the EU's external relations. Finally, I should add a *Dank schee* to my new colleagues from near and far in Munich.

It was both a privilege and a productive challenge to write this book concurrently with several EU-funded projects. Still, I tried to find a fresh approach to the topic, neither reproducing the powerful narratives that the European institutions have invented about themselves, nor following any other well-trodden paths of interpretation.

Many colleagues helped me in fine-tuning this new approach and in developing a new language to write about the history of the EU. The book first came out in German, and I am particularly grateful to a group of German-speaking colleagues who each read a chapter: Philipp Dann, Jost Dülffer, Jens Hacke, Heinz-Gerhard Haupt, Konrad H. Jarausch, Hartmut Kaelble, Jürgen Kocka, Sandrine Kott, Jacob Krumrey, Wilfried Loth, Martin Rempe, Thomas Risse, Hans Christian Röhl, Heike Schweitzer, Philipp Ther, Heike Wieters and Heinrich August Winkler. I have much profited from the constructive criticism of these colleagues from three academic generations and three disciplines, and, with each of them, links go beyond shared academic interests. Having said all this, I obviously bear the responsibility for any remaining problems.

A long list of other colleagues also deserve mention, most importantly Holger Afflerbach, Oriane Calligaro, Martin Conway, Peter Fäßler, Heike Friedman, Laura Frader, Didier Georgakakis, Liesbeth van de Grift, Stephen Gross, Pablo del Hierro, Stefan-Ludwig Hoffmann, Liesbet Hooghe, Konrad H. Jarausch, Jan-Holger Kirsch, John Krige, Ferenc Laczo, Vincent Lagendijk, Anne Lammers, Charles S. Maier, Harold Marcuse, Marco Mariano, Gary Marks, Ben Martill, Veera Mitzner,

Nico Randeraad, Ute Schneider, Frank Schorkopf, Johan Schot, Bruno Settis, Uta Staiger, Daniel Stinsky, Eckart Stratenschulte, Paul Sutter, Helmuth Trischler, Antoine Vauchez, Andreas Wirsching, Laurent Warlouzet and Kenneth Weisbrode. Their speaking invitations in too long a list of places to mention here, their publication projects, comments and advice have all ultimately helped to improve this book. As research assistants, special thanks go to Jonas Brendebach, Max Grönegräs, Ismay Milford, Alexia Philippart de Foy and Alexandros Sianos, as well as to Anna Reyneri di Lagnasco and Eva Durlinger, all in Maastricht.

I would also like to thank the staff of the archives I visited in the course of this project. Special thanks go to Knud Piening at the Politisches Archiv des Auswärtigen Amtes in Berlin for advice (and tea), to the team at the EUI in Florence, and to Jocelyn Collonval at the archive of the European Commission and Carlos van Lerberghe at the archive of the European Council in Brussels.

Meredith Dale, with whom I have worked for over a decade on a long list of texts, translated this book from German to English. It has always been a great pleasure to work with him, but never did I enjoy it as much as on this book. Meredith often knew better what I was trying to say than I did myself. His mix of British humour, German precision and a cosmopolitan sense for language made all the difference.

At Cambridge, special thanks go to Michael Watson for believing in a book on a topic that most people consider to be somewhere between dull and toxic, and to Emily Sharp and Ruth Boyes for their excellent work. I am also very grateful to the Cambridge's anonymous reviewers and to Julene Knox, who copy-edited the book with granular precision. Finally, I would like to thank my new team at Munich for support in preparing this English version, most importantly Jessica Hall and David Irion.

Words do not suffice to express what I owe to my family and especially to Christina. For many years, I have paid back my absences from home to our children Nina, Emma and Ben by writing stories about Betty Boden, a character we once invented. Dozens of stories and hundreds of pages have come together over the years. In reality, however, I wrote *this* book for you – and for anyone else trying to make sense of the history of a process that often seems inconceivably remote and complicated, while also shaping the everyday lives of hundreds of millions as well as European and international politics more generally: the process that eventually led to today's European Union.

NOTES

Prologue

1. https://bit.ly/1fFuNue (accessed 1 July 2019).
2. See for example James, *Europe Reborn*; Mazower, *Dark Continent*; with greater attention to the history of European integration, Judt, *Postwar*; Jarausch, *Out of Ashes*.
3. On this issue, see Gilbert, 'Narrating the Process'; Dülffer, 'The History of European Integration'.
4. Milward, *The European Rescue of the Nation-State*.
5. *Die große Politik der europäischen Kabinette*, vol. 2, p. 87.
6. Schot and Scranton, *Making Europe*.
7. For a contrary perspective, see Rosato, *Europe United*.
8. Brill, *Abgrenzung und Hoffnung*, p. 266.
9. See for example the EEC Treaty.
10. Keohane and Hoffmann, 'Institutional Change in Europe in the 1980s', p. 8.

Europe and European Integration

1. https://bit.ly/31URPtK (accessed 1 July 2019).
2. Patel and Kaiser, 'Continuity and Change in European Cooperation during the Twentieth Century'.
3. Own calculations based on *Yearbook of International Organizations* 1 (1948), pp. 182–394.
4. AAB, Aake Anker-Ording Papers, ARK-1025, D-L0104, A. Ording, Service Center for International Non-Governmental Organizations, undated [1949]. I am grateful to Nico Randeraad for pointing me to this. On the wider context, see Randeraad and Post, 'Carving Out a Role'.
5. *Yearbook of International Organizations* 23 (1986/87), vol. 2, figs. 2 and 3; Iriye, *Global Community*, pp. 37–59; Mazower, *Governing the World*.
6. Speich Chassé, 'Towards a Global History of the Marshall Plan', pp. 199–200.
7. The metaphor is from Stinsky, 'Sisyphus' Palace', which deals with the UNECE as a whole; on the implications for the history of integration, see also Georgakakis,

'European Integration'; Warlouzet, 'Dépasser la crise de l'histoire de l'intégration européenne'.
8. Schildt, 'German Angst'; see also Geyer, 'Der Kalte Krieg, die Deutschen und die Angst'.
9. Duranti, *The Conservative Human Rights Revolution.*
10. Patel, *The New Deal*, pp. 278–285.
11. Brinkley, *Dean Acheson*, pp. 41–42.
12. Milward, *The United Kingdom and the European Community*, vol. 1; Ellison, *Threatening Europe.*
13. Richardson, 'The Concept of Atlantic Community', p. 1.
14. Winkler, *Geschichte des Westens*, vol. 3.
15. AAPD, 1951, pp. 327–331.
16. Kott, 'Par-delà la guerre froide'.
17. In brief, for example, Segers, 'Preparing Europe for the Unforeseen'.
18. Translated from Grosser, *Wie anders sind die Deutschen*, p. 200.
19. Reynaud, *Unite or Perish*, pp. xvi–xvii.
20. TNA, PREM 15/868, British Embassy, Oslo, report, 4 October 1972.
21. Press review in TNA, FCO 30/1556, British Embassy Moscow to FCO, 2 October 1972.
22. Translated from PAAA, B 20-200/95B, Vertretung der Bundesrepublik beim Europarat an AA, 15 May 1957.
23. HAEU, OEEC, 207, Note from Gian Gaspare Cittadini Cesi to René Sergent, 12 February 1958.
24. Patel, 'Provincialising European Union'.
25. On the definition question, see Thiemeyer and Tölle, 'Supranationalität im 19. Jahrhundert'.
26. Translated from AAPD, 1950, pp. 250–253, quote 251.
27. For example Ludlow, *The European Community and the Crises of the 1960s*, pp. 118–124.
28. Thiemeyer and Tölle, 'Supranationalität im 19. Jahrhundert'.
29. Joint Declaration of the Ministers Signatory to the Treaty Establishing the European Coal and Steel Pool (18 April 1951), available online via www.cveu.eu (accessed 1 July 2019).
30. Hallstein, *United Europe*, p. 28.
31. Vauchez, *L'Union par le droit*; on German scholarship on European law: Stolleis, *Geschichte des öffentlichen Rechts in Deutschland*, vol. 4, pp. 609–629.
32. Lindsay, *European Assemblies*; de Puig, *International Parliaments*; on the relationship with the WEU, see Rohan, *The Western European Union*, p. 42.
33. Loth, *Charles de Gaulle*, pp. 223–248.
34. See the impressive analysis in Warlouzet, *Le choix de la CEE par la France*; also Segers, 'Preparing Europe for the Unforeseen'.
35. For example, for the Federal Republic, Patel, 'Germany and European Integration since 1945'; on Dutch criticisms of federalism, for example, Harryvan, van der Harst, Mans and Kersten, 'Dutch Attitudes towards European Military, Political and Economic Integration'.
36. Patel and Schot, 'Twisted Paths to European Integration'; on the distinction between *traité loi* and *traité cadre*, see for example Lenaerts and Van Nuffel, *Europees Recht in Hoofdlijnen*, p. 43.
37. On the conflict over the Director of the Financial Division, see above all HAEU, PM-130, Skribanowitz à Malvestiti, 28 October 1959; also Spierenburg and Poidevin, *The History of the High Authority of the European Coal and Steel Community*, pp. 379–387.

38. Spierenburg and Poidevin, *The History of the High Authority of the European Coal and Steel Community*, pp. 568–570.
39. Dumoulin, Guillen and Vaïsse, *L'Énergie nucléaire en Europe.*
40. Bloch, *The Principle of Hope*, vol. 2, pp. 664–665; on the context, see for example Radkau, *Aufstieg und Krise der deutschen Atomwirtschaft*, esp. pp. 78–100; Hecht, *The Radiance of France.*
41. Translated from DPII, Nr. 44: Ministerio degli affari esteri, Nota ufficiosa, 7 July 1955, quote p. 83.
42. Bossuat, *Faire l'Europe sans défaire la France*, pp. 57–65; Loth, *Building Europe*, pp. 56–74.
43. Spierenburg and Poidevin, *The History of the High Authority of the European Coal and Steel Community*, p. 651. The second was the coal crisis of the late 1950s; see Chapter 2, 'Peace and Security'.
44. For more detail on relations with the United States, see Chapter 8, 'The Community and its World'.
45. Krumrey, *The Symbolic Politics of European Integration*, pp. 37–41.
46. Krumrey, *The Symbolic Politics of European Integration*, pp. 157–206; Trunk, *Europa, ein Ausweg*, pp. 116–131; Göldner, *Politische Symbole der europäischen Integration*, pp. 157–207.
47. Dumoulin and Lethé, 'The Question of Location', pp. 273–286.
48. AD, Courneuve, 248QO/268, Télégramme Ministère des affaires étrangères à ambassades de France, 24 October 1962.
49. Spierenburg and Poidevin, *The History of the High Authority of the European Coal and Steel Community*, pp. 573–576.
50. Samuel Pufendorf on the Holy Roman Empire, 1667, translated from Latin.
51. Karl Theodor von Dalberg, 1795, translated from Wesel, *Geschichte des Rechts in Europa*, p. 319.
52. On minor complications in the WEU, see PAAA, B 130/8429A.
53. Ludlow, *The European Community and the Crises of the 1960s*, pp. 112–114.
54. Quoted from Nafpliotis, *Britain and the Greek Colonels*, p. 50; on the similar attitude in Bonn, see Rock, *Macht, Märkte und Moral*, pp. 99–105. The case at point, the Greek military coup of 1967, is addressed in greater detail in Chapter 5, 'Values and Norms', in this volume.
55. See for example PAAA, B 130/8429B on corresponding discussions in 1966.
56. TNA, FO 371/154539, esp. Letter Bevan to Haigh, 20 May 1960 with appendix; also TNA, DG 1/83; TNA, FO 371/154501.
57. Hünemörder, *Die Frühgeschichte der globalen Umweltkrise und die Formierung der deutschen Umweltpolitik*; Kaiser and Meyer, *International Organizations and Environmental Protection*; Risso, 'NATO and the Environment'.
58. This is especially apparent in DPII, Serie A: Il 'Rilancio dell'Europa' dalla conferenza di Messina ai trattati di Roma.
59. Spaak, *The Continuing Battle.*
60. Kaiser and Schot, *Writing the Rules for Europe*, pp. 208–210.
61. Kaiser, 'Transnational Practices Governing European Integration'.
62. Marjolin, *Le travail d'une vie.*
63. Patel, *Europäisierung wider Willen*, p. 216.
64. Kaiser and Schot, *Writing the Rules for Europe*, pp. 79–217.
65. Brenke, 'Europakonzeptionen im Widerstreit'; Kaiser, *Using Europe, Abusing the Europeans*, pp. 61–107.
66. Krumrey, *The Symbolic Politics of European Integration*, pp. 136–138.
67. Bariéty and Bled, 'Du Plan Fouchet au Traité franco-allemand de janvier 1963'.

68. Wassenberg, *History of the Council of Europe*, pp. 19–32; Bitsch, *Jalons pour une histoire du Conseil de l'Europe*.
69. Duranti, 'European Integration, Human Rights, and Romantic Internationalism', p. 444; more extensive, Duranti, *The Conservative Human Rights Revolution*.
70. Spaak, *The Continuing Battle*, pp. 271–291.
71. Translated from PAAA, B 20-200/95B, Vertretung der Bundesrepublik beim Europarat an AA, 15 May 1957.
72. Translated from the French original: https://bit.ly/2nUQtur ('solidarité de fait'). The published English is 'de facto solidarity': https://bit.ly/2daphop (both accessed 1 July 2019).
73. See also Herbst, 'Die zeitgenössische Integrationstheorie und die Anfänge der europäischen Einigung'; on the transition to the EC, see Patel, 'Europäische Integration', pp. 353–359.
74. Translated from 'Die Unterschrift', *Frankfurter Allgemeine Zeitung*, 26 March 1957; see also for example 'Ministers ondertekenen in Rome Euromarkt-verdrag', *De Telegraaf*, 25 March 1957; Arnaldo Cortesi, 'West Europeans Sign Pacts Today', *New York Times*, 25 March 1957.
75. See the analysis in Herzer, 'The Rise of Euro-journalism'.
76. For example Lundestad, *The United States and Western Europe since 1945*; Neuss, *Geburtshelfer Europas?*, and Chapter 8, 'The Community and its World', in this volume.
77. Krumrey, *The Symbolic Politics of European Integration*, p. 47.
78. Dickhaus, 'It Is Only the Provisional that Lasts'; Boel, 'The European Productivity Agency'.
79. Gordon, 'The Organization for European Economic Cooperation', p. 1.
80. Leimgruber and Schmelzer, *The OECD and the International Political Economy since 1948*; Schmelzer, *The Hegemony of Growth*; Griffiths, *Explorations in OEEC History*.
81. Opinion surveys in Deutsch, 'Integration and Arms Control in the European Political Environment', p. 360.
82. Translated from Snoy et d'Oppuers, *Rebâtir l'Europe*, pp. 201–202; see also Dumoulin, 'Milieux patronaux belges et construction européenne autour de 1960'.
83. Investigated systematically in Patel and Kaiser, 'Multiple Connections in European Cooperation'.
84. For the classic neo-functionalist take, see Haas, *The Uniting of Europe*.
85. On agricultural policy, see for example Ludlow, 'The Making of the CAP'; on environmental policy, Kaiser and Meyer, *International Organizations and Environmental Protection*; on cultural policy, Staiger, 'The European Capitals of Culture in Context'.
86. See Chapter 6, 'Superstate or Tool of Nations?', in this volume.
87. Weiler, *The EU, the WTO, and the NAFTA*.
88. See for example Meyer, 'Who Should Pay for Pollution?'; more general, De Witte and Thies, 'Why Choose Europe?'
89. CAC, Cambridge, GBR/0014/DSND, 9/14, Letter Tončić-Sorinj to Sandys, 24 July 1972.
90. Shackleton, *Financing the European Community*; Knudsen, 'Delegation as a Political Process'.
91. Spierenburg and Poidevin, *The History of the High Authority of the European Coal and Steel Community*, p. 475.
92. Merriënboer, *Mansholt*; comparative, Patel and Schot, 'Twisted Paths to European Integration'.

93. Knudsen, 'The European Parliament and Political Careers at the Nexus of European Integration and Transnational History'; on the effects of exchange between these parliaments and assemblies, see Patel and Calligaro, 'The True "EURESCO"?'
94. Pardo, 'The Year that Israel Considered Joining the European Economic Community'; see also PAAA, B 130/3293A; PAAA, B20-200/528.
95. Translated from PAAA, B 20-200/381, AA, Obermayer an Vertretung der Bundesrepublik bei der EWG, 5 February 1960 with appendix.
96. Fernández Soriano, *Le fusil et l'olivier*, pp. 93–95.
97. PAAA, B 20-200/528, EWG, Rat, Auszug aus dem Protokollentwurf der Sitzung im engeren Rahmen, 25–27 September 1961.
98. 'Pledge of Aid by Commission', *Times*, 2 August 1961.
99. Herzer, 'The Rise of Euro-journalism', esp. pp. 161–241; see also Brill, *Abgrenzung und Hoffnung*; Meyer, *The European Public Sphere*.
100. William Rees Mogg, 'The Next 25 Years', *Times*, 6 January 1976.
101. For a summary, see Patel and Schot, 'Twisted Paths to European Integration'.
102. Warlouzet, *Governing Europe in a Globalizing World*.
103. PAAA, B 130/8520A, AA, Ergebnisniederschrift deutsch-französische Konsultationen v, 27–28 April 1967, 9 May 1967.
104. Pevehouse, Nordstrom and Warnke, 'The Correlates of War'; on the WEU, Bailes and Messervy-Whiting, *Death of an Institution*.
105. PAAA, B 30/3290A, AA, Aufzeichnung, 20 August 1960.
106. Also, but with a more negative slant, Zielonka, *Is the EU Doomed?*, p. 29.
107. Haberler, *Economic Growth and Stability*, p. 156; two decades later, with a similar argument, Strange, 'Why Do International Organizations Never Die?'
108. See the protocol on inner-German trade in: *Kommentar zum EWG-Vertrag*, ed. von der Groeben and von Boeckh, vol. 2, p. 537; on this, Patel, *Europäisierung wider Willen*, pp. 334–345.
109. Kitzinger, *Diplomacy and Persuasion*, pp. 128–145.
110. Translated from Brandt, *Berliner Ausgabe*, vol. 9, Dokument 5, pp. 98–113, here p. 108.
111. Stubb, *Negotiating Flexibility in the European Union*, pp. 34–35; Tuytschaever, *Differentiation in European Union Law*, pp. 7–23; on the discussion today, de Witte, Ott and Vos, *Between Flexibility and Disintegration*.
112. See Chapter 3, 'Growth and Prosperity', in this volume.
113. Ludlow, *The Making of the European Monetary System*; Stubb, *Negotiating Flexibility in the European Union*, pp. 34–39; Mourlon-Druol, *A Europe Made of Money*, esp. pp. 228–260.
114. European Council Meeting at Fontainebleau, 25 and 26 June 1984, Conclusions of the Presidency, online: https://bit.ly/2pQNnxM (accessed 1 July 2019).
115. Pudlat, *Schengen*; Pudlat, 'Der lange Weg zum Schengen-Raum'; see also Zaiotti, *Cultures of Border Control*.
116. Fossum, 'Democracy and Differentiation in Europe'.
117. Müller, 'Failed and Forgotten?'
118. Research is only beginning to address this issue; for history, see Patel and Kaiser, 'Multiple Connections in European Cooperation'; for politics, see for example Biermann and Koops, *Palgrave Handbook of Inter-Organizational Relations in World Politics*; for law, de Witte and Thies, 'Why Choose Europe?'; in general, see also Hartley, *European Union Law in a Global Context*, esp. pp. xv–xvi.
119. See Chapter 8, 'The Community and its World', in this volume.

Peace and Security

1. Translated from 'Kuuban kriisi kärjistynyt uhkaavasti', *Uusi Suomi*, 24 October 1962.
2. Translated from 'Militaire Blokkade van Cuba: Vragen', *Het Vrije Volk*, 22 October 1962.
3. 'Kto dał St. Zjednowczonym prawo decydowania o losach innych krajów?', *Głos Pracy*, 24 October 1962.
4. Translated from 'Atmosphère de crise à Washington', *Le Monde*, 23 October 1962; 'Ein tiefer Eingriff', *Frankfurter Allgemeine Zeitung*, 24 October 1962.
5. Translated from 'Decisione Tardiva', *Corriere della Sera*, 24 October 1962.
6. HAEU, CM2/1962–71, 81e session du Conseil de la CEE, Bruxelles, 9–10 October 1962.
7. Translated from HAEU, CM2/1962–72, 82e session du Conseil de la CEE, Bruxelles, 22–23 October 1962.
8. HAEU, CM2/1962–73, Réunion restreinte à l'occasion de la 82e session du Conseil de la CEE, Bruxelles, 22–23 October 1962.
9. AD, Courneuve, 248QO/268, Ministère des affaires étrangères, Compte-rendue de la réunion des ministres des affaires étrangères tenue à Bruxelles le 23 Octobre 1962, 7 November 1962; see also Vaïsse, 'Une hirondelle', pp. 89–107.
10. See the various contributions in Vaïsse, *L'Europe et la crise de Cuba*; Gioe, Scott and Andrew, *An International History*.
11. Sondersitzung, 29 October 1962, in KPBR, vol. 15, pp. 477–478, quote p. 477.
12. See most recently, for example, Börzel and Risse, 'Three Cheers', p. 638; also Haftel, *Regional Economic Institutions*; Pinder, 'Community against Conflict', pp. 147–196; Nye, *Peace in Parts*.
13. https://bit.ly/2BhluBH (accessed 12 October 2019).
14. Zubok, *A Failed Empire*, pp. 72–74; see also Schain, *The Marshall Plan*.
15. Translated from 'Regierung der UdSSR erklärt', *Dokumentation der Zeit, hrsg.* v. *Deutsches Institut für Zeitgeschichte, Berlin (Ost)*, 20 April 1957.
16. Faraldo, Gulińska-Jurgiel and Domnitz, *Europa im Ostblock*; Domnitz, *Hinwendung nach Europa*.
17. Ratka, 'Die Assoziierungspolitik der Neutralen'; see also the controversial discussion in PAAA, B 20-200/736, Ergebnisprotokoll über die Ressortbesprechung im AA, 19 February 1962.
18. On Finland, see Mitzner, 'Almost in Europe?', pp. 481–504; on Austria, see Gehler, *Der lange Weg*.
19. Gehler and Steininger, *Die Neutralen*; on Ireland, see Fanning, 'Irish Neutrality', pp. 27–38.
20. With a similar argument recently, Hermann Lübbe, 'Der verspätete Kontinent', *Frankfurter Allgemeine Zeitung*, 23 June 2016; on the wider context, Dülffer, *Jalta, 4. Februar 1945*.
21. Lundestad, *The United States and Western Europe since 1945*, and Chapter 8, 'The Community and its World', in this volume.
22. The quote cited here is a direct translation from the French original; see Spaak, *Combats inachevées*, vol. 2, p. 422: 'J'avais contribué, par l'Alliance atlantique, à assurer la paix en Europe et j'avais contribué à l'édification de l'Europe unie'. The published English translation reads: 'By playing my part in forging the Atlantic Alliance, I had promoted the cause of peace in Europe and European unity.' See Spaak, *The Continuing Battle*, p. 495.
23. Rasmussen, 'Joining the European Communities'.
24. FRUS, 1955–1957, vol. 4, pp. 362–364, quote p. 364.

25. Wilhelm Röpke, 'Gefahr der schleichenden Inflation II', *Das Neue Journal*, 24 April 1957; on Röpke, see Warneke, *Die europäische Wirtschaftsintegration aus der Perspektive Wilhelm Röpkes*.
26. EP, Débats. Compte rendu in extenso des séances, 20 March 1958, p. 36.
27. Printed in an English translation in: Nelsen and Stubb, *The European Union*, pp. 13–14.
28. Europa-Archiv, Dokumentation, 20 May 1951, here p. 3991.
29. EEC Treaty, p. 153.
30. Francois Hollande, 'L'Europe que je veux', *Le Monde*, 8 May 2014.
31. With a different interpretation, see for example most recently Stråth, *Europe's Utopias of Peace*.
32. Wilkens, *Le plan Schuman*; Kipping, *Zwischen Kartellen*.
33. Loth, *Building Europe*, pp. 1–8.
34. Spierenburg and Poidevin, *The History of the High Authority of the European Coal and Steel Community*, esp. pp. 252–272; see also the various contributions to Rasch and Düwell, *Anfänge und Auswirkungen*.
35. Carruth, *Industrial Policy*, pp. 92–102.
36. Translated from Schwabe, 'Die Gründung', pp. 13–30, here p. 26.
37. Gillingham, 'The European Coal and Steel Community', here p. 152; see also Gillingham, *Coal, Steel, and the Rebirth of Europe*.
38. Spaak, *Combats inachevées*, vol. 2, p. 60 (this section was not included in the book's English version); Dulles: FRUS, 1952–1954, vol. 5, part 2, pp. 1120–1122.
39. Trausch, *Die Europäische Integration*.
40. Schwabe, 'Die Gründung', pp. 13–30.
41. Schwabe, 'The Cold War and European Integration', pp. 18–34; Ludlow, *European Integration and the Cold War*.
42. Trachtenberg, *A Constructed Peace*; Westad, *The Global Cold War*; Westad, *The Cold War*.
43. EEC Treaty, p. 207; Loth and Bitsch, 'The Hallstein Commission', pp. 51–78.
44. Badel, Jeannesson and Ludlow, *Les administrations nationales*; Kaiser, Leucht and Rasmussen, *The History of the European Union*; for further detail, see Chapter 6, 'Superstate or Tool of Nations?', in this volume.
45. van Middelaar, *The Passage to Europe*, p. 303.
46. PAAA, B 130/8431A, esp. Brentano an Adenauer, 9 July 1959; PAAA, B 130, 3263A, Carstens, AA an Deutsche Botschaft Paris, 24 June 1959.
47. See for example PAAA, B 130/10105A, Monnet an Brandt, 12 May 1967.
48. Translated from 'Bemühungen in Brüssel', *Frankfurter Allgemeine Zeitung*, 29 December 1961.
49. Hallstein, *United Europe*, p. 55.
50. PAAA, B 20–200/1315, EWG, Generalsekretariat, Dokumentationsblatt, 8 January1965; on the wider context, see Varsori, *La Cenerentola*, pp. 187–203; Craveri and Varsori, *L'Italia nella costruzione europea*.
51. Ludlow, *The European Community and the Crises of the 1960s*.
52. Translated from BA/K, B 116/14009, AA, Aufzeichnung Lahr, 1 April 1966.
53. 'Alas, Poor Europe', *Economist*, 20 March 1982.
54. Warlouzet, *Le choix de la CEE par la France*.
55. See for example BA/K, B 136/8319; on this issue, Patel, *Europäisierung wider Willen*, esp. pp. 265–288.
56. See Chapter 3, 'Growth and Prosperity', in this volume.
57. Patel and Schweitzer, *The Historical Foundations*.
58. See Chapter 3, 'Growth and Prosperity', in this volume.

59. Knudsen, *Farmers on Welfare*; Patel, *Europäisierung wider Willen*.
60. Oberloskamp, *Codename TREVI*.
61. Raymond Aron, 'La victoire de l'idée européenne', *Le Figaro*, 27 December 1963.
62. Patel, 'Provincialising European Union', pp. 649–673.
63. De Gaulle, *Discours et messages*, 1958–1962, pp. 430–431, here p. 431 (8 July 1962); see also Miard-Delacroix, *Im Zeichen der europäischen Einigung*; Marcowitz and Miard-Delacroix, *50 ans de relations franco-allemandes*.
64. 'Reims Rites End Visit of Adenauer', *Washington Post*, 9 July 1962.
65. Pfeil, 'Der Händedruck', pp. 498–505.
66. Only in certain academic debates is the OECD associated with a specific form of peace; see for example Senghaas, *Zum irdischen Frieden*.
67. Möckli, *European Foreign Policy*; Gainar, *Aux origines de la diplomatie européenne*; Mourlon-Druol and Romero, *International Summitry and Global Governance*.
68. http://aei.pitt.edu/5576/1/5576.pdf (accessed 1 July 2019); see also Gfeller, 'A European Voice', pp. 659–676.
69. *Document on the European Identity*, 14 December 1973: https://bit.ly/30WXPAD (accessed 1 July 2019).
70. Möckli, *European Foreign Policy*.
71. Above all Romano, *The European Community*; Romano, 'The EC and the Socialist World'; Kansikas, *Socialist Countries*.
72. Text of the Stuttgart Declaration: http://aei.pitt.edu/1788/1/stuttgart_declaration_1983.pdf (accessed 1 July 2019); see also Bonvicini, 'The Genscher-Colombo Plan and the "Solemn Declaration on European Union"'; Ludlow, 'More than just a Single Market'.
73. Tavani, 'The Détente Crisis', pp. 49–68.
74. Demidova, 'The Deal of the Century', pp. 59–82.
75. Ludlow, 'The Unnoticed Apogee', pp. 17–38.
76. Romano and Romero, 'European Socialist Regimes Facing Globalisation and European Co-operation'.
77. https://bit.ly/2M1D7va (accessed 1 July 2019).
78. 'Völlig schnuppe', *Spiegel*, 22 March 1982; see also Tavani, 'The Détente Crisis'.
79. TNA, FCO 7/4590, FCO to British Embassies, 10 April 1982; see also for example PAAA, Zwischenarchiv, 136665, AA, DG 41, Vermerk, 6 April 1982; PAAA, Zwischenarchiv, 136666, esp. AA, Abteilung 5 an Staatssekretär, 16 April 1982; TNA, FCO 7/5874.
80. TNA, FCO 7/4591, UK Permanent Representative on the North Atlantic Council to FCO, 13 April 1982.
81. TNA, FCO 98/1201, FCO, Bayne, to FCO, Giffard, 3 April 1982.
82. Martin, 'Institutions and Cooperation', pp. 143–178; Bleckmann, 'Zur Rechtmäßigkeit'; on Germany, see also for example Gespräch Schmidt mit Elias, 2 July 1982, in AAPD 1982, vol. 2, pp. 1048–1059; on Italy, for example, HAEU, EN-2361, Note Noël for Schaub, 14 May 1982; on the positions of the various other member states, TNA, FCO 7/4590–4593; FCO 98/1201–1207; on the United States, FRUS, 1981–1988, vol. XIII, esp. doc. 270: Memorandum Fontaine and Blair for Clark, 17 May 1982.
83. Stavridis and Hill, *Domestic Sources*.
84. This in turn was followed very closely by the West, see for example PAAA, Zwischenarchiv, 130423, Deutsche Botschaft Moskau an AA, 10 May 1982.
85. See Chapter 5, 'Values and Norms', in this volume.
86. Karamouzi, *Greece, the EEC and the Cold War*.

87. FRUS, 1969–1976, vol. xxx, doc. 56: U.S. and Allied Security Policy in Southern Europe, 15 December 1975, pp. 194–207, quote p. 206.
88. Pinto and Severiano Teixeira, 'From Africa to Europe'; del Pero, 'A European Solution for a European Crisis'; Trouvé, *L'Espagne et l'Europe*; Muñoz Sánchez, 'A European Answer to the Spanish Question'.
89. Lejeune and Brüll, *Grenzerfahrungen*.
90. Quoted in Keogh, 'Managing Membership', p. 148.
91. Hayward, 'Reiterating National Identities'.
92. Gold, *Gibraltar*.
93. Quoted in Sarotte, *The Struggle*, p. 27.
94. Bozo, *Mitterrand, la fin de la guerre froide et l'unification allemande*; Schwarz, *Helmut Kohl*, esp. pp. 489–618.
95. https://bit.ly/2MbofN4 (accessed 1 July 2019).
96. On this, see Teltschik, *329 Tage*, p. 211; also Loth, *Building Europe*, pp. 300–310.
97. 'Durch die Hintertür', *Spiegel*, 23 April 1990; more generally Ritter, *Der Preis der deutschen Einheit*, pp. 55–61.
98. Mayhew, 'L'Assistance financière à l'Europe centrale et orientale'; Gehler, 'Mehr Europäisierung in Umbruchszeiten?'
99. Judt, 'The Rediscovery of Central Europe'; Domnitz, *Hinwendung nach Europa*.
100. See also Ludlow, 'European Integration in the 1980s'.
101. Dan Diner, 'Sind wir wieder im 19. Jahrhundert', *Frankfurter Allgemeine Zeitung*, 15 September 2016.
102. Quoted in Silber and Little, *Yugoslavia*, p. 159; see also for example Edwards, 'The Potential', p. 173–195.
103. Wirsching, *Der Preis der Freiheit*, pp. 121–152.

Growth and Prosperity

1. European Union, *The EU in the World. 2016 Edition*; for an overview of consumer spending, see Haupt, 'Der Siegeszug der Konsumgesellschaft'.
2. https://bit.ly/2daphop (accessed 1 July 2019).
3. *Rapport des chefs de délégation aux ministres des affaires étrangères*, p. 9.
4. Today there are other, very different ways to measure prosperity and standard of living, such as the UN's Human Development Index. Here I begin by focusing on GDP, in line with the contemporaneous perspective, but broaden the discussion over the course of the chapter.
5. Translated from 'Gemeinsamer Markt', *Spiegel*, 24 November 1969.
6. Recently for example Phinnemore, 'Crisis-Ridden, Battered and Bruised', pp. 61–74, here p. 66; Campos, Coricelli and Moretti, *Economic Growth and Political Integration*.
7. Translated from HAEU, MK 1, Letter Kohnstamm an Monnet, 1 August 1953.
8. Fourastié, *Les Trente Glorieuses*. The term was soon applied to other countries too.
9. Doering-Manteuffel and Raphael, *Nach dem Boom*.
10. For the criticisms, see for example Pessis, Topçu and Bonneuil, *Une autre histoire des 'Trente glorieuses'*; Goschler and Graf, *Europäische Zeitgeschichte*, pp. 79–82.
11. Translated from Fourastié, *Les Trente Glorieuses*, p. 267.
12. Ambrosius, *Wirtschaftsraum Europa*, pp. 10–12. The precise figures are influenced by the chosen definition of Western Europe; slightly different figures are found for example in Eichengreen, *The European Economy since 1945*, pp. 16–17; see also Crafts and Toniolo, *Economic Growth in Europe since 1945*.
13. Kaelble, *Sozialgeschichte Europas*; Jarausch, *Out of Ashes*.

14. Translated from 'Discours de Pierre Pflimlin, 5 February 1997', in Collowald, *J'ai vu naître l'Europe*, pp. 137–150, here p. 141.
15. Own calculation based on Maddison, *The World Economy*, pp. 272–284; see also Eichengreen, *The European Economy since 1945*, p. 17. See also Table 1 in this chapter.
16. On the United States, see Crafts and Toniolo, 'Les Trente Glorieuses', pp. 356–378; on Japan and the world Szirmai, 'Industrialisation as an Engine of Growth', p. 408.
17. On the causes with more detailed observations, see for example Eichengreen, *The European Economy since 1945*, pp. 15–47; Crafts and Toniolo, *Economic Growth in Europe since 1945*; Judt, *Postwar*, pp. 324–330.
18. Crafts and Toniolo, 'Les Trente Glorieuses', pp. 359–361.
19. Figures from Crafts and Toniolo, 'Les Trente Glorieuses', p. 373.
20. See also Milward, *The Reconstruction of Western Europe*; Hogan, *The Marshall Plan*; Maier, *The Marshall Plan and Germany*; Schain, *The Marshall Plan*.
21. Eichengreen, *Reconstructing Europe's Trade and Payments*.
22. James, 'The IMF and the Bretton Woods System', pp. 93–126.
23. Moggridge, *The Collected Writings of John Maynard Keynes*, vol. XXV, p. 2; see also Fonzi, 'La "Großraumwirtschaft" e l'Unione Europea dei Pagamenti', pp. 131–153; James, 'The Multiple Contexts of Bretton Woods', pp. 411–430.
24. Stinsky, 'Sisyphus' Palace'.
25. Irwin, 'The GATT's Contribution to Economic Recovery', pp. 127–150; on the Kennedy Round, Coppolaro, *The Making of a World Trading Power*; Brusse, 'The Failure of European Tariff Plans in GATT', pp. 99–114.
26. Boyer and Sallé, 'The Liberalization of Intra-European Trade', pp. 179–216, esp. p. 211.
27. Crafts, 'West European Economic Integration', pp. 6–7.
28. Bayoumi and Eichengreen, 'Is Regionalism Simply a Diversion?'; see also Badinger and Breuss, 'The Quantitative Effects', pp. 285–315.
29. Eichengreen, *The European Economy since 1945*, p. 181.
30. Balassa, 'Trade Creation and Diversion in the European Common Market', pp. 79–118.
31. Badinger, 'Growth Effects of Economic Integration', pp. 50–78; Eichengreen and Boltho, 'The Economic Impact of European Integration', pp. 267–295, here p. 282; see also Jarausch, *Out of Ashes*, p. 516: 'highly successful'.
32. Landau, 'The Contribution of the European Common Market', pp. 774–782, referring to the entire period from 1950 to 1990; for measurability issues and an overview of the debate, see also Campos, Coricelli and Moretti, *Economic Growth and Political Integration*.
33. Plumpe and Steiner, 'Dimensionen wirtschaftlicher Integrationsprozesse in West- und Osteuropa', pp. 21–38. For a similar thrust following a different line of argument, see Gillingham, *European Integration*.
34. Eichengreen and Boltho, 'The Economic Impact of European Integration', p. 295; see also Crafts and Toniolo, 'Les Trente Glorieuses'.
35. For a revealing comparative analysis of trade in the inter-war and post-war periods, see Alker and Puchala, 'Trends in Economic Partnership', pp. 287–316.
36. Judt, *Postwar*, p. 326.
37. Plumpe, 'Europäische Krisenpolitik auf dem Prüfstand', pp. 73–74.
38. Anthony Harris, 'Euro Gloom', *Guardian*, 21 January 1972.
39. Henrekson, Torstensson and Torstensson, 'Growth Effects of European Integration', pp. 1537–1557.
40. Badinger, 'Growth Effects of Economic Integration', pp. 50–78.

41. Crafts, 'West European Economic Integration', p. 10; see also van Ark and Crafts, *Quantitative Aspects of Post-War European Economic Growth*; Bayoumi and Eichengreen, 'Is Regionalism Simply a Diversion?'
42. For a compact summary of the causes and effects of the crisis, see Berend, 'A Restructured Economy', pp. 406–422.
43. Henrekson, Torstensson and Torstensson, 'Growth Effects of European Integration'; Bayoumi and Eichengreen, 'Is Regionalism Simply a Diversion?'
44. 8/74, *Staatsanwaltschaft* v. *Benoît u. Gustave Dassonville*, Urteil; 120/78, *Rewe-Zentral-AG* v. *Bundesmonopolverwaltung für Branntwein* (*Cassis de Dijon*).
45. Monnier, 'The European Union at the Time of Enlargement'.
46. Patel and Schweitzer, *The Historical Foundations of EU Competition Law*, p. 192.
47. Gwartney and Lawson, *Economic Freedom of the World*, pp. 19–21 (but note the source's strong ideological bias).
48. James, *Making the European Monetary Union*, pp. 61–210; Mourlon-Druol, *A Europe Made of Money*; see also Allen, Gasiorek and Smith, 'The Competition Effects of the Single Market in Europe', pp. 440–486; Eichengreen and Boltho, 'The Economic Impact of European Integration', pp. 284–287.
49. This 'shift in mood' was even felt in the United States, see Gilbert, 'A Shift in Mood', pp. 243–264; see also European Commission, DG for Economic and Financial Affairs, *The Economics of 1992*; see also for example Eichengreen, *The European Economy since 1945*, pp. 335–366; recently on Delors, Bitumi, 'An Uplifting Tale of Europe'.
50. See for example Crafts, 'West European Economic Integration since 1950'.
51. 'Gemeinsamer Markt', *Spiegel*, 24 November 1969.
52. Knudsen, 'European Integration in the Image and the Shadow of Agriculture', pp. 189–215; Tyers and Anderson, *Disarray in World Food Markets*; Sanderson, *Agricultural Protectionism in the Industrialized World*; on the national differences, see Eichengreen and Boltho, 'The Economic Impact of European Integration', p. 282.
53. Campos, Coricelli and Moretti, *Economic Growth and Political Integration*.
54. Crafts, 'West European Economic Integration since 1950', pp. 12–13.
55. Boltho, 'Growth', pp. 9–35.
56. Clavin and Patel, 'The Role of International Organizations in Europeanization', pp. 110–131.
57. Speich Chassé, *Die Erfindung des Bruttosozialprodukts*.
58. Heintz, 'Numerische Differenz'.
59. Statistisches Amt der EG, *Die Wirtschaftsrechnungen der Arbeiterfamilien der EGKS 1956/57*, pp. 50–51; on this set of problems, see also Lammers, 'Daten für das "Europa der Sechs"'.
60. Translated from HAEU, CEAB 12/1104, Melle A. Devaux, Etude statistique sur l'évolution dans les pays du marché commun et dans quelques autres pays européens, Paris, 1962, here p. 60.
61. Translated from Wagenführ, 'Die Statistik in der Integration der Sechs', pp. 51–73, quote p. 52.
62. Statistisches Amt der EG, *Volkswirtschaftliche Gesamtrechnungen 1957–1966*, esp. p. 36.
63. Wagenführ, 'Die industrielle Weltproduktion', pp. 5–60, quote p. 48.
64. Statistisches Amt der EG, *Jahrbuch der Industriestatistik*, for example vol. 1974/1975, 1984.
65. See for example HAEU, BAC 94/1985, 395, Communauté économique européenne, Commission, Note d'information, 20 October 1964; HAEU, CEAB

4/122; see also for example EGKS, Hohe Behörde, *Die E.G.K.S.* The author of the latter study was Rolf Wagenführ.
66. Translated from Statistisches Amt der EG, *Statistische Informationen 6/1960*, p. 588.
67. Translated from EGKS, Hohe Behörde, *Die E.G.K.S.*, p. 50.
68. Translated from Wagenführ, 'Die Statistik in der Integration der Sechs', pp. 51–73, quote p. 51.
69. See for example European Commission, DG for Economic and Financial Affairs, *The Economics of 1992*, p. 19.
70. Fourastié, *Les Trente Glorieuses*, pp. 267, 28.
71. OECD, *OECD Historical Statistics*, pp. 30, 42; see also Mitchell, *International Historical Statistics*, pp. 149–160.
72. Nora, 'Comment écrire l'histoire de France', pp. 9–32.
73. Although naturally certain rules were agreed; see for example Commission of the EC, *The European Community and the Textile Arrangements*.
74. Fischer, 'Wirtschaft, Gesellschaft und Staat in Europa', pp. 133–136.
75. Knudsen, *Farmers on Welfare*; Patel, *Europäisierung wider Willen*.
76. Bairoch, *Victoires et déboires*, p. 199.
77. Monnet, *Memoirs*, p. 292.
78. For example Milward, *The Reconstruction of Western Europe*, pp. 126–167; Gillingham, *Coal, Steel, and the Rebirth of Europe*.
79. Gualtieri, 'L'Europa come vincolo esterno'; Varsori, *La Cenerentola*; for Portugal, see del Pero, 'La transizione portoghese'.
80. Translated from HAEU, MK 1, Letter Kohnstamm an Monnet, 1 August 1953.
81. Toffler, *Future Shock*, p. 398.
82. HAEU, GR 142, Mansholt to Malfatti, 9 February 1972; see also van der Harst, 'Mansholt', pp. 175–178.
83. Schmelzer, *The Hegemony of Growth*.
84. Maier, 'The Politics of Productivity', pp. 607–633.
85. COM(2010) 2020 final.
86. See for example Hantrais, *Social Policy in the European Union*; Kleinman, *A European Welfare State?*, esp. pp. 82–92; Barbier, *The Road to Social Europe*; Denord and Schwartz, *L'Europe sociale n'aura pas lieu*.
87. Cayet and Rosental, 'Politiques sociales et marché(s)', pp. 3–16.
88. Now see Fertikh and Wieters, 'Harmonisierung der Sozialpolitik in Europa'.
89. Above all Verschueren, *Fermer les mines*.
90. Kreyssig, 'Die sozialpolitische Fundierung der Montanunion', pp. 217–223, quote p. 219.
91. For a summary, see Kaelble, 'Geschichte des sozialen Europa'.
92. Summary in Group of Experts, 'Social Aspects of European Economic Co-operation', pp. 99–123.
93. Mechi, 'Managing the Labour Market in an Open Economy'; Mechi, 'Du BIT à la politique sociale européenne', pp. 17–30; Kott, 'Un modèle international de protection sociale est-il possible?'; on the issue of harmonisation, see Fertikh and Wieters, 'Harmonisierung der Sozialpolitik in Europa'.
94. League of Nations, Report on the First Two Sessions of the Committee, C.381. M214.1932.VIII, 15 April 1932 and Circular Concerning Programmes of Important Public Works, C.736.M341, 9 October 1931; on this issue, Schipper, *Driving Europe*, pp. 83–157.
95. EEC Treaty, p. 196.
96. Ciampani and Gabaglio, *L'Europa sociale e la Confederazione europea dei sindacati*; Leonardi and Varsori, *Lo spazio sociale europeo*.

97. Fertikh, 'La construction d'un "droit social européen"'.
98. For an analysis of the phase under discussion here – through until the Treaty of Maastricht – see for example Pillinger, *Feminising the Market*; for the EU's perspective on the question today, see for example Foubert, *The Gender Pay Gap*.
99. Translated from Wagenführ, 'Die Statistik in der Integration der Sechs', pp. 51–73, quote p. 51.
100. Comte, *The History of the European Migration Regime*; see also Berlinghoff, *Das Ende der 'Gastarbeit'*; Calandri, Paoli and Varsori, 'Peoples and Borders'.
101. Fertikh, 'La construction d'un "droit social européen"'; Glootz, *Alterssicherung im europäischen Wohlfahrtsstaat*, pp. 187–265; and, already at the time, Gerig, 'European Multilateral Social Security Treaties'.
102. Kaelble, 'Geschichte des sozialen Europa'.
103. 1408/71/EEC; see also Leboutte, *Histoire économique et sociale de la construction européenne*, esp. pp. 619–682; Varsori, 'Le rôle de la formation et de l'enseignement', pp. 70–85.
104. For this period, see for example Majone, 'The European Community between Social Policy and Social Regulation'.
105. Mechi, 'Du BIT à la politique sociale européenne', pp. 28–30; Kleinman, *A European Welfare State?*, pp. 86–92.
106. Trades Union Congress 1988, speech by Jacques Delors, '1992: The Social Dimension': https://europa.eu/rapid/press-release_SPEECH-88-66_en.htm (accessed 1 July 2019).
107. Bitumi, 'An Uplifting Tale of Europe'.
108. Eurostat, *Revue 1977–1986*, p. 24. During this period the number of annual sessions fluctuated between fifty-eight and ninety-nine.
109. Kaelble, *Sozialgeschichte Europas*, pp. 332–357; Kaelble, *Mehr Reichtum, mehr Armut*.
110. Gilpin, *The Political Economy of International Relations*, p. 355 (with reference to James Mayall); on the context, see also Tsoukalis, *The New European Economy*; Berend, *An Economic History of Twentieth-Century Europe*, pp. 190–212.
111. McCann, *The Political Economy of the European Union*, p. 22.
112. Patel and Schweitzer, *The Historical Foundations of EU Competition Law*; Warlouzet, 'The Centralization of EU Competition Policy', pp. 725–741.
113. Recently esp. Warlouzet, *Governing Europe in a Globalizing World*; also Maes, 'History of Economic Thought and Policy-Making at the European Commission', pp. 38–52; Maes, *Economic Thought and the Making of European Monetary Union*.
114. Lazar, *Maisons rouges*.
115. De L'Écotais, *L'Europe sabotée*, p. 203.
116. Recently esp. Warlouzet, *Governing Europe in a Globalizing World*.
117. Above all Basosi, 'The European Community and International Reaganomics', pp. 133–153.
118. Favier and Martin-Roland, *La décennie Mitterrand*, vol. 1, esp. pp. 418–503.
119. Suzuki, 'The Rise of Summitry and EEC–Japan Trade Relations', pp. 164–165; Maes, *Economic Thought and the Making of European Monetary Union*.
120. Patel and Schweitzer, *The Historical Foundations of EU Competition Law*; Ther, 'Der Neoliberalismus, Version: 1.0'; McCann, *The Political Economy of the European Union*, pp. 28–39; Tsoukalis, *The New European Economy*; on neoliberals' split views of the EC, now see Slobodian, *Globalists*, pp. 184–217.
121. Petit, de Benedictis, Britton, de Groot, Henrichsmeyer and Lechi, *Agricultural Policy Formation in the European Community*.

122. Ther, *Die neue Ordnung auf dem alten Kontinent*, pp. 47–57; also Stråth, *Europe's Utopias of Peace*, pp. 343–406.
123. Article 100a, Single European Act (SEA); on this, for example Tsoukalis, *The New European Economy*, pp. 46–69, 148–174.
124. Loth, *Building Europe*, pp. 271–289; Endo, *The Presidency of the European Commission under Jacques Delors*.
125. 'Kurt Schmücker', *Spiegel*, 2 March 1964.
126. See for example the rather obscure example of cultural policy in Patel, *The Cultural Politics of Europe*.
127. Kocka, *Geschichte des Kapitalismus*.
128. Lindberg and Scheingold, *Europe's Would-Be Polity*, p. 31.
129. TNA, T 340/16, esp. Cmnd. 4289: Britain and the European Communities: An Economic Assessment, February 1970; see also Ludlow, *The European Community and the Crises of the 1960s*, pp. 72–93.
130. See for example the debates in CEAH, BAC 86/2005 454, EC, Delegation de la Commission des Communautés Européennes, J. Linthort Homan, Rapport 855, 3 December 1970.

Participation and Technocracy

1. Quotes (including activists' statement) translated from 'Zu stabil für den Abbruch', *Spiegel*, 10 August 1950; see also eyewitness report of Heister, *Der Studentensturm auf die Grenzen 1950*, and HAEU, GR 3.
2. Ludwig, 'Westwallbau und Kriegsgeschehen', pp. 33–136.
3. HAEU, GR 3, Manifestation: Aux Délégués de l'Assemblée Consultative du Conseil de l'Europe, November 1950.
4. 'Studenten breken een stukje grens... ', *Het Vrije Volk*, 7 August 1950.
5. See for example Speech by Kohl, 4 October 1995, *Bulletin des Presse- und Informationsamtes der Bundesregierung* 76 (1995); on Kohl, see also Schwarz, *Helmut Kohl*, pp. 56–57.
6. See for example Hooghe and Marks, 'A Postfunctionalist Theory', pp. 1–23; Chalmers, Davies and Monti, *European Union Law*, p. 28; Laursen, 'The Not-So-Permissive Consensus', pp. 295–317; now see also Kaelble, *Der verkannte Bürger*.
7. Schmale, *Geschichte Europas*; Conway and Patel, *Europeanization in the Twentieth Century*; Stråth and Wagner, *European Modernity*; Greiner, *Wege nach Europa*.
8. Patel, 'William Penn und sein Essay', pp. 330–357.
9. Cited from Ziegerhofer-Prettenthaler, *Botschafter Europas*, pp. 516–524, here p. 516; see also Coudenhove-Kalergi, *Pan-Europe*; for an English version of the manifesto: https://bit.ly/2OEtHrz (accessed 1 July 2019).
10. Anonymous, *Paneuropa Union*; for membership figures, see Ziegerhofer-Prettenthaler, *Botschafter Europas*, p. 104.
11. Badel, 'Les promoteurs français', pp. 17–29.
12. Above all Schulz, 'Europa-Netzwerke'.
13. Joachim von Ribbentrop, Speech, 26 November 1941, in: Lipgens, *Documents on the History of European Integration*, vol. 1, doc. 16, quote p. 91 (English), German original on microfiche.
14. See for example Kletzin, *Europa aus Rasse und Raum*; Grunert, *Der Europagedanke*.
15. Translated from Bourdet, Frenay and Hauriou, 'Das "Combat"-Programm', p. 197.

16. Milward, *The European Rescue of the Nation-State*, esp. pp. 21–45; Mazower, *Hitler's Empire*, pp. 553–575.
17. Niess, *Die europäische Idee*, pp. 55–59, 72–91; Pistone, *The Union of European Federalists*, figures p. 33; also Lipgens, *Die Anfänge der europäischen Einigungspolitik*.
18. Grob-Fitzgibbon, *Continental Drift*, pp. 34–59; Niess, *Die europäische Idee*, pp. 130–151.
19. Pfahl-Traughber, 'Zeitschriftenporträt', pp. 305–322.
20. On the German example, see Conze, *Das Europa der Deutschen*; recently also Großmann, *Die Internationale der Konservativen*.
21. Cited from Gross, 'Peace Planning', pp. 168–179, here p. 171.
22. Hendrik Brugmans, 'Europe's Own Task', in: Lipgens, *Documents on the History of European Integration*, vol. 3, doc. 111, quote p. 385. The translation given by Lipgens ('Europe must be independent of both East and West') is heavily abbreviated; the Dutch original is: 'Europese vredespolitiek eist onafhanklijkheidspolitiek. Naar beide kanten'.
23. The figures given here are for support as a proportion of all those who received the survey, rather than respondents. Final figures from Coudenhove-Kalergi, *Kampf um Europa*, p. 267; see also the analysis in Lipgens, *Die Anfänge der europäischen Einigungspolitik*, pp. 438–444 (percentages deviate slightly, as Lipgens does not use the final figures).
24. On Nice, see Pfister, *Europa im Bild*, p. 198; on the Italian petition, Vayssière, *Vers une Europe fédérale?*, pp. 251–255; on Amsterdam, Niess, *Die europäische Idee*, p. 218.
25. Pasquinucci, 'Nella "direzione del movimento storico"', pp. 395–415; on the complexity of the first post-war years, see D'Ottavio, 'Il discorso politico sull'Europa nell'immediato dopoguerra'.
26. Kaiser, *Christian Democracy and the Origins of European Union*, esp. pp. 291–294; Gehler and Kaiser, *Transnationale Parteienkooperation der europäischen Christdemokraten*; on the debates among federalists, see for example HAEU, UEF-97.
27. French Council of the European Movement, April 1950, in: Lipgens, *Documents on the History of European Integration*, vol. 3, doc. 36, quotes pp. 114–115.
28. For their demands, see HAEU, UEF-101; see also Norwig, *Die erste europäische Generation*, pp. 72–81.
29. Translated from Spinelli, *L'Europa non cade dal cielo*, pp. 307, 26; see also Morelli and Spinelli, *Il pensiero*.
30. De Rougemont, *Ecrits sur l'Europe*, vol. 2, p. 259.
31. Neißkenwirth, *'Die Europa-Union wird Avantgarde bleiben'*, esp. pp. 215–346; on Arendt, see Verovšek, 'Unexpected Support for European Integration'; Selinger, 'The Politics of Arendtian Historiography', pp. 417–446.
32. Kaelble, *Sozialgeschichte Europas*, p. 392.
33. Norwig, *Die erste europäische Generation*, p. 72.
34. Neißkenwirth, *'Die Europa-Union wird Avantgarde bleiben'*, p. 318.
35. For overviews, see Pasquinucci and Verzichelli, *Contro l'Europa?*; Wassenberg, Clavert and Hamman, *Contre l'Europe?*; Gainar and Libera, *Contre l'Europe?*
36. Available online: https://bit.ly/32wW7aL (accessed 1 July 2019); on the role of empires during this period, see Burbank and Cooper, *Empires in World History*.
37. Merseburger, *Kurt Schumacher*.
38. Harryvan, *In Pursuit of Influence*.
39. Cruciani, *L'Europa delle sinistre*; Cruciani, *Il socialismo europeo e il processo di integrazione*.

40. Translated from 'Adenauer: Ces traites nous remplissent d'espoir', *L'Humanité*, 26 March 1957.
41. Bussière, Dumoulin and Schirmann, *Europe organisée, Europe du libre-échange?*; Wegmann, *Früher Neoliberalismus und europäische Integration*.
42. Norwig, *Die erste europäische Generation*.
43. 'Zu stabil für den Abbruch', *Spiegel*, 10 August 1950. Other contemporary sources give her name as 'Lüthi'.
44. Garavini, *Dopo gli imperi*, p. 130; on the broader context, but with a rather problematic link to the EC, see also Jobs, 'Youth Movements', pp. 376–404.
45. Ali, *The Coming British Revolution*, esp. pp. 14–15.
46. EP, Débats. Compte rendu in extenso des séances, 20 March 1958, p. 37.
47. Pasquinucci and Verzichelli, *Contro l'Europa?*; Wassenberg, Clavert and Hamman, *Contre l'Europe?*; Gainar and Libera, *Contre l'Europe?*
48. Großmann, *Die Internationale der Konservativen*.
49. Bautz, 'Die Auslandsbeziehungen der deutschen Kommunen im Rahmen der europäischen Kommunalbewegung in den 1950er und 1960er Jahren'; on Colombes and Frankenthal, see Dümmer, 'Die Städtepartnerschaft Frankenthal – Colombes (1958) und die Bedeutung transnationaler Kommunalverbände'; see also Wassenberg, 'Between Cooperation and Competitive Bargaining'.
50. Jobs, *Backpack Ambassadors*, esp. pp. 42–44, 161, 233–234.
51. Corbett, 'Ideas, Institutions and Policy Entrepreneurs'.
52. Above all Milward, *The European Rescue of the Nation-State*.
53. For a different approach, see Moravcsik, *The Choice for Europe*.
54. Kaelble, *Sozialgeschichte Europas*, esp. pp. 299–328; Therborn, *European Modernity and Beyond*.
55. Plotkin and Tilman, *Political Ideas*.
56. Loeb, *Life in a Technocracy*, p. xliii.
57. On technocratic internationalism, see Schot and Lagendijk, 'Technocratic Internationalism', pp. 196–217; see also Kaiser and Schot, *Writing the Rules for Europe*; see also Chabot, 'Technocratie et construction européenne', pp. 7–20; from a legal vantage point, see Peters and Peter, 'International Organizations'.
58. Schipper, *Driving Europe*, pp. 104–116.
59. Cohen, 'Why Call It a "European Community"?'; see also Gosewinkel, *Anti-liberal Europe*.
60. Schwabe, 'Die Gründung der Montanunion', pp. 13–30, here pp. 28–29.
61. Translated from Neißkenwirth, '*Die Europa-Union wird Avantgarde bleiben*', p. 223.
62. *Kommentar zum EWG-Vertrag*, ed. von der Groeben and von Boeckh, vol. 2, p. 161.
63. Ritleng, 'The Independence and Legitimacy of the European Court of Justice', pp. 83–124, esp. pp. 102–104; one of many reform proposals: Laffranque, 'Dissenting Opinion in the European Court of Justice', pp. 14–23.
64. Davies and Nicola, 'Introduction to EU Law Stories'; Davies and Rasmussen, 'Towards a New History of European Law', pp. 305–475; Cohen, 'Constitutionalism without Constitution', pp. 109–135.
65. Vauchez, 'The Transnational Politics of Judicialization', pp. 11–28; Rasmussen, 'From *Costa* v. *ENEL* to the Treaties of Rome', pp. 69–85.
66. For example HAEU, FD 494, Courrier socialiste européen, La primauté du droit communautaire, 18 May 1965.
67. AdsD, PV/352, Protokoll Wirtschaftspolitischer Ausschuss, 8/9 February 1957.
68. Haas, *The Uniting of Europe*, p. 17.

69. Commission des Communautés Européennes, *Les Européens et l'unification de l'Europe*, p. i.
70. Garavini, *Dopo gli imperi*, p. 130.
71. Above all Spierenburg and Poidevin, *The History of the High Authority of the European Coal and Steel Community.*
72. Buiter, 'Le point de vue des Syndicats Libres', p. 146.
73. De Gaulle, *Discours et messages*, 1962–1965, p. 378 (9 September 1965); English translation: http://aei.pitt.edu/5356/1/5356.pdf (accessed 1 July 2019); see also Bossuat, *Faire l'Europe sans défaire la France*, pp. 83–118.
74. Garavini, *Dopo gli imperi*, p. 130.
75. Rittberger, 'No Integration without Representation'; more generally, Rittberger, *Building Europe's Parliament.*
76. van den Braak, 'Een Nederlandse machtspoliticus machteloos in Brussel'.
77. Roos, 'Far Beyond the Treaties' Clauses'; Rittberger, *Building Europe's Parliament*; Knudsen, 'The European Parliament and Political Careers at the Nexus of European Integration and Transnational History'.
78. See for example van der Eijk and Franklin, *The European Electorate and National Politics*; Reif and Schmitt, 'Nine Second-Order National Elections', pp. 3–44.
79. Kaelble, *Wege zur Demokratie.*
80. Luzzatto Fegiz, *Il volto sconosciuto dell'Italia*, p. 783; Commission des Communautés Européennes, *Les Européens et l'unification de l'Europe*, p. 55.
81. See for example Bitsch, Loth and Barthel, *Cultures politiques*; on the role of national filters, see for example Medrano, *Framing Europe.*
82. These much researched questions are of less interest here. Although they permit further differentiation, they overlook the gulf between general approval on the one hand and concrete knowledge and acceptance of specific policy areas on the other.
83. *Jahrbuch der öffentlichen Meinung*, 1965, pp. 542–543; documents in HAEU, CEAB 3/767; BDFD, vol. 4, p. 57; Guillen, 'La France et la négociation du traité d'Euratom', pp. 391–412, here p. 391; Guillen, 'Frankreich und der europäische Wiederaufschwung', pp. 1–19, here p. 1; see also D'Ottavio, *Europa mit den Deutschen*, pp. 71–78; with a different claim, see Vanke, *Europeanism and European Union.*
84. HAEU, CEAB 2/2174, Gallup International, L'opinion publique et l'Europe des six, Paris, 1962, quote p. 4; also Lindberg and Scheingold, *Europe's Would-Be Polity*, p. 42, fn. 23.
85. Commission des Communautés Européennes, *Les Européens et l'unification de l'Europe*, pp. 201, 55.
86. For more detail on the differences between member states, see Anderson and Kaltenthaler, 'The Dynamics of Public Opinion toward European Integration', pp. 175–199, here p. 180.
87. Lindberg and Scheingold, *Europe's Would-Be Polity*, esp. pp. 24–63, 249–278, quote p. 41; taken up for example in *Eurobarometer* 40 (1993), p. ix; term originally coined by Key in *Public Opinion and American Democracy*; see also Almond, *The American People and Foreign Policy.*
88. Definition from Merriam–Webster, online. See also Patel, 'Wie Europa seine Bürger verlor', pp. 22–28. Of course in the strict Stoic interpretation, 'adiaphora' meant everything between vice and virtue. In that sense the term is used metaphorically here.
89. Imig, 'Contestation in the Streets', pp. 216–234, here p. 224.
90. HAEU, CEAB 2/2174, Gallup International, L'opinion publique et l'Europe des six, Paris, 1962; also HAEU, UEF-488; on this and more broadly, esp. Aldrin, 'L'invention de l'opinion publique européenne', pp. 79–101; on the role of the United States, Puchala, 'The Common Market and Political Federation', pp. 32–59.

91. HAEU, CEAB 3/767, Klunhaar, Renseignement tirés des sondages d'opinion sur la Communauté Européenne de Charbon et de l'Acier, 29 October 1957.
92. See for example COM(2006) 35; more broadly, see also Reinfeldt, *Unter Ausschluss der Öffentlichkeit?*
93. Commission des Communautés Européennes, *Les Européens et l'unification de l'Europe*, for example pp. 13, 18, 65.
94. See the analysis in Aldrin, 'L'invention de l'opinion publique européenne'; the concrete example is from *Eurobarometer* 3 (1975), p. 29.
95. On the way terms like 'Europe' and 'European integration' remained polysemantic, see for example, de Lassalle, 'European Worlds', pp. 175–195.
96. Inglehart, Rabier and Reif, 'The Evolution of Public Attitudes toward European Integration', pp. 135–155, here p. 136.
97. For figures, see Hug, *Voices of Europe*, esp. pp. 23–45; on Norway, see for example Lie, 'Masters and Servants'.
98. McCutcheon, 'The Irish Constitution and Ratification of the Single European Act'; see also for example PAAA, Zwischenarchiv, 209200, esp. Irische Botschaft an AA, Verbalnote, 10 April 1987.
99. Pinto and Severiano Teixeira, 'From Africa to Europe', p. 39.
100. *Eurobarometer* 16 (1981), p. 48; on 1982–1985, see Inglehart, Rabier and Reif, 'The Evolution of Public Attitudes toward European Integration'; on falling approval in the 1980s in certain states, see also van Ingelgom, 'Mesurer l'indifférence', pp. 1–20.
101. Allers, *Besondere Beziehungen*, pp. 338–344.
102. This perspective is shared for example by Laursen, 'The Not-So-Permissive Consensus'.
103. Siune and Svensson, 'The Danes and the Maastricht Treaty', pp. 99–111; for a summary of public responses, see for example 'Europa reageert verbijsterd op Deens "ne"', *Leeuwarder Courant*, 3 June 1992.
104. See also Chapter 2, 'Peace and Security', and Chapter 3, 'Growth and Prosperity', in this volume.
105. Schönberger, 'Die Bürgerschaft der Europäischen Union', pp. 664–665; now see also, though with a slightly different argument, Kaelble, *Der verkannte Bürger*.
106. Dulphy and Manigand, 'L'opinion publique française face aux élargissements', pp. 125–145, here p. 127.
107. For example Brill, *Abgrenzung und Hoffnung*; Meyer, *The European Public Sphere*; Frank, *Un espace public européen en construction*; Seidendorf, *Europäisierung nationaler Identitätsdiskurse?*; Gerhards, 'Westeuropäische Integration und die Schwierigkeiten der Entstehung einer europäischen Öffentlichkeit'; Herzer, 'The Rise of Euro-journalism'.

Values and Norms

1. European Convention, *Draft Treaty Establishing a Constitution for Europe*, p. 3.
2. Winkler, *Quo vadis Europa?*
3. Thuc 2.65.
4. Lehmann, *Perikles*, pp. 7–29; da Silva, 'Thucydide II, 37 et le préambule de la Constitution européenne'; Bosworth, 'The Historical Context of Thucydides' Funeral Oration', pp. 1–16.
5. Bossuat, 'Histoire d'une controverse', pp. 68–82; Naumann, *Eine religiöse Referenz*.
6. European Convention, *Draft Treaty Establishing a Constitution for Europe*, p. 3.

7. CONV806/03, contrib 363, contribution by Edmund Wittbrodt and Marta Fogler, 10 March 2003; for these and further contributions to the debate, see http://european-convention.europa.eu (accessed 1 July 2019); on this issue, see also for example Bogdandy, 'The Preamble', p. 3–10; on the broader context, see Winkler, *Geschichte des Westens*, vol. 4, pp. 264–270.
8. For one example of such simplification, see European Union Agency for Fundamental Rights, *The European Union as a Community of Values*; see also (with a very specific understanding of 'normative') Manners, 'Normative Power Europe', pp. 235–258; for a very different perspective, also Nicolaïdis, Vergerio, Fisher Onar and Viehoff, 'From Metropolis to Microcosmos', pp. 718–745.
9. Which was naturally known at the time; see for example Scheuner, 'Fundamental Rights in European Community Law and in National Constitutional Law', pp. 171–191, here p. 186; see also Schulz-Forberg and Stråth, *The Political History of European Integration.*
10. De Búrca, 'The Language of Rights and European Integration', pp. 29–54.
11. I leave that question to one side here; see Chapter 2, 'Peace and Security', in this volume.
12. On the search for an ethos, see also Weiler, 'Does Europe Need a Constitution?', pp. 265–294, esp. p. 266.
13. www.echr.coe.int/Documents/Convention_ENG.pdf (accessed 1 July 2019); on the Convention, see Duranti, *The Conservative Human Rights Revolution*; see also Simpson, *Human Rights and the End of Empire.*
14. Niess, *Die europäische Idee*, esp. pp. 181–220; Wassenberg, *History of the Council of Europe*, pp. 33–37; Greppi, 'Il Consiglio d'Europa', pp. 87–116, here pp. 107–111.
15. www.nato.int/cps/en/natohq/official_texts_17072.htm (accessed 1 July 2019).
16. Einaudi, *Octobre 1961*. The exact figures remain controversial.
17. Buchanan, 'Human Rights, the Memory of War and the Making of a "European" Identity', pp. 157–171; Eckel, *Die Ambivalenz des Guten*, pp. 156–179; on Kenya and Algeria, see Klose, *Menschenrechte im Schatten kolonialer Gewalt.*
18. Mazower, *Dark Continent.*
19. See esp. Articles 2, 3, 45; treaty text in Ducci and Olivi, *L'Europa incompiuta*; see also de Búrca, *The Evolution of EU Human Rights Law*, pp. 465–497 for the broader context of the EPC and the Comité d'études pour la constitution européenne.
20. *Rapport des chefs de délégation aux ministres des affaires étrangères*; see also Thomas, 'Constitutionalization through Enlargement', pp. 1190–1210, here p. 1194.
21. Article 119, EEC Treaty, p. 196.
22. Article 3, EEC Treaty, p. 155; see also Barnard, *The Substantive Law of the EU.*
23. Fernández Soriano, *Le fusil et l'olivier*, pp. 71–76, also describing a unilateral Italian initiative in 1964.
24. 1/58, *Stork* v. *High Authority.*
25. Chalmers, Davies and Monti, *European Union Law*, pp. 232–233.
26. 26/62, *van Gend & Loos*; 6/64, *Costa* v. *ENEL.*
27. Eckel, *Die Ambivalenz des Guten*; Moyn, *The Last Utopia*; Gosewinkel, *Schutz und Freiheit?*, pp. 479–518.
28. Article 63: Grondwet en Statuut voor het Koninkrijk der Nederlanden (1963); on the context and earlier reforms, see van Leeuwen, 'On Democratic Concerns and Legal Traditions'; more generally, see Stone Sweet, *Governing with Judges.*
29. Wengler, 'Grundrechtsminimum und Äquivalenz der Grundrechtsschutzsysteme', pp. 327–329; Rupp, 'Die Grundrechte und das Europäische Gemeinschaftsrecht', pp. 353–359.

30. Kaiser, Badura, Evers and Fuss, *Bewahrung und Veränderung demokratischer und rechtsstaatlicher Verfassungsstruktur in den internationalen Gemeinschaften.*
31. HAEU, AH-67, Commission Constitutionelle, Quatrième session, Groupe de travail, 11 February 1953; see also EP Report A0-0110/66 (Fernand Dehousse, Report Legal Sub-Committee, 7 July 1966); see also European Parliament/CARDOC, *Ein Europa der Rechte*, pp. 10–11; on Dehousse's role in the negotiations about EPC, see Carlier, 'Fernand Dehousse et le projet d'Union Politique', pp. 365–377.
32. On the administrative court (Verwaltungsgericht Frankfurt), see for example Zuleeg, 'Fundamental Rights and the Law of the European Communities'.
33. 11/70, *Internationale Handelsgesellschaft* v. *Einfuhr- und Vorratsstelle für Getreide und Futtermittel.*
34. 35/67, *Van Eick* v. *Commission*; 29/69, *Stauder* v. *Ulm*; 4/73, *Nold* v. *Commission.* The *Stauder* case was pursued by a German recipient of war victims' assistance; it concerned details of the German practice of supplying subsidised butter to recipients of particular social benefits; *Nold* involved minimum sale quantities in trade regulations.
35. Translated from 29/69, *Stauder* v. *Ulm.*
36. The gap was already clear at the time; see for example Dauses, 'The Protection of Fundamental Rights'.
37. Williams, *EU Human Rights Policies*, pp. 128–161; Smismans, 'The European Union's Fundamental Rights Myth', pp. 45–66; see also Bergeron, 'An Ever Whiter Myth', pp. 3–26; Verney, 'Creating the Democratic Tradition of European Integration', pp. 97–127.
38. Translated from BVerfG, 29 May 1974 – 2 BVL 52/71 (Solange I); see also for example Scheuner, 'Fundamental Rights in European Community Law and in National Constitutional Law'; Chalmers, Davies and Monti, *European Union Law*, p. 234.
39. Patel, 'Germany and European Integration since 1945', pp. 775–794.
40. BVerfG, 22 October 1986 – 2 BvR 197/83 (Solange II).
41. Frowein, 'Solange II', pp. 201–206; Kokott, 'Report on Germany', pp. 77–131.
42. This dimension is sometimes overlooked in the political and legal discussion; see for example Schimmelfennig, 'Competition and Community', pp. 1247–1264.
43. Article 237, EEC Treaty, p. 228.
44. EP, Débats. Compte rendu in extenso des séances, 20 March 1958, esp. p. 38; see also DDF, 1960, Tome 1, pp. 73–90.
45. See Chapters 7 and 8, in this volume.
46. Cited from Thomas, 'Constitutionalization through Enlargement', p. 1196; see also the documents in HAEU, MAEF 35, especially Ministère des affaires étrangères, Wormser, Note, 27 January 1961: in France it was assumed that the relationship would be association.
47. Powell, 'The Long Road to Europe', pp. 21–44; Guirao, *Spain and the Reconstruction of Western Europe.*
48. HAEU, MAEF 35, Ministère des affaires étrangères, Wormser, Note, 4 December 1961; HAEU, MAEF 35, Ambassade de France en Espagne, Note, 3 February 1962.
49. Cited from PAAA, 206/162, 3 July 1962; see also HAEU, MAEF 35; Aschmann, 'The Reliable Ally', pp. 37–52; Thomas, 'Constitutionalization through Enlargement'; on Merkatz, see Großmann, *Die Internationale der Konservativen*, pp. 183–186.
50. Quote translated from Gliech, 'Bio-bibliographische Grunddaten zu den Referenten und Generalsekretären des IAI', pp. 571–609, here p. 587.
51. Thomas, 'Constitutionalization through Enlargement', pp. 1190–1210; see also Fernández Soriano, 'La CEE face à l'Espagne franquiste', pp. 85–98.

52. EP, Documents de séance, 15 January 1962, doc. 122, quotes p. 5 (originally in German).
53. Translated from HAEU, BAC 26/1969, 667/1, Lettre Castiella à Couve de Murville, 9 February 1962; on the secret communication with the member states, see for example PAAA, B 130/2377A, Botschaft Madrid an AA, 19 January 1962.
54. Sanz, 'Fernando M[a] Castiella', pp. 393–427; on the broader context, see Großmann, '"Baroque Spain" as Metaphor'.
55. Verney, 'Creating the Democratic Tradition of European Integration', p. 111; on the Dutch context, see Eckel, *Die Ambivalenz des Guten*, pp. 440–462.
56. Translated from HKNAW, S01571, Jitta, Ministerie van Buitenlandse Zaken, 23 November 1962, online: https://bit.ly/2p7UOAg (accessed 1 July 2019); on the broader context, see Eckel, *Die Ambivalenz des Guten*, pp. 440–462.
57. Fernández Soriano, *Le fusil et l'olivier*, pp. 77–104; Thomas, 'Constitutionalization through Enlargement'.
58. EP, Débats. Compte rendu in extenso des séances, 27–30 March 1962, p. 81.
59. Pinto and Severiano Teixeira, 'From Africa to Europe', pp. 3–40; Andresen-Leitão, 'Portugal's European Integration Policy', pp. 25–35; Tsoukalis, *The European Community and Its Mediterranean Enlargement*, pp. 50–74; on the trade agreement with Spain, see Trouvé, *L'Espagne et l'Europe*, pp. 99–180.
60. Translated from 'Der Bundeskanzler vor der Weltpresse', *Bulletin des Presse- und Informationsamtes der Bundesregierung* 19 (1951), pp. 133–135, here p. 134.
61. Schimmelfennig, 'The Community Trap', pp. 47–80; see also Rittberger and Schimmelfennig, 'Explaining the Constitutionalization of the European Union', pp. 1148–1167.
62. On the many trade union protests against the Franco regime, see for example Fernández Soriano, *Le fusil et l'olivier*, pp. 133–136; on popular support for the EC, see Chapter 4, 'Participation and Technocracy', in this volume.
63. Quote (translated) from the preparatory talks, PAAA, B 130/3293A, Ophuels an AA, 22 June 1959; in its application for association, Greece cited strong economic arguments, but also laid out geopolitical and security grounds; PAAA, B 20–200/242, Christidis an Hallstein, 8 June 1959. An almost identical formulation appears in France in AD, Courneuve, 189QO/233, Ministère des affaires étrangères, Note, 20 June 1961.
64. AD, Courneuve, 189QO/233, Conseils des Communautés européennes, Note d'information, 16 May 1967; see also de Angelis and Karamouzi, 'Enlargement and the Historical Origins of the European Community's Identity', pp. 439–458.
65. Fernández Soriano, *Le fusil et l'olivier*, pp. 147–223; Pedaliu, 'Human Rights and International Security', pp. 1014–1039; see also Tsoukalis, *The European Community and Its Mediterranean Enlargement*.
66. TNA, FCO 30/1328, Report on Lord Limerick's Visit to Greece, 22 November 1972; see also TNA, FCO 30/1328, FCO, Note A. Brooke Turner, 12 October 1972. This was the first official visit by a British minister since the coup; on the broader context, see Nafpliotis, *Britain and the Greek Colonels*.
67. Verney, 'Creating the Democratic Tradition of European Integration', pp. 104–107, 115–125; Kjærsgaard, 'Confronting the Greek Military Junta'.
68. On the Order, see AD, Courneuve, 189QO/235; on this, see Fernández Soriano, Facing the Greek Junta; see also Eckel, *Die Ambivalenz des Guten*, pp. 169–178.
69. Translated from PAAA, B 20–200/524, EWG, Rat, Protokoll über die Sitzung im engeren Rahmen, 20/21 March 1961.

70. See for example PAAA, B 130/3256A, AA, Aufzeichnung Hartlieb, 12 January 1960; with many details, see PAAA, B 20–200/524; on Soviet offers, see for example PAAA, B 20–200/608.
71. Fernández Soriano, *Le fusil et l'olivier*, pp. 57–60.
72. Commission of the EC, *SEC(89) 2290 final*, p. 7.
73. Yılmaz, 'Europeanisation and Its Discontents', pp. 53–64; Savaşan, 'The Credibility of EU Human Rights Conditionality', pp. 45–70; Hughes, *Turkey's Accession to the European Union*, pp. 20–44.
74. Plassmann, *Comme dans une nuit des Paques?*; Pelt, *Tying Greece to the West*, pp. 281–335.
75. Translated from AD, Courneuve, 189QO/290, Ministère des affaires étrangères, Note, 14 February 1975.
76. EP, Debates, 4 April 1973, pp. 17–19.
77. http://aei.pitt.edu/4545/1/epc_identity_doc.pdf (accessed 1 July 2019).
78. *Bulletin of the EC*, Supplement 1/76, Report by Leo Tindemans to the European Council; see also Bergeron, 'An Ever Whiter Myth'.
79. Weiler, *The Constitution of Europe.*
80. Fernández Soriano, *Le fusil et l'olivier.*
81. Villaume, Mariager and Porsdam, *The 'Long 1970s'*; Thomas, *The Helsinki Effect*, pp. 39–54; Romano, *From Détente in Europe to European Détente.*
82. Duchêne, 'The European Community and the Uncertainties of Interdependence', pp. 1–21, quote p. 20; see also Duchêne, 'Europe's Role in World Peace', pp. 32–47.
83. Mayne, 'The Europe We Want', p. 348.
84. Translated from de Rougemont, *Ecrits sur l'Europe*, vol. 2, p. 256.
85. See for example the criticism of Duchêne in Orbie, 'Civilian Power Europe', pp. 123–128.
86. For an early reflection on the circumstances that shaped this debate, see Bull, 'Civilian Power Europe', pp. 149–164; see also de Angelis and Karamouzi, 'Enlargement and the Historical Origins of the European Community's Identity'.
87. C 103/1, 27 April 1977; now see also the exact analysis in Williams, *EU Human Rights Policies*, pp. 151–153.
88. Winkler, *Zerbricht der Westen?*, pp. 61–72; Grimm, *Europa ja – aber welches?*
89. European Parliament/CARDOC, *Ein Europa der Rechte*, pp. 15–19.
90. See the argument in Fernández Soriano, *Le fusil et l'olivier.*
91. Translated from AD, Courneuve, 189QO/290, Communication de M. Caramanlis aux ambassadeurs de la C.E.E., 12 June 1975.
92. *Bulletin of the EC*, Supplement 2/76, p. 6; see also CMA, CM5 ADH ADH2.1.
93. Translated from Barre, 'Grand Témoin', pp. 132–137, here p. 135.
94. HKNAW, Z00144, Notulen Ministerraad, 13 June 1975, online: https://bit.ly/33bvsQO; see also HKNAW, Z00174, Notulen Ministerraad, 6 February 1976, online: https://bit.ly/33jdxb3 (both accessed 1 July 2019).
95. Karamouzi, *Greece, the EEC and the Cold War*; see also for example Tsoukalis, *The European Community and Its Mediterranean Enlargement*, pp. 105–115, 133–162.
96. *Bulletin of the EC*, Supplement 1/78, p. 6.
97. Cunha, 'O Alargamento Ibérico da Comunidade Económica Europeia'; Trouvé, *L'Espagne et l'Europe*, pp. 181–370; de la Guardia, 'In Search of Lost Europe', pp. 99–118; Severiano Teixeira, *The International Politics of Democratization*; del Pero, Gavín, Guirao and Varsori, *Democrazie.*

98. De Angelis and Karamouzi, 'Enlargement and the Historical Origins of the European Community's Identity', p. 452.
99. Fierro, *The EU's Approach to Human Rights Conditionality*, pp. 41–59; Williams, *EU Human Rights Policies*, pp. 22–52; Dann, *Entwicklungsverwaltungsrecht*, pp. 84–88; Bartels, *Human Rights Conditionality in the EU's International Agreements*; Lister, *The European Community and the Developing World*.
100. L 169, 29 June 1987; see also Smismans, 'The European Union's Fundamental Rights Myth', p. 49.
101. C 191, 29 July 1992.
102. Williams, *EU Human Rights Policies*; Smismans, 'The European Union's Fundamental Rights Myth'.
103. See also Ricoeur, 'Quel éthos nouveau pour l'Europe?', pp. 107–116.
104. C 103/1, 27 April 1977; on the relationship to the Convention, see for example Schimmelfennig, 'Competition and Community'.
105. TNA, FCO 30/5607, FCO, Eileen Denza, Proposed Accession of the Communities to the European Convention on Human Rights, 2 February 1981; see also for example TNA, FCO 30/5608.
106. Anderson and Murphy, 'The Charter of Fundamental Rights', p. 155.
107. On this ambivalence, see Dauses, 'The Protection of Fundamental Rights'.
108. On both points, see de Búrca, 'The Evolution of EU Human Rights Law', pp. 465–497.
109. Gehler, *Der lange Weg*, pp. 437–475; Leconte, 'The Fragility of the EU as a "Community of Values"', pp. 620–649.
110. This line of thought was to culminate in Fukuyama, *The End of History and the Last Man*.
111. For example Dauses, 'The Protection of Fundamental Rights'.
112. See for example Donner, 'The Constitutional Powers of the Court of Justice', pp. 127–140.
113. See also de Búrca, 'The Language of Rights and European Integration'.
114. See also Schimmelfennig, 'Competition and Community', pp. 1247–1264.
115. Hodenberg, *Konsens und Krise*; Herzer, 'The Rise of Euro-Journalism'.
116. De Búrca, 'The Language of Rights and European Integration', pp. 50–52.
117. Moravcsik, 'The Origins of Human Rights Regimes', pp. 217–252.
118. See for example Weiler, *The Constitution of Europe*, pp. 102–129.
119. Schnädelbach, *Analytische und postanalytische Philosophie*, esp. pp. 266–281.
120. Translated from Dahrendorf, *Auf der Suche nach einer neuen Ordnung*, p. 121.
121. Börzel and Risse, 'Three Cheers for Comparative Regionalism', pp. 621–647, here p. 628.

Superstate or Tool of Nations?

1. Küsters, *Die Gründung der Europäischen Wirtschaftsgemeinschaft*, p. 432.
2. Margaret Thatcher's Bruges speech, 20 September 1988, in: *Documents on European Integration*, pp. 243–244.
3. Thatcher, *Statecraft*, p. 324.
4. Cited from Vaïsse, *La grandeur*, p. 33.
5. Spierenburg and Poidevin, *The History of the High Authority of the European Coal and Steel Community*, p. 651.
6. On the Council meeting, see HAEU, CM2/1963-1-2.
7. Milward, *The European Rescue of the Nation-State*; on the agenda of this chapter, see also Palmowski, 'The Europeanization of the Nation-State'.

8. Weber, *Economy and Society*, p. 220.
9. Cited from Hoffman, *Queen Juliana*, p. 115.
10. Lacey, *Monarch*, pp. 178–186.
11. Ullrich, *Der Weimar-Komplex*.
12. Judt, *Postwar*, pp. 63–77; Kaelble, *Sozialgeschichte Europas*, pp. 332–357; Jarausch, *Out of Ashes*, esp. pp. 560–584.
13. Flora, *Growth to Limits*, vol. 1, pp. 305–309 and vol. 2, pp. 15–19, 164–169, 393–396; summarising also Ambrosius and Hubbard, *A Social and Economic History of Twentieth-Century Europe*, pp. 255–260.
14. Translated from 'Prinses Juliana als moeder', *De West*, 7 September 1948.
15. Lacey, *Monarch*, p. 180.
16. Translated from 'Proclamatie van Koningin Juliana', *De West*, 7 September 1948; for the broader context, see Moore, 'Decolonization by Default'.
17. Milward, *The European Rescue of the Nation-State*.
18. Spierenburg and Poidevin, *The History of the High Authority of the European Coal and Steel Community*, p. 58.
19. Dumoulin and Lethé, 'The Question of Location'.
20. Wessels, *Die Öffnung des Staates*, pp. 201–203.
21. Spierenburg and Poidevin, *The History of the High Authority of the European Coal and Steel Community*, p. 649.
22. All figures from Mangenot and Seidel, 'Consolidating the European Civil Service', pp. 61–70 and Commission of the EC, *General Report on the Activities of the European Communities*, various years.
23. Hay, *The European Commission and the Administration of the Community*, p. 31.
24. Strasser, *Les finances de l'Europe*, p. 283. This figure is based on the ECU data, and thus more precise than calculations using the currency of a member state. The EC's overall budget in 1992 was sixty-four billion ECUs, Commission of the EC, *General Report on the Activities of the European Communities*, 1992, p. 403.
25. Dumoulin, 'The Commissioners'; Seidel, *The Process of Politics in Europe*; Dumoulin, 'The Administration'; Cini, *The European Commission*.
26. All figures from Mangenot and Seidel, 'Consolidating the European Civil Service'.
27. Hix, Noury and Roland, *Democratic Politics in the European Parliament*, p. 13.
28. For an analysis encompassing the other institutions, see esp. Wessels, *Die Öffnung des Staates*, pp. 195–260.
29. Shore, *Building Europe*, pp. 177–203; Seidel, *The Process of Politics in Europe*, pp. 9–62.
30. Quotes translated from HAEU, INT 231, p. 29 and Buzzonetti, 'Merci, Monsieur Noël', p. 269.
31. Seidel, *The Process of Politics in Europe*; Shore, *Building Europe*, pp. 177–187; Mangenot, 'La revendication d'une paternité'; Cini, *The European Commission*, pp. 51–68.
32. For example, Versluis, van Keulen and Stephenson, *Analyzing the European Union Policy Process*.
33. HAEU, CM2 1970–448; HAEU, CM2 1970–29/ab, EWG, Rat, Zusammenfassung der Ratsbeschlüsse v. 13., 14., 20. April 1970.
34. Wessels, *Die Öffnung des Staates*, p. 204.
35. For a historical perspective, see Knudsen and Rasmussen, 'A European Political System in the Making'; see also Wessels, *Die Öffnung des Staates*, pp. 233–241; Christiansen and Larsson, *The Role of Committees in the Policy-Process of the European Union*.
36. Wessels, *Die Öffnung des Staates*, pp. 212–227.

37. TNA, FCO 13/1114, Telegram British Embassy Rome to FCO, 24 July 1981; see also TNA, FCO 13/1558 on the preparations in 1982.
38. Translated from PAAA, Zwischenarchiv, 130399, AA, Stavenhagen an Bundesministerium für Wirtschaft, Schlecht, 4 July 1986.
39. TNA, FCO 9/2981, Telegram FCO, Carrington, to British Embassy Athens, 28 November 1980.
40. Patel, *Europäisierung wider Willen*.
41. Article 85, EEC Treaty, p. 184.
42. Regulation 17/62, 21 February 1962.
43. Regulation 1/2003, 16 December 2002; see also Cini and McGowan, *Competition Policy in the European Union*, p. 215; see also Patel and Schweitzer, *The Historical Foundations of EU Competition Law*.
44. See Chapter 4, 'Participation and Technocracy', in this volume. Also Grimm, *Europa ja – aber welches?*
45. For detail, see Scharpf, 'Negative and Positive Integration in the Political Economy of European Welfare States'.
46. Eichener, 'Effective European Problem-Solving'; in general, on the following esp. Barnard, *The Substantive Law of the EU*.
47. Above all Article 30, EEC Treaty, p. 165.
48. 120/78, *Rewe-Zentral-AG* v. *Bundesmonopolverwaltung für Branntwein* (*Cassis de Dijon*).
49. Allan Dashwood's 'functional parallelism' is to my mind more precise, but has failed to find broader acceptance.
50. 8/74, *Staatsanwaltschaft* v. *Benoît u. Gustave Dassonville*; on this, for example, Weiler, 'The Constitution of the Common Market Place'.
51. For example, Communication from the Commission in 1980/C 256/2, 3 October 1980; overall Nicolaïdis, 'The Cassis Legacy'.
52. COM (85) 310; see also Pelkmans, 'Mutual Recognition in Goods and Services'; on the role of the Commission, see also CEAH, BAC 224/1994 25; CEAH, BAC 224/1994 31 with references to *Cassis*.
53. COM (85) 310, p. 55.
54. Barnard, *The Substantive Law of the EU*, pp. 11–12; as an example of the charged nature of the discussion concerning the Single Market Programme, see Delors, *Das neue Europa*, pp. 109–156.
55. Cowles, 'Setting the Agenda for a New Europe'; Tsoukalis, *The New European Economy*, pp. 47–55; on the Ligue, CEAH, BAC 224/1994 27, Lettre Président de la Ligue Européenne de Coopération Economique to European Commission, 10 July 1985.
56. Moravcsik, *The Choice for Europe*, pp. 314–378; see also Craig, 'The Evolution of the Single Market'.
57. CEAH, BAC 224/1994 31, Commission of the EC, Fortescue, Office of Lord Cockfield to Mr Braun et al., 3 May 1985.
58. CEAH, BAC 224/1994 27, Commission of the EC, Legal Service, Ehlermann, Note to Lord Cockfield, 23 July 1985.
59. See also Schorkopf, 'Rechtsgeschichte der europäischen Integration'.
60. 188/84, *Commission* v. *France*, Judgment (*Wood-working machines*).
61. 85/C 136/01, 7 May 1985; see also the earlier Low Voltage Directive, 73/23/EEC, 19 February 1973.
62. Di Fabio, *Produktharmonisierung durch Normung und Selbstüberwachung* (also addressing broader issues); Barnard, *The Substantive Law of the EU*, pp. 636–641; Joerges, Falke, Micklitz and Brüggemeier, *Die Sicherheit von*

Konsumgütern und die Entwicklung der Europäischen Gemeinschaft, esp. pp. 305–386.

63. Röhl, *Akkreditierung und Zertifizierung im Produktsicherheitsrecht*, pp. 3–22.
64. For the perspective of a central participant, see Cockfield, *The European Union* (albeit emphasising primarily his own role and that of the Commission).
65. Translated from CEAH, BAC 224/1994 27, Lettre Wogau à Delors, 11 April 1985. CEN stands for Comité européen de normalisation; CENELEC for Comité européen de normalisation en électronique et en électrotechnique.
66. For a contemporary account conveying a sense of the breadth of possibilities, see for example Pelkmans, 'The New Approach to Technical Harmonization and Standardization'; on this issue, see also Nicolaïdis, 'The Cassis Legacy', pp. 281–282.
67. L 169/1, 29 June 1987; on the internal negotiations and debates, see PAAA, Zwischenarchiv, 130392–130401; PAAA, Zwischenarchiv, 209200–209201; CEAH, BAC 193/2001, 103; CEAH, BAC 408/1991, 306; CEAH, BAC 193/2001 103; CEAH, BAC 408/1991 306; CEAH, BAC 408/1991 227.
68. Weiler, *The Constitution of Europe*, pp. 68–75; strictly speaking, the latter concerned an amendment to the Council's Rules of Procedure on the basis of Article 100a, see 87/508/Euratom, EGKS, EWG, 20 July 1987.
69. Nicolaïdis, 'The Cassis Legacy', pp. 290–293; also addressing the long-term economic consequences, see Micossi, 'Thirty Years of the Single European Market'.
70. For example Dehousse, 'Completing the Internal Market', pp. 335–336.
71. http://aei.pitt.edu/1113/1/internal_market_wp_COM_85_310.pdf (accessed 1 July 2019).
72. C 316, 12 December 1988, p. 11.
73. On the media reporting, see for example 'Europese Rekenkamer signaleert fraude met exportsubsidies', *De Telegraaf*, 6 September 1985; see also for example 'EG geeft miljarden landbouwsubsidies uit zonder controle', *Leeuwarder Courant*, 9 January 1982; on one especially spectacular case, see C 316, Court of Auditors, Annual Report Concerning 1987, 12 December 1988, p. 69.
74. 'Fraude kost EG per jaar ruim f 7 mld.', *Nederlands Dagblad*, 10 April 1987; on the budget, see C 316, 12 December 1988.
75. Grant, *The Common Agricultural Policy*, p. 99; Sieber, 'Euro-fraud' (the latter also addressing other forms of fraud); some experts put the figure as high as 20 per cent; see also de Doelder, *Bestrijding van EEG-fraude*.
76. Ulrich, *Wege nach Europa*, esp. pp. 61–87, 110–114; Stephenson, 'Starting from Scratch?'; Stephenson, 'Sixty-Five Years of Auditing Europe'; C 316, 12 December 1988, p. 7 for the figures for 1987. Alongside the fraud cases, the EC's own resources (from 1970) were a central factor in the expansion of the Court of Auditors.
77. C 316, 12 December 1988, p. 74.
78. C 316, 12 December 1988, p. 68.
79. See the analysis in 85/C 215/01, 7 May 1985; for other reasons, see also Passas and Nelken, 'The Thin Line between Legitimate and Criminal Enterprises'.
80. 283/72 EEC; see also Carey, 'Fraud and the Common Agricultural Policy'.
81. For example Tiedemann, *Subventionskriminalität in der Bundesrepublik*, esp. pp. 80–97.
82. Neuhann, *Im Schatten der Integration*, pp. 29–42.
83. For a contemporary account, see Joerges, Falke, Micklitz and Brüggemeier, *Die Sicherheit von Konsumgütern und die Entwicklung der Europäischen Gemeinschaft*,

pp. 276–280; Krislov, Ehlermann and Weiler, 'The Political Organs and the Decision-Making Process in the United States and the European Community'.

84. Versluis, van Keulen and Stephenson, *Analyzing the European Union Policy Process*, pp. 180–184.
85. Own calculations using data from http://eur-lex.europa.eu (accessed 1 July 2019).
86. For the starting point, see Regulation 543/69, 25 March 1969.
87. Philip, 'The Application of the EEC Regulations on Drivers' Hours and Tachographs'; Cosgrove Twitchett, 'Harmonisation and Road Freight Transport'.
88. 128/78, *Commission* v. *United Kingdom of Great Britain and Northern Ireland* (*Tachograph*).
89. *Hansard*, vol. 976, 19 December 1979.
90. Wessels, *Die Öffnung des Staates*, pp. 242–246.
91. Pelkmans, 'The European Single Market'.
92. For the first major systematic project, see Siedentopf and Ziller, *Making European Policies Work*.
93. O'Toole, 'Policy Recommendations for Multi-Actor Implementation'.
94. For more recent overviews of the research history, see Treib, 'Implementing and Complying with EU Governance Outputs'; Mastenbroek, 'EU Compliance'; on the reasons behind the change of direction in research, see Seibel, *Verwaltung verstehen*, pp. 155–158.
95. Giuliani and Piattoni, 'Italy'; on the context, see Varsori, *La Cenerentola*, pp. 159–374.
96. Castelnau, 'Le SGCI'.
97. On the example of agriculture, see Patel, *Europäisierung wider Willen*; see also Wessels, *Die Öffnung des Staates*.
98. Contemporary: Weiler, 'The White Paper and the Application of Community Law', pp. 355–356.
99. Summarising Tallberg, 'Paths to Compliance', p. 615.
100. Masing, *Die Mobilisierung des Bürgers für die Durchsetzung des Rechts*, esp. pp. 19–53; Bergeron, 'An Ever Whiter Myth'.
101. For example Börzel, 'Why There Is No "Southern Problem"'.
102. 75/117/EEC, 10 February 1975.
103. For detail on the administrations, see Seibel, *Verwaltung verstehen*; taking a different angle, see Lindseth, *Power and Legitimacy*.
104. Wessels, *Die Öffnung des Staates*.
105. Kropp, *Kooperativer Föderalismus und Politikverflechtung*, pp. 161–162.
106. Christensen, 'EU Legislation and National Regulation', p. 11.
107. Patel, *Europäisierung wider Willen*, p. 83.
108. Maier, *Once within Borders*, p. 275; also Maier, *Leviathan 2.0*; in relation to the EU, see Jureit and Tietze, *Postsouveräne Territorialität*.
109. Salvatore Vicario, 'Francesco Borrelli, incisore', *Wall Street International* (Italian), 25 September 2017.
110. See Chapter 4, 'Participation and Technocracy', in this volume.

Disintegration and Dysfunctionality

1. TNA, FCO 33/4669, Statement Motzfeldt, 2 October 1981.
2. COM(83) 66 final; see also Weiss, 'Greenland's Withdrawal from the European Communities', pp. 173–185.
3. Article 240, EEC Treaty, p. 228. Only the ECSC Treaty was term-limited, to fifty years; on the contemporary discussions around this question, see for

example Feinberg, 'Unilateral Withdrawal from an International Organization', pp. 189–219.

4. Reproduced in Ducci and Olivi, *L'Europa incompiuta*, p. 220.
5. 2007/C 306/01, Treaty of Lisbon, Article 50; on the Article's history, see Galloro, 'Der Rücktritt gemäß Art. 50 EUV', pp. 150–161.
6. Nicolaides, 'Withdrawal from the European Union', pp. 209–219; see also Weiler, 'Alternatives to Withdrawal', pp. 282–298.
7. TNA, FCO 33/4670, Duncan, FCO, to Hogger, FCO, 20 October 1981.
8. Harhoff, 'Greenland's Withdrawal from the European Communities', pp. 13–33.
9. L 29/1; Treaty Amending the Treaties, 1 February 1985; L 29/14, Protocol on Fishing, 12 January 1985.
10. PAAA, Zwischenarchiv, 130417, esp. AA an BMWi u.a., 20 March 1984; PAAA, Zwischenarchiv, 121995, esp. AA, Vermerk über das Gespräch zwischen MP Joergensen und StS Wischnewski, 2 September 1982; overall PAAA, Zwischenarchiv, 121995, 121996, 121997; also AD, Courneuve, 1930INVA/5120; CMA, CM2CC, CEEA 1984.11; now see also Jensen and Heinrich, 'Fra hjemmestyre til selvstyre'.
11. European Commission, Directorate-General for Trade, EU Trade in Goods with Greenland, 20 October 2015; https://bit.ly/20Vruoh (accessed 1 July 2019); see also Gad, 'Greenland Projecting Sovereignty', pp. 217–234; 'Grønland udskyder selvstændighed', *Information*, 22 April 2015.
12. PAAA, Zwischenarchiv, 121995, 410–420.10 DAN, Sachstand, 2 September 1982; TNA, FCO, 33/4670, Hatford, British Embassy Copenhagen, to Spreckley, FCO, 6 November 1981; see also TNA, FCO 33/4669; TNA, FCO 33/5469.
13. See for example Gespräch Genscher mit Olesen, 19 April 1982, in AAPD 1982, vol. 2, pp. 597–602; figure from PAAA, Zwischenarchiv, 121995, AA, 410–420.10 DAN, Aufzeichnung, 2 September 1982; on the same issue, see also for example PAAA, Zwischenarchiv, 130416; on the position of the Dutch government, for which fishery was also key, HKNAW, Z00778, M. Timmerman, DMP/EG, Memorandum, 18 August 1983, online: https://bit.ly/313ThZr (accessed 1 July 2019).
14. Above all PAAA, Zwischenarchiv, 121996, AA, 410, Sachstand, 9 March 1983.
15. *Bulletin of the European Communities*, Supplement 1/83: Status of Greenland, 2 February 1983, p. 10; see also CEAH, 78/1986 99; CEAH, BAC 159/1991 94; CEAH, BAC 416/1991 930.
16. See for example Harhoff, 'Greenland's Withdrawal from the European Communities'.
17. Hallstein from 'Western Europe: Pulling Apart', *Time*, 14 February 1969.
18. See for example Gad, 'Greenland Projecting Sovereignty', pp. 217–234, which describes Greenland as the first such case.
19. Jansen, *Erobern und Erinnern*, pp. 467–468; on the broader context, see also Cooper, *Citizenship between Empire and Nation*, and Connelly, *A Diplomatic Revolution*.
20. Article 227(2), EEC Treaty, p. 225.
21. For one of the rare exceptions, see Tatham, 'Don't Mention Divorce at the Wedding, Darling!', pp. 128–154.
22. Adi and Sherwood, *Pan-African History*, pp. 7–10.
23. Ben Bella, *Discours du Président Ben Bella*, pp. 7, 16, 12.
24. HAEU, CM2/1963, 885, Lettre Ben Bella à Hallstein, 24 December 1962. This important question is overlooked in Byrne's otherwise excellent *Mecca of Revolution*.

25. Translated from HAEU, CM2/1963, 885, Communauté économique européenne, Conseil, Note, secret, 25 June 1963; from the EP's perspective, see also HAEU, PEO-8310.
26. Naylor, *France and Algeria*, pp. 47–73; Cooper, *Citizenship between Empire and Nation*.
27. HAEU, CM2/1963, 885, Communauté économique européenne, Le Conseil, Note, secret, 20 January 1963; see also AN, Pierrefitte, 19880053/185, Communautés européennes, Le Conseil Groupe 'Algerie – Maroc – Tunisie', Note, 20 July 1967; ibid., 19880053/186, Communautés européennes, Le Conseil, Note: Déclaration de la délegation italienne, 2 June 1967.
28. See for example HAEU, CM2/1972, 1701; ibid., 1702–1714.
29. Translated from HAEU, CM2/1972, 1701, EWG, Rat, Einleitende Aufzeichnung, 27 November 1965.
30. For a summary of developments, see HAEU, CM2/1972, 1709, EG, Rat, Beziehungen zu Algerien, 30 January 1968.
31. HAEU, CM2/1972, 1709, EG, Rat, Beziehungen zu Algerien, 30 January 1968.
32. Translated from Mameri, 'L'adhésion de l'Algérie à la Communauté Economique Européenne', p. 429.
33. See for example HAEU, CM2/1972, 1713, EG, Kommission, Beziehungen zwischen der Gemeinschaft und Algerien, 14 April 1970; see also ibid., 1711, Algerischer Botschafter an Präsident der Europäischen Kommission, 25 March 1968; ibid., 1714, EWG, Rat, Beziehungen zu Algerien, 15 October 1971; AN, Pierrefitte, 19880053/186, Communautés européennes, Le Conseil, Note: Déclaration de la délegation italienne, 2 June 1967; on the French stance, see AN, Pierrefitte, 19880053/196, Ministère de l'economie et des finances, Note, 6 December 1967.
34. Isnard, 'Le commerce extérieur de l'Algérie', pp. 93–98; Meloni and Swinnen, 'The Rise and Fall', pp. 3–33.
35. Ben Bella as quoted in Merle, *Ahmed Ben Bella*, p. 162.
36. Scioldo-Zürcher, *Devenir métropolitain*, p. 45.
37. Meloni and Swinnen, 'The Political Economy of European Wine Regulations', pp. 244–284; see also Rat der EG, *Protokolle zum Kooperationsabkommen EWG–Algerien*.
38. See Caruso and Geneve, 'Trade and History: The Case of EU–Algeria Relations' (with certain inexactitudes, for example concerning the prior existence of discrimination); HAEU, CM2/1972, 1709, EG, Rat, Beziehungen zu Algerien, 30 January 1968; generally, on the pre-1970 wine sector rules in relation to Algeria, AN, Pierrefitte, 19880053/186, Communauté économique européenne, Le Conseil, Relations avec le Maroc et la Tunesie, 8 April 1965, which also deals in detail with Algeria; see also ibid., 19880053/197–198 and CEAH, BAC 3–1978 1456–1457.
39. Translated from HAEU, CM2/1972, 1714, Memorandum der Algerischen Regierung über die Beziehungen zwischen Algerien und den Europäischen Gemeinschaften, 17 March 1972.
40. Translated from AN, Pierrefitte, 19880053/197, Lettre du chef de la mission d'Algérie à R. Dahrendorf, 11 December 1971.
41. Translated from AN, Pierrefitte, 19880053/197, Basdevant, Ministère des affaires étrangères, Télégramme, 29 October 1971.
42. Meloni and Swinnen, 'The Rise and Fall', pp. 3–33; for detail on the negotiations, see AN, Pierrefitte, 19880053/196–198.
43. Meloni and Swinnen, 'The Rise and Fall'; for detail on the negotiations, see for example AD, Courneuve, 0034SUP/90; AD, Courneuve, 0035SUP/265; TNA, FCO 30/2182.

44. EEC Treaty, p. 153.
45. See EEC Council Regulation 816/70; see also the analysis in Meloni and Swinnen, 'The Rise and Fall'.
46. For trade figures, see AN, Pierrefitte, 19880053/196, Communauté économique européenne, Le Conseil, Relations avec l'Algérie, 21 May 1965; HAEU, CM2/1972, 1703, Communauté économique européenne, Commission, Relations de la CEE avec les pays du Maghreb, 14 December 1966; European Commission, Directorate-General for Trade, EU Trade in Goods with Algeria, 20 October 2015; http://trade.ec.europa.eu/doclib/docs/2006/september/tradoc_113343.pdf (accessed 1 July 2019).
47. Wall, *The Official History of Britain and the European Community*, pp. 511–590; on the scenarios for a 'leave' vote, see TNA, FV 61/32; TNA, FCO 30/2944–2949; TNA, T 355/274–275; now see also Saunders, *Yes to Europe!*
48. On the question of withdrawal before the Treaty of Lisbon, see also for example Wagner, 'Verrechtlichung durch Integration', pp. 67–83.
49. Despite decades of debate on European integration, conceptualisation of European disintegration remains rudimentary; for example Schmitter and Lefkofridi, 'Neo-Functionalism as a Theory of Disintegration'; Vollaard, 'Explaining European Disintegration'; Eppler and Scheller, *Zur Konzeptionalisierung europäischer Desintegration*; Webber, 'How Likely Is It that the European Union Will *Dis*integrate?'; Georgakakis, 'European Integration'.
50. Lindberg, *The Political Dynamics of European Economic Integration*, p. 10; see also Rosamond, 'The Uniting of Europe and the Foundation of EU Studies'.
51. Articles 74–84, EEC Treaty, pp. 181–183; for a comparative perspective, see Henrich-Franke, *Gescheiterte Integration im Vergleich*; Patel and Schot, 'Twisted Paths to European Integration', pp. 383–403.
52. For example Rosamond, *Theories of European Integration*, pp. 50–68; Schmitter, 'Neo-Neofunctionalism', pp. 45–74.
53. HAEU, KM/22, EWG, Ausarbeitung, undated [1964]; PAAA, B 20–200/1536, Aufzeichnung U. Weinstock, Europäische Agrarpolitik und Währungsfragen, 1969; see also Hill, *The Common Agricultural Policy*, pp. 60–72.
54. ACDP, NL 01–283/19/1, BML, Neef, Aufzeichnung, 15 August 1969; see also Patel, *Europäisierung wider Willen*, pp. 404–406.
55. Cited from Bodo Radke, 'Marathondebatte über den Grabstein für den Agrarmarkt', *Welt*, 13 August 1969; see also 'Un enterrement', *Le Monde*, 13 August 1969.
56. See for example 'Einde van een EEG-illusie', *Limburgsch dagblad*, 16 August 1969; Thomas Löffelholz, 'Rückschlag für Europa', *Stuttgarter Zeitung*, 13 August 1969; Karl-Peter Krause, 'Das Dilemma des "grünen Dollar"', *Frankfurter Allgemeine Zeitung*, 13 August 1969.
57. HAEU, CM2/1969–45/ad, EWG, Rat, Protokoll Ratstagung, 6 October 1969.
58. Eichengreen, *The European Economy since 1945*, pp. 242–251.
59. Mourlon-Druol, *A Europe Made of Money*, pp. 15–29; Schmitz, 'L'Influence de l'élite monétaire européenne'.
60. Gleske, 'Nationale Geldpolitik auf dem Weg zur europäischen Währungsunion', pp. 745–788.
61. https://bit.ly/33HZdsP (accessed 1 July 2019); on the Plan, see *Bulletin des Communautés européennes*, Supplément 11/1970, Werner Report, final, 8 October 1970.
62. Mourlon-Druol, *A Europe Made of Money*.
63. Marx, *Society and Social Change*, p. 115.
64. Jay, 'Europe', pp. 63–72, here p. 66.
65. Monnet, *Memoirs*, p. 417.

66. Hallstein, *Europe in the Making*, p. 328.
67. For a contemporaneous account on inactivity of international organisations, see for example Feinberg, 'Unilateral Withdrawal from an International Organization'.
68. PAAA, B 20–200/1320, Sachs, Ständige Vertretung, an AA, 1 July 1965.
69. Article 5, EEC Treaty, p. 156.
70. On the Empty Chair Crisis, see esp. Palayret, Wallace and Winand, *Visions, Votes and Vetoes*; Ludlow, *The European Community and the Crises of the 1960s*, esp. pp. 68–124.
71. Weiler, 'Alternatives to Withdrawal'.
72. Article 8, EEC Treaty, p. 156; on the French demand and the outcome, see HAEU, CM2/1966–1/ac, EWG, Rat, Protokoll über die außerordentliche Ratstagung am 17/18/27/28 January 1966.
73. On this time dimension – which has been largely ignored in the conventional historiography – see Patel, 'Rivalisierende Raum-Zeit-Ordnungen', pp. 61–77; fundamental: Koselleck, *Futures Past*; on time regimes in the integration process, see also Howlett and Goetz 'Time, Temporality and Timescapes', pp. 477–492, with pointers to further literature.
74. 2010/718/EU, 29 October 2010.
75. See Chapter 2, 'Peace and Security', in this volume.
76. Spierenburg and Poidevin, *The History of the High Authority of the European Coal and Steel Community*, esp. pp. 404–414.
77. Translated from 'Das Krisenmanifest', *Spiegel*, 4 March 1959.
78. There were of course other processes of disintegration and dysfunctionality that had nothing at all to do with the EC; these remain outside the scope of the present discussion.
79. See Chapter 2, 'Peace and Security', in this volume.
80. Rasmussen, 'Joining the European Communities', pp. 67–82; see also PAAA, B 20–200/528, AA, Aufzeichnung zu handelspolitischen Aspekten des Beitritts Dänemarks, 17 October 1961.

The Community and its World

1. Ludlow, *Roy Jenkins and the European Commission Presidency*, pp. 141–170; on Haferkamp, see for example 'Hey, Big Spender', *Economist*, 27 January 1979; see also S. van der Zee, 'Financiële capriolen van EG-commissaris mikpunt van kritiek', *NRC Handelsblad*, 31 January 1979.
2. Interaction with the Eastern Bloc and other parts of Europe are discussed in various parts of this book, first and foremost Chapter 2, 'Peace and Security'.
3. Möckli and Mauer, *European–American Relations and the Middle East*; Calandri, 'Understanding the EEC Mediterranean Policy'.
4. See Chapter 1, 'Europe and European Integration', in this volume.
5. Quoted from Kennedy, *Freedom from Fear*, p. 381.
6. See for example Lundestad, *The United States and Western Europe since 1945*, pp. 22–59; Winand, *Eisenhower, Kennedy, and the United States of Europe*, pp. 1–23.
7. Ferrell, 'The Truman Era and European Integration'; Neuss, *Geburtshelfer Europas?*, pp. 26–58; Schain, *The Marshall Plan*; on the period immediately before the US policy shift, see Weisbrode, *The Year of Indecision.*
8. Kissinger, *Diplomacy*, p. 821.
9. See for example DBPO, Series II, vol. 1, pp. 105–106, 128–129.
10. Schwabe, 'Ein Akt konstruktiver Staatskunst'; Romero, 'U.S. Attitudes towards Integration and Interdependence'; Bossuat and Vaicbourdt, *Etats-Unis, Europe et*

Union européenne; on EC competition law, see Leucht, 'Transatlantic Policy Networks in the Creation of the First European Anti-Trust Law'; Leucht and Marquis, 'American Influences on EEC Competition Law'.

11. Quote from Dulles, FRUS, 1952–1954, vol. V, part 1, p. 463; more generally, Neuss, *Geburtshelfer Europas?*, pp. 84–275; Lundestad, *The United States and Western Europe since 1945*, p. 80–83; Mélandri, 'Le rôle de l'unification européenne dans la politique extérieure des Etats-Unis 1948–1950'.
12. Giauque, *Grand Designs and Visions of Unity*, pp. 19–33; Neuss, *Geburtshelfer Europas?*, pp. 286–344.
13. FRUS, 1955–1957, vol. IV, part 1, p. 432; this source alone contains more than 300 pages on the topic.
14. FRUS, 1955–1957, vol. IV, part 1, p. 543: ('highly gratified'); NARA, RG 59/250/62/32/07, Box 2, State Department, Memorandum, undated [1957]: ('a truly historical event').
15. On the US Mission, see Winand, 'The US Mission to the EU in "Brussels D.C.", the European Commission Delegation in Washington D.C. and the New Transatlantic Agenda'; on the EC's representation in Washington, ibid. and Krumrey, *The Symbolic Politics of European Integration*, pp. 90–95.
16. See for example the accounts in the files of the State Department Bureau of European Affairs: NARA, RG 59/250/62/33/1–3, Boxes 2–15; NARA, RG 59/150/69/20/01, Boxes 23–24; NARA, RG 59/250/5/4/2.
17. Schwabe, *Jean Monnet*, pp. 19–74.
18. NARA, RG 59/250/62/33/1–3, Box 4, EEC, Mozer to US Mission Brussels, Zaglits, 3 June 1963.
19. NARA, RG 59/150/69/28/05–07, Box 5, US Mission Brussels, Fessenden to US Embassy Bonn, Hillenbrand, 30 January 1964; ibid., Box 6, US Mission Brussels, Fessenden to State Department, Hinton, 7 February 1964.
20. Krüger, *Sicherheit durch Integration?*, pp. 367–508; Dietl, *Emanzipation und Kontrolle*; Loth, *Der Weg nach Europa*.
21. On the latter, FRUS, 1961–1963, vol. XIII, for example pp. 162–165.
22. Servan-Schreiber, *The American Challenge*.
23. See for example a comparative study on non-tariff agricultural protectionism that was especially critical of the EC; BA/K, B 102, Deutsche Botschaft Washington an AA, 13 September 1963; more generally, Patel, *Europäisierung wider Willen*, pp. 237–251, there also on the aforementioned 'Chicken War', which is also discussed in Talbot, *The Chicken War*.
24. Kennedy quoted in Sorensen, *Kennedy*, p. 412.
25. See, from a French perspective, Bougeard, *René Pleven*, pp. 247–271.
26. Quoted in Pineau, *1956, Suez*, p. 191; on the wider context, see Loth, *Building Europe*, pp. 64–74; Bossuat, *Faire l'Europe sans défaire la France*, pp. 65–70; Thiemeyer, *Vom 'Pool Vert' zur Europäischen Wirtschaftsgemeinschaft*, pp. 218–223; Thiemeyer dates the breakthrough in the negotiations earlier, to September 1956.
27. Quoted in Monnet, *Memoirs*, p. 534.
28. Aubourg, Bossuat and Scott-Smith, *European Community, Atlantic Community?*; Scott-Smith and Aubourg, *Atlantic, Euratlantic, or Europe-America?*
29. Lundestad, *The United States and Western Europe since 1945*.
30. Hallstein, *Europe in the Making*, p. 21.
31. Mourlon-Druol, *A Europe Made of Money*; Zimmermann, *Money and Security*.

32. Conze, *Die gaullistische Herausforderung*; with a different interpretation, see Giauque, *Grand Designs and Visions of Unity*.
33. FRUS, 1969–1975, vol. E–15, part 2, pp. 36–37, here p. 37; a few years earlier Nixon was considerably more positive, see for example NARA, NP, NSC, CF-E, Box 682, Memorandum of Conversation, Nixon–Kiesinger, 8 August 1969; see also NARA, NP, NSC, VIP Visits, Talking Points for Visit of Kiesinger, undated [July or August 1969]; AAPD, 1969, pp. 906–909; see also Nichter, *Richard Nixon and Europe*.
34. Schulz and Schwartz, *The Strained Alliance*; on the document, see Chapter 2, 'Peace and Security', in this volume; for a relevant case study, see Bitumi, *Un ponte sull'Atlantico*.
35. Lundestad, *The United States and Western Europe since 1945*, p. 201.
36. See Chapter 2, 'Peace and Security', in this volume.
37. See the various contributions in Patel and Weisbrode, *European Integration and the Atlantic Community in the 1980s*; Westad, *The Cold War*, esp. pp. 516–526; on the summits, see Mourlon-Druol and Romero, *International Summitry and Global Governance*; see also Murray, 'View from the United States'.
38. See Articles 110–116, EEC Treaty, pp. 193–195.
39. Coppolaro, *The Making of a World Trading Power*; Zeiler, *American Trade and Power in the 1960s*; on the Dillon Round, Alkema, 'Regionalism in a Multilateral Framework'.
40. See for example TNA, FO 371/150287, US State Department, Dillon, to Dutch Foreign Minister, Luns, 15 April 1960; more generally, see Winand, *Eisenhower, Kennedy, and the United States of Europe*, pp. 112–114; Romero, 'Interdependence and Integration in American Eyes'.
41. JFKL, CAHF, Box 6, Background Paper on Erhard Visit, 19 September 1966; see also for example JFKL, WHSF, Box 8A, Scope Paper on Kennedy Round, 4 March 1964.
42. NL-HaNA, Buza, Code-archief 1965–1974, 2.05.313, inv. no. 15238, Concept-interventie Luns, undated [1967]; see also NL-HaNA, Buza, Code-archief 1965–1974, 2.05.313, inv. no. 15226.
43. Coppolaro, *The Making of a World Trading Power*; on agriculture Patel, *Europäisierung wider Willen*, pp. 345–357.
44. Gees, *Die Schweiz im Europäisierungsprozess*.
45. Winham, *International Trade and the Tokyo Round Negotiation*; Meunier, *Trading Voices*; Josling, Tangermann and Warley, *Agriculture in the GATT*.
46. See the extensive records in FRUS, 1977–1980, vol. 3, pp. 101–115; on the conflicts over Jenkins' role within the EC, see Ludlow, *Roy Jenkins and the European Commission Presidency*, pp. 101–109.
47. See Chapter 7, 'Disintegration and Dysfunctionality' in this volume.
48. See for example Davies, *Europe*, p. 1068.
49. Cooper, *Colonialism in Question*; Thomas, *Fight or Flight*.
50. https://bit.ly/2daphop (accessed 1 July 2019).
51. Laak, *Imperiale Infrastruktur*.
52. Coudenhove-Kalergi, *Pan-Europe*, p. 34; see also Coudenhove-Kalergi, *Das Wesen des Antisemitismus*.
53. Fundamental: Mazower, *Dark Continent*.
54. Beckert, 'American Danger'; Odijie, 'The Fear of "Yellow Peril" and the Emergence of European Federalist Movement'; Greiner, *Wege nach Europa*, pp. 244–351; see also Reinhard, *Die Unterwerfung der Welt*.

55. Hansen and Jonsson, *Eurafrica*, pp. 17–69, although they overstate the importance of the debate in the inter-war years; see also the contributions in Bitsch and Bossuat, *L'Europe unie et l'Afrique*.
56. Morone, *L'ultima colonia*.
57. Especially Cooper, *Citizenship between Empire and Nation*, pp. 202–210.
58. Kojève, 'Kolonialismus in europäischer Sicht', p. 136; on the wider context, see Montarsolo, *L'Eurafrique*.
59. Schmitt, 'Die Ordnung der Welt nach dem zweiten Weltkrieg', p. 27.
60. On this and other international organisations, see Hansen and Jonsson, *Eurafrica*, pp. 112–120.
61. Duranti, *The Conservative Human Rights Revolution*, pp. 197–210; Klose, *Menschenrechte im Schatten kolonialer Gewalt*; see also Schmale, 'Before Self-Reflexivity'.
62. Quoted from Richard, 'The Consultative Assembly of the Council of Europe as a Platform for African Interests'; on neoliberal criticism of Eurafrique, see Slobodian, *Globalists*, pp. 193–202.
63. Rempe, *Entwicklung im Konflikt*, pp. 36–37; Garavini, 'The European Community's Development Policy'; see also Hansen and Jonsson, *Eurafrica*.
64. Article 131, EEC Treaty, p. 200.
65. Vahsen, *Eurafrikanische Entwicklungskooperation*, pp. 55–107; Hansen and Jonsson, *Eurafrica*, pp. 147–238; Bitsch and Bossuat, *L'Europe unie et l'Afrique*; see also Adebajo and Whiteman, *The EU and Africa*.
66. Summary in Williams, *EU Human Rights Policies*, pp. 23–25; on France, see Montarsolo, *L'Eurafrique*, pp. 197–258.
67. See for example 'Frankrijk voelt in Eurafrika kans op nieuwe grootheid', *Nieuwsblad van het Noorden*, 17 January 1959; on the West German government's perspective, see for example, 172. Kabinettssitzung of 21 February 1957, in KPBR, vol. 10, pp. 154–162; PAAA, B 20–200/119, AA, Hartlieb, Aufzeichnung, 12 June 1958.
68. Translated from HKNAW, S00544, Drees, Coördinatie Commissie voor Integratie, Ter Behandeling in de ministerraad, 29 November 1956, online: https://bit.ly/2OBp8ya (accessed 1 July 2019); on the wider context, see de Bruin, *Elastisch Europa*, pp. 167–189; de Bruin, 'Indonesian Decolonisation and the Dutch Attitude towards the Establishment of the EEC's Association Policy'; see also Segers, *Reis naar het continent*, pp. 103–131.
69. Zischka, *Afrika*; on Zischka, see Laak, *Imperiale Infrastruktur*, pp. 345–349.
70. Contemporary: Wallerstein, *Africa*, pp. 141, 147; see also Schenk, 'Decolonization and European Economic Integration'; May, *Britain, the Commonwealth and Europe*.
71. Quoted from Martin, *Africa in World Politics*, p. 9; contemporary: see also Mazrui, 'African Attitudes to the European Economic Community'; now see also Gerits, 'When the Bull Elephants Fight'; Aqui, 'Macmillan, Nkrumah and the 1961 Application for European Economic Community Membership'.
72. Rempe, *Entwicklung im Konflikt*, pp. 42–52.
73. See for example PAAA, B 20–200/242, Dt. Botschaft Tunis, Gregor an AA, 23 January 1959.
74. As argued by Rempe, *Entwicklung im Konflikt*; for a different take, see for example Vahsen, *Eurafrikanische Entwicklungskooperation*; Migani, *La France et l'Afrique Sub-Saharienne*; see also the negotiations in DDF, 1960, Tome 1, pp. 584–599.

75. For greater detail on the negotiations, see for example Vahsen, *Eurafrikanische Entwicklungskooperation*; see also Zartman, *The Politics of Trade Negotiations between Africa and the European Economic Community*.
76. Heller, *The United Nations under Dag Hammarskjöld*, pp. 91–114.
77. Pasture, *Imagining European Unity since 1000 AD*, pp. 185–195; on the wider context, see Buettner, *Europe after Empire*; Nicolaïdis, Sèbe and Maas, *Echoes of Empire*.
78. Dimier, *The Invention of a European Development Aid Bureaucracy*; Turpin, 'Alle origini della politica europea di cooperazione allo sviluppo'.
79. Rempe, *Entwicklung im Konflikt*.
80. See the apposite US assessment in NARA, RG 59/250/62/33/1–3, Box 5, State Department, Hinton, Background Paper, 27 December 1963.
81. See for example NL-HaNA, Buza, Code-archief 1965–1974, 2.05.313, inv. no. 15233, Buza, Kennedy Ronde, F/7573/67, undated [1967]; see also NL-HaNA, Buza, Code-archief 1965–1974, 2.05.313, inv. no. 15230, Buza, van Schaik aan leden van de coördinatie Commissie, 28 May 1967 met bijlage.
82. On the EC's market organisation, see BA/K, B 136/3546, Ständige Vertretung der Bundesrepublik bei der EG, Sachs, an AA, 24 July 1966; on Senegal and these issues more broadly, see Rempe, 'Decolonization by Europeanization?'; Rempe, 'Airy Promises'.
83. See also Vahsen, *Eurafrikanische Entwicklungskooperation*, pp. 37, 247–261.
84. Garavini, 'The European Community's Development Policy'; more generally, see Garavini, *Dopo gli imperi*.
85. Spinelli, *L'Europa non cade dal cielo*, p. 295.
86. Vahsen, *Eurafrikanische Entwicklungskooperation*, pp. 175–177, 223–233.
87. Vahsen, *Eurafrikanische Entwicklungskooperation*, pp. 333–392; Bartels, 'The Trade and Development Policy of the European Union', pp. 726–728.
88. Dinkel, *Die Bewegung Bündnisfreier Staaten*, pp. 149–242.
89. For example, on the Dutch preparations for the talks, see HKNAW, Z00095, Ministerraad, Notulen, 18 July 1974, online: https://bit.ly/2Mv1bpj (accessed 1 July 2019).
90. On the preparation phase, see for example CMA, CM6 EAMA, ACP ACP.4.1–11; CMA, CM6 EAMA, ACP ACP.6.1–5; literature: Dimier, *The Invention of a European Development Aid Bureaucracy*; Gilman, 'The New International Economic Order'; Dann, *Entwicklungsverwaltungsrecht*, pp. 65–70; Migani, 'Lomé and the North–South Relations'; Migani, 'The EEC and the Challenge of the ACP States' Industrialization'; Palayret, 'Mondialisme contre régionalisme'; Dimier, *Eurafrica and Its Business*.
91. Garavini, *Dopo gli imperi*, pp. 149–188.
92. Calandri, 'Understanding the EEC Mediterranean Policy'.
93. Dann, *Entwicklungsverwaltungsrecht*, pp. 65–70.
94. Migani, 'Lomé and the North–South Relations'; on the wider context, see for example, Gilman, 'The New International Economic Order'.
95. Gerlach, 'Fortress Europe'; Patel, *Europäisierung wider Willen*, pp. 446–452; Baldwin, 'Regulatory Protectionism, Developing Nations, and a Two-Tier World Trade System'; Cosgrove-Sacks, 'Europe, Diplomacy and Development Co-operation with the ACP Group', pp. 272–276; on the United States and Japan, see for example Maswood, *Trade, Development and Globalization*, pp. 69–71.
96. Ferrari, 'The European Community as a Promoter of Human Rights in Africa and Latin America'; Lister, *The European Community and the Developing World*; Grilli, *The European Community and the Developing Countries*, pp. 35–43.

97. Gundlach, Hiemenz, Langhammer and Nunnenkamp, *Regional Integration in Europe and Its Effects on Developing Countries*, p. 8.
98. Elgström, 'Lomé and Post-Lomé', p. 178.
99. Grilli, *The European Community and the Developing Countries*, pp. 225–290; on Spain, which from the mid-1980s advocated especially for closer relations with Latin America, see Sotillo, 'América Latina en las negociaciones del ingreso de *España* en la Comunidad Europea'.
100. https://ec.europa.eu/europeaid/regions/octs_en (accessed 1 July 2019); as well as Greenland, these today include the Falkland Islands, Curaçao and Aruba.
101. Quoted from McIntosh, *Japan Re-armed*, p. 132; see also for example Theo Sommer, 'Unbehagen unterm Sonnenbanner', *Zeit*, 7 June 1991.
102. 'Grausam, aber gut', *Spiegel*, 26 May 1969.
103. Gilson, *Japan and the European Union*, pp. 11–22; Rothacher, *Economic Diplomacy between the European Community and Japan*, esp. pp. 132–133; Rothacher, 'The EC and Japan'.
104. Rothacher, *Economic Diplomacy between the European Community and Japan*, pp. 83–143; Rothacher, 'The EC and Japan'.
105. Suzuki, 'Negotiating the Japan–EC Trade Conflict'; Hardy, '1970–1982'.
106. Möhler and van Rij, '1983–1987'; Suzuki, 'Negotiating the Japan–EC Trade Conflict'; Keck, '1987–1990'. Vehicles produced within the EC were also affected by Italian restrictions, see Jones and North, 'Japanese Motor Industry Transplants'.
107. Quoted from Hardy, '1970–1982', p. 34.
108. Rothacher, 'Europa–Giappone'; see also Möhler and van Rij, '1983–1987'; Frattolillo, *Diplomacy in Japan–EU Relations*, pp. 45–51.
109. Mourlon-Druol, 'Steering Europe'.
110. Bussière, 'Devising a Strategy' (esp. the contribution by Sigfrido Ramírez-Pérez on pp. 274–275); Fridenson, 'Stratégies des groupes automobiles et structure du marché en Europe 1979–1992'; van Laer, 'Forschung'; for a Japanese perspective on the car talks, see Abe, *Japan and the European Union*, esp. pp. 55–85; for an example of lobbying, see PAAA, Zwischenarchiv, 130399, CCMC/CLCA, Pressemitteilung, 20 May 1986.
111. Quoted from Scott, 'China–EU Convergence 1957–2003', p. 218; also see Fardella, 'The EC and China'.
112. Quoted from Scott, 'China–EU Convergence 1957–2003', p. 218.
113. Chenard, 'The European Community's Policy towards the People's Republic of China'; Albers, 'Partners but not Allies'; Möller, 'Diplomatic Relations and Mutual Strategic Perceptions'; on technology imports, see Zuqian, 'China's Commercial Relations with Europe', pp. 235–236; see also Kapur, *China and the European Economic Community*.
114. See figures in Redmond and Lan, 'The European Community and China', pp. 144, 149; Fardella, 'The EC and China'.
115. Möller, 'Diplomatic Relations and Mutual Strategic Perceptions'; see also COM (1995) 279 final.
116. De Gaulle, *Discours et messages*, 1962–1965, pp. 222–237, here p. 228 (23 July 1964).
117. HAEU, BAC 48/1984, 235, Commission of the EC, DG for External Relations, I–A, General Background Brief, 1 April 1977.
118. On the comment attributed to Kissinger, see Markus C. Schulte von Drach, 'Wen ruft man an, wenn man die EU anruft?', *Süddeutsche Zeitung*, 12 December 2012.

119. See for example Galtung, *The European Community*; Kohnstamm and Hager, *A Nation Writ Large?*; Duchêne, 'Europe's Role in World Peace'; de la Serre, 'Foreign Policy of the European Community'.
120. Jones and North, 'Japanese Motor Industry Transplants', p. 188.

Epilogue

1. 'Vele journalisten en politici geveld door Eurotop-ziekte', *Limburgs Dagblad*, 26 March 1981; on the medical aspect, see Beckers et al., 'Twee explosies van Salmonella indiana te Maastricht'.
2. 'Eurotop Maastricht ontsnapt aan voedselvergiftiging', *Nieuwsblad van het Noorden*, 28 December 1992.
3. See for example Dinan, *Ever Closer Union*, p. 136; Winkler, *Geschichte des Westens*, vol. 4, p. 19.
4. NL-HaNA, PV EG Brussel, 2.05.281, inv. no. 15, Europa Instituut, University of Amsterdam, the Dutch and the Presidency, July 1983.
5. Bulletin der EG, 3/1981, Conclusions of the Maastricht European Council; CMA, CM2 CEE, CEAA, 1981 1.1–4, esp. CMA, CM2 CEE, CEAA, 1981 1.4, General Secretariat of the Council, Note for the file, 30 March 1981; on Dutch planning, see NL-HaNA, PV EG Brussel, 2.05.281, inv. no. 14.
6. Ludlow, 'European Integration in the 1980s'; on the negotiations, see Dyson and Featherstone, *The Road to Maastricht*; James, *Making the European Monetary Union*.
7. Lappenküper, 'Hans-Dietrich Genscher, Emilio Colombo und der Kampf gegen die "Eurosklerose"'; Cuccia, 'The Genscher–Colombo Plan'; Bonvicini, 'The Genscher–Colombo Plan and the "Solemn Declaration on European Union"'.
8. Puetter, 'Europe's Deliberative Intergovernmentalism'; Bickerton, Hodson and Puetter, 'The New Intergovernmentalism'.
9. Mourlon-Druol, 'Steering Europe'.
10. CMA, CM2 CEE, CEAA, 1981, 1.4, General Secretariat of the Council, Note for the file, 30 March 1981.
11. Winkler, *Geschichte des Westens*, vol. 4, esp. pp. 152–164; see also Geppert, *Ein Europa, das es nicht gibt*; Brunnermeier, James and Landau, *The Euro and the Battle of Ideas*.
12. Dinan, 'From Treaty Revision to Treaty Revision'. For the sake of completeness mention must also be made of the Treaty on the Functioning of the European Union, whose origins also lie in the original EEC Treaty.
13. Paradoxically, the history of European integration since the end of the Cold War has been treated more thoroughly than, for example, developments during the 1980s; see for instance Wirsching, *Der Preis der Freiheit*, pp. 153–225; Rödder, *21.0.*, pp. 266–337.
14. De Witte, Ott and Vos, *Between Flexibility and Disintegration*; Fossum, 'Democracy and Differentiation in Europe'.
15. Bröckling, *Gute Hirten führen sanft*, pp. 113–139; see also for example Höhler, 'Resilienz'; Walker and Cooper, 'Genealogies of Resilience'.
16. See also for example Jean-Claude Juncker's concept of 'polycrisis': http://europa.eu/rapid/press-release_SPEECH-16-2293_de.htm (accessed 1 July 2019).
17. Mazower, *Dark Continent*.
18. Pocock, 'The Atlantic Archipelago and the War of the Three Kingdoms', p. 78.

19. See also Hooghe and Marks, 'A Postfunctionalist Theory of European Integration'.
20. *Eurobarometer* 89, 2 (2018), esp. pp. 22–25.
21. See Winkler, *Geschichte des Westens*, vol. 3, p. 1060.
22. Or, as Nigel Farage put it in the Brexit referendum campaign: 'Membership of this union stops us acting in our own national interest, forcing us to be represented by unelected old men in Brussels.' *Daily Express*, 21 June 2016.
23. Meunier and Nicolaïdis, 'The European Union as a Trade Power'; Larik, 'No Mixed Feelings'.
24. Koselleck, *Futures Past*, pp. 36–42; Herzog, 'Historia magistra vitae'; Repgen, 'Vom Nutzen der Historie'; Hölscher, *Die Entdeckung der Zukunft*.
25. On Dahrendorf in Brussels, see Meifort, *Ralf Dahrendorf*, pp. 190–197.

BIBLIOGRAPHY

1. Archival Materials

Belgium

Commission Européenne, Archives Historiques, Brussels (CEAH)

Council of Ministers Archives, Brussels (CMA)

Germany

Archiv für Christlich-Demokratische Politik der Konrad-Adenauer Stiftung, St. Augustin (ACDP)
NL 01–283 (Fritz Neef Papers)

Archiv der sozialen Demokratie der Friedrich-Ebert-Stiftung, Bonn (AdsD)
PV (Parteivorstand)

Bundesarchiv Koblenz (BA/K)
B 102 (Bundesministerium für Wirtschaft)
B 116 (Bundesministerium für Ernährung, Landwirtschaft und Forsten)
B 136 (Bundeskanzleramt)

Politisches Archiv des Auswärtigen Amtes, Berlin (PAAA)
B 130 (Verschlusssachen)
B 20–200 (Referat 200, later renamed to IA2)
B 30 (Vereinte Nationen)
Zwischenarchiv

France

Archives Nationales (AN), Site Pierrefitte-sur-Saine

Archives Diplomatiques (AD), La Courneuve

Italy

Historical Archives of the European Union, Florence (HAEU)
AH (Assemblée ad hoc)
BAC (CEE/CEEA Commissions – Fonds BAC)
CEAB (Haute Autorité CECA)
CM2 (Conseil des ministres CEE et Euratom)
EN (Emile Noël Papers)
FD (Fernand Dehousse Papers)
GR (Georges Rencki Papers)
INT 231 (Interview Eduardo Peña Abizanda)
KM (Klaus Meyer Papers)
MAEF (Ministère des affaires étrangères français)
MK (Max Kohnstamm Papers)
OEEC (Organization for European Economic Co-operation)
PEO (Assemblée parlementaire européenne et Parlement européen avant l'élection directe)
PM (Piero Malvestiti Papers)
UEF (Union européenne des fédéralistes)

Netherlands

Nationaal Archief, Den Haag (NL-HaNA)
Ministerie van Buitenlandse Zaken (Buza)
Nederlandse Permanente Vertegenwoordiging bij de Europese Gemeenschappen te Brussel (PV EG Brussel)

Huygens, KNAW, Nederland en de Europese integratie, 1950–1986 (HKNAW, online collection of documents from Dutch archives)

Norway

Arbeiderbevegelsens Arkiv og Bibliotek, Oslo (AAB)
Aake Anker-Ording Papers

United Kingdom

The National Archives of the United Kingdom, Kew (TNA)
DG (Records of International Organisations)
FCO (Foreign and Commonwealth Office)
FO (Foreign Office)
FV (Department of Trade and Industry and Department of Trade)
PREM (Records of the Prime Minister's Office)
T (Treasury)

Churchill Archives Centre (CAC), Cambridge
DSND (Duncan Sandys Papers)

United States of America

National Archives and Record Administration, College Park, MD (NARA)
RG 59 (Department of State Central Files)
Nixon Papers (NP, now at Nixon Library, Yorba Linda, CA)

John F. Kennedy Library, Boston, MA (JFKL)
Christian A. Herter Files (CAHF)
Papers of President John F. Kennedy, White House Staff Files (WHSF)

2. Official Printed Material and Edited Sources

Endnote entries beginning with the capital letters L or C, or taking the form 1408/71/EEC originate from the *Official Journal of the European Union* (see below), or its predecessors. The *Official Journal* is available online and the individual documents are not listed in the bibliography. Newspaper articles, decisions of the ECJ and rulings of the German Federal Constitutional Court (Bundesverfassungsgericht, BVerG) are cited in the usual form in the endnotes but not listed in the bibliography. Certain EU documents that are available online are also cited directly in the notes.

Akten zur Auswärtigen Politik der Bundesrepublik Deutschland, ed. by Institut für Zeitgeschichte (Munich: Oldenbourg, various years). (=AAPD)
Bulletin des Presse- und Informationsamtes der Bundesregierung, ed. by Bundesregierung (Bonn: Deutscher Bundesverlag, various years).
Bulletin of the European Communities, Supplements, ed. by European Commission (Luxembourg: Office for Official Publications of the EC, various years).
Bundesrepublik Deutschland und Frankreich: Dokumente 1949–1963, ed. by Horst Möller and Klaus Hildebrand, 4 vols. (Munich: K. G. Saur, 1997–1999). (=BDFD)

Commission des Communautés Européennes, *Les Européens et l'unification de l'Europe* (Brussels: European Commission, 1972).
Commission of the EC, *General Report on the Activities of the European Communities* (Luxembourg: Office for Official Publications of the European Communities, various years).
Commission of the European Communities, *SEC(89) 2290 final: Commission Opinion on Turkey's Request for Accession to the Community* (Luxembourg: Office for Official Publications of the EC, 1989).
Commission of the European Communities, *The European Community and the Textile Arrangements* (Luxembourg: Office for Official Publications of the EC, 1979).
Die große Politik der europäischen Kabinette, 1871–1914, vol. 2, ed. by Johannes Lepsius, Albrecht Mendelssohn Bartholdy and Friedrich Thimme (Berlin: Deutsche Verlags-Gesellschaft für Politik und Geschichte, 1927).
Documenti sulla politica internazionale dell'Italia, Series A: Il Rilancio dell'Europa dalla conferenza di Messina ai trattati di Roma, ed. by Ministerio degli affari esteri e della cooperazione internazionale (Rome: Istituto poligrafico e zecca dello stato, 2017). (=DPII)
Documents Diplomatiques Français, ed. by Ministère des affaires étrangères, Commission de publication des documents français (Paris: Imprimerie nationale, various years). (=DDF)
Documents on British Policy Overseas, ed. by Roger Bullen et al. (London: Her Majesty's Stationery Office, various years). (=DBPO)
Documents on European Integration, ed. by Anjo G. Harryvan and Jan van der Harst (Houndmills: Macmillan, 1997).
EGKS, Hohe Behörde, *Die E.G.K.S. 1952–1962. Die ersten 10 Jahre einer Teilintegration* (Luxembourg: EGKS, 1963).
Eurobarometer, ed. by European Commission (Luxembourg: Office for Official Publications of the European Communities, various years).
Europa-Archiv, ed. by Deutsche Gesellschaft für Auswärtige Politik (Bonn: Deutsche Gesellschaft für Auswärtige Politik, various years).
Europäische Kommission, *Außen- und Intrahandel der Europäischen Union – Statistisches Jahrbuch, Daten 1958–2001* (Luxembourg: Amt für amtliche Veröffentlichungen der EG, 2002).
European Commission, *35 Years of Eurobarometer: European Integration as seen by Public Opinion in the Member States of the European Union, 1973–2008* (Luxembourg: Office for Official Publications of the European Communities, 2008).
European Commission, DG for Economic and Financial Affairs, *The Economics of 1992: An Assessment of the Potential Economic Effects of Completing the Internal Market of the European Community (Emerson Report)*, CB-AR-88–035-EN-C, 1988.
European Convention, *Draft Treaty Establishing a Constitution for Europe* (Luxembourg: Office for Official Publications of the European Communities, 2003).
European Parliament/CARDOC, *Ein Europa der Rechte: Geschichte der europäischen Charta* (Luxembourg: Office for Publications of the EU, 2012).
European Parliament, Débats. *Compte rendu in extenso des séances* (Luxembourg: Office for Official Publications of the European Communities, various years). (=EP, Débats).
European Union, *The EU in the World. 2016 Edition* (Luxembourg: Publications Office of the European Union, 2016).
European Union Agency for Fundamental Rights, *The European Union as a Community of Values: Safeguarding Fundamental Rights in Times of Crisis* (Luxembourg: Office for Official Publications of the EU, 2013).

Eurostat, *External and Intra-European Union Trade. Statistical Yearbook – Data 1958–2006* (Luxembourg: Office for Official Publications of the European Communities, 2008).
Eurostat, *Revue 1977–1986* (Luxembourg: Statistical Office of the EC, 1988).
Foreign Relations of the United States, ed. by U.S. Department of State (Washington, DC: United States Government Printing Office, various years). (=FRUS)
Grondwet en Statuut voor het Koninkrijk der Nederlanden (1963), ed. by E. van Raalte (Alphen aan den Rijn: N. Samson N.V., 1964).
Hansard: Official Report of Parliamentary Debates, United Kingdom (London: HMSO, various years).
Jahrbuch der öffentlichen Meinung, ed. by Elisabeth Noelle and Erich Peter Neumann (Allensbach: Verlag für Demoskopie, various years).
Kabinettsprotokolle der Bundesregierung, ed. for the Bundesarchiv by Hans Booms et al. (Munich: Oldenbourg, various years). (=KPBR)
Kommentar zum EWG-Vertrag, ed. by Hans von der Groeben and Hans von Boeckh, 2 vols. (Baden-Baden: Verlag August Lutzeyer, 1958/1960).
League of Nations, Circular Concerning Programmes of Important Public Works, C.736. M341, 9.10.1931.
League of Nations, Report on the First Two Sessions of the Committee, C.381. M214.1932.VIII.
Lipgens, Walter (ed.), *Documents on the History of European Integration*, 4 vols. (Berlin: Walter de Gruyter, 1985–1991).
OECD, *OECD Historical Statistics, 1960–1997* (Paris: OECD, 1999).
Official Journal of the European Union, ed. by the European Union (Brussels: Office for Official Publications of the EU, various years).
Rapport des chefs de délégation aux ministres des affaires étrangères, ed. by the Comité intergouvernemental créé par la conference de Messine (Brussels: Comité, 1956).
Rat der EG, *Protokolle zum Kooperationsabkommen EW–Algerien sowie andere grundlegende Texte* (Luxembourg: Amt für amtliche Veröffentlichungen der EG, 1990).
Statistisches Amt der EG, *Die Wirtschaftsrechnungen der Arbeiterfamilien der EGKS 1956/57* (Luxembourg: Statistisches Amt der EG, 1960).
Statistisches Amt der EG, *Jahrbuch der Industriestatistik* (Luxembourg: Amt für amtliche Veröffentlichungen der EG, various years).
Statistisches Amt der EG, *Statistische Informationen 6/1960* (Brussels: Statistisches Amt der EG, 1960).
Statistisches Amt der EG, *Volkswirtschaftliche Gesamtrechnungen 1957–1966* (Brussels: Statistisches Amt der EG, 1967).
www.cvce.eu with several original sources (accessed 1 July 2019).
Yearbook of International Organizations (Brussels: Union of International Associations, various years).

3. Literature

Abe, Atsuko, *Japan and the European Union: Domestic Politics and Transnational Relations* (London: Athlone Press, 1999).
Adebajo, Adekeye and Kaye Whiteman (eds.), *The EU and Africa: From Eurafrique to Afro-Europa* (New York: Columbia University Press, 2012).
Adi, Hakim and Marika Sherwood, *Pan-African History: Political Figures from Africa and the Diaspora since 1787* (London: Routledge, 2003).
Albers, Martin, 'Partners but not Allies: West European Co-Operation with China, 1978–1982', in: *Diplomacy & Statecraft* 25 (2014), 688–707.

Aldrin, Philippe, 'L'Invention de l'opinion publique européenne. Genèse intellectuelle et politique de l'Eurobaromètre (1950–1973)', in: *Politix* 89 (2010), 79–101.

Ali, Tariq, *The Coming British Revolution* (London: Cape, 1972).

Alkema, Ynze, 'Regionalism in a Multilateral Framework: The EEC, the United States and the GATT Confronting Trade Policies, 1957–1962' (unpubl. PhD thesis, European University Institute, Florence, 1997).

Alker, Hayward and Donald Puchala, 'Trends in Economic Partnership: The North Atlantic Area, 1928–1963', in: J. David Singer (ed.), *Quantitative International Politics: Insights and Evidence* (New York: Free Press, 1968), 287–316.

Allen, Chris, Michael Gasiorek and Alasdair Smith, 'The Competition Effects of the Single Market in Europe', in: *Economic Policy* 27 (1998), 439–486.

Allers, Robin M., *Besondere Beziehungen. Deutschland, Norwegen und Europa in der Ära Brandt (1966–1974)* (Bonn: Dietz, 2009).

Almond, Gabriel A., *The American People and Foreign Policy* (New York: Praeger, 1960).

Ambrosius, Gerold, *Wirtschaftsraum Europa. Vom Ende der Nationalökonomien* (Frankfurt am Main: Fischer, 1998).

Ambrosius, Gerold and William H. Hubbard, *A Social and Economic History of Twentieth-Century Europe* (Cambridge, MA: Harvard University Press, 1989).

Anderson, Christopher J. and Karl C. Kaltenthaler, 'The Dynamics of Public Opinion toward European Integration, 1973–93', in: *European Journal of International Relations* 2 (1996), 175–199.

Anderson, David and Cian C. Murphy, 'The Charter of Fundamental Rights', in: Andrea Biondi, Piet Eeckhout and Stefanie Ripley (eds.), *EU Law after Lisbon* (Oxford: Oxford University Press, 2012), 155–179.

Andresen-Leitão, Nicolau, 'Portugal's European Integration Policy, 1947–72', in: *Journal of European Integration History* 7 (2001), 25–35.

Anonymous, *Paneuropa Union* (Vienna: Paneuropa Verlag, no date).

Aqui, Lindsay, 'Macmillan, Nkrumah and the 1961 Application for European Economic Community Membership', in: *International History Review* 39 (2017), 575–591.

Aschmann, Birgit, 'The Reliable Ally: Germany Supports Spain's European Integration Efforts, 1957–67', in: *Journal of European Integration History* 7 (2001), 37–52.

Aubourg, Valérie, Gérard Bossuat and Giles Scott-Smith (eds.), *European Community, Atlantic Community?* (Paris: Soleb, 2008).

Badel, Laurence, 'Les promoteurs français d'une union économique et douanière de l'Europe dans l'entre-deux-guerres', in: Antoine Fleury and Lubor Jílek (eds.), *Le Plan Briand d'Union fédérale européenne: Perspectives nationales et transnationales, avec documents* (Bern: Peter Lang, 1998), 17–29.

Badel, Laurence, Stanislas Jeannesson and N. Piers Ludlow (eds.), *Les administrations nationales et la construction européenne: Une approche historique (1919–1975)* (Brussels: Peter Lang, 2005).

Badinger, Harald, 'Growth Effects of Economic Integration: Evidence from the EU Member States', in: *Review of World Economics* 141 (2005), 50–78.

Badinger, Harald and Fritz Breuss, 'The Quantitative Effects of European Post-War Economic Integration', in: Miroslav N. Jovanović (ed.), *International Handbook on the Economics of Integration*, vol. III (Cheltenham: Edward Elgar, 2011), 285–315.

Bailes, Alyson J. K. and Graham Messervy-Whiting, *Death of an Institution: The End for Western European Union, a Future for European Defence?* (Gent: Academia Press, 2011).

Bairoch, Paul, *Victoires et déboires. Histoire économique et sociale du monde du XVIe siècle à nos jours*, vol. III (Paris: Gallimard, 1997).

Balassa, Béla, 'Trade Creation and Diversion in the European Common Market: An Appraisal of the Evidence', in Béla Balassa (ed.), *European Economic Integration* (Amsterdam: North-Holland Publishing Company, 1975), 79–118.

Baldwin, Richard E., 'Regulatory Protectionism, Developing Nations, and a Two-Tier World Trade System', in: *Brookings Trade Forum* (2000), 237–293.

Barbier, Jean-Claude, *The Road to Social Europe: A Contemporary Approach to Political Cultures and Diversity in Europe* (London: Routledge, 2013).

Bariéty, Jacques and Jean-Paul Bled (eds.), 'Du Plan Fouchet au Traité franco-allemand de janvier 1963', in: *Revue d'Allemagne et des Pays de Langue Allemande* 29, 2 (1997) (special issue).

Barnard, Catherine, *The Substantive Law of the EU: The Four Freedoms*, 4th ed. (Oxford: Oxford University Press, 2013).

Barre, Raymond, 'Grand Témoin', in: Serge Bernstein and Jean-François Sirinelli (eds.), *Les années Giscard. Valéry Giscard d'Estaing et l'Europe, 1974–1981* (Paris: Armand Colin, 2006), 132–137.

Bartels, Lorand, *Human Rights Conditionality in the EU's International Agreements* (Oxford: Oxford University Press, 2005).

Bartels, Lorand, 'The Trade and Development Policy of the European Union', in: *European Journal of International Law* 18 (2007), 715–756.

Basosi, Duccio, 'The European Community and International Reaganomics, 1981–85', in: Kiran Klaus Patel and Kenneth Weisbrode (eds.), *European Integration and the Atlantic Community in the 1980s* (Cambridge: Cambridge University Press, 2013), 133–153.

Bautz, Ingo, 'Die Auslandsbeziehungen der deutschen Kommunen im Rahmen der europäischen Kommunalbewegung in den 1950er und 1960er Jahren' (unpubl. PhD diss., Siegen University, 2002).

Bayoumi, Tamim and Barry Eichengreen, 'Is Regionalism Simply a Diversion? Evidence from the Evolution of the EC and EFTA', in: NBER Working Paper, No. 5283 (1995).

Beckers, H. J. et al., 'Twee explosies van Salmonella indiana te Maastricht; een overzicht van de salmonellose ten tijde van de Eurotop-conferentie', in: *Nederlands Tijdschrift voor Geneeskunde* 126 (1982), 1305–1311.

Beckert, Sven, 'American Danger: United States Empire, Eurafrica, and the Territorialization of Industrial Capitalism, 1870–1950', in: *American Historical Review* 122 (2017), 1137–1170.

Ben Bella, Ahmed, *Discours du Président Ben Bella: Du 28 Septembre au 12 Décembre 1962* (Algiers: Publication du Ministère de l'information, 1963).

Berend, Ivan T., *An Economic History of Twentieth-Century Europe: Economic Regimes from Laissez-faire to Globalization* (Cambridge: Cambridge University Press, 2006).

Berend, Ivan T., 'A Restructured Economy: From the Oil Crisis to the Financial Crisis, 1973–2009', in: Dan Stone (ed.), *The Oxford Handbook of Postwar European History* (Oxford: Oxford University Press, 2012), 406–422.

Bergeron, James Henry, 'An Ever Whiter Myth: The Colonization of Modernity in European Community Law', in: Peter Fitzpatrick and James Henry Bergeron (eds.), *Europe's Other: European Law between Modernity and Postmodernity* (Aldershot: Asghate, 1998), 3–26.

Berlinghoff, Marcel, *Das Ende der 'Gastarbeit'. Europäische Anwerbestopps 1970–1974* (Paderborn: Schöningh, 2013).

Bickerton, Christopher J., Dermot Hodson and Uwe Puetter, 'The New Intergovernmentalism: European Integration in the Post-Maastricht Era', in: *Journal of Common Market Studies* 53 (2015), 703–722.

Biermann, Rafael and Joachim A. Koops (eds.), *Palgrave Handbook of Inter-Organizational Relations in World Politics* (New York: Palgrave Macmillan, 2017).

Bitsch, Marie-Thérèse (ed.), *Jalons pour une histoire du Conseil de l'Europe: Actes du Colloque de Strasbourg, 8–10 juin 1995* (Brussels: Peter Lang, 1997).
Bitsch, Marie-Thérèse and Gérard Bossuat (eds.), *L'Europe unie et l'Afrique. De l'idée d'Eurafrique à la convention de Lomé* I (Brussels: Bruylant, 2005).
Bitsch, Marie-Thérèse, Wilfried Loth and Charles Barthel (eds.), *Cultures politiques, opinion publiques et intégration européenne* (Brussels: Bruylant, 2007).
Bitumi, Alessandra, *Un ponte sull'Atlantico. Il 'Programma di visitatori' e la diplomazia pubblica della Comunità europea negli anni Settanta* (Bologna: Il Mulino, 2014).
Bitumi, Alessandra, 'An Uplifting Tale of Europe: Jacques Delors and the Commitment to Social Europe', in: *Journal of Transatlantic Studies* 16 (2018), 203–221.
Bleckmann, Albert, 'Zur Rechtmäßigkeit der EG-Sanktionen gegen Argentinien nach allgemeinem Völkerrecht und dem Recht der Europäischen Gemeinschaft', in: Georg Ress and Michael R. Will (eds.), *Vorträge, Reden und Berichte aus dem Europa-Institut der Universität des Saarlandes*, vol. 4 (Saarbrücken: Europainstitut, 1982), 3–31.
Bloch, Ernst, *The Principle of Hope*, vol. 2 (Oxford: Blackwell, 1986).
Boel, Bent, 'The European Productivity Agency, 1953–1961', in: Richard Griffiths (ed.), *Explorations in OEEC History* (Paris: OECD, 1997), 113–122.
Bogdandy, Armin von, 'The Preamble', in: Bruno de Witte (ed.), *Ten Reflections on the Constitutional Treaty for Europe* (Florence: EUI, 2003), 3–10.
Boltho, Andrea, 'Growth', in: Andrea Boltho (ed.), *The European Economy: Growth and Crisis* (Oxford: Oxford University Press, 1982), 9–37.
Bonvicini, Gianni, 'The Genscher–Colombo Plan and the "Solemn Declaration on European Union": (1981–1983)', in: Roy Pryce (ed.), *The Dynamics of European Union* (London: Routledge, 1989), 174–187.
Börzel, Tanja A., 'Why There Is No 'Southern Problem': On Environmental Leaders and Laggards in the European Union', in: *Journal of European Public Policy* 7 (2000), 141–162.
Börzel, Tanja A. and Thomas Risse, 'Three Cheers for Comparative Regionalism', in: Tanja A. Börzel and Thomas Risse (eds.), *Oxford Handbook of Comparative Regionalism* (Oxford: Oxford University Press, 2016), 621–649.
Bossuat, Gérard, *Faire l'Europe sans défaire la France. 60 ans de politique d'unité européenne des gouvernements et des présidents de la République française (1943–2003)* (Brussels: Peter Lang, 2005).
Bossuat, Gérard, 'Histoire d'une controverse. La référence aux héritages spirituels dans la Constitution européenne', in: *Matériaux pour l'Histoire de Notre Temps* 78 (2005), 68–82.
Bossuat, Gérard and Nicolas Vaicbourdt (eds.), *Etats-Unis, Europe et Union européenne. Histoire et avenir d'un partenariat difficile (1945–1999)* (Brussels: Peter Lang, 2001).
Bosworth, Albert B., 'The Historical Context of Thucydides' Funeral Oration', in: *Journal of Hellenic Studies* 120 (2000), 1–16.
Bougeard, Christian, *René Pleven: Un Français libre en politique* (Rennes: Presses universitaires de Rennes, 1994).
Bourdet, Claude, Henri Frenay and André Hauriou, 'Das "Combat"-Programm', in: Walter Lipgens (ed.), *Europa-Föderationspläne der Widerstandsbewegungen 1940–1945. Eine Dokumentation* (Munich: Oldenbourg, 1968), 197.
Boyer, Frederic and J. P. Sallé, 'The Liberalization of Intra-European Trade in the Framework of OEEC', in: *Staff Papers* (International Monetary Fund) 4 (1955), 179–216.
Bozo, Frédéric, *Mitterrand, la fin de la guerre froide et l'unification allemande: De Yalta à Maastricht* (Paris: Odile Jacob, 2005).
Brandt, Willy, *Berliner Ausgabe*, vol. 9: *Die Entspannung unzerstörbar machen*, redacted by Frank Fischer, ed. by Helga Grebing, Gregor Schöllgen and Heinrich August Winkler (Bonn: Dietz, 2003).

Brenke, Gabiele, 'Europakonzeptionen im Widerstreit. Die Freihandelszonenverhandlungen 1956–1958', in: *Vierteljahrshefte für Zeitgeschichte* 42 (1994), 595–633.

Brill, Ariane, *Abgrenzung und Hoffnung. 'Europa' in der deutschen, britischen und amerikanischen Presse 1945–1980* (Göttingen: Wallstein, 2014).

Brinkley, Douglas, *Dean Acheson: The Cold War Years, 1953–71* (New Haven, CT: Yale University Press, 1992).

Bröckling, Ulrich, *Gute Hirten führen sanft. Über Menschenregierungskünste* (Frankfurt am Main: Suhrkamp, 2017).

Brunnermeier, Markus K., Harold James and Jean-Pierre Landau, *The Euro and the Battle of Ideas* (Princeton, NJ: Princeton University Press, 2016).

Brusse, Wendy Asbeek, 'The Failure of European Tariff Plans in GATT (1951–1954)', in: Gilbert Trausch (ed.), *Die Europäische Integration vom Schuman-Plan bis zu den Verträgen von Rom: Pläne und Initiativen, Enttäuschungen und Mißerfolge* (Baden-Baden: Nomos, 1993), 99–114.

Buchanan, Tom, 'Human Rights, the Memory of War and the Making of a "European" Identity, 1945–75', in: Martin Conway and Kiran Klaus Patel (eds.), *Europeanisation in the Twentieth Century: Historical Approaches* (Basingstoke: Palgrave Macmillan, 2010), 157–171.

Buettner, Elizabeth, *Europe after Empire: Decolonization, Society and Culture* (Cambridge: Cambridge University Press, 2016).

Buiter, Harm, 'Le point de vue des Syndicats Libres', in: *Les élections européennes au suffrage universel direct* (Brussels: Editions de l'Institut de Sociologie Solvay, 1960), 145–148.

Bull, Hedley, 'Civilian Power Europe: A Contradiction in Terms?', in: *Journal of Common Market Studies* 21 (1982), 149–164.

Burbank, Jane and Frederick Cooper, *Empires in World History: Power and the Politics of Difference* (Princeton, NJ: Princeton University Press, 2010).

Bussière, Eric, 'Devising a Strategy: The Internal Market and Industrial Policy', in: Eric Bussière et al. (eds.), *The European Commission 1973–1986: History and Memories of an Institution* (Luxembourg: Publications Office of the European Union, 2014), 263–276.

Bussière, Eric, Michel Dumoulin and Sylvain Schirmann (eds.), *Europe organisée, Europe du libre-échange? Fin XIXe siècle–années 1960* (Brussels: Peter Lang, 2006).

Buzzonetti, Marcello, 'Merci, Monsieur Noël', in: Stephen Martin (ed.), *The Construction of Europe: Essays in Honour of Emile Noël* (Dordrecht: Kluwer, 1994), 269–270.

Byrne, Jeffrey James, *Mecca of Revolution: Algeria, Decolonization, and the Third World Order* (Oxford: Oxford University Press, 2016).

Calandri, Elena, 'Understanding the EEC Mediterranean Policy: Trade, Security, Development and the Redrafting of Mediterranean Boundaries', in: Claudia Hiepel (ed.), *Europe in a Globalising World* (Baden-Baden: Nomos, 2014), 165–184.

Calandri, Elena, Simone Paoli and Antonio Varsori (eds.), 'Peoples and Borders: Seventy Years of Migration in Europe, from Europe, to Europe (1945–2015)', in: *Journal of European Integration History* 23 (2017) (special issue).

Campos, Nauro F., Fabrizio Coricelli and Luigi Moretti, 'Economic Growth and Political Integration: Estimating the Benefits from Membership in the European Union Using the Synthetic Counterfactuals Method', *CEPR Discussion Paper*, No. 9968 (2014).

Carey, Charles J., 'Fraud and the Common Agricultural Policy', in: Hans de Doelder (ed.), *Bestrijding van EEG-fraude* (Antwerp: Kluwer, 1990), 11–20.

Carlier, Philippe, 'Fernand Dehousse et le projet d'Union Politique', in: Gilbert Trausch (ed.), *Die Europäische Integration vom Schuman-Plan bis zu den Verträgen von Rom. Pläne und Initiativen, Enttäuschungen und Mißerfolge* (Baden-Baden: Nomos, 1993), 365–377.

Carruth, Reba Anne, *Industrial Policy Coordination in International Organizations: The Case of Steel Policy in the OECD and the EEC* (Frankfurt am Main: Lang, 1989).

Caruso, Daniela and Joanna Geneve, 'Trade and History: The Case of EU–Algeria Relations', in: *Boston University International Law Journal Online* (17 February 2015; online https://bit.ly/2M6sB6h, accessed 1 July 2019).

Castelnau, Anne de, 'Le SGCI. Une réponse administrative aux défis européens de l'après-guerre', in: Laurence Badel, Stanislas Jeanneson and N. Piers Ludlow (eds.), *Les administrations nationales et la construction européenne. Une approche historique 1919–1975* (Brussels: Peter Lang, 2005), 307–335.

Cayet, Thomas and Paul-André Rosental, 'Politiques sociales et marché(s). Filiations et variations d'un registre transnational d'action, du BIT des années 1920 à la construction européenne et à la Chine contemporaine', in: *Le Mouvement Social* 244 (2013), 3–16.

Chabot, Jean-Luc, 'Technocratie et construction européenne', in: *Les Cahiers: Série Cahiers du CUREI* 15 (2001), 7–20.

Chalmers, Damian, Gareth T. Davies and Giorgio Monti, *European Union Law: Cases and Materials*, 2nd ed. (Cambridge: Cambridge University Press, 2010).

Chalmers, Damian, Gareth T. Davies and Giorgio Monti (eds.), *European Union Law: Texts and Materials*, 3rd ed. (Cambridge: Cambridge University Press, 2014).

Chenard, Marie Julie, 'The European Community's Policy towards the People's Republic of China: Establishing Diplomatic Relations (December 1973–May 1975)', in: Pascaline Winand, Andrea Benvenuti and Max Guderzo (eds.), *The External Relations of the European Union: Historical and Contemporary Perspectives* (Brussels: Peter Lang, 2015), 189–204.

Christensen, Jørgen Grønnegaard, 'EU Legislation and National Regulation: Uncertain Steps towards a European Public Policy', in: *Public Administration* 88 (2010), 3–17.

Christiansen, Thomas and Torbjörn Larsson (eds.), *The Role of Committees in the Policy-Process of the European Union: Legislation, Implementation and Deliberation* (Cheltenham: Edward Elgar, 2007).

Ciampani, Andrea and Emilio Gabaglio (eds.), *L'Europa sociale e la Confederazione europea dei sindacati* (Bologna: Il Mulino, 2010).

Cini, Michelle, *The European Commission: Leadership, Organisation and Culture in the EU Administration* (Manchester: Manchester University Press, 1996).

Cini, Michelle and Lee McGowan, *Competition Policy in the European Union*, 2nd ed. (Houndmills: Palgrave Macmillan, 2009).

Clavin, Patricia and Kiran Klaus Patel, 'The Role of International Organizations in Europeanization: The Case of the League of Nations and the European Economic Community', in: Martin Conway and Kiran Klaus Patel (eds.), *Europeanization in the Twentieth Century: Historical Approaches* (Basingstoke: Palgrave Macmillan, 2010), 110–131.

Cockfield, Francis Arthur, *The European Union: Creating the Single Market* (London: Wiley Chancery Law, 1994).

Cohen, Antonin, 'Constitutionalism without Constitution: Transnational Elites Between Political Mobilization and Legal Expertise in the Making of a Constitution for Europe (1940s–1960s)', in: *Law & Social Enquiry* 32 (2007), 109–135.

Cohen, Antonin, 'Why Call It a "European Community"? Ideological Continuities and Institutional Design of Nascent European Organisations', in: *Contemporary European History* 27 (2018), 326–344.

Collowald, Paul, *J'ai vu naître l'Europe. De Strasbourg à Bruxelles, le parcours d'un pionnier de la construction européenne* (Strasbourg: Editions La Nuée Bleue, 2014).

Comte, Emmanuel, *The History of the European Migration Regime: Germany's Strategic Hegemony* (London: Routledge, 2018).

Connelly, Matthew James, *A Diplomatic Revolution: Algeria's Fight for Independence and the Origins of the Post-Cold War Era* (Oxford: Oxford University Press, 2002).

Conway, Martin and Kiran Klaus Patel (eds.), *Europeanization in the Twentieth Century: Historical Approaches* (Basingstoke: Palgrave Macmillan, 2010).

Conze, Eckart, *Die gaullistische Herausforderung. Die deutsch-französischen Beziehungen in der amerikanischen Europapolitik 1958–1963* (Munich: Oldenbourg, 1995).

Conze, Vanessa, *Das Europa der Deutschen. Ideen von Europa in Deutschland zwischen Reichstradition und Westorientierung (1920–1970)* (Munich: Oldenbourg, 2005).

Cooper, Frederick, *Colonialism in Question: Theory, Knowledge, History* (Berkeley: University of California Press, 2005).

Cooper, Frederick, *Citizenship between Empire and Nation: Remaking France and French Africa, 1945–1960* (Princeton, NJ: Princeton University Press, 2014).

Coppolaro, Lucia, *The Making of a World Trading Power: The European Economic Community (EEC) in the GATT Kennedy Round Negotiations (1963–67)* (Farnham: Ashgate, 2013).

Corbett, Anne, 'Ideas, Institutions and Policy Entrepreneurs: Towards a New History of Higher Education in the European Community', in: *European Journal of Education* 38 (2003), 315–330.

Cosgrove Twitchett, Carol, 'Harmonisation and Road Freight Transport', in: Carol Cosgrove Twitchett (ed.), *Harmonisation in the EEC* (London: Macmillan, 1981), 63–77.

Cosgrove-Sacks, Carol, 'Europe, Diplomacy and Development Cooperation with the ACP Group', in: Carol Cosgrove-Sacks (ed.), *Europe, Diplomacy and Development: New Issues in EU Relations with Developing Countries* (Houndmills: Palgrave Macmillan, 2001), 259–286.

Coudenhove-Kalergi, Richard Nikolaus, *Pan-Europa* (Vienna: Paneuropa Verlag, 1923).

Coudenhove-Kalergi, Richard Nikolaus, *Pan-Europe* (New York: Alfred A. Knopf, 1926).

Coudenhove-Kalergi, Richard Nikolaus, *Das Wesen des Antisemitismus* (Vienna: Paneuropa Verlag, 1929).

Coudenhove-Kalergi, Richard Nikolaus, *Kampf um Europa. Aus meinem Leben* (Zurich: Atlantis Verlag, 1949).

Cowles, Maria Green, 'Setting the Agenda for a New Europe: The ERT and EC 1992', in: *Journal of Common Market Studies* 33 (1995), 501–526.

Crafts, Nicholas, 'Economic Growth in East Asia and Western Europe since 1950: Implications for Living Standards', in: *National Institute Economic Review* 162 (1997), 75–84.

Crafts, Nicholas, 'West European Economic Integration since 1950', in: Volker Nisch and Harald Badinger (eds.), *Routledge Handbook of the Economics of European Integration* (London: Taylor & Francis, 2015), 3–21.

Crafts, Nicholas and Gianni Toniolo (eds.), *Economic Growth in Europe since 1945* (Cambridge: Cambridge University Press, 1996).

Crafts, Nicholas and Gianni Toniolo, 'Les Trente Glorieuses: From the Marshall Plan to the Oil Crisis', in: Dan Stone (ed.), *Postwar European History* (Oxford: Oxford University Press, 2012), 356–378.

Craig, Paul, 'The Evolution of the Single Market', in: Catherine Barnard and Joanne Scott (eds.), *The Law of the Single European Market: Unpacking the Premises* (Oxford: Hart, 2002), 1–40.

Craveri, Piero and Antonio Varsori (eds.), *L'Italia nella costruzione europea. Un bilancio storico (1957–2007)* (Milan: FrancoAngeli, 2009).

Cruciani, Sante, *L'Europa delle sinistre. La nascita del Mercato comune europeo attraverso i casi francese e italiano (1955–1957)* (Rome: Carocci, 2007).

Cruciani, Sante (ed.), *Il socialismo europeo e il processo di integrazione: Dai Trattati di Roma alla crisi politica dell'Unione (1957–2016)* (Milan: FrancoAngeli, 2016).

Cuccia, Deborah, 'The Genscher–Colombo Plan: A Forgotten Page in the European Integration History', in: *Journal of European Integration History* 24 (2018), 59–78.

Cunha, Alice, 'O Alargamento Ibérico da Comunidade Económica Europeia: A Experiência Portuguesa' (unpubl. PhD diss., Universidade Nova de Lisboa, 2012).

da Silva, Glaydson José, 'Thucydide II, 37 et le préambule de la Constitution européenne', in: *Histoire Antique* 40 (2008), 38–44.

Dahrendorf, Ralf, *Auf der Suche nach einer neuen Ordnung: Vorlesungen zur Politik der Freiheit im 21. Jahrhundert* (Munich: C. H. Beck, 2003).

Dann, Philipp, *Entwicklungsverwaltungsrecht. Theorie und Dogmatik des Rechts der Entwicklungszusammenarbeit, untersucht am Beispiel der Weltbank, der EU und der Bundesrepublik Deutschland* (Tübingen: Mohr Siebeck, 2012).

Dauses, Manfred A., 'The Protection of Fundamental Rights in the Community Legal Order', in: *European Law Review* 10 (1985), 398–419.

Davies, Bill and Fernanda Nicola, 'Introduction to EU Law Stories: Contextual and Critical Histories in European Jurisprudence', in: Fernanda Nicola and Bill Davies (eds.), *EU Law Stories: Contextual and Critical Histories in European Jurisprudence* (Cambridge: Cambridge University Press, 2017), 1–18.

Davies, Bill and Morten Rasmussen (eds.), 'Towards a New History of European Law', in: *Contemporary European History* 21, 3 (2012) (special issue).

Davies, Norman, *Europe: A History* (Oxford: Oxford University Press, 1996).

de Angelis, Emma and Eirini Karamouzi, 'Enlargement and the Historical Origins of the European Community's Identity, 1961–1978', in: *Contemporary European History* 25 (2016), 439–458.

de Bruin, Robin, *Elastisch Europa. De integratie van Europa en de Nederlandse politiek, 1947–1968* (Amsterdam: Wereldbibliotheek, 2014).

de Bruin, Robin, 'Indonesian Decolonisation and the Dutch Attitude towards the Establishment of the EEC's Association Policy, 1945–1963', in: *Journal of European Integration History* 23 (2017), 211–226.

de Búrca, Gráinne, 'The Language of Rights and European Integration', in: Jo Shaw and Gillian More (eds.), *New Legal Dynamics of European Union* (Oxford: Oxford University Press, 1995), 29–54.

de Búrca, Gráinne, 'The Evolution of EU Human Rights Law', in: Paul P. Craig and Gráinne de Búrca (eds.), *The Evolution of EU Law*, 2nd ed. (Oxford: Oxford University Press, 2011), 465–497.

de Doelder, Hans (ed.), *Bestrijding van EEG-fraude* (Antwerp: Kluwer, 1990).

de Gaulle, Charles, *Discours et messages*, vol. 3 (1958–1962) and vol. 4 (1962–1965) (Paris: Plon, 1970).

de la Guardia, Ricardo Martín, 'In Search of Lost Europe: Spain', in: Wolfram Kaiser and Jürgen Elvert (eds.), *European Union Enlargement: A Comparative History* (Routledge: London, 2004), 99–118.

de la Serre, Françoise, 'Foreign Policy of the European Community', in: Roy C. Macridis (ed.), *Foreign Policy in World Politics*, 6th ed. (Englewood Cliffs, NJ: Prentice-Hall, 1985), 411–435.

de Lassalle, Marine, 'European Worlds', in: Daniel Gaxie, Nicolas Hubé and Jay Rowell (eds.), *Perceptions of Europe: A Comparative Sociology of European Attitudes* (Colchester: ECPR Press, 2011), 175–195.

de L'Écotais, Yann, *L'Europe sabotée* (Brussels: Rossel Edition, 1976).

de Puig, Lluís Maria, *International Parliaments* (Strasbourg: Europarat, 2008).

de Rougemont, Denis, *Ecrits sur l'Europe*, vol. 2 (1962–1986) (Paris: Editions de la Différence, 1994).

de Witte, Bruno, Andrea Ott and Ellen Vos (eds.), *Between Flexibility and Disintegration: The Trajectory of Differentiation in EU Law* (Northampton, MA: Edward Elgar, 2017).

de Witte, Bruno and Anne Thies, 'Why Choose Europe? The Place of the European Union in the Architecture of International Legal Cooperation', in: Bart van Vooren, Steven Blockmans and Jan Wouters (eds.), *The EU's Role in Global Governance: The Legal Dimension* (Oxford: Oxford University Press, 2013), 23–38.

Dehousse, Renaud, 'Completing the Internal Market: Institutional Constraints and Challenges', in: Roland Bieber et al. (eds.), *1992: One European Market?* (Baden-Baden: Nomos, 1988), 311–336.

del Pero, Mario, 'A European Solution for a European Crisis: The International Implications of Portugal's Revolution', in: *Journal of European Integration History* 15 (2009), 15–34.

del Pero, Mario, 'La transizione portoghese', in: Mario del Pero, Víctor Gavín, Fernando Guirao and Antonio Varsori, *Democrazie. L'Europa meridionale e la fine delle dittature* (Milan: Mondadori, 2010), 95–174.

del Pero, Mario, Víctor Gavín, Fernando Guirao and Antonio Varsori, *Democrazie. L'Europa meridionale e la fine delle dittature* (Milan: Mondadori, 2010).

Delors, Jacques, *Das neue Europa* (Munich: Carl Hanser, 1993).

Demidova, Ksenia, 'The Deal of the Century: The Reagan Administration and the Soviet Pipeline', in: Kiran Klaus Patel and Kenneth Weisbrode (eds.), *European Integration and the Atlantic Community in the 1980s* (Cambridge: Cambridge University Press, 2013), 59–82.

Denord, François and Antoine Schwartz, *L'Europe sociale n'aura pas lieu* (Paris: Raisons d'Agir, 2009).

Deutsch, Karl W., 'Integration and Arms Control in the European Political Environment', in: *American Political Science Review* 60 (1966), 354–365.

di Fabio, Udo, *Produktharmonisierung durch Normung und Selbstüberwachung* (Cologne: Heymanns, 1996).

Dickhaus, Monika, '"It Is only the Provisional that Lasts": The European Payments Union', in: Richard Griffiths (ed.), *Explorations in OEEC History* (Paris: OECD, 1997), 183–200.

Dietl, Ralph, *Emanzipation und Kontrolle. Europa in der westlichen Sicherheitspolitik 1948–1963*, 2 vols. (Stuttgart: Franz Steiner Verlag, 2006).

Dimier, Véronique, *The Invention of a European Development Aid Bureaucracy: Recycling Empire* (Basingstoke: Palgrave Macmillan, 2014).

Dimier, Véronique, 'Eurafrica and Its Business: The European Development Fund Between the Member States, the European Commission and European Firms', in: *Journal of European Integration History* 23 (2017), 187–210.
Dinan, Desmond, *Ever Closer Union: An Introduction to European Integration*, 2nd ed. (Houndmills: Palgrave, 1999).
Dinan, Desmond, 'From Treaty Revision to Treaty Revision: The Legacy of Maastricht', in: *Journal of European Integration History* 19 (2013), 123–139.
Dinkel, Jürgen, *Die Bewegung Bündnisfreier Staaten. Genese, Organisation und Politik (1927–1992)* (Berlin: de Gruyter Oldenbourg, 2015).
Doering-Manteuffel, Anselm and Lutz Raphael, *Nach dem Boom: Perspektiven auf die Zeitgeschichte seit 1970* (Göttingen: Vandenhoeck & Ruprecht, 2008).
Domnitz, Christian, *Hinwendung nach Europa. Öffentlichkeitswandel im Staatssozialismus 1975–1989* (Bochum: Winkler, 2015).
Donner, André M., 'The Constitutional Powers of the Court of Justice of the European Communities', in: *Common Market Law Review* 127 (1974), 127–140.
D'Ottavio, Gabriele, *Europa mit den Deutschen. Die Bundesrepublik und die europäische Integration (1949–1966)* (Berlin: Duncker & Humblot, 2016).
D'Ottavio, Gabriele, 'Il discorso politico sull'Europa nell'immediato dopoguerra (1945–1947)', in: Giovanni Bernardini, Maurizio Cau, Gabriele D'Ottavio and Cecilia Nubola (eds.), *L'Età costituente. Italia 1945–1948* (Bologna: Il Mulino, 2017), 397–424.
Ducci, Roberto and Bino Olivi (eds.), *L'Europa incompiuta* (Padua: CEDAM, 1970).
Duchêne, François, 'Europe's Role in World Peace', in: Richard Mayne (ed.), *Europe Tomorrow: Sixteen Europeans Look Ahead* (London: Fontana, 1972), 32–47.
Duchêne, François, 'The European Community and the Uncertainties of Interdependence', in: Max Kohnstamm and Wolfgang Hager (eds.), *A Nation Writ Large? Foreign Policy Problems before the European Community* (London: Macmillan, 1973), 1–21.
Dülffer, Jost, *Jalta, 4. Februar 1945: Der Zweite Weltkrieg und die Entstehung der bipolaren Welt* (Munich: DTV, 1999).
Dülffer, Jost, 'The History of European Integration: From Integration History to the History of Integrated Europe', in: Wilfried Loth (ed.), *Experiencing Europe: 50 Years of European Construction 1957–2007* (Baden-Baden: Nomos, 2007), 17–32.
Dulphy, Anne and Christine Manigand, 'L'Opinion publique française face aux élargissements', in: Marie-Thérèse Bitsch, Wilfried Loth and Charles Barthel (eds.), *Cultures politiques, opinion publiques et intégration européenne* (Brussels: Bruylant, 2007), 125–145.
Dümmer, Barbara, 'Die Städtepartnerschaft Frankenthal – Colombes (1958) und die Bedeutung transnationaler Kommunalverbände', in: Corine Defrance, Michael Kißener and Pia Nordblom (eds.), *Wege der Verständigung zwischen Deutschen und Franzosen nach 1945. Zivilgesellschaftliche Annäherungen* (Tübingen: Narr, 2010), 189–203.
Dumoulin, Michel, 'Milieux patronaux belges et construction européenne autour de 1960', in: Eric Bussière, Michel Dumoulin and Sylvain Schirmann (eds.), *Europe organisée, Europe du libre-échange? Fin XIXe siècle–années 1960* (Brussels: Peter Lang, 2006), 149–163.
Dumoulin, Michel, 'The Administration', in: Michel Dumoulin (ed.), *The European Commission, 1958–72: History and Memories* (Luxembourg: Office for Official Publications of the European Communities, 2007), 219–239.

Dumoulin, Michel, 'The Commissioners', in: Eric Bussière et al. (eds.), *The European Commission 1973–1986: History and Memories of an Institution* (Luxembourg: Publications Office of the European Union, 2014), 77–85.
Dumoulin, Michel, Pierre Guillen and Maurice Vaïsse (eds.), *L'Energie nucléaire en Europe: Des origines à Euratom* (Bern: Peter Lang, 1994).
Dumoulin, Michel and Matthieu Lethé, 'The Question of Location', in: Michel Dumoulin (ed.), *The European Commission 1958–72: History and Memories* (Luxembourg: Office for Official Publications of the European Communities, 2007), 273–286.
Duranti, Marco, 'European Integration, Human Rights, and Romantic Internationalism', in: Nicholas Doumanis (ed.), *The Oxford Handbook of European History, 1914–1945* (Oxford: Oxford University Press, 2016), 440–458.
Duranti, Marco, *The Conservative Human Rights Revolution: European Identity, Transnational Politics, and the Origins of the European Convention* (Oxford: Oxford University Press, 2017).
Dyson, Kenneth and Kevin Featherstone, *The Road to Maastricht: Negotiating Economic and Monetary Union* (Oxford: Oxford University Press, 1999).
Eckel, Jan, *Die Ambivalenz des Guten. Menschenrechte in der internationalen Politik seit den 1940ern* (Göttingen: Vandenhoeck & Ruprecht, 2014).
Edwards, Geoffrey, 'The Potential and Limits of the CFSP: The Yugoslav Example', in: Elfriede Regelsberger, Philippe de Schoutheete de Tervarent and Wolfgang Wessels (eds.), *Foreign Policy of the European Union: From EPC to CFSP and Beyond* (Boulder, CO: Lynne Rienner, 1997), 173–195.
Eichener, Volker, 'Effective European Problem-Solving: Lessons from the Regulation of Occupational Safety and Environmental Protection', in: *Journal of European Public Policy* 4 (1997), 591–608.
Eichengreen, Barry, *Reconstructing Europe's Trade and Payments: The European Payments Union* (Manchester: Manchester University Press, 1993).
Eichengreen, Barry, *The European Economy since 1945: Coordinated Capitalism and Beyond* (Princeton, NJ: Princeton University Press, 2007).
Eichengreen, Barry and Andrea Boltho, 'The Economic Impact of European Integration', in: Stephen Broadberry and Kevin H. O'Rourke (eds.), *The Cambridge Economic History of Modern Europe*, vol. 2: *1870 to the Present* (Cambridge: Cambridge University Press, 2010), 267–295.
Einaudi, Jean-Luc, *Octobre 1961: Un massacre à Paris* (Paris: Fayard, 2001).
Elgström, Ole, 'Lomé and Post-Lomé: Asymmetric Negotiations and the Impact of Norms', in: *European Foreign Affairs Review* 5 (2000), 175–195.
Ellison, James, *Threatening Europe: Britain and the Creation of the European Community, 1955–58* (Houndmills: Macmillan, 2000).
Endo, Ken, *The Presidency of the European Commission under Jacques Delors: The Politics of Shared Leadership* (New York: St. Martin's Press, 1999).
Eppler, Annegret and Henrik Scheller (eds.), *Zur Konzeptionalisierung europäischer Desintegration. Zug- und Gegenkräfte im europäischen Integrationsprozess* (Baden-Baden: Nomos, 2013).
Fanning, Ronan, 'Irish Neutrality: An Historical Review', in: *Irish Studies in International Affairs* 1 (1982), 27–38.
Faraldo, José M., Paulina Gulińska-Jurgiel and Christian Domnitz (eds.), *Europa im Ostblock. Vorstellungen und Diskurse (1945–1991)* (Vienna: Böhlau, 2008).
Fardella, Enrico, 'The EC and China: Rise and Demise of a Strategic Relationship', in: Ulrich Krotz, Kiran Klaus Patel and Federico Romero (eds.), *Europe's Cold War Relations: The EC Towards a Global Role* (London: Bloomsbury, 2020), 91–110.

Favier, Pierre and Michel Martin-Roland, *La décennie Mitterrand*, vol. 1: *Les ruptures (1981–1984)* (Paris: Editions du Seuil, 1990).
Feinberg, Nathan, 'Unilateral Withdrawal from an International Organization', in: *British Yearbook of International Law* 39 (1963), 189–219.
Fernández Soriano, Víctor, 'La CEE face à l'Espagne franquiste. De la mémoire de la guerre à la construction politique de l'Europe', in: *Vingtième Siècle* 108 (2010), 85–98.
Fernández Soriano, Víctor, *Le fusil et l'olivier. Les droits de l'Homme en Europe face aux dictatures méditerranéennes (1949–1977)* (Brussels: Editions de l'Université de Bruxelles, 2015).
Ferrari, Lorenzo, 'The European Community as a Promoter of Human Rights in Africa and Latin America, 1970–80', in: *Journal of European Integration History* 21 (2015), 217–230.
Ferrell, Robert H., 'The Truman Era and European Integration', in: Francis H. Heller and John R. Gillingham (eds.), *The United States and the Integration of Europe: Legacies of the Postwar Era* (New York: St. Martin's Press, 1996), 25–44.
Fertikh, Karim, 'La construction d'un "droit social européen". Socio-histoire d'une catégorie transnationale (années 1950–années 1970)', in: *Politix* 115 (2016), 201–224.
Fertikh, Karim and Heike Wieters, 'Harmonisierung der Sozialpolitik in Europa. Socio-histoire einer sozialpolitischen Kategorie der EWG', in: Karim Fertikh, Heike Wieters and Bénédicte Zimmermann (eds.), *Ein soziales Europa als Herausforderung. Von der Harmonisierung zur Koordination sozialpolitischer Kategorien* (Frankfurt am Main: Campus, 2018), 49–86.
Fierro, Elena, *The EU's Approach to Human Rights Conditionality in Practice* (the Hague: Kluwer Law International, 2003).
Fischer, Wolfram, 'Wirtschaft, Gesellschaft und Staat in Europa 1914–1980', in: Wolfram Fischer (ed.), *Handbuch der europäischen Wirtschafts- und Sozialgeschichte*, vol. 6 (Stuttgart: Klett-Cotta, 1987), 1–221.
Flora, Peter (ed.), *Growth to Limits: The Western European Welfare States since World War II*, vols. 1 and 2 (Berlin: Walter de Gruyter, 1986).
Fonzi, Paolo, 'La "Großraumwirtschaft" e l'Unione Europea dei Pagamenti: Continuità nella cultura economica tedesca a cavallo del 1945', in: *Ricerche di Storia Politica* 2 (2012), 131–153.
Fossum, John Erik, 'Democracy and Differentiation in Europe', in: *Journal of European Public Policy* 22 (2015), 799–815.
Foubert, Petra, *The Gender Pay Gap in Europe from a Legal Perspective* (Luxembourg: Publications Office of the European Union, 2010).
Fourastié, Jean, *Les Trente Glorieuses, ou la révolution invisible de 1946 à 1975* (Paris: Fayard, 1979).
Frank, Robert et al. (eds.), *Un espace public européen en construction. Des années 1950 à nos jours* (Brussels: Lang, 2010).
Frattolillo, Oliviero, *Diplomacy in Japan–EU Relations: From the Cold War to the Post-Bipolar Era* (London: Routledge, 2013).
Fridenson, Patrick, 'Stratégies des groupes automobiles et structure du marché en Europe 1979–1992', in: Éric Bussière, Michel Dumoulin and Sylvain Schirmann (eds.), *Milieux économiques et intégration européenne au XXe siècle. La relance des années quatre-vingt (1979–1992)* (Paris: Comité pour l'histoire économique et financière de la France, 2007), 333–347.
Frowein, Jochen Abraham, 'Solange II (BVerfGE 73, 339). Constitutional Complaint Firma W.', in: *Common Market Law Review* 25 (1988), 201–206.
Fukuyama, Francis, *The End of History and the Last Man* (New York: Free Press, 1992).

Gad, Ulrik Pram, 'Greenland Projecting Sovereignty – Denmark Protecting Sovereignty Away', in: Rebecca Adler-Nissen and Ulrik Pram Gad (eds.), *European Integration and Postcolonial Sovereignty Games: The EU Overseas Countries and Territories* (London: Routledge, 2013), 217–234.

Gainar, Maria, *Aux origines de la diplomatie européenne: Les Neuf et la Coopération politique européenne de 1973 à 1980* (Brussels: Peter Lang, 2012).

Gainar, Maria and Martial Libera (eds.), *Contre l'Europe? Anti-européisme, euroscepticisme et alter-européisme dans la construction européenne de 1945 à nos jours*, vol. 2 (Stuttgart: Franz Steiner Verlag, 2013).

Galloro, Carmine, 'Der Rücktritt gemäß Art. 50 EUV unter rechtshistorischen Aspekten. Der Fall des sog. "Brexit"', in: *Journal on European History of Law* 7 (2016), 150–161.

Galtung, Johan, *The European Community: A Superpower in the Making* (London: George Allen & Unwin, 1973).

Garavini, Giuliano, *Dopo gli imperi: L'integrazione europea nello scontro Nord-Sud* (Florence: Le Monnier, 2009).

Garavini, Giuliano, 'The European Community's Development Policy: The Eurafrica Factor', in: Ulrich Krotz, Kiran Klaus Patel and Federico Romero (eds.), *Europe's Cold War Relations: The EC Towards a Global Role* (London: Bloomsbury, 2020), 205–228.

Gees, Thomas, *Die Schweiz im Europäisierungsprozess. Wirtschafts- und gesellschaftspolitische Konzepte am Beispiel der Arbeitsmigrations-, Agrar- und Wissenschaftspolitik 1947–1974* (Zurich: Chronos, 2006).

Gehler, Michael, *Der lange Weg nach Europa. Österreich vom Ende der Monarchie bis zur EU* (Vienna: StudienVerlag, 2002).

Gehler, Michael, 'Mehr Europäisierung in Umbruchzeiten? Die Europäische Politische Zusammenarbeit (EPZ) und die revolutionären Ereignisse in Mittel-, Ost- und Südosteuropa Ende der 1980er Jahre', in: Gabriele Clemens (ed.), *Die Suche nach Europäisierung. Ein komplexer Prozess in interdisziplinärer Perspektive* (Stuttgart: Franz Steiner Verlag, 2017), 87–116.

Gehler, Michael and Wolfram Kaiser (eds.), *Transnationale Parteienkooperation der europäischen Christdemokraten: Dokumente 1945–1965* (Munich: Saur, 2004).

Gehler, Michael and Rolf Steininger (eds.), *Die Neutralen und die europäische Integration, 1945–1995* (Vienna: Böhlau, 2000).

Georgakakis, Didier, 'European Integration', in: William Outhwaite and Stephen Turner (eds.), *The SAGE Handbook of Political Sociology*, vol. 2 (London: SAGE, 2018), 1083–1103.

Geppert, Dominik, *Ein Europa, das es nicht gibt. Die fatale Sprengkraft des Euro* (Berlin: Europaverlag, 2013).

Gerhards, Jürgen, 'Westeuropäische Integration und die Schwierigkeiten der Entstehung einer europäischen Öffentlichkeit', in: *Zeitschrift für Soziologie* 22 (1993), 96–110.

Gerig, Daniel S., 'European Multilateral Social Security Treaties', in: *Social Security Bulletin* 22 (1959), 12–14.

Gerits, Frank, '"When the Bull Elephants Fight": Kwame Nkrumah, Non-Alignment, and Pan-Africanism as an Interventionist Ideology in the Global Cold War (1957–66)', in: *International History Review* 37 (2015), 951–969.

Gerlach, Christian, 'Fortress Europe: The EEC in the World Food Crisis, 1972–1975', in: Kiran Klaus Patel (ed.), *Fertile Ground for Europe? The History of European Integration and the Common Agricultural Policy since 1945* (Baden-Baden: Nomos, 2009), 241–256.

Geyer, Michael, 'Der Kalte Krieg, die Deutschen und die Angst. Die westdeutsche Opposition gegen Wiederbewaffnung und Kernwaffen', in: Klaus Naumann (ed.), *Nachkrieg in Deutschland* (Hamburg: Hamburger Edition, 2001), 267–318.

Gfeller, Aurélie E., 'A European Voice in the Arab World: France, the Superpowers and the Middle East, 1970–74', in: *Cold War History* 11 (2011), 659–676.

Giauque, Jeffrey Glen, *Grand Designs and Visions of Unity: The Atlantic Powers and the Reorganization of Western Europe, 1955–1963* (Chapel Hill: University of North Carolina Press, 2002).

Gilbert, Mark, 'Narrating the Process: Questioning the Progressive Story of European Integration', in: *Journal of Common Market Studies* 46 (2008), 641–662.

Gilbert, Mark, 'A Shift in Mood: The 1992 Initiative and Changing U.S. Perceptions of the European Community, 1988–1989', in: Kiran Klaus Patel and Kenneth Weisbrode (eds.), *European Integration and the Atlantic Community in the 1980s* (Cambridge: Cambridge University Press, 2013), 243–264.

Gillingham, John, *Coal, Steel, and the Rebirth of Europe, 1945–1955: The Germans and French from Ruhr Conflict to Economic Community* (Cambridge: Cambridge University Press, 1991).

Gillingham, John, 'The European Coal and Steel Community: An Object Lesson?', in: Barry Eichengreen (ed.), *Europe's Post-War Recovery* (Cambridge: Cambridge University Press, 1995), 151–168.

Gillingham, John, *European Integration, 1950–2003: Superstate or New Market Economy?* (Cambridge: Cambridge University Press, 2003).

Gilman, Nils, 'The New International Economic Order: A Reintroduction', in: *Humanity* 6 (2015), 1–16.

Gilpin, Robert, *The Political Economy of International Relations* (Princeton, NJ: Princeton University Press, 1987).

Gilson, Julie, *Japan and the European Union: A Partnership for the Twenty-First Century?* (New York: St. Martin's Press, 2000).

Gioe, David, Len Scott and Christopher Andrew (eds.), *An International History of the Cuban Missile Crisis: A 50-year Retrospective* (London: Routledge, 2014).

Giuliani, Marco and Simona Piattoni, 'Italy: Both Leader and Laggard', in: Eleanor E. Zeff and Ellen B. Pirro (eds.), *The European Union and the Member States: Cooperation, Coordination, and Compromise* (London: Lynne Rienner, 2001), 115–142.

Gleske, Leonhard, 'Nationale Geldpolitik auf dem Weg zur europäischen Währungsunion', in: Deutsche Bundesbank (ed.), *Währung und Wirtschaft in Deutschland 1876–1975* (Frankfurt am Main: Fritz Knapp, 1976), 745–788.

Gliech, Oliver, 'Bio-bibliographische Grunddaten zu den Referenten und Generalsekretären des IAI, 1929–1945', in: Reinhard Liehr, Günther Maihold and Günter Vollmer (eds.), *Ein Institut und sein General: Wilhelm Faupel und das Ibero-Amerikanische Institut in der Zeit des Nationalsozialismus* (Frankfurt am Main: Vervuert, 2003), 571–609.

Glootz, Tanja Anette, *Alterssicherung im europäischen Wohlfahrtsstaat. Etappen ihrer Entwicklung im 20. Jahrhundert* (Frankfurt am Main: Campus Verlag, 2005).

Gold, Peter, *Gibraltar: British or Spanish?* (London: Routledge, 2005).

Göldner, Markus, *Politische Symbole der europäischen Integration. Fahne, Hymne, Hauptstadt, Paß, Briefmarke, Auszeichungen* (Frankfurt am Main: Lang, 1988).

Gordon, Lincoln, 'The Organization for European Economic Cooperation', in: *International Organization* 10 (1956), 1–11.

Goschler, Constantin and Rüdiger Graf, *Europäische Zeitgeschichte seit 1945* (Berlin: Akademie Verlag, 2010).

Gosewinkel, Dieter (ed.), *Anti-liberal Europe: A Neglected Story of Europeanization* (New York: Berghahn, 2015).
Gosewinkel, Dieter, *Schutz und Freiheit? Staatsbürgerschaft in Europa im 20. und 21. Jahrhundert* (Frankfurt am Main: Suhrkamp, 2016).
Grant, Wyn, *The Common Agricultural Policy* (Houndmills: Macmillan, 1997).
Greiner, Florian, *Wege nach Europa. Deutungen eines imaginierten Kontinents in deutschen, britischen und amerikanischen Printmedien 1914–1945* (Göttingen: Wallstein, 2014).
Greppi, Edoardo, 'Il Consiglio d'Europa: L'istituzionalizzazione della cooperazione politica tra stati sovrani', in: Romain H. Rainero (ed.), *Storia dell'integrazione europea*, vol. 1: *L'integrazione europea dalle origini alla nascita della Cee* (Rome: Marzorati, 1997), 87–116.
Griffiths, Richard T. (ed.), *Explorations in OEEC History* (Paris: OECD, 1997).
Grilli, Enzo R., *The European Community and the Developing Countries* (Cambridge: Cambridge University Press, 1993).
Grimm, Dieter, *Europa ja – aber welches? Zur Verfassung der europäischen Demokratie* (Munich: Beck, 2016).
Grob-Fitzgibbon, Benjamin, *Continental Drift: Britain and Europe from the End of Empire to the Rise of Euroscepticism* (Cambridge: Cambridge University Press, 2016).
Gross, Feliks, 'Peace Planning for Central and Eastern Europe', in: *Annals of the American Academy of Political and Social Science* 232 (1944), 169–176.
Grosser, Alfred, *Wie anders sind die Deutschen?* (Munich: C. H. Beck, 2002).
Großmann, Johannes, '"Baroque Spain" as Metaphor: *Hispanidad*, Europeanism and Cold War Anti-Communism in Francoist Spain', in: *Bulletin of Spanish Studies* 91 (2014), 755–771.
Großmann, Johannes, *Die Internationale der Konservativen. Transnationale Elitenzirkel und private Außenpolitik in Westeuropa seit 1945* (Munich: Oldenbourg, 2014).
Group of Experts, 'Social Aspects of European Economic Co-operation', in: *International Labour Review* 74 (1956), 99–123.
Grunert, Robert, *Der Europagedanke westeuropäischer faschistischer Bewegungen 1940–1945* (Paderborn: Ferdinand Schöningh, 2012).
Gualtieri, Roberto, 'L'Europa come vincolo esterno', in: Piero Craveri and Antonio Varsori (eds.), *L'Italia nella costruzione europea: Un bilancio storico (1957–2007)* (Milan: FrancoAngeli, 2009), 313–331.
Guillen, Pierre, 'Frankreich und der europäische Wiederaufschwung: Vom Scheitern der EVG zur Ratifizierung der Verträge von Rom', in: *VfZ* 28 (1980), 1–19.
Guillen, Pierre, 'La France et la négociation du traité d'Euratom', in: *Relations Internationales* 44 (1985), 391–412.
Guirao, Fernando, *Spain and the Reconstruction of Western Europe, 1945–1957: Challenge and Response* (New York: St. Martin's Press, 1998).
Gundlach, Erich, Ulrich Hiemenz, Rolf J. Langhammer and Peter Nunnenkamp, *Regional Integration in Europe and Its Effects on Developing Countries* (Tübingen: J. C. B. Mohr, 1994).
Gwartney, James D. and Robert A. Lawson, *Economic Freedom of the World: 2006 Annual Report* (Vancouver: Fraser Institute, 2006).
Haas, Ernst B., *The Uniting of Europe: Political, Social, and Economic Forces 1950–1957* (Stanford, CA: Stanford University Press, 1958).
Haberler, Gottfried, *Economic Growth and Stability: An Analysis of Economic Change and Policies* (Los Angeles: Nash Publ., 1974).

Haftel, Yoram Z., *Regional Economic Institutions and Conflict Mitigation: Design, Implementation, and the Promise of Peace* (Ann Arbor: University of Michigan Press, 2012).

Hallstein, Walter, *United Europe: Challenge and Opportunity* (Cambridge, MA: Harvard University Press, 1962).

Hallstein, Walter, *Europe in the Making* (London: George Allen & Unwin, 1972).

Hansen, Peo and Stefan Jonsson, *Eurafrica: The Untold History of European Integration and Colonialism* (London: Bloomsbury, 2015).

Hantrais, Linda, *Social Policy in the European Union*, 3rd ed. (Houndmills: Palgrave Macmillan, 2007).

Hardy, Michael, '1970–1982: Growing Difficulties and the GATT Procedure', in: Jörn Keck, Dimitri Vanoverbeke and Franz Waldenberger (eds.), *EU–Japan Relations, 1970–2012: From Confrontation to Global Partnership* (London: Routledge, 2013), 27–57.

Harhoff, Frederik, 'Greenland's Withdrawal from the European Communities', in: *Common Market Law Review* 20 (1983), 13–33.

Harryvan, Anjo G., *In Pursuit of Influence: The Netherland's European Policy during the Formative Years of the European Union, 1952–1973* (Brussels: Peter Lang, 2009).

Harryvan, Anjo G., Jan van der Harst, G. M. V. Mans and A. E. Kersten, 'Dutch Attitudes towards European Military, Political and Economic Integration (1950–1954)', in: Gilbert Trausch (ed.), *Die europäische Integration vom Schuman-Plan bis zu den Verträgen von Rom* (Baden-Baden: Nomos, 1993), 321–347.

Hartley, Trevor C., *European Union Law in a Global Context* (Cambridge: Cambridge University Press, 2004).

Haupt, Heinz-Gerhard, 'Der Siegeszug der Konsumgesellschaft', in: Martin Sabrow and Peter Ulrich Weiß (eds.), *Das 20. Jahrhundert vermessen. Signaturen eines vergangenen Zeitalters* (Göttingen: Wallstein, 2016), 219–240.

Hay, Richard, *The European Commission and the Administration of the Community* (Luxembourg: Office for Official Publications of the European Communities, 1989).

Hayward, Katy, 'Reiterating National Identities: The European Union Conception of Conflict Resolution in Northern Ireland', in: *Cooperation and Conflict* 41 (2006), 261–284.

Hecht, Gabrielle, *The Radiance of France: Nuclear Power and National Identity after World War II* (Cambridge, MA: MIT Press, 1998).

Heintz, Bettina, 'Numerische Differenz. Überlegungen zu einer Soziologie des (quantitativen) Vergleichs', in: *Zeitschrift für Soziologie* 39 (2010), 162–181.

Heister, Matthias W. M., *Der Studentensturm auf die Grenzen 1950. Für ein föderales Europa. Fakten – Probleme – Hintergründe – Konsequenzen* (Bonn: Iduso, 2015).

Heller, Peter B., *The United Nations under Dag Hammarskjöld, 1953–1961* (Lanham, MD: Scarecrow Press, 2001).

Henrekson, Magnus, Johan Torstensson and Rasha Torstensson, 'Growth Effects of European Integration', in: *European Economic Review* 41 (1997), 1537–1557.

Henrich-Franke, Christian, *Gescheiterte Integration im Vergleich: Der Verkehr – ein Problemsektor gemeinsamer Rechtsetzung im Deutschen Reich (1871–1879) und der Europäischen Wirtschaftsgemeinschaft (1958–1972)* (Stuttgart: Franz Steiner Verlag, 2012).

Herbst, Ludolf, 'Die zeitgenössische Integrationstheorie und die Anfänge der europäischen Einigung 1947–1950', in: *Vierteljahrshefte für Zeitgeschichte* 34 (1986), 161–205.

Herzer, Martin, 'The Rise of Euro-journalism: The Media and the European Communities, 1950s–1970s' (unpubl. PhD thesis, European University Institute, Florence, 2017).
Herzog, Benjamin, 'Historia magistra vitae', in: Stefan Jordan (ed.), *Lexikon Geschichtswissenschaft. Hundert Grundbegriffe* (Stuttgart: Reclam, 2002), 145–147.
Hill, Brian E., *The Common Agricultural Policy: Past, Present, and Future* (London: Methuen, 1984).
Hix, Simon, Abdul Noury and Gérard Roland, *Democratic Politics in the European Parliament* (Cambridge: Cambridge University Press, 2007).
Hodenberg, Christina von, *Konsens und Krise. Eine Geschichte der westdeutschen Medienöffentlichkeit 1945–1973* (Göttingen: Wallstein, 2006).
Hoffman, William, *Queen Juliana: The Story of the Richest Woman in the World* (New York: Harcourt Brace Jovanovich, 1979).
Hogan, Michael J., *The Marshall Plan: America, Britain, and the Reconstruction of Western Europe, 1947–1952* (Cambridge: Cambridge University Press, 1987).
Höhler, Sabine, 'Resilienz: Mensch – Umwelt – System. Eine Geschichte der Stressbewältigung von der Erholung zur Selbstoptimierung', in: *Zeithistorische Forschungen* 11 (2014), 425–443.
Hölscher, Lucian, *Die Entdeckung der Zukunft* (Frankfurt am Main: Fischer, 1999).
Hooghe, Liesbet and Gary Marks, 'A Postfunctionalist Theory of European Integration: From Permissive Consensus to Constraining Dissensus', in: *British Journal of Political Science* 39 (2009), 1–23.
Howlett, Michael and Klaus H. Goetz, 'Time, Temporality and Timescapes in Administration and Policy: Introduction', in: *International Review of Administrative Sciences* 80 (2014), 477–492.
Hug, Simon, *Voices of Europe: Citizens, Referendums, and European Integration* (Lanham, MD: Rowman & Littlefield, 2002).
Hughes, Edel, *Turkey's Accession to the European Union: The Politics of Exclusion?* (Abingdon: Routledge, 2010).
Hünemörder, Kai, *Die Frühgeschichte der globalen Umweltkrise und die Formierung der deutschen Umweltpolitik (1950–1973)* (Stuttgart: Franz Steiner Verlag, 2004).
Imig, Doug, 'Contestation in the Streets: European Protest and the Emerging Euro-Polity', in: Gary Marks and Marco R. Steenbergen (eds.), *European Integration and Political Conflict* (Cambridge: Cambridge University Press, 2004), 216–234.
Inglehart, Ronald, 'An End to European Integration?', in: *American Political Science Review* 61 (1967), 91–105.
Inglehart, Ronald, Jacques-René Rabier and Karlheinz Reif, 'The Evolution of Public Attitudes toward European Integration: 1970–1986', in: *Journal of European Integration* 10 (1987), 135–155.
Iriye, Akira, *Global Community: The Role of International Organizations in the Making of the Contemporary World* (Berkeley: University of California Press, 2002).
Irwin, Douglas A., 'The GATT's Contribution to Economic Recovery in Post-War Western Europe', in: Barry Eichengreen (ed.), *Europe's Post-War Recovery* (Cambridge: Cambridge University Press, 1995), 127–150.
Isnard, Hildebert, 'Le commerce extérieur de l'Algérie en 1960', in: *Méditerranée* 2 (1961), 93–98.
James, Harold, 'The IMF and the Bretton Woods System, 1944–58', in: Barry Eichengreen (ed.), *Europe's Post-War Recovery* (Cambridge: Cambridge University Press, 1995), 93–126.
James, Harold, *Europe Reborn: A History, 1914–2000* (Harlow: Longman, 2003).

James, Harold, *Making the European Monetary Union: The Role of the Committee of Central Bank Governors and the Origins of the European Central Bank* (Cambridge, MA: Belknap Press, 2012).
James, Harold, 'The Multiple Contexts of Bretton Woods', in: *Oxford Review of Economic Policy* 28 (2012), 411–430.
Jansen, Jan C., *Erobern und Erinnern. Symbolpolitik, öffentlicher Raum und französischer Kolonialismus in Algerien 1830–1950* (Munich: Oldenbourg, 2013).
Jarausch, Konrad H., *Out of Ashes: A New History of Europe in the Twentieth Century* (Princeton, NJ: Princeton University Press, 2015).
Jay, Peter, 'Europe: Periclean League of Democracies, Bonaparte's Third French Empire or Carolingian Fourth Reich', in: Kurt Almqvist and Alexander Linklater (eds.), *The Pursuit of Europe: Perspectives from the Engelberg Seminar 2012* (Stockholm: Ax:son Foundation, 2013), 63–72.
Jensen, Einar Lund and Jens Heinrich, 'Fra hjemmestyre til selvstyre, 1979–2009', in: Hans Christian Gulløv (ed.), *Danmark og kolonierne: Grønland* (Copenhagen: GADs Forlag, 2017), 374–421.
Jobs, Richard Ivan, 'Youth Movements: Travel, Protest, and Europe in 1968', in: *American Historical Review* 114 (2009), 376–404.
Jobs, Richard Ivan, *Backpack Ambassadors: How Youth Travel Integrated Europe* (Chicago: University of Chicago Press, 2017).
Joerges, Christian, Josef Falke, Hans-Wolfgang Micklitz and Gert Brüggemeier, *Die Sicherheit von Konsumgütern und die Entwicklung der Europäischen Gemeinschaft* (Baden-Baden: Nomos, 1988).
Jones, Philip N. and John North, 'Japanese Motor Industry Transplants: The West European Dimension', in: *Economic Geography* 67 (1991), 105–123.
Josling, Timothy E., Stefan Tangermann and Thorald K. Warley, *Agriculture in the GATT* (New York: St. Martin's Press, 1996).
Judt, Tony, 'The Rediscovery of Central Europe', in: *Daedalus* 119 (1990), 23–54.
Judt, Tony, *Postwar: A History of Europe since 1945* (New York: Penguin, 2005).
Jureit, Ulrike and Nikola Tietze (eds.), *Postsouveräne Territorialität. Die Europäische Union und ihr Raum* (Hamburg: Hamburger Edition, 2015).
Kaelble, Hartmut, *Wege zur Demokratie. Von der Französischen Revolution zur Europäischen Union* (Stuttgart: DVA, 2001).
Kaelble, Hartmut, *Sozialgeschichte Europas. 1945 bis zur Gegenwart* (Munich: C. H. Beck, 2007).
Kaelble, Hartmut, *Mehr Reichtum, mehr Armut. Soziale Ungleichheit in Europa vom 20. Jahrhundert bis zur Gegenwart* (Frankfurt am Main: Campus, 2017).
Kaelble, Hartmut, *Der verkannte Bürger. Eine andere Geschichte der europäischen Integration seit 1950* (Frankfurt am Main: Campus, 2019).
Kaelble, Hartmut, 'Geschichte des sozialen Europa. Erfolge oder verpasste Chancen?', in: Gabriele Metzler and Michael Werner (eds.), *Europa neu besehen. Geistes- und sozialwissenschaftliche Einblicke* (Frankfurt am Main: Campus, forthcoming).
Kaiser, Joseph H., Peter Badura, Hans-Ulrich Evers and Ernst-Werner Fuss, *Bewahrung und Veränderung demokratischer und rechtsstaatlicher Verfassungsstruktur in den internationalen Gemeinschaften (Tagung der Vereinigung der Deutschen Staatsrechtslehrer 1964)* (Berlin: de Gruyter, 1966).
Kaiser, Wolfram, *Using Europe, Abusing the Europeans: Britain and European Integration, 1945–63* (Houndmills: Macmillan, 1999).
Kaiser, Wolfram, *Christian Democracy and the Origins of European Union* (Cambridge: Cambridge University Press, 2007).

Kaiser, Wolfram, 'Transnational Practices Governing European Integration: Executive Autonomy and Neo-Corporatist Concertation in the Steel Sector', in: *Contemporary European History* 27 (2018), 239–257.

Kaiser, Wolfram, Brigitte Leucht and Morten Rasmussen (eds.), *The History of the European Union: Origins of a Trans- and Supranational Polity, 1950–72* (New York: Routledge, 2009).

Kaiser, Wolfram and Jan-Henrik Meyer (eds.), *International Organizations and Environmental Protection: Conservation and Globalization in the Twentieth Century* (New York: Berghahn, 2016).

Kaiser, Wolfram and Johan Schot, *Writing the Rules for Europe: Experts, Cartels, and International Organizations* (Houndmills: Palgrave Macmillan, 2014).

Kansikas, Suvi, *Socialist Countries Face the European Community: Soviet-Bloc Controversies over East–West Trade* (Frankfurt am Main: Lang, 2014).

Kapur, Harish, *China and the European Economic Community: The New Connection* (Dordrecht: Nijhoff, 1986).

Karamouzi, Eirini, *Greece, the EEC and the Cold War, 1974–1979: The Second Enlargement* (Houndmills: Palgrave Macmillan, 2014).

Keck, Jörn, '1987–1990: Keeping Relations on an Even Keel', in: Jörn Keck, Dimitri Vanoverbeke and Franz Waldenberger (eds.), *EU–Japan Relations, 1970–2012: From Confrontation to Global Partnership* (London: Routledge, 2013), 78–110.

Kennedy, David M., *Freedom from Fear: The American People in Depression and War, 1929–1945* (Oxford: Oxford University Press, 1999).

Keogh, Aoife, 'Managing Membership: Ireland and the European Economic Community 1973–1979' (unpubl. PhD thesis, European University Institute, Florence, 2015).

Keohane, Robert O. and Stanley Hoffmann, 'Institutional Change in Europe in the 1980s', in: Robert O. Keohane and Stanley Hoffmann (eds.), *The New European Community: Decision-making and Institutional Change* (Boulder, CO: Westview Press, 1991), 1–39.

Key, Valdimer O., *Public Opinion and American Democracy* (New York: Alfred A. Knopf, 1961).

Kipping, Matthias, *Zwischen Kartellen und Konkurrenz. Der Schuman-Plan und die Ursprünge der europäischen Einigung 1944–1952* (Berlin: Duncker & Humblot, 1996).

Kissinger, Henry A., *Diplomacy* (New York: Simon & Schuster, 1994).

Kitzinger, Uwe, *Diplomacy and Persuasion: How Britain Joined the Common Market* (London: Thames & Hudson, 1973).

Kjærsgaard, Kristine, 'Confronting the Greek Military Junta: Scandinavian Joint Action under the European Commission on Human Rights, 1967–70', in: Poul Villaume, Rasmus Mariager and Helle Porsdam (eds.), *The 'Long 1970s': Human Rights, East–West Détente and Transnational Relations* (New York: Routledge, 2016), 51–70.

Kleinman, Mark, *A European Welfare State? European Union Social Policy in Context* (Houndmills: Palgrave Macmillan, 2002).

Kletzin, Birgit, *Europa aus Rasse und Raum. Die nationalsozialistische Idee der Neuen Ordnung* (Münster: Lit, 2000).

Klopotek, Felix, 'Projekt', in: Ulrich Bröcking, Susanne Krasmann and Thomas Lemke (eds.), *Glossar der Gegenwart* (Frankfurt am Main: Suhrkamp, 2004), 216–220.

Klose, Fabian, *Menschenrechte im Schatten kolonialer Gewalt. Die Dekolonisierungskriege in Kenia und Algerien 1945–1962* (Munich: Oldenbourg, 2009).

Knudsen, Ann-Christina, 'Delegation as a Political Process: The Case of the Inter-Institutional Debate over the Budget Treaty', in: Wolfram Kaiser, Brigitte Leucht and Morten Rasmussen (eds.), *The History of the European Union: Origins of a Trans- and Supranational Polity 1950–72* (New York: Routledge, 2009), 167–188.

Knudsen, Ann-Christina, 'The European Parliament and Political Careers at the Nexus of European Integration and Transnational History', in: Johnny Laursen (ed.), *The Institutions and Dynamics of the European Community, 1973–83* (Baden-Baden: Nomos, 2014), 76–97.

Knudsen, Ann-Christina L., *Farmers on Welfare: The Making of Europe's Common Agricultural Policy* (Ithaca, NY: Cornell University Press, 2009).

Knudsen, Ann-Christina L., 'European Integration in the Image and the Shadow of Agriculture', in: Desmond Dinan (ed.), *Origins and Evolution of the European Union*, 2nd ed. (Oxford: Oxford University Press, 2014), 189–216.

Knudsen, Ann-Christina L. and Morten Rasmussen, 'A European Political System in the Making, 1958–1970: The Relevance of Emerging Committee Structures', in: *Journal of European Integration History* 14 (2008), 51–69.

Kocka, Jürgen, *Geschichte des Kapitalismus* (Munich: C. H. Beck, 2013).

Kohnstamm, Max and Wolfgang Hager (eds.), *A Nation Writ Large? Foreign Policy Problems before the European Community* (London: Macmillan, 1973).

Kojève, Alexandre, 'Kolonialismus in europäischer Sicht', in: Piet Tommissen (ed.), *Schmittiana: Beiträge zu Leben und Werk Carl Schmitts*, vol. VI (Berlin: Duncker & Humblot, 1996), 126–140.

Kokott, Juliane, 'Report on Germany', in: Anne-Marie Slaughter, Alec Stone Sweet and J. H. H. Weiler (eds.), *The European Court and National Courts: Doctrine and Jurisprudence* (London: Bloomsbury Publishing, 1998), 77–131.

Koselleck, Reinhart, *Futures Past: On the Semantics of Historical Time* (New York: Columbia University Press, 2004).

Kott, Sandrine, 'Par-delà la guerre froide. Les organisations internationales et les circulations Est-Ouest (1947–1973)', in: *Vinctième Siècle* 109 (2011), 142–154.

Kott, Sandrine, 'Un modèle international de protection sociale est-il possible? L'OIT entre assurance et sécurité sociale (1919–1952)', in: *Revue d'Histoire de la Protection Sociale* 10 (2017), 62–83.

Kreyssig, Gerhard, 'Die sozialpolitische Fundierung der Montanunion', in: *Gewerkschaftliche Monatshefte* 9 (1958), 217–223.

Krislov, Samuel, Claus-Dieter Ehlermann and Joseph Weiler, 'The Political Organs and the Decision-Making Process in the United States and the European Community', in: Mauro Cappelletti, Monica Seccombe and Joseph Weiler (eds.), *Integration through Law: Europe and the American Federal Experience*, vol. 1, book 2 (Berlin: de Gruyter, 1986), 3–110.

Kropp, Sabine, *Kooperativer Föderalismus und Politikverflechtung* (Wiesbaden: VS Verlag, 2010).

Krotz, Ulrich, Kiran Klaus Patel and Federico Romero (eds.), *Europe's Cold War Relations: The EC Towards a Global Role* (London: Bloomsbury, 2020).

Krüger, Dieter, *Sicherheit durch Integration? Die wirtschaftliche und politische Zusammenarbeit Westeuropas 1947 bis 1957/58* (Munich: Oldenbourg, 2003).

Krumrey, Jacob, *The Symbolic Politics of European Integration: Staging Europe* (Basingstoke: Palgrave Macmillan, 2018).

Küsters, Hanns Jürgen, *Die Gründung der Europäischen Wirtschaftsgemeinschaft* (Baden-Baden: Nomos, 1982).

Laak, Dirk van, *Imperiale Infrastruktur. Deutsche Planungen für eine Erschließung Afrikas 1880 bis 1960* (Paderborn: Schöningh, 2004).

Lacey, Robert, *Monarch: The Life and Reign of Elizabeth II* (New York: Free Press, 2002).

Laffranque, Julia, 'Dissenting Opinion in the European Court of Justice – Estonia's Possible Contribution to the Democratisation of the European Union Judicial System', in: *Juridica International* 9 (2004), 14–23.

Lammers, Anne, 'Daten für das "Europa der Sechs": Sozialstatistiken für die Europäischen Gemeinschaften der 1950er- und 1960er-Jahre', in: *Themenportal Europäische Geschichte* (2013; online www.europa.clio-online.de/essay/id/artikel-3760, accessed 1 July 2019).

Landau, Daniel, 'The Contribution of the European Common Market to the Growth of Its Member Countries: An Empirical Test', in: *Weltwirtschaftliches Archiv* 131 (1995), 774–782.

Lappenküper, Ulrich, 'Hans-Dietrich Genscher, Emilio Colombo und der Kampf gegen die 'Eurosklerose'', in: Michael Gehler and Maddalena Guiotto (eds.), *Italien, Österreich und die Bundesrepublik Deutschland in Europa. Ein Dreiecksverhältnis in seinen wechselseitigen Beziehungen und Wahrnehmungen von 1945/49 bis zur Gegenwart* (Vienna: Böhlau Verlag, 2012), 225–242.

Larik, Joris, 'No Mixed Feelings: The Post-Lisbon Common Commercial Policy in *Daiichi Sankyo* and *Commission* v. *Council (Conditional Access Convention)*', in: *Common Market Law Review* 52 (2015), 779–800.

Laursen, Finn, 'The Not-So-Permissive Consensus: Thoughts on the Maastricht Treaty and the Future of European Integration', in: Finn Laursen and Sophie Vanhoonacker (eds.), *The Ratification of the Maastricht Treaty: Issues, Debates and Future Implications* (Dordrecht: Martinus Nijhoff, 1994), 295–317.

Lazar, Marc, *Maisons rouges. Les partis communistes français et italien de la Libération à nos jours* (Paris: Aubier, 1992).

Leboutte, René, *Histoire économique et sociale de la construction européenne* (Brussels: Peter Lang, 2008).

Leconte, Cécile, 'The Fragility of the EU as a "Community of Values": Lessons from the Haider Affair', in: *West European Politics* 28 (2005), 620–649.

Lehmann, Gustav Adolf, *Perikles. Staatsmann und Stratege im klassischen Athen* (Munich: C. H. Beck, 2008).

Leimgruber, Matthieu and Matthias Schmelzer (eds.), *The OECD and the International Political Economy since 1948* (New York: Palgrave Macmillan, 2017).

Lejeune, Carlo and Christoph Brüll (eds.), *Grenzerfahrungen: Eine Geschichte der Deutschsprachigen Gemeinschaft Belgiens*, vol. 5: *Säuberung, Wiederaufbau, Autonomiediskussionen (1945–1973)* (Eupen: Grenz-Echo Verlag, 2014).

Lenaerts, Koen and Piet Van Nuffel, *Europees Recht in Hoofdlijnen* (Antwerp: Maklu, 2003).

Leonardi, Laura and Antonio Varsori (eds.), *Lo spazio sociale europeo. Atti del convegno internazionale di studi, Fiesole (Fi), 10–11 ottobre 2003* (Florence: Firenze University Press, 2005).

Leucht, Brigitte, 'Transatlantic Policy Networks in the Creation of the First European Anti-Trust Law: Mediating between American Anti-Trust and German Ordo-Liberalism', in: Wolfram Kaiser, Brigitte Leucht and Morten Rasmussen (eds.), *The History of the European Union: Origins of a Trans- and Supranational Polity 1950–72* (New York: Routledge, 2009), 56–73.

Leucht, Brigitte and Mel Maquis, 'American Influences on EEC Competition Law: Two Paths, How Much Dependence?', in: Kiran Klaus Patel and Heike Schweitzer (eds.), *The Historical Foundations of EU Competition Law* (Oxford: Oxford University Press, 2013), 125–161.

Lie, Einar, 'Masters and Servants: Economists and Bureaucrats in the Dispute over Norwegian EEC Membership in 1972', in: *Contemporary European History* 24 (2015), 279–300.

Lindberg, Leon N., *The Political Dynamics of European Economic Integration* (Stanford, CA: Standford University Press, 1963).

Lindberg, Leon N. and Stuart A. Scheingold, *Europe's Would-Be Polity: Patterns of Change in the European Community* (Engelwood Cliffs, NJ: Prentice-Hall, 1970).

Lindsay, Kenneth, *European Assemblies: The Experimental Period, 1949–1959* (London: Stevens, 1960).

Lindseth, Peter L., *Power and Legitimacy: Reconciling Europe and the Nation-State* (Oxford: Oxford University Press, 2010).

Lipgens, Walter, *Die Anfänge der europäischen Einigungspolitik 1945–1950*, 2 vols. (Stuttgart: Ernst Klett Verlag, 1977).

Lister, Marjorie, *The European Community and the Developing World: The Role of the Lomé Convention* (Aldershot: Avebury, 1988).

Loeb, Harold, *Life in a Technocracy: What It Might Be Like* (New York: Syracuse University Press, 1996).

Loth, Wilfried, *Der Weg nach Europa. Geschichte der europäischen Integration 1939–1957*, 3rd ed. (Göttingen: Vandenhoeck & Ruprecht, 1996).

Loth, Wilfried, *Building Europe: A History of European Unification* (Berlin: de Gruyter, 2015).

Loth, Wilfried, *Charles de Gaulle* (Stuttgart: Kohlhammer, 2015).

Loth, Wilfried and Marie-Thérèse Bitsch, 'The Hallstein Commission, 1958–67', in: European Commission (ed.), *The European Commission 1958–72: History and Memories* (Luxembourg: Office for Official Publications of the European Communities, 2007), 57–86.

Ludlow, N. Piers, 'The Making of the CAP: Towards a Historical Analysis of the EU's First Major Policy', in: *Contemporary European History* 14 (2005), 347–371.

Ludlow, N. Piers, *The European Community and the Crises of the 1960s: Negotiating the Gaullist Challenge* (London: Routledge, 2006).

Ludlow, N. Piers (ed.), *European Integration and the Cold War: Ostpolitik–Westpolitik, 1965–1973* (London: Routledge, 2007).

Ludlow, N. Piers, 'European Integration in the 1980s: On the Way to Maastricht?', in: *Journal of European Integration History* 19 (2013), 11–22.

Ludlow, N. Piers, 'The Unnoticed Apogee of Atlanticism? U.S.–Western European Relations during the Early Reagan Era', in: Kiran Klaus Patel and Kenneth Weisbrode (eds.), *European Integration and the Atlantic Community in the 1980s* (Cambridge: Cambridge University Press, 2013), 17–38.

Ludlow, N. Piers, *Roy Jenkins and the European Commission Presidency 1976–1980: At the Heart of Europe* (Basingstoke: Palgrave Macmillan, 2016).

Ludlow, N. Piers, 'More than just a Single Market: European Integration, Peace and Security in the 1980s', in: *The British Journal of Politics and International Relations* 19 (2017), 48–62.

Ludlow, Peter, *The Making of the European Monetary System: A Case Study of the Politics of the European Community* (London: Butterworth, 1982).

Ludwig, Karl, 'Westwallbau und Kriegsgeschehen in der Südpfalz. Der Otterbachabschnitt 1936–1945', in: Rolf Übel and Oliver Röller (eds.), *Der Westwall in der Südpfalz: Otterbach-Abschnitt* (Ludwigshafen: Pro Message, 2012), 33–136.

Lundestad, Geir, *The United States and Western Europe since 1945: From 'Empire' by Invitation to Transatlantic Drift* (Oxford: Oxford University Press, 2003).

Luzzatto Fegiz, Pierpaolo, *Il volto sconosciuto dell'Italia* (Milan: Giuffrè Editore, 1956).
Maddison, Angus, *The World Economy: A Millennial Perspective* (Paris: OECD, 2001).
Maes, Ivo, *Economic Thought and the Making of European Monetary Union: Selected Essays of Ivo Maes* (Cheltenham: Edward Elgar, 2002).
Maes, Ivo, 'History of Economic Thought and Policy-Making at the European Commission', in: Volker Nisch and Harald Badinger (eds.), *Routledge Handbook of the Economics of European Integration* (London: Taylor & Francis, 2015), 38–52.
Maier, Charles S., 'The Politics of Productivity: Foundations of American International Economic Policy after World War II', in: *International Organization* 31 (1977), 607–633.
Maier, Charles S. (ed.), *The Marshall Plan and Germany: West German Development within the Framework of the European Recovery Program* (New York: Berg, 1991).
Maier, Charles S., *Leviathan 2.0: Inventing Modern Statehood* (Cambridge, MA: Belknap Press, 2012).
Maier, Charles S., *Once within Borders: Territories of Power, Wealth, and Belonging since 1500* (Cambridge, MA: Belknap Press, 2016).
Majone, Giandomenico, 'The European Community between Social Policy and Social Regulation', in: *Journal of Common Market Studies* 31 (1993), 153–170.
Mameri, Aflakh, 'L'Adhésion de l'Algérie à la Communauté Economique Européenne', in: *Revue Algérienne des Sciences Juridiques, Economiques et Politiques* 5 (1968), 429–435.
Mangenot, Michel, 'La revendication d'une paternité: Les hauts fonctionnaires français et le "style" administratif de la Commission européenne (1958–1988)', in: *Pôle Sud* 15 (2001), 33–46.
Mangenot, Michel and Katja Seidel, 'Consolidating the European Civil Service', in: Eric Bussière et al. (eds.), *The European Commission 1973–1986: History and Memories of an Institution* (Luxembourg: Publications Office of the European Union, 2014), 61–70.
Manners, Ian, 'Normative Power Europe: A Contradiction in Terms?', in: *Journal of Common Market Studies* 40 (2002), 235–258.
Marcowitz, Reiner and Hélène Miard-Delacroix (eds.), *50 ans de relations franco-allemandes* (Paris: Nouveau Monde Editions, 2013).
Marjolin, Robert, *Le travail d'une vie: Mémoires, 1911–1986* (Paris: Laffont, 1986).
Martin, Guy, *Africa in World Politics: A Pan-African Perspective* (Trenton, NJ: Africa World Press, 2002).
Martin, Lisa L., 'Institutions and Cooperation: Sanctions during the Falkland Islands Conflict', in: *International Security* 16 (1992), 143–178.
Marx, Karl, *On Society and Social Change*, ed. by Neil J. Smelser (Chicago: Chicago University Press, 1973).
Masing, Johannes, *Die Mobilisierung des Bürgers für die Durchsetzung des Rechts. Europäische Impulse für eine Revision der Lehre vom subjektiv-öffentlichen Recht* (Berlin: Duncker & Humblot, 1997).
Mastenbroek, Ellen, 'EU Compliance: Still a "Black Hole"?', in: *Journal of European Public Policy* 12 (2005), 1103–1120.
Maswood, S. Javed, *Trade, Development and Globalization* (New York: Routledge, 2014).
May, Alex (ed.), *Britain, the Commonwealth and Europe: The Commonwealth and Britain's Application to Join the European Communities* (Houndmills: Palgrave Macmillan, 2001).
Mayhew, Alan, 'L'Assistance financière à l'Europe centrale et orientale. Le programme Phare', in: *Revue d'Etudes Comparatives Est-Ouest* 27 (1996), 135–157.

Mayne, Richard, 'The Europe We Want', in: Richard Mayne (ed.), *Europe Tomorrow: Sixteen Europeans Look Ahead* (London: Fontana, 1972), 340–348.
Mazower, Mark, *The Dark Continent: Europe's Twentieth Century* (New York: Alfred A. Knopf, 1998).
Mazower, Mark, *Hitler's Empire: Nazi Rule in Occupied Europe* (London: Allen Lane, 2008).
Mazower, Mark, *Governing the World: The History of an Idea* (New York: Penguin, 2012).
Mazrui, Ali A., 'African Attitudes to the European Economic Community', in: *International Affairs* 39 (1963), 24–36.
McCann, Dermot, *The Political Economy of the European Union: An Institutionalist Perspective* (Cambridge: Polity Press, 2010).
McCutcheon, J. Paul, 'The Irish Constitution and Ratification of the Single European Act', in: Paul Brennan (ed.), *Ireland, Europe and 92* (Paris: Presses Sorbonne Nouvelle, 1992), 19–41.
McIntosh, Malcolm, *Japan Re-armed* (London: F. Pinter, 1986).
Mechi, Lorenzo, 'Du BIT à la politique sociale européenne: Les origines d'un modèle', in: *Le Mouvement Social* 244 (2013), 17–30.
Mechi, Lorenzo, 'Managing the Labour Market in an Open Economy: From the International Labour Organisation to the European Communities', in: *Contemporary European History* 27 (2018), 221–238.
Medrano, Juan Díez, *Framing Europe: Attitudes to European Integration in Germany, Spain, and the United Kingdom* (Princeton, NJ: Princeton University Press, 2003).
Meifort, Franziska, *Ralf Dahrendorf. Eine Biographie* (Munich: C. H. Beck, 2017).
Mélandri, Pierre, 'Le rôle de l'unification européenne dans la politique extérieure des Etats-Unis 1948–1950', in: Raymond Poidevin (ed.), *Histoire des débuts de la construction européenne* (Brussels: Bruylant, 1986), 25–45.
Meloni, Giulia and Johan Swinnen, 'The Political Economy of European Wine Regulations', in: *Journal of Wine Economics* 8 (2013), 244–284.
Meloni, Giulia and Johan Swinnen, 'The Rise and Fall of the World's Largest Wine Exporter – and Its Institutional Legacy', in: *Journal of Wine Economics* 9 (2014), 3–33.
Merle, Robert, *Ahmed Ben Bella* (Paris: Gallimard, 1965).
Merriënboer, Johan van, *Mansholt: Een biografie* (Amsterdam: Boom, 2006).
Merseburger, Peter, *Kurt Schumacher: Patriot, Volkstribun, Sozialdemokrat* (Munich: Pantheon Verlag, 2010).
Meunier, Sophie, *Trading Voices: The European Union in International Commercial Negotiations* (Oxford: Oxford University Press, 2006).
Meunier, Sophie and Kalypso Nicolaïdis, 'The European Union as a Trade Power', in: Christopher Hill, Michael Smith and Sophie Vanhoonacker (eds.), *International Relations and the European Union*, 3rd ed. (Oxford: Oxford University Press, 2017), 209–234.
Meyer, Jan-Henrik, *The European Public Sphere: Media and Transnational Communication in European Integration 1969–1991* (Stuttgart: Franz Steiner Verlag, 2010).
Meyer, Jan-Henrik, 'Who Should Pay for Pollution? The OECD, the European Communities and the Emergence of Environmental Policy in the early 1970s', in: *European Review of History* 24 (2017), 377–398.
Miard-Delacroix, Hélène, *Im Zeichen der europäischen Einigung. 1963 bis in die Gegenwart* (Darmstadt: WBG, 2011).

Micossi, Stefano, 'Thirty Years of the Single European Market', in: *CEPS Special Report* 148 (2016), 1–33.
Migani, Guia, *La France et l'Afrique Sub-Saharienne, 1957–1963: Histoire d'une décolonisation entre idéaux eurafricains et politique de puissance* (Brussels: Peter Lang, 2008).
Migani, Guia, 'The EEC and the Challenge of the ACP States' Industrialization, 1972–1975', in: Christian Grabas and Alexander Nützenadel (eds.), *Industrial Policy in Europe after 1945: Wealth, Power and Economic Development in the Cold War* (Houndmills: Palgrave Macmillan, 2014), 256–276.
Migani, Guia, 'Lomé and the North–South Relations (1975–1984): From the "New International Economic Order" to a New Conditionality', in: Claudia Hiepel (ed.), *Europe in a Globalising World: Global Challenges and European Responses in the 'Long' 1970s* (Baden-Baden: Nomos, 2014), 123–145.
Milward, Alan S., *The Reconstruction of Western Europe, 1945–51* (Berkeley: University of California Press, 1984).
Milward, Alan S., *The European Rescue of the Nation-State*, 2nd ed. (London: Routledge, 2000).
Milward, Alan S., *The United Kingdom and the European Community*, vol. I: *The Rise and Fall of a National Strategy, 1945–1963* (London: Routledge, 2002).
Mitchell, B. R., *International Historical Statistics: Europe 1750–2000* (Houndmills: Palgrave Macmillan, 2003).
Mitzner, Veera, 'Almost in Europe? How Finland's Embarrassing Entry into Eureka Captured Policy Change', in: *Contemporary European History* 25 (2016), 481–504.
Möckli, Daniel, *European Foreign Policy during the Cold War: Heath, Brandt, Pompidou and the Dream of Political Unity* (London: I. B. Tauris, 2009).
Möckli, Daniel and Victor Mauer (eds.), *European–American Relations and the Middle East: From Suez to Iraq* (New York: Routledge, 2011).
Moggridge, Donald E., (ed.), *The Collected Writings of John Maynard Keynes*, vol. XXV: *Activities 1940–1944* (Basingstoke: Macmillan, 1980).
Möhler, Rolf and Jan van Rij, '1983–1987: Export Moderation as a Panacea or Can Japan Change?', in: Jörn Keck, Dimitri Vanoverbeke and Franz Waldenberger (eds.), *EU–Japan Relations, 1970–2012: From Confrontation to Global Partnership* (London: Routledge, 2013), 58–77.
Möller, Kay, 'Diplomatic Relations and Mutual Strategic Perceptions: China and the European Union', in: *China Quarterly* 169 (2002), 10–32.
Monnet, Jean, *Memoirs* (Garden City, NY: Doubleday, 1979).
Monnier, Alain, 'The European Union at the Time of Enlargement', in: *Population (English Edition)* 59 (2004), 315–336.
Montarsolo, Yves, *L'Eurafrique, contrepoint de l'idée d'Europe* (Aix-en-Provence: Publications de l'Université de Provence, 2010).
Moore, Bob, 'Decolonization by Default: Suriname and the Dutch Retreat from Empire', in: *Journal of Imperial and Commonwealth History* 28 (2000), 228–250.
Moravcsik, Andrew, *The Choice for Europe: Social Purpose and State Power from Messina to Maastricht* (Ithaca, NY: Cornell University Press, 1998).
Moravcsik, Andrew, 'The Origins of Human Rights Regimes: Democratic Delegation in Postwar Europe', in: *International Organization* 54 (2000), 217–252.
Morelli, Umberto and Altiero Spinelli, *Il pensiero e l'azione per la federazione europea* (Milan: Giuffrè Editore, 2010).
Morone, Antonio M., *L'ultima colonia: Come l'Italia è tornata in Africa 1950–1960* (Rome: Laterza, 2011).

Mourlon-Druol, Emmanuel, *A Europe Made of Money: The Emergence of the European Monetary System* (Ithaca, NY: Cornell University Press, 2012).

Mourlon-Druol, Emmanuel, 'Steering Europe: Explaining the Rise of the European Council, 1975–1986', in: *Contemporary European History* 25 (2016), 409–437.

Mourlon-Druol, Emmanuel and Federico Romero (eds.), *International Summitry and Global Governance: The Rise of the G7 and the European Council, 1974–1991* (London: Routledge, 2014).

Moyn, Samuel, *The Last Utopia: Human Rights in History* (Cambridge, MA: Belknap Press of Harvard University Press, 2010).

Müller, Uwe, 'Failed and Forgotten? New Perspectives on the History of the Council for Mutual Economic Assistance', in: *Comparativ* 27 (2017), 7–25.

Muñoz Sánchez, Antonio, 'A European Answer to the Spanish Question: The SPD and the End of the Franco Dictatorship', in: *Journal of European Integration History* 15 (2009), 77–93.

Murray, Christopher W., 'View from the United States: Common Foreign and Security Policy as a Centerpiece of U.S. Interest in European Political Union', in: Reinhardt Rummel (ed.), *Toward Political Union: Planning a Common Foreign and Security Policy in the European Community* (Boulder, CO: Westview Press, 1992), 213–227.

Nafpliotis, Alexandros, *Britain and the Greek Colonels: Accommodating the Junta in the Cold War* (London: I. B. Tauris, 2013).

Naumann, Kolja, *Eine religiöse Referenz in einem Europäischen Verfassungsvertrag* (Tübingen: Mohr Siebeck, 2008).

Naylor, Philip C., *France and Algeria: A History of Decolonization and Transformation* (Gainesville: University Press of Florida, 2000).

Neißkenwirth, Frederike, *'Die Europa-Union wird Avantgarde bleiben'. Transnationale Zusammenarbeit in der niederländischen und deutschen Europabewegung (1945–1958)* (Münster: Waxmann, 2016).

Nelsen, Brent F. and Alexander Stubb (eds.), *The European Union: Readings on the Theory and Practice of European Integration* (Houndmills: Macmillan, 2003).

Neuhann, Florian, *Im Schatten der Integration. OLAF und die Bekämpfung von Korruption in der Europäischen Union* (Baden-Baden: Nomos, 2005).

Neuss, Beate, *Geburtshelfer Europas? Die Rolle der Vereinigten Staaten im europäischen Integrationsprozeß 1945–1958* (Baden-Baden: Nomos, 2000).

Nichter, Luke A., *Richard Nixon and Europe: The Reshaping of the Postwar Atlantic World* (Cambridge: Cambridge University Press, 2015).

Nicolaïdis, Kalypso, 'The Cassis Legacy: Kir, Banks, Plumbers, Drugs, Criminals and Refugees', in: Fernanda Nicola and Bill Davies (eds.), *EU Law Stories: Contextual and Critical Histories of European Jurisprudence* (Cambridge: Cambridge University Press, 2017), 278–300.

Nicolaïdis, Kalypso, Berny Sèbe and Gabrielle Maas (eds.), *Echoes of Empire: Memory, Identity and Colonial Legacies* (London: I. B. Tauris, 2015).

Nicolaïdis, Kalypso, Claire Vergerio, Nora Fisher Onar and Juri Viehoff, 'From Metropolis to Microcosmos: The EU's New Standards of Civilisation', in: *Millennium: Journal of International Studies* 42 (2014), 718–745.

Nicolaides, Phedon, 'Withdrawal from the European Union: A Typology of Effects', in: *Maastricht Journal* 20 (2013), 209–219.

Niess, Frank, *Die europäische Idee – aus dem Geist des Widerstands* (Frankfurt am Main: Suhrkamp, 2001).

Nora, Pierre, 'Comment écrire l'histoire de France?', in: Pierre Nora (ed.), *Les lieux de mémoire:* III *Les France*, vol. 1 (Paris: Gallimard, 1992), 11–32.

Norwig, Christina, *Die erste europäische Generation. Europakonstruktionen in der Europäischen Jugendkampagne 1951–1958* (Göttingen: Wallstein, 2016).

Nye, Joseph S., *Peace in Parts: Integration and Conflict in Regional Organization* (Boston: Little, Brown and Company, 1971).

Oberloskamp, Eva, *Codename TREVI. Terrorismusbekämpfung und die Anfänge einer europäischen Innenpolitik in den 1970er Jahren* (Munich: Oldenbourg, 2017).

Odijie, Michael, 'The Fear of "Yellow Peril" and the Emergence of European Federalist Movement', in: *International History Review* 40 (2018), 358–375.

Orbie, Jan, 'Civilian Power Europe: Review of the Original and Current Debates', in: *Cooperation and Conflict* 41 (2006), 123–128.

O'Toole, Laurence J. Jr., 'Policy Recommendations for Multi-Actor Implementation: An Assessment of the Field', in: *Journal of Public Policy* 6 (1986), 181–210.

Palayret, Jean-Marie, 'Mondialisme contre régionalisme: CEE et ACP dans les négociations de la convention de Lomé 1970–75', in: Antonio Varsori (ed.), *Inside the European Community: Actors and Policies in European Integration 1957–1972* (Baden-Baden: Nomos, 2006), 369–397.

Palayret, Jean-Marie, Helen Wallace and Pascaline Winand (eds.), *Visions, Votes and Vetoes: The Empty Chair Crisis and the Luxembourg Compromise Forty Years On* (Brussels: Lang, 2006).

Palmowski, Jan, 'The Europeanization of the Nation-State', in: *Journal of Contemporary History* 46 (2011), 631–657.

Pardo, Sharon, 'The Year that Israel Considered Joining the European Economic Community', in: *Journal of Common Market Studies* 51 (2013), 901–915.

Pasquinucci, Daniele, 'Nella "direzione del movimento storico". Il contributo federalista alla europeizzazione dell'Italia', in: Piero Craveri and Antonio Varsori (eds.), *L'Italia nella costruzione europea. Un bilancio storico (1957–2007)* (Milan: FrancoAngeli, 2009), 395–415.

Pasquinucci, Daniele and Luca Verzichelli (eds.), *Contro l'Europa? I diversi scetticismi verso l'integrazione europea* (Bologna: Il Mulino, 2016).

Passas, Nikos and David Nelken, 'The Thin Line between Legitimate and Criminal Enterprises: Subsidy Fraud in the European Community', in: *Crime, Law & Social Change* 19 (1993), 223–243.

Pasture, Patrick, *Imagining European Unity since 1000* AD (Houndmills: Palgrave Macmillan, 2015).

Patel, Kiran Klaus, 'Wie Europa seine Bürger verlor. Europäisierung und die Defizite der Integration', in: *Internationale Politik* 60 (2005), 22–28.

Patel, Kiran Klaus, *Europäisierung wider Willen: Die Bundesrepublik Deutschland in der Agrarintegration der EWG 1955–1973* (Munich: Oldenbourg, 2009).

Patel, Kiran Klaus, 'Germany and European Integration since 1945', in: Helmut Walser Smith (ed.), *The Oxford Handbook of Modern German History* (Oxford: Oxford University Press, 2011), 775–794.

Patel, Kiran Klaus, 'Rivalisierende Raum-Zeit-Ordnungen. Verhandeln im Europäischen Integrationsprozess im 20. Jahrhundert', in: Günther Heeg (ed.), *Globalizing Areas, kulturelle Flexionen und die Herausforderung der Geisteswissenschaften* (Stuttgart: Franz Steiner Verlag, 2011), 61–77.

Patel, Kiran Klaus, 'Europäische Integration', in: Jost Dülffer and Wilfried Loth (eds.), *Dimensionen internationaler Geschichte* (Munich: Oldenbourg, 2012), 353–372.

Patel, Kiran Klaus, 'William Penn und sein Essay *Towards the Present and Future Peace of Europe* (1693): Friedensfürst, Vordenker europäischer Einigung oder Machtpolitiker?', in: *Historische Zeitschrift* 295 (2012), 330–357.

Patel, Kiran Klaus (ed.), *The Cultural Politics of Europe: European Capitals of Culture and European Union since the 1980s* (London: Routledge, 2013).

Patel, Kiran Klaus, 'Provincialising European Union: Co-operation and Integration in Europe in a Historical Perspective', in: *Contemporary European History* 22 (2013), 649–673.

Patel, Kiran Klaus, *The New Deal: A Global History* (Princeton, NJ: Princeton University Press, 2016).

Patel, Kiran Klaus and Oriane Calligaro, 'The True "EURESCO"? The Council of Europe, Transnational Networking and the Emergence of European Community Cultural Policies, 1970–90', in: *European Review of History* 24 (2017), 399–422.

Patel, Kiran Klaus and Wolfram Kaiser (eds.), 'Multiple Connections in European Cooperation: International Organizations, Policy Ideas, Practices and Transfers 1967–1992', in: *European Review of History* 24, 3 (2017) (special issue).

Patel, Kiran Klaus and Wolfram Kaiser, 'Continuity and Change in European Cooperation during the Twentieth Century', in: *Contemporary European History* 27 (2018), 165–182.

Patel, Kiran Klaus and Johan Schot, 'Twisted Paths to European Integration: Comparing Agriculture and Transport in a Transnational Perspective', in: *Contemporary European History* 20 (2011), 383–403.

Patel, Kiran Klaus and Heike Schweitzer (eds.), *The Historical Foundations of EU Competition Law* (Oxford: Oxford University Press, 2013).

Patel, Kiran Klaus and Kenneth Weisbrode (eds.), *European Integration and the Atlantic Community in the 1980s* (Cambridge: Cambridge University Press, 2013).

Pedaliu, Effie G. H., 'Human Rights and International Security: The International Community and the Greek Dictators', in: *International History Review* 38 (2016), 1014–1039.

Pelkmans, Jacques, 'The New Approach to Technical Harmonization and Standardization', in: *Journal of Common Market Studies* 25 (1987), 249–269.

Pelkmans, Jacques, 'Mutual Recognition in Goods and Services: An Economic Perspective', in: *Economics Working Papers* No. 016, European Network of Economic Policy Research Institutes (2003).

Pelkmans, Jacques, 'The European Single Market – How Far from Completion?', in: *Intereconomics* 46 (2011), 64–81.

Pelt, Mogens, *Tying Greece to the West: US–West German–Greek Relations, 1949–1974* (Copenhagen: Museum Tusculanum Press, 2006).

Pessis, Céline, Sezin Topçu and Christophe Bonneuil (eds.), *Une autre histoire des 'Trente glorieuses'. Modernisation, contestations et pollutions dans la France d'après-guerre* (Paris: La Découverte, 2013).

Peters, Anne and Simone Peter, 'International Organizations: Between Technocracy and Democracy', in: Bardo Fassbender and Anne Peters (eds.), *The Oxford Handbook of the History of International Law* (Oxford: Oxford University Press, 2012), 170–197.

Petit, Michel, Michele de Benedictis, Denis Britton, Martijn de Groot, Wilhelm Henrichsmeyer and Francesco Lechi, *Agricultural Policy Formation in the European Community: The Birth of Milk Quotas and CAP Reform* (Amsterdam: Elsevier, 1987).

Pevehouse, Jon C., Timothy Nordstrom and Kevin Warnke, 'The Correlates of War 2 International Governmental Organizations Data Version 2.0', in: *Conflict Management and Peace Science* 21 (2004), 101–119.

Pfahl-Traughber, Armin, 'Zeitschriftenporträt: Nation Europa', in: *Jahrbuch Extremismus & Demokratie* 12 (2000), 305–322.

Pfeil, Ulrich, 'Der Händedruck von Verdun. Pathosformel der deutsch-französischen Versöhnung', in: Gerhard Paul (ed.), *Das Jahrhundert der Bilder. 1949 bis heute* (Göttingen: Vandenhoeck & Ruprecht, 2008).

Pfister, Eugen, *Europa im Bild: Imaginationen Europas in Wochenschauen in Deutschland, Frankreich, Großbritannien und Österreich 1948–1959* (Göttingen: Vandenhoeck & Ruprecht, 2014).

Philip, Alan Butt, 'The Application of the EEC Regulations on Drivers' Hours and Tachographs', in: Heinrich Siedentopf and Jacques Ziller (eds.), *Making European Policies Work: The Implementation of Community Regulation in the Member States*, vol. 1 (London: SAGE, 1988), 88–129.

Phinnemore, David, 'Crisis-Ridden, Battered and Bruised: Time to Give Up on the EU?', in: *Journal of Common Market Studies* 53 (2015), 61–74.

Pillinger, Jane, *Feminising the Market: Women's Pay and Employment in the European Community* (Houndmills: Palgrave Macmillan, 1992).

Pinder, John, 'Community against Conflict: The European Community's Contribution to Ethno-National Peace in Europe', in: Abram Chayes and Antonia Handler Chayes (eds.), *Preventing Conflict in the Post-Communist World: Mobilizing International and Regional Organizations* (Washington, D.C.: Brookings Institution, 1996).

Pineau, Christian, *1956, Suez* (Paris: R. Laffont, 1976).

Pinto, Antonio Costa and Nuno Severiano Teixeira, 'From Africa to Europe: Portugal and European Integration', in: Antonio Costa Pinto and Nuno Severiano Teixeira (eds.), *Southern Europe and the Making of the European Union 1945–1980s* (New York: Columbia University Press, 2002), 3–40.

Pistone, Sergio, *The Union of European Federalists: From the Foundation to the Decision on Direct Election of the European Parliament (1946–1974)* (Milan: Giuffrè Editore, 2008).

Plassmann, Lorenz, *Comme dans une nuit des Paques? Les relations franco-grecques, 1944–1981* (Brussels: Lang, 2012).

Plotkin, Sidney and Rick Tilman, *The Political Ideas of Thorstein Veblen* (New Haven, CT: Yale University Press, 2011).

Plumpe, Werner, 'Europäische Krisenpolitik auf dem Prüfstand. Die Europäische Integration aus wirtschaftshistorischer Sicht', in: Winfried Brömmel, Helmut König and Manfred Sicking (eds.), *Europa, wie weiter? Perspektiven eines Projekts in der Krise* (Bielefeld: transcript, 2015), 61–77.

Plumpe, Werner and André Steiner, 'Dimensionen wirtschaftlicher Integrationsprozesse in West- und Osteuropa nach dem Zweiten Weltkrieg', in: *Jahrbuch für Wirtschaftsgeschichte* 2 (2008), 21–38.

Pocock, J. G. A., 'The Atlantic Archipelago and the War of the Three Kingdoms (1996)', in: J. G. A. Pocock, *The Discovery of Islands: Essays in British History* (Cambridge: Cambridge University Press, 2005), 77–93.

Powell, Charles, 'The Long Road to Europe: Spain and the European Community, 1957–1986', in: Joaquín Roy and María Lorca-Susino (eds.), *Spain in the European Union: The First Twenty-Five Years (1986–2011)* (Miami: EU Centre, 2011), 21–44.

Puchala, Donald J., 'The Common Market and Political Federation in Western European Public Opinion', in: *International Studies Quarterly* 14 (1970), 32–59.

Pudlat, Andreas, 'Der lange Weg zum Schengen-Raum: Ein Prozess im Vier-Phasen-Modell', in: *Journal of European Integration History* 17 (2011), 303–326.

Pudlat, Andreas, *Schengen. Zur Manifestation von Grenze und Grenzschutz* (Hildesheim: Olms, 2013).

Puetter, Uwe, 'Europe's Deliberative Intergovernmentalism: The Role of the Council and European Council in EU Economic Governance', in: *Journal of European Public Policy* 19 (2012), 161–178.

Radkau, Joachim, *Aufstieg und Krise der deutschen Atomwirtschaft 1945–1975* (Hamburg: Reinbek, 1983).

Randeraad, Nico and Philip Post, 'Carving Out a Role: The UIA after the Second World War', in: Daniel Laqua, Wouter Van Acker and Christophe Verbruggen (eds.), *International Organizations and Global Civil Society: Histories of the Union of International Associations* (London: Bloomsbury Academic, 2019), 73–90.

Rasch, Manfred and Kurt Düwell (eds.), *Anfänge und Auswirkungen der Montanunion auf Europa. Die Stahlindustrie in Politik und Wirtschaft* (Essen: Klartext, 2007).

Rasmussen, Morten, 'Joining the European Communities: Denmark's Road to EC-Membership, 1961–1973' (unpubl. PhD thesis, European University Institute, Florence, 2004).

Rasmussen, Morten, 'From *Costa v ENEL* to the Treaties of Rome: A Brief History of a Legal Revolution', in: Miguel Poiares Maduro and Loïc Azoulai (eds.), *The Past and Future of EU Law: The Classics of EU Law Revisited on the 50th Anniversary of the Rome Treaty* (Oxford: Hart, 2008), 69–85.

Ratka, Thomas, 'Die Assoziierungspolitik der Neutralen 1961–1963 und der österreichische Alleingang 1963–1967', in: Michael Gehler (ed.), *Vom gemeinsamen Markt zur europäischen Unionsbildung. 50 Jahre Römische Verträge 1957–2007* (Vienna: Böhlau, 2009), 283–306.

Redmond, John and Zou Lan, 'The European Community and China: New Horizons', in: *Journal of Common Market Studies* 25 (1986), 133–155.

Reif, Karlheinz and Hermann Schmitt, 'Nine Second-Order National Elections: A Conceptual Framework for the Analysis of European Election Results', in: *European Journal of Political Research* 8 (1980), 3–44.

Reinfeldt, Alexander, *Unter Ausschluss der Öffentlichkeit? Akteure und Strategien supranationaler Informationspolitik in der Gründungsphase der europäischen Integration 1952–1972* (Stuttgart: Franz Steiner Verlag, 2014).

Reinhard, Wolfgang, *Die Unterwerfung der Welt. Globalgeschichte der europäischen Expansion, 1415–2015* (Munich: C. H. Beck, 2016).

Rempe, Martin, 'Airy Promises: The Senegal and the EEC's Common Agricultural Policy in the 1960s', in: Kiran Klaus Patel (ed.), *Fertile Ground for Europe? The History of European Integration and the Common Agricultural Policy since 1945* (Baden-Baden: Nomos, 2009), 221–240.

Rempe, Martin, 'Decolonization by Europeanization? The Early EEC and the Transformation of French–African Relations', in: Working Paper Series, No. 27 Kolleg-Forschergruppe (KFG), 'The Transformative Power of Europe', Freie Universität Berlin (2011).

Rempe, Martin, *Entwicklung im Konflikt. Die EWG und der Senegal 1957–1975* (Cologne: Böhlau, 2012).

Repgen, Konrad, 'Vom Nutzen der Historie', in: Amalie Fössel and Christoph Kampmann (eds.), *Wozu Historie heute? Beiträge zu einer Standortbestimmung im fachübergreifenden Gespräch* (Cologne: Böhlau, 1996), 167–183.

Reynaud, Paul, *Unite or Perish* (New York: Simon & Schuster, 1951).

Richard, Anne-Isabelle, 'The Consultative Assembly of the Council of Europe as a Platform for African Interests' (unpubl. paper at the conference 'From Empires to Empire? European Integration in Global Context, 1950s to 1990s', Berlin, 7–8 April 2016).

Richardson, James, 'The Concept of Atlantic Community', in: *Journal of Common Market Studies* 3 (1964), 1–22.
Ricoeur, Paul, 'Quel éthos nouveau pour l'Europe?', in: Peter Koslowski (ed.), *Imaginer l'Europe. Le marché intérieur européen, tâche culturelle et économique* (Paris: Les Editions du Cerf, 1992), 107–116.
Risso, Linda, 'NATO and the Environment: The Committee on the Challenges of Modern Society', in: *Contemporary European History* 25 (2016), 505–535.
Ritleng, Dominique, 'The Independence and Legitimacy of the European Court of Justice', in: Dominique Ritleng (ed.), *Independence and Legitimacy in the Institutional System of the European Union* (Oxford: Oxford University Press, 2016), 83–124.
Rittberger, Berthold, *Building Europe's Parliament: Democratic Representation beyond the Nation State* (Oxford: Oxford University Press, 2005).
Rittberger, Berthold, '"No Integration without Representation!" European Integration, Parliamentary Democracy, and Two Forgotten Communities', in: *Journal of European Public Policy* 13 (2006), 1211–1229.
Rittberger, Berthold and Frank Schimmelfennig, 'Explaining the Constitutionalization of the European Union', in: *Journal of European Public Policy* 13 (2006), 1148–1167.
Ritter, Gerhard A., *Der Preis der deutschen Einheit. Die Wiedervereinigung und die Krise des Sozialstaats* (Munich: C. H. Beck, 2007).
Rock, Philipp, *Macht, Märkte und Moral. Zur Rolle der Menschenrechte in der Außenpolitik der Bundesrepublik in den sechziger und siebziger Jahren* (Frankfurt am Main: Lang, 2010).
Rödder, Andreas, *21.0. Eine kurze Geschichte der Gegenwart* (Munich: C. H. Beck, 2015).
Rohan, Sally, *The Western European Union: International Politics between Alliance and Integration* (London: Routledge, 2014).
Röhl, Hans Christian, *Akkreditierung und Zertifizierung im Produktsicherheitsrecht. Zur Entwicklung einer neuen Europäischen Verwaltungsstruktur* (Berlin: Springer, 2000).
Romano, Angela, *From Détente in Europe to European Détente: How the West Shaped the Helsinki CSCE* (Brussels: Lang, 2009).
Romano, Angela, *The European Community and Eastern Europe in the Cold War: Overcoming the East–West Divide* (London: Routledge, 2016).
Romano, Angela, 'The EC and the Socialist World: The Ascent of a Key Player in Cold War Europe', in: Ulrich Krotz, Kiran Klaus Patel and Federico Romero (eds.), *Europe's Cold War Relations: The EC Towards a Global Role* (London: Bloomsbury, 2020), 51–69.
Romano, Angela and Federico Romero, 'European Socialist Regimes Facing Globalisation and European Co-operation: Dilemmas and Responses', in: *European Review of History* 21 (2014), 157–164.
Romero, Federico, 'Interdependence and Integration in American Eyes: From the Marshall Plan to Currency Convertibility', in: Alan S. Milward (ed.), *The Frontier of National Sovereignty: History and Theory, 1945–1992* (London: Routledge, 1993), 155–182.
Romero, Federico, 'U.S. Attitudes towards Integration and Interdependence: The 1950s', in: Francis H. Heller and John R. Gillingham (eds.), *The United States and the Integration of Europe: Legacies of the Postwar Era* (New York: St. Martin's Press, 1996), 103–121.

Roos, Mechthild, 'Far Beyond the Treaties' Clauses: The European Parliament's Gain in Power, 1952–1979', in: *Journal of Contemporary European Research* 13 (2017), 1055–1075.
Rosamond, Ben, *Theories of European Integration* (Houndmills: Palgrave Macmillan, 2000).
Rosamond, Ben, 'The Uniting of Europe and the Foundation of EU Studies: Revisiting the Neofunctionalism of Ernst B. Haas', in: *Journal of European Public Policy* 12 (2005), 237–254.
Rosato, Sebastian, *Europe United: Power Politics and the Making of the European Community* (Ithaca, NY: Cornell University Press, 2011).
Rothacher, Albrecht, *Economic Diplomacy between the European Community and Japan, 1959–1981* (Aldershot: Gower, 1983).
Rothacher, Albrecht, 'Europa–Giappone: Dietro il sipario di bambù', in: *Relazioni Internazionali* 6 (1993), 16–23.
Rothacher, Albrecht, 'The EC and Japan: From Mutual Neglect to Trade Conflicts and Beyond', in: Ulrich Krotz, Kiran Klaus Patel and Federico Romero (eds.), *Europe's Cold War Relations: The EC Towards a Global Role* (London: Bloomsbury, 2020), 111–124.
Rupp, Hans Heinrich, 'Die Grundrechte und das Europäische Gemeinschaftsrecht', in: *Neue Juristische Wochenschrift* 23 (1970), 353–359.
Sanderson, Fred. H. (ed.), *Agricultural Protectionism in the Industrialized World* (Baltimore: Johns Hopkins University Press, 1990).
Sanz, Rosa Pardo, 'Fernando Mª Castiella: Una larga travesía hacia el liberalismo', in: Juan Avilés Farré (ed.), *Historia, política y cultura. Homenaje a Javier Tusell* (Madrid: UNED, 2009), 393–427.
Sarotte, Mary E., *1989: The Struggle to Create Post-Cold War Europe* (Princeton, NJ: Princeton University Press, 2009).
Saunders, Robert, *Yes to Europe! The 1975 Referendum and Seventies Britain* (Cambridge: Cambridge University Press, 2018).
Savaşan, Zerrin, 'The Credibility of EU Human Rights Conditionality: Turkey's Case', in: Belgin Akçay and Bahri Yilmaz (eds.), *Turkey's Accession to the European Union: Political and Economic Challenges* (Lanham, MD: Lexington Books, 2013), 45–70.
Schain, Martin (ed.), *The Marshall Plan: Fifty Years After* (New York: Palgrave Macmillan, 2001).
Scharpf, Fritz W., 'Negative and Positive Integration in the Political Economy of European Welfare States', in: Gary Marks, Fritz W. Scharpf, Philippe C. Schmitter and Wolfgang Streeck (eds.), *Governance in the European Union* (London: SAGE, 1996), 15–39.
Schenk, Catherine R., 'Decolonization and European Economic Integration: The Free Trade Area Negotiations, 1956–58', in: James D. Le Sueur (eds.), *The Decolonization Reader* (London: Routledge, 2003), 139–155.
Scheuner, Ulrich, 'Fundamental Rights in European Community Law and in National Constitutional Law', in: *Common Market Law Review* 12 (1975), 171–191.
Schildt, Axel, '"German Angst": Überlegungen zur Mentalitätsgeschichte der Bundesrepublik', in: Daniela Münkel and Jutta Schwarzkopf (eds.), *Geschichte als Experiment. Studien zu Politik, Kultur und Alltag im 19. und 20. Jahrhundert* (Frankfurt am Main: Campus, 2004), 87–97.
Schimmelfennig, Frank, 'The Community Trap: Liberal Norms, Rhetorical Action, and the Eastern Enlargement of the European Union', in: *International Organization* 55 (2001), 47–80.

Schimmelfennig, Frank, 'Competition and Community: Constitutional Courts, Rhetorical Action, and the Institutionalization of Human Rights in the European Union', in: *Journal of European Public Policy* 13 (2006), 1247–1264.

Schipper, Frank, *Driving Europe: Building Europe on Roads in the 20th Century* (Amsterdam: Aksant, 2008).

Schmale, Wolfgang, *Geschichte Europas* (Vienna: Böhlau, 2001).

Schmale, Wolfgang, 'Before Self-Reflexivity: Imperialism and Colonialism in the Early Discourses of European Integration', in: Menno Spiering and Michael Wintle (eds.), *European Identity and the Second World War* (Houndmills: Palgrave Macmillan, 2011), 186–201.

Schmelzer, Matthias, *The Hegemony of Growth: The OECD and the Making of the Economic Growth Paradigm* (Cambridge: Cambridge University Press, 2016).

Schmitt, Carl, 'Die Ordnung der Welt nach dem zweiten Weltkrieg', in: Piet Tommissen (ed.), *Schmittiana II* (Brussels: K. de Rooms, 1990), 11–30.

Schmitter, Philippe C., 'Neo-Neofunctionalism', in: Antje Wiener and Thomas Diez (eds.), *European Integration Theory* (Oxford: Oxford University Press, 2004), 45–74.

Schmitter, Philippe C. and Zoe Lefkofridi, 'Neo-Functionalism as a Theory of Disintegration', *Chinese Political Science Review* 1 (2016), 1–29.

Schmitz, Stéphanie, 'L'influence de l'élite monétaire européenne et des réseaux informels sur la coopération des Six en matière d'intégration économique (1958–1969)' (unpubl. PhD thesis, European University Institute, Florence, 2014).

Schnädelbach, Herbert, *Analytische und postanalytische Philosophie. Vorträge und Abhandlungen* 4 (Frankfurt am Main: Suhrkamp, 2004).

Schönberger, Christoph, 'Die Bürgerschaft der Europäischen Union. Anmerkungen zu einem multinationalen Bürgerrecht in historisch-vergleichender Perspektive', in: *Geschichte und Gesellschaft* 42 (2016), 651–668.

Schorkopf, Frank, 'Rechtsgeschichte der europäischen Integration. Ein Themengebiet für Grundlagenforschung in der Rechtswissenschaft', in: *Juristenzeitung* 69 (2014), 421–431.

Schot, Johan and Vincent Lagendijk, 'Technocratic Internationalism in the Interwar Years: Building Europe on Motorways and Electricity Networks', in: *Journal of Modern European History* 6 (2008), 196–217.

Schot, Johan and Phil Scranton (eds.), *Making Europe: Technology and Transformations, 1850–2000*, 6 vols. (New York: Palgrave Macmillan, 2013–2019).

Schulz, Matthias, 'Europa-Netzwerke und Europagedanke in der Zwischenkriegszeit', in: Europäische Geschichte Online; www.ieg-ego.eu/schulzm-2010-de (accessed 1 July 2019).

Schulz, Matthias and Thomas A. Schwartz (eds.), *The Strained Alliance: U.S.–European Relations from Nixon to Carter* (Cambridge: Cambridge University Press, 2010).

Schulz-Forberg, Hagen and Bo Stråth, *The Political History of European Integration: The Hypocrisy of Democracy-through-Market* (London: Routledge, 2010).

Schwabe, Klaus, '"Ein Akt konstruktiver Staatskunst". Die USA und die Anfänge des Schuman-Plans', in: Klaus Schwabe (ed.), *Die Anfänge des Schuman-Plans 1950/51* (Baden-Baden: Nomos, 1988), 211–240.

Schwabe, Klaus, 'The Cold War and European Integration, 1947–63', in: *Diplomacy & Statecraft* 12 (2001), 18–34.

Schwabe, Klaus, 'Die Gründung der Montanunion aus deutscher und französischer Sicht', in: Manfred Rasch and Kurt Düwell (eds.), *Anfänge und Auswirkungen der Montanunion auf Europa. Die Stahlindustrie in Politik und Wirtschaft* (Essen: Klartext, 2007), 13–30.

Schwabe, Klaus, *Jean Monnet: Frankeich, die Deutschen und die Einigung Europas* (Baden-Baden: Nomos, 2016).

Schwarz, Hans-Peter, *Helmut Kohl. Eine politische Biographie* (Stuttgart: DVA, 2012).

Scioldo-Zürcher, Yann, *Devenir métropolitain: Politique d'intégration et parcours de rapatriés d'Algérie en metropole (1954–2005)* (Paris: Editions de l'Ecole des hautes études en sciences sociales, 2010).

Scott, David, 'China–EU Convergence 1957–2003: Towards a "Strategic Partnership"', in: *Asia Europe Journal* 5 (2007), 217–233.

Scott-Smith, Giles and Valérie Aubourg (eds.), *Atlantic, Euratlantic, or Europe-America?* (Paris: Soleb, 2011).

Segers, Mathieu, 'Preparing Europe for the Unforeseen, 1958–63. De Gaulle, Monnet, and European Integration beyond the Cold War: From Co-operation to Discord in the Matter of the Future of the EEC', in: *International History Review* 34 (2012), 347–370.

Segers, Mathieu, *Reis naar het continent. Nederland en de Europese integratie, 1950 tot heden* (Amsterdam: Bakker, 2013).

Seibel, Wolfgang, *Verwaltung verstehen. Eine theoriegeschichtliche Einführung* (Frankfurt am Main: Suhrkamp, 2017).

Seidel, Katja, *The Process of Politics in Europe: The Rise of European Elites and Supranational Institutions* (London: I. B. Tauris, 2010).

Seidendorf, Stefan, *Europäisierung nationaler Identitätsdiskurse? Ein Vergleich französischer und deutscher Printmedien* (Baden-Baden: Nomos, 2007).

Selinger, William, 'The Politics of Arendtian Historiography: European Federation and the *Origins of Totalitarianism*', in: *Modern Intellectual History* 13 (2016), 417–446.

Senghaas, Dieter, *Zum irdischen Frieden: Erkenntnisse und Vermutungen* (Frankfurt am Main: Suhrkamp, 2004).

Servan-Schreiber, Jean-Jacques, *The American Challenge* (New York: Atheneum, 1979, French orig.: *Le défi américain*, 1967).

Severiano Teixeira, Nuno (ed.), *The International Politics of Democratization: Comparative Perspectives* (London: Routledge, 2008).

Shackleton, Michael, *Financing the European Community* (London: Pinter, 1990).

Shore, Cris, *Building Europe: The Cultural Politics of European Integration* (London: Routledge, 2000).

Sieber, Ulrich, 'Euro-fraud: Organised Fraud against the Financial Interests of the European Union', in: *Crime, Law & Social Change* 30 (1998), 1–42.

Siedentopf, Heinrich and Jacques Ziller (eds.), *Making European Policies Work: The Implementation of Community Legislation in the Member States*, 2 vols. (London: SAGE, 1988).

Silber, Laura and Allan Little, *Yugoslavia: Death of a Nation* (New York: TV Books, 1996).

Simpson, A. W. Brian, *Human Rights and the End of Empire: Britain and the Genesis of the European Convention* (Oxford: Oxford University Press, 2001).

Siune, Karen and Palle Svensson, 'The Danes and the Maastricht Treaty: The Danish EC Referendum of June 1992', in: *Electoral Studies* 12 (1993), 99–111.

Slobodian, Quinn, *Globalists: The End of Empire and the Birth of Neoliberalism* (Cambridge, MA: Harvard University Press, 2018).

Smismans, Stijn, 'The European Union's Fundamental Rights Myth', in: *Journal of Common Market Studies* 48 (2010), 45–66.

Snoy et d'Oppuers, Jean-Charles, *Rebâtir l'Europe: Mémoires* (Paris: Duculot, 1989).

Sorensen, Theodore C., *Kennedy* (New York: Harper & Row, 1965).

Sotillo Lorenzo, José Angel, 'América Latina en las negociaciones del ingreso de España en la Comunidad Europea', in: *Política y Sociedad* 4 (1989), 25–32.

Spaak, Paul-Henri, *The Continuing Battle: Memoirs of a European, 1936–1966* (London: Weidenfeld & Nicolson, 1971, French orig.: *Combats inachevées*, 2 vols., 1969).

Speich Chassé, Daniel, *Die Erfindung des Bruttosozialprodukts. Globale Ungleichheit in der Wissensgeschichte der Ökonomie* (Göttingen: Vandenhoeck & Ruprecht, 2013).

Speich Chassé, Daniel, 'Towards a Global History of the Marshall Plan: European Post-War Reconstruction and the Rise of Development Economic Expertise', in: Christian Grabas and Alexander Nützenadel (eds.), *Industrial Policy in Europe after 1945: Wealth, Power and Economic Development in the Cold War* (New York: Palgrave Macmillan, 2014), 187–212.

Spierenburg, Dirk and Raymond Poidevin, *The History of the High Authority of the European Coal and Steel Community* (London: Weidenfeld & Nicolson, 1994).

Spinelli, Altiero, *L'Europa non cade dal cielo* (Bologna: Il Mulino, 1960).

Staiger, Uta, 'The European Capitals of Culture in Context: Cultural Policy and the European Integration Process', in: Kiran Klaus Patel (ed.), *The Cultural Politics of Europe: European Capitals of Culture and European Union since the 1980s* (London: Routledge, 2013), 19–38.

Stavridis, Stelios and Christopher Hill (eds.), *Domestic Sources of Foreign Policy: West European Reactions to the Falklands Conflict* (Oxford: Berg, 1996).

Stephenson, Paul, 'Sixty-Five Years of Auditing Europe', in: *Journal of Contemporary European Research* 12 (2016), 467–485.

Stephenson, Paul, 'Starting from Scratch? Analysing Early Institutionalization Processes: The Case of Audit Governance', in: *Journal of European Public Policy* 23 (2016), 1481–1501.

Stinsky, Daniel, 'Sisyphus' Palace: The United Nations Economic Commission on Europe, 1947–60' (unpubl. PhD thesis, Maastricht University, 2019).

Stolleis, Michael, *Geschichte des öffentlichen Rechts in Deutschland*, vol. 4 (Munich: C. H. Beck, 2012).

Stone Sweet, Alec, *Governing with Judges: Constitutional Politics in Europe* (Oxford: Oxford University Press, 2000).

Strange, Susan, 'Why Do International Organizations Never Die?', in: Bob Reinalda and Bertjan Verbeek (eds.), *Autonomous Policy Making by International Organizations* (London: Routledge, 1998), 213–220.

Strasser, Daniel, *Les finances de l'Europe. Le droit budgétaire et financier des communautés européennes* (Paris: Librairie générale de droit et de jurisprudence, 1990).

Stråth, Bo, *Europe's Utopias of Peace: 1815, 1919, 1951* (London: Bloomsbury, 2016).

Stråth, Bo and Peter Wagner, *European Modernity: A Global Approach* (London: Bloomsbury, 2017).

Stubb, Alexander, *Negotiating Flexibility in the European Union: Amsterdam, Nice and Beyond* (Houndmills: Palgrave, 2002).

Suzuki, Hitoshi, 'Negotiating the Japan–EC Trade Conflict: The Role and Presence of the European Commission, the Council of Ministers, and Business Groups in Europe and Japan, 1970–1982', in: Claudia Hiepel (ed.), *Europe in a Globalising World: Global Challenges and European Responses in the 'Long' 1970s* (Baden-Baden: Nomos, 2014), 201–229.

Suzuki, Hitoshi, 'The Rise of Summitry and EEC–Japan Trade Relations', in: Emmanuel Mourlon-Druol and Federico Romero (eds.), *International Summitry and*

Global Governance: The Rise of the G7 and the European Council, 1974–1991 (London: Routledge, 2014), 152–173.
Szirmai, Adam, 'Industrialisation as an Engine of Growth in Developing Countries, 1950–2005', in: *Structural Change and Economic Dynamics* 23 (2012), 406–420.
Talbot, Ross B., *The Chicken War: An International Trade Conflict between the United States and the European Economic Community 1961–64* (Ames: Iowa State University Press, 1978).
Tallberg, Jonas, 'Paths to Compliance: Enforcement, Management, and the European Union', in: *International Organization* 56 (2002), 609–643.
Tatham, Allan F., '"Don't Mention Divorce at the Wedding, Darling!" EU Accession and Withdrawal after Lisbon', in: Andrea Biondi, Piet Eeckhout and Stefanie Ripley (eds.), *EU Law after Lisbon* (Oxford: Oxford University Press, 2012), 128–154.
Tavani, Sara, 'The Détente Crisis and the Emergence of a Common European Foreign Policy: The "Common European Polish Policy"', in: Claudia Hiepel (ed.), *Europe in a Globalising World: Global Challenges and European Responses in the 'Long' 1970s* (Baden-Baden: Nomos, 2014), 49–68.
Teltschik, Horst, *329 Tage. Innenansichten der Einigung* (Berlin: Siedler, 1991).
Thatcher, Margaret, *Statecraft: Strategies for a Changing World* (New York: HarperCollins, 2002).
Ther, Philipp, *Die neue Ordnung auf dem alten Kontinent. Eine Geschichte des neoliberalen Europa* (Berlin: Suhrkamp, 2014).
Ther, Philipp, 'Der Neoliberalismus, Version: 1.0', in: Docupedia-Zeitgeschichte (5 July 2016; online: http://docupedia.de/zg/ther_neoliberalismus_v1_de_2016, accessed 1 July 2019).
Therborn, Göran, *European Modernity and Beyond: The Trajectory of European Societies, 1945–2000* (London: SAGE, 1995).
Thiemeyer, Guido, *Vom 'Pool Vert' zur Europäischen Wirtschaftsgemeinschaft. Europäische Integration, Kalter Krieg und die Anfänge der Gemeinsamen Europäischen Agrarpolitik 1950–1957* (Munich: Oldenbourg, 1999).
Thiemeyer, Guido and Isabel Tölle, 'Supranationalität im 19. Jahrhundert? Die Beispiele der Zentralkommission für die Rheinschifffahrt und des Octroivertrages 1804–1832', in: *Journal of European Integration History* 17 (2011), 177–196.
Thomas, Daniel C., *The Helsinki Effect: International Norms, Human Rights, and the Demise of Communism* (Princeton, NJ: Princeton University Press, 2001).
Thomas, Daniel C., 'Constitutionalization through Enlargement: The Contested Origins of the EU's Democratic Identity', in: *Journal of European Public Policy* 13 (2006), 1190–1210.
Thomas, Martin, *Fight or Flight: Britain, France, and their Roads from Empire* (Oxford: Oxford University Press, 2014).
Tiedemann, Klaus, *Subventionskriminalität in der Bundesrepublik. Erscheinungsformen, Ursachen, Folgerungen* (Reinbek: Rowohlt, 1972).
Toffler, Alvin, *Future Shock* (London: Bodley Head, 1970).
Trachtenberg, Marc, *A Constructed Peace: The Making of the European Settlement, 1945–1963* (Princeton, NJ: Princeton University Press, 1999).
Trausch, Gilbert (ed.), *Die Europäische Integration vom Schuman-Plan bis zu den Verträgen von Rom* (Baden-Baden: Nomos, 1993).
Treib, Oliver, 'Implementing and Complying with EU Governance Outputs', in: *Living Reviews in European Governance* 9 (2014), 5–47.
Trouvé, Matthieu, *L'Espagne et l'Europe. De la dictature de Franco à l'Union européenne* (Brussels: Lang, 2008).

Trunk, Achim, *Europa, ein Ausweg. Politische Eliten und europäische Identität in den 1950er Jahren* (Munich: Oldenbourg, 2007).
Tsoukalis, Loukas, *The European Community and Its Mediterranean Enlargement* (London: George Allen & Unwin, 1981).
Tsoukalis, Loukas, *The New European Economy: The Politics and Economics of Integration* (Oxford: Oxford University Press, 1993).
Turpin, Frédéric, 'Alle origini della politica europea di cooperazione allo sviluppo: La Francia e la politica di associazione Europa-Africa (1957–1975)', in: *Ventunesimo Secolo* 6 (2007), 135–150.
Tuytschaever, Filip, *Differentiation in European Union Law* (Oxford: Hart, 1999).
Tyers, Rodney and Kym Anderson, *Disarray in World Food Markets: A Quantitative Assessment* (Cambridge: Cambridge University Press, 1992).
Ullrich, Sebastian, *Der Weimar-Komplex. Das Scheitern der ersten deutschen Demokratie und die politische Kultur der frühen Bundesrepublik 1945–1959* (Göttingen: Wallstein, 2009).
Ulrich, Laura Christine, *Wege nach Europa. Heinrich Aigner und die Anfänge des Europäischen Rechnungshofes* (St. Otilien: EOS, 2015).
Vahsen, Urban, *Eurafrikanische Entwicklungskooperation: Die Assoziierungspolitik der EWG gegenüber dem subsaharischen Afrika in den 1960er Jahren* (Stuttgart: Franz Steiner Verlag, 2010).
Vaïsse, Maurice (ed.), *L'Europe et la crise de Cuba* (Paris: Armand Colin, 1993).
Vaïsse, Maurice, 'Une hirondelle ne fait pas le printemps: La France et la crise de Cuba', in: Maurice Vaïsse (ed.), *L'Europe et la Crise de Cuba* (Paris: Armand Colin, 1993), 89–107.
Vaïsse, Maurice, *La grandeur. Politique étrangère du général de Gaulle, 1958–1969* (Paris: Fayard, 1998).
van Ark, Bart and Nicholas Crafts (eds.), *Quantitative Aspects of Post-War European Economic Growth* (Cambridge: Cambridge University Press, 1996).
van den Braak, Bert, 'Een Nederlandse machtspoliticus machteloos in Brussel: Henk Vredeling, lid van de Europese Commissie (1977–1981)', in: Gerrit Voerman, Bert van den Braak and Carla van Baalen (eds.), *De Nederlandse eurocommissarissen* (Amsterdam, Boom: 2010), 175–205.
van der Eijk, Cees and Mark N. Franklin (eds.), *The European Electorate and National Politics in the Face of Union* (Ann Arbor: Michigan University Press, 1996).
van der Harst, Jan, 'Sicco Mansholt: Courage and Conviction', in: Michel Dumoulin (ed.), *The European Commission, 1958–72: History and Memories* (Luxembourg: Office for Official Publications of the European Communities, 2007), 165–180.
van Ingelgom, Virginie, 'Mesurer l'indifférence. Intégration européenne et attitudes des citoyens', in: *Sociologie* 1 (2012), 1–20.
van Laer, Arthe, 'Forschung: Für eine neue gemeinsame Politik', in: Eric Bussière et al. (eds.), *Die Europäische Kommission 1973–1986. Geschichte und Erinnerungen einer Institution* (Luxembourg: Amt für Veröffentlichungen der Europäischen Kommission, 2014), 287–301.
van Leeuwen, Karen, 'On Democratic Concerns and Legal Traditions: The Dutch 1953 and 1956 Constitutional Reforms "Towards Europe"', in: *Contemporary European History* 21 (2012), 357–374.
van Middelaar, Luuk, *The Passage to Europe: How a Continent Became a Union* (New Haven, CT: Yale University Press, 2013).
Vanke, Jeffrey W., *Europeanism and European Union: Interests, Emotions, and Systemic Integration into the Early Economic Community* (Palo Alto, CA: Academica Press, 2010).

Varsori, Antonio, 'Le rôle de la formation et de l'enseignement professionnels dans la politique sociale européenne et le Cedefop', in: *Formation Professionelle* 32 (2004), 70–85.
Varsori, Antonio, *La Cenerentola d'Europa? L'Italia e l'integrazione europea dal 1947 a oggi* (Soveria Mannelli: Rubbettino, 2010).
Vauchez, Antoine, 'The Transnational Politics of Judicialization: Van Gend en Loos and the Making of EU Polity', in: *European Law Journal* 16 (2010), 1–28.
Vauchez, Antoine, *L'Union par le droit. L'invention d'un programme institutionnel pour l'Europe* (Paris: Presses de la Fondation des sciences politiques, 2013).
Vayssière, Bertrand, *Vers une Europe fédérale? Les espoirs et les actions fédéralistes au sortir de la seconde guerre mondiale* (Brussels: Peter Lang, 2006).
Verney, Susannah, 'Creating the Democratic Tradition of European Integration: The South European Catalyst', in: Helene Sjursen (ed.), *Enlargement and the Finality of the EU* (Oslo: Arena, 2002), 97–127.
Verovšek, Peter J., 'Unexpected Support for European Integration: Memory, Rupture, and Totalitarianism in Arendt's Political Theory', in: *The Review of Politics* 76 (2014), 389–413.
Verschueren, Nicolas, *Fermer les mines en construisant l'Europe. Une histoire sociale de l'intégration européenne* (Brussels: Lang, 2013).
Versluis, Esther, Mendeltje van Keulen and Paul Stephenson, *Analyzing the European Union Policy Process* (Houndmills: Palgrave Macmillan, 2011).
Villaume, Poul, Rasmus Mariager and Helle Porsdam (eds.), *The 'Long 1970s': Human Rights, East–West Détente, and Transnational Relations* (New York: Routledge, 2016).
Vollaard, Hans, 'Explaining European Disintegration', in: *Journal of Common Market Studies* 52 (2014), 1142–1159.
Wagenführ, Rolf, 'Die industrielle Weltproduktion – 1950 bis 1964', in: *Statistisches Amt der EG, Statistische Informationen 4/1965* (Luxembourg: Statistisches Amt der EG, 1965), 5–60.
Wagenführ, Rolf, 'Die Statistik in der Integration der Sechs', in: *Statistische Hefte* 7 (1966), 51–73.
Wagner, Helmut, 'Verrechtlichung durch Integration. Erwägungen zu verfassungsrechtlichen Verfahren der EU über den Beitritt und Austritt, den Ausschluss und die Auflösung', in: Heiner Timmermann (ed.), *Eine Verfassung für die Europäische Union. Beiträge zu einer grundsätzlichen und aktuellen Diskussion* (Opladen: Leske + Budrich, 2001), 67–83.
Walker, Jeremy and Melinda Cooper, 'Genealogies of Resilience: From Systems Ecology to the Political Economy of Crisis Adaptation', in: *Security Dialogue* 42 (2011), 143–160.
Wall, Stephen, *The Official History of Britain and the European Community*, vol. 2: *From Rejection to Referendum, 1963–1975* (London: Routledge, 2013).
Wallerstein, Immanuel, *Africa: The Politics of Independence* (New York: Vintage Books, 1961).
Warlouzet, Laurent, *Le choix de la CEE par la France: L'Europe économique en débat de Mendès France à de Gaulle, 1955–1969* (Paris: CHEFF, 2011).
Warlouzet, Laurent, 'Dépasser la crise de l'histoire de l'intégration européenne', in: *Politique Européenne* 44 (2014), 98–122.
Warlouzet, Laurent, 'The Centralization of EU Competition Policy: Historical Institutionalist Dynamics from Cartel Monitoring to Merger Control (1956–91)', in: *Journal of Common Market Studies* 54 (2016), 725–741.
Warlouzet, Laurent, *Governing Europe in a Globalizing World: Neoliberalism and its Alternatives Following the 1973 Oil Crisis* (London: Routledge, 2017).

Warneke, Sara, *Die europäische Wirtschaftsintegration aus der Perspektive Wilhelm Röpkes* (Stuttgart: Lucius & Lucius, 2013).

Wassenberg, Birte, *History of the Council of Europe* (Strasbourg: Council of Europe, 2013).

Wassenberg, Birte, 'Between Cooperation and Competitive Bargaining: The Council of Europe, Local and Regional Networking, and the Shaping of the European Community's Regional Policies, 1970s–90s', in: *European Review of History* 24 (2017), 423–444.

Wassenberg, Birte, Frédéric Clavert and Philippe Hamman (eds.), *Contre l'Europe? Anti-européisme, euroscepticisme et alter-européisme dans la construction européenne de 1945 à nos jours* (Stuttgart: Franz Steiner Verlag, 2010).

Webber, Douglas, 'How Likely Is It that the European Union Will *Dis*integrate? A Critical Analysis of Competing Theoretical Perspectives', in: *European Journal of International Relations* 20 (2014), 341–365.

Weber, Max, *Economy and Society: An Outline of Interpretive Sociology* (Berkeley: University of California Press, 1978).

Wegmann, Milène, *Früher Neoliberalismus und europäische Integration. Interdependenz der nationalen, supranationalen und internationalen Ordnung von Wirtschaft und Gesellschaft (1932–1965)* (Baden-Baden: Nomos, 2002).

Weiler, Joseph H. H., 'Alternatives to Withdrawal from an International Organization: The Case of the European Economic Community', in: *Israel Law Review* 20 (1985), 282–298.

Weiler, Joseph H. H., 'The White Paper and the Application of Community Law', in: Roland Bieber et al. (eds.), *1992: One European Market?* (Baden-Baden: Nomos, 1988), 337–358.

Weiler, Joseph H.H ., 'Does Europe Need a Constitution? Reflections on Demos, Telos and Ethos in the German Maastricht Decision', in: Peter Gowan and Perry Anderson (eds.), *The Question of Europe* (London: Verso, 1997), 265–294.

Weiler, Joseph H. H., 'The Constitution of the Common Market Place: Text and Context in the Evolution of the Free Movements of Goods', in: Paul P. Craig and Gráinne de Búrca (eds.), *The Evolution of EU Law* (Oxford: Oxford University Press, 1999), 349–376.

Weiler, Joseph H. H., *The Constitution of Europe: 'Do the New Clothes Have an Emperor?' and Other Essays on European Integration* (Cambridge: Cambridge University Press, 1999).

Weiler, Joseph H. H. (ed.), *The EU, the WTO, and the NAFTA: Towards a Common Law of International Trade?* (Oxford: Oxford University Press, 2000).

Weisbrode, Kenneth, *The Year of Indecision, 1946: A Tour through the Crucible of Harry Truman's America* (New York: Viking, 2016).

Weiss, Friedl, 'Greenland's Withdrawal from the European Communities', in: *European Law Review* 10 (1985), 173–185.

Wengler, Wilhelm, 'Grundrechtsminimum und Äquivalenz der Grundrechtsschutzsysteme', in: *Juristenzeitung* 10 (1968), 327–329.

Wesel, Uwe, *Geschichte des Rechts in Europa. Von den Griechen bis zum Vertrag von Lissabon* (Munich: C. H. Beck, 2010).

Wessels, Wolfgang, *Die Öffnung des Staates. Modelle und Wirklichkeit grenzüberschreitender Verwaltungspraxis* (Wiesbaden: Leske + Budrich, 2000).

Westad, Odd Arne, *The Global Cold War: Third World Interventions and the Making of Our Times* (Cambridge: Cambridge University Press, 2005).

Westad, Odd Arne, *The Cold War: A World History* (New York: Basic Books, 2017).

Wilkens, Andreas (ed.), *Le plan Schuman dans l'histoire. Intérêts nationaux et projet européen* (Brussels: Bruylant, 2004).

Williams, Andrew, *EU Human Rights Policies: A Study in Irony* (Oxford: Oxford University Press, 2004).

Winand, Pascaline, *Eisenhower, Kennedy, and the United States of Europe* (London: Macmillan, 1993).

Winand, Pascaline, 'The US Mission to the EU in "Brussels D.C.", the European Commission Delegation in Washington D.C. and the New Transatlantic Agenda', in: Éric Philippart and Pascaline Winand (eds.), *Ever Closer Partnership: Policy-Making in US–EU Relations* (Brussels: Peter Lang, 2001), 107–153.

Winham, Gilbert R., *International Trade and the Tokyo Round Negotiation* (Princeton, NJ: Princeton University Press, 1986).

Winkler, Heinrich August, *Quo vadis Europa? Die Europäische Union zwischen Erweiterung und Vertiefung* (Warsaw: Friedrich-Ebert-Stiftung-Büro Warschau, 2007).

Winkler, Heinrich August, *Geschichte des Westens*, vol. 3: *Vom Kalten Krieg zum Mauerfall* (Munich: C. H. Beck, 2014).

Winkler, Heinrich August, *Geschichte des Westens*, vol. 4: *Die Zeit der Gegenwart* (Munich: C. H. Beck, 2015).

Winkler, Heinrich August, *Zerbricht der Westen? Über die gegenwärtige Krise in Europa und Amerika* (Munich: C. H. Beck, 2017).

Wirsching, Andreas, *Der Preis der Freiheit. Geschichte Europas in unserer Zeit* (Munich: C. H. Beck, 2012).

Yılmaz, Hakan, 'Europeanisation and Its Discontents: Turkey, 1959–2007', in: Constantine Arvanitopoulos (ed.), *Turkey's Accession to the European Union: An Unusual Candidacy* (Berlin: Springer, 2009), 53–64.

Zaiotti, Ruben, *Cultures of Border Control: Schengen and the Evolution of European Frontiers* (Chicago: University of Chicago Press, 2011).

Zartman, I. William, *The Politics of Trade Negotiations between Africa and the European Economic Community: The Weak Confront the Strong* (Princeton, NJ: Princeton University Press, 1971).

Zeiler, Thomas W., *American Trade and Power in the 1960s* (New York: Columbia University Press, 1992).

Ziegerhofer-Prettenthaler, Anita, *Botschafter Europas: Richard Nikolaus Coudenhove-Kalergi und die Paneuropa-Bewegung in den zwanziger und dreißiger Jahren* (Vienna: Böhlau Verlag, 2004).

Zielonka, Jan, *Is the EU Doomed?* (London: Polity Press, 2014).

Zimmermann, Hubert, *Money and Security: Troops, Monetary Policy, and West Germany's Relations with the United States and Britain, 1950–1971* (Cambridge: Cambridge University Press, 2002).

Zischka, Anton, *Afrika. Europas Gemeinschaftsaufgabe Nr. 1* (Oldenburg: Gerhard Stalling Verlag, 1951).

Zubok, Vladislav M., *A Failed Empire: The Soviet Union in the Cold War from Stalin to Gorbachev* (Chapel Hill: University of North Carolina Press, 2009).

Zuleeg, Manfred, 'Fundamental Rights and the Law of the European Communities', in: *Common Market Law Review* 8 (1971), 446–461.

Zuqian, Zhang, 'China's Commercial Relations with Europe', in: David Shambaugh, Eberhard Sandschneider and Zhoug Hong (eds.), *China–Europe Relations: Perceptions, Policies and Prospects* (New York: Taylor & Francis, 2008), 231–248.

INDEX